# Climbing
# ROCK
# AND ICE

# Climbing
# ROCK
# AND ICE

## Learning the
## Vertical Dance

*Text and Illustrations by*

# JERRY
# CINNAMON

Ragged Mountain Press
*Camden, Maine*

*This book is dedicated to the friends*

*and fellow climbers who helped shape my*

*vision of what is possible.*

Published by Ragged Mountain Press, a division of McGraw-Hill, Inc.

10 9 8 7 6 5 4 3

**Library of Congress Cataloging-in-Publication Data**
Cinnamon, Jerry.
    Climbing rock & ice : learning the vertical dance / Jerry Cinnamon.
        p.    cm.
    Includes index.
    ISBN 0-87742-405-5
    1. Rock climbing. 2. Snow and ice climbing.
I. Title.
II. Title: Climbing rock and ice.
GV200.2.C55   1993
796.5'223–dc20                                        93-28175
                                                                    CIP

Questions regarding the content of this book should be addressed to:
Ragged Mountain Press
P.O. Box 220
Camden, ME  04843

Questions regarding the ordering of this book should be addressed to:

McGraw-Hill, Inc.
Customer Service Department
P. O. Box 547
Blacklick, OH  43004
Retail Customers: 1-800-822-8158
Bookstores: 1-800-722-4726

*Climbing Rock and Ice* is printed on 60-pound Renew Opaque Vellum, a recycled paper containing a minimum of 50% total recycled fiber with 10% post-consumer de-inked fiber. ♻

Printed by R. R. Donnelley, Crawfordsville, IN
Design by Joyce C. Weston
Production and page layout by Janet S. Robbins
Edited by Dorcas Susan Miller, Nancy N.
    Green, and Pamela Benner

A percentage of the price of this product is donated to the Access Fund. The Access Fund is a national, nonprofit climbers' organization working exclusively to protect the natural resources used by climbers and climbers' access to those resources.

the ACCESS FUND
*...preserving America's diverse*
*climbing resources.*

# Contents

# Acknowledgments

I wish to take this opportunity to thank the following individuals who have contributed to my personal growth or have directly contributed to the success of this book by sharing adventures, modeling for photographs, critiquing illustrations and text, or providing support: Jeff Alexander, Rich Baker, Tom Davis, Jim Ewing, Gene Francis, Dave Getchell Jr., Dave Getchell Sr., Eric Harms, Geoff Heath, Damon Johnston, Scott Kimball, Dan Koch, Matt Lawler, Jon Leonard, Heather Lindquist, Laurie Little, Mike Lockett, Dan Lowell, Dodi Marvell, Doug McMullin, Dorcas Miller, Chris Misavage, Jim F. Morrisey, Marty O'Keefe, Nick Prvulov, Dot Quimby, Ed Raiola, James Reed, David Smith, Debbie Sugerman, Mark Tenney, Shawn Tierney, Ben Townsend, Steve Tweito, Marjory Ulin, Kathy Dixon-Wallace, Peter Wallace, Mary Ward, and others who were inadvertently left off this list. Thanks to the Unity College Board of Trustees, who granted a semester of free time to initiate this book, and to other members of the college community for their support.

I wish to thank the following individuals and their organizations for reviewing the text, transmitting information, making it possible for me to further my education on subjects related to specific chapters: Roger Damon and the Eastern Division of the National Ski Patrol; Paul DiBello and the National Sports Center for the Disabled, Blind Climbing Program; and John (Jed) E. Williamson and the American Alpine Club.

Thanks also go to the following individuals and organizations for permission to use copyrighted works: Michael L. Benge, managing editor of *Climbing* magazine, to quote from Dick Dorworth's article on John Donlou in volume 36, and from an article by Paul Piana in volume 110 on the Salathé Wall; Yvon Chouinard to quote from his book, *Climbing Ice*, concerning the origin of the radically drooped ice-axe pick; Bruce Temper, editor of *The Avalanche Review*, to quote from the 1991 article "White Death: A Review of Fatal Accidents in Colorado, 1950–91" by Dale Atkins; Jay Mather, photographer, for use of his photograph to draw Figure 2-1; Anthony Herr, photographer, for use of his photograph to draw Figure 2-2A; S. Peter Lewis, photographer, for use of his photograph to draw Figure 2-2B; Paul DiBello to draw Figure 2-3, based on the video *Reach for the Peak*; Tom Zierk and Project Adventure to sketch Figure 2-4, based on the cover photograph of Mark S. Haven's book, *Bridges to Accessibility*; John (Jed) E. Williamson and the American Alpine Club to quote individual case studies from *Accidents in American Mountaineering*.

Finally, I wish to thank the generations of climbers before me who have contributed to the literature, technique, and knowledge of climbing.

# Preface

This book grew out of many years of teaching climbing to individuals, many of whom have become masters of the sport. My premise has been that novices begin to learn under the tutelage of an experienced friend, instructor, or guide, and eventually reach a point of mastery where they can climb safely with peers, and perhaps teach others.

This book should remain valuable to you throughout your climbing career for review, as a guide to skill presentation, as a source of additional references, and to introduce you to new areas to master, such as working with groups.

You can enjoy and practice climbing throughout your life at whatever level of athletic ability or conditioning you possess as long as you are aware of your own limits. More than athletic ability, climbing demands thought and decision-making. This book tries to show currently accepted techniques and procedures of climbing, but it can never replace your own judgment as to how to apply them in the fluid situations that climbing offers.

The book is divided into four parts. Part One focuses on climbing movement, since the central focus of climbing is movement in the vertical world, supported by companions, gear, and techniques. Chapter 1 teaches individual movement techniques and sequences and when to use them. Chapter 2 describes the efforts of individuals with disabilities who have adapted through special techniques to climb very well. These people are opening up new opportunities for others with disabilities, and their success inspires us all to put forth our best effort as we train and climb.

Part Two focuses on the tools to climb rock: basic knots, harnesses, rope, protection, and anchor systems, as well as the techniques of belaying and rappelling. A chapter on leading rock and a discussion of fall forces round out this section.

Part Three covers the special skills needed for movement on ice and snow, the kinds and use of protection in this environment, the nature of ice, and the techniques of climbing on steep ice. In Part Three I have assumed that the reader is already familiar with the information in Part Two, especially the sections concerning ropes, belaying, and anchors as used in rock climbing. Part Three also deals with avalanches, an environmental hazard that occurs in terrain where snow and ice climbing take place.

Part Four is written for experienced climbers who wish to help manage a climbing site when working with organized groups, and who recognize that the dangers of climbing also require management for safety.

Appendices on fitness, lightning, pulleys, and first-aid programs conclude the book.

The climbing community has come to recognize that great climbs can be accomplished by both women and men. Results depend largely on the amount of time and effort that individuals wish to spend learning, training, and putting skills to use. Throughout the book I have attempted to use gender-inclusive terminology, except when referring to a specific, illustrated climber.

# Introduction

Climbing is about having fun. It is about pumping adrenaline, exposure to the outdoors, ascending impossibly vertical or smooth walls, viewing space beneath our feet, sitting quietly on a ledge reflecting on nature, and sharing tall tales and adventures with friends, but at its heart climbing is about moving our bodies from one spot to another, at our best, with the accomplished, graceful steps of a dancer.

Dancers are not born as masters with the gift of springing into the air and landing softly again on their toes to hold an audience in rapture. Like dancers, climbers start as apprentices; we rehearse our steps time and again to move fluidly and develop grace. We practice by climbing whenever we can, at the cliffs, on rock walls, or in the gym. One type of climbing, bouldering, was originally practiced on small glacial boulders but can be practiced on any climbing surface low enough to safely jump from. Bouldering frees us from encumbering ropes, rope partners, and tools. We use our hands, climbing shoes, and bodies to move for long periods of time and to try movement problems at our current limit. This promotes muscular endurance and power, increases fluidity of motion, and allows us to spend time doing what we enjoy most. Practice gives us the opportunity to incorporate thinking about climbing technique, or mind knowledge, into actual climbing, or body knowledge.

Climbing was once the pastime of a few privileged Victorians with the money and leisure to climb mountains. Its popularity gradually spread in the 1900s to a wider public looking for physical challenges. In the 1960s, with the introduction of advances in ice tools, ice climbing became a separate sport from mountain climbing. A rapid revolution of tools, protection, boots, and clothing followed to make this cold-weather sport more enjoyable and safer than ever before. During the 1980s "sport" cliffs, indoor climbing walls, "sticky" shoes, and technologically advanced gear made rock climbing accessible to tens of thousands of climbers.

Currently, novices—men and women alike—can begin the sport close to home, under the supervision of accomplished friends, climbing gym personnel, school climbing clubs, or guide services. Anyone of average physical ability can profitably spend their first climbing season under the tutelage of a seasoned climber to gain familiarity with the sport. If you want to do advanced intermediate climbs, you will need to develop a general fitness program that involves endurance and strength training. This program can become highly specialized as you train to climb at an advanced level.

Climbing includes a number of disciplines, including bouldering, rock climbing on small and large cliffs, sport climbing, water-ice climbing, and mountaineering. These disciplines present opportunities to develop new skills and knowledge; to encounter diverse internal responses to the effort demanded, ranging from exhaustion to heightened states of awareness; and to gain new summits. The view from the top of any climb is both beautiful and far. On the way to the top, you will see new places, meet new people, make new friends, and experience successes as well as failures. All of these experiences will seep into you, and, upon reflection, enrich your daily life.

As you read and as you practice climbing, think positive thoughts and enjoy yourself!

# PART ONE

# Focus on Climbers

# 1

# Movement

## Face Climbing

Cliffs range from low-angle to very steep indeed. Climbers began exploring cliffs by using cracks that split otherwise featureless faces: the cracks provided handholds, or *jams,* and places to insert artificial *protection*—anchors used to shorten a fall—to safeguard the climber. (This is known as *crack climbing,* and we will come to it later in this chapter.) Climbers did venture out onto the rock face, but often were limited by the scarcity of protection. Today you have a multitude of specialized protection pieces that, in combination with sticky climbing shoes, safeguard you in what was once an alien place. As a result, you can find many of today's *test pieces*—climbs on the cutting edge of the sport—as well as fun climbs on faces, where you need precise footwork, concentration, and excellent balance.

## Basic Moves

When you climb, you use your feet in combination with your hands to keep yourself on the rock. Since good balance requires that you position your feet below your hands and not off to the side, you must often make a choice between using the largest footholds available or using the largest handholds. When resting, you will probably choose the largest footholds to stand on. When attempting to pull up with your arms on a steep wall, you will often use the largest handholds and whatever small footholds are directly underneath your hands. On less steep walls with positive, or jutting, footholds, you may find that you can balance from foothold to foothold without much use of your hands to support your body weight. As handholds get smaller and the wall gets steeper, take shorter steps a few inches apart to help maintain balance. As a general rule, the higher you step, the larger the handhold you will need to maintain balance. The two common techniques used on these small holds are *edging* and *smearing*.

When small positive edges or the tops of semi-detached rock flakes are available, you edge on these, as shown in Figure 1-1. This means that you use the inside edge of your shoe, adjacent to the big toe; on bigger holds, you use the inside ball of your foot. When you take this stance with both feet turned outward, you can bring your body closer to the rock while remaining upright. Alternatively, you can stand on the outside edge of your foot, which puts much of your weight directly over the

outside edge

inside edge

*Figure 1-1. **Edging:** The left foot, at the lower right corner of the figure, is edging on the inside. This places body weight directly over the inside of the big toe. The right foot, at the upper left corner of the figure, is edging on the outside of the foot. Body weight is over the outside of the ball of the foot.*

*Figure 1-2. **Smearing on Rounded Holds***

bone structure of your foot but usually feels less secure than inside edging because your foot and ankle tend to roll. You can counteract this by tensing involved muscles. Most climbers use an outside edge as a transitory move on small holds while trying to get to better holds where they can pause.

When the rock on steep faces and slabs offers you holds that are rounded so you cannot edge, you place your entire foot on the hold, at right angles to the fall line—the most direct line up and down the cliff—to create the maximum contact area between the bottom of your foot and the rock. You use the maximum surface area of the bottom of your foot. This is called *smearing*. You can use any small surface that is of a lower angle than the overall cliff (Figure 1-2).

On low-angle rock slabs, extend both the smearing concept and shoe-to-rock surface contact by pointing the toe of your shoe up the fall line (Figure 1-3). This is the *friction foothold*. Do not attempt to edge on rounded holds, as edging reduces the area of the shoe making contact with the rock.

For any single friction move there are usually places to step on that are less steep than the general overall angle of the rock. Place your foot on one of these spots and then shift your body weight over your foot. You want a smooth shift from one foot to the other, as if you were ice skating. Climb by linking these moves until you get to a resting place where you can place protection and start over. Moving directly up the slope is easier than moving sideways, where a pronounced weight shift is necessary to transfer from one foot to the other. If the route requires you to move sideways, it is almost always easier to plan ahead and ascend in a diagonal line rather than a horizontal one.

### Handholds and Finger Holds

You can grip handholds and finger holds in many ways, as shown in Figure 1-4. Possible grips include the open, cling, vertical, pinch, finger grip, and finger wrap.

In the open grip (A) you use a maximum amount of surface area of your fingers and hand to grip a hold; this works well on large and rounded holds. You can use the friction of your palm, called *palming*, to increase the security of the hold. Use a cling grip (B) when the pads of your fingers fit on the hold. You can stabilize the grip by placing your thumb over the adjacent finger to provide support and additional strength.

On narrow positive holds, use the vertical grip (C). Bend your fingers at the second joint and fold the first two joints into the third, forming your hand into a hold-grabbing hook. This grip transfers your weight to the rock through your fingertips. The hold does place stress on the bone structure and tendons of your fingers, so using this grip extensively can damage finger tendons. The ends of your fingers are also likely to hurt. The vertical grip does allow you to *crank*—pull your hardest—on the smallest of positive holds and to feel relatively secure while you do. On very small holds

*Figure 1-3. Frictioning*

Figure 1-4. *Hand and Finger Holds: A—Open grip; B—Cling grip with thumb as stabilizer; C—Vertical grip; D—Pinch grip; E—Finger wrap; F—Finger grip.*

you can make the vertical grip more secure by hooking your fingernails over the rock crystals to provide a powerful but potentially painful hold.

Use the pinch, or squeeze, grip (D) on holds with two surfaces that you can pinch together. On large holds this grip can engage the whole hand; on holds the size of a pebble you use a couple of fingers. On small holds pinch the hold between your thumb and the side of your index finger for the greatest holding power.

You can often more securely hold protruding rounded knobs and even large protruding crystals that you might otherwise pinch-grip by using a finger wrap (E). Wrap your small finger, and as many other fingers as you can, around the knob to create maximum surface contact between your fingers and the rock. Maximize contact between the side of your small finger and the rock, and hook the bend in the second joint of this finger over an upper sharp bend in the knob. Pressing your thumb against either your fingers or the knob may help to stabilize the wrap.

You can use a finger grip (F) in thin cracks, piton scars, and small pockets. Insert a finger into the hole and *cam,* or twist, your finger. Combine this with a pull to the side to enhance the cam. Fitting two or more fingers side by side in the hole increases the strength of the grip. Stack fingers on top of each other in holes that are taller than they are wide. Experiment with different ways of inserting your fingers to determine what works best. Remember that handholds should help you maintain balance, while footwork actually moves you up the cliff. Pulling up mostly on finger strength can be very strenuous and may lead to injury.

### Balance and Progression in Face Climbing

Once you know individual foot and hand techniques, you need to put them together. Do you use a vertical grip while edging with the inside of your left foot, or do you use an open grip while smearing with both feet? Is it better to go fast or slow? How do you transfer body weight from one hold to another? To use the dance analogy, these problems are like knowing the individual steps to a dance, and then learning how to link them together into a graceful choreographed pattern that flows over the dance floor.

Face climbing, like dance, emphasizes balance over the feet and smooth body shifts. By standing upright over your feet, you use gravity to stay on the rock, as shown in Figure 1-5. If you stand upright on a slab, the downward force of gravity pulls you into the rock. If you lean into the rock, on the other hand, gravity pulls your feet away from the rock, resulting in a slide down the rock face.

correct:
upright position

incorrect:
leaning position

*Figure 1-5. Gravity and Balance on Slabs*

Small steps, often measured in inches, help you maintain balance. They also bring the power of large leg muscles into play and substitute leg strength for that of weaker forearm and upper-arm muscles, so you will not need to hang off small finger holds as much.

### The Hand Traverse on a Slab

In a hand traverse, you have positive holds for your hands while your feet smear, friction, or occasionally edge. A classic hand traverse leading diagonally, right to left, across a slab illustrates how you put together different foot and hand techniques. The climber in Figure 1-6 maintains his center of gravity by squatting over his feet and leaning back on his arms. This stance keeps his body weight over his feet so that they do not slide out from under him. He uses a vertical grip on the small holds available but will switch to open grip, cling, finger, or pinch technique as he encounters appropriate holds. He frictions with his feet, but will smear on rounded holds and stand on his inside shoe edge if appropriate holds appear at points on crossing the slab. When hand-traversing a slab, you often cross hands to make long reaches from one good hold to another as you shuffle your feet beneath your body.

*Figure 1-6. A Classic Hand Traverse Across a Slab, Moving from Right to Left*

### Mantleshelves

A mantleshelf is a rock shelf with a wall behind it. (The shelf found above a fireplace is a mantelshelf.) When you approach this shelf from below, it first provides handholds. Climbing past the shelf presents problems of balance that become greater if the shelf slopes outward, if it has a rounded edge, and if the wall behind gets steeper and more featureless.

Mantling, the act of surmounting the shelf, is a skill that can be broken up into a number of steps. For a wide shelf (Figure 1-7A), mantle facing the rock. From below, feel around on the shelf for the best finger holds so you can start pulling yourself upward; leave room for your foot on the shelf so you do not step on your hand. If the shelf is not too high, you may be able to place your palm on the shelf to bear weight as you move up in the next step.

In the second step, hoist your upper body as high as possible to enable you to cock your arm next to the wall. You can use small footholds or friction with your feet to assist upward movement. You need to get high enough to lean your upper body over your cocked arm and the palm of your hand. This places your body's center of gravity over your hands and allows you to straighten your

arm. This position also uses your triceps efficiently to push your body weight upward. If you do not get high enough to get your body weight over your cocked arm, the mantle move will fail and you will have to reverse the movement in order not to fall. To succeed in mantling you must commit to an active, forceful, or dynamic move (as opposed to a slow-motion, near-static move) and a vulnerable position of balance to get your body weight well over your palm. This challenge makes hard mantles interesting.

As you move your body upward, you can rotate your hand on the shelf to bear your body weight over your palm if you could not do so in the initial setup. It takes coordination to hoist yourself and turn your hand at the same time. Getting as much friction as possible on the palm of your hand is important when the shelf slopes outward and is slippery.

You can mantle onto small shelves by turning your body sideways (Figure 1-7B), a position that allows you room to lean forward. If the shelf is very small, you can place one hand on top of the other to leave room for your foot. Otherwise you may find that you have to place your foot on top of your hand, making it difficult to stand. (Some experienced climbers have actually fallen and broken bones after standing on their own hands.) Once you are positioned sideways, hoist yourself upward and lean forward to get your body weight over your cocked arm. Stabilize your balance in this position before attempting to bring a foot up onto the shelf. Then press your body upward to complete the mantle sequence. Finish by bringing a foot up onto the mantleshelf and standing up.

Small handholds or finger holds above the shelf that enable you to pull downward or to the side will greatly enhance this final move onto the shelf. In the absence of positive holds, you can try smearing the palm of your hand on the steep wall behind the shelf to create a tenuous friction hold. While you are using one hand on the wall behind the shelf, you can use the other hand to push up off the shelf or even off your foot (which is on the shelf) to help you stand. The act of standing is easier if your foot is underneath your body, rather than out to

Figure 1-7. *Two Sequences of Mantling onto a Shelf:*
*A—Directly; B—On one side.*

the side. This movement means you need to use your leg muscles to help walk your foot sideways, in a series of small movements, until you can load it fully.

On some steep face routes, climbers run into a situation where there is a large positive foothold slightly off to the side, but almost no handholds to help you stand up. You can overcome this problem by placing your instep and heel, rather than the ball of your foot, over the hold before standing up, using leg power to lift you over the hold. This maneuver works because it places your center of gravity over your foot as you attempt to stand. Combine it with mantle technique and side pulls to aid in standing.

### Counterforces: Underclings, Liebacks, and Stemming

Counterforce is a general technique applied to many types of climbing. You generate forces that act in opposite, or counter, directions to create friction and provide balance. You can create these forces by opposing your hands, as if you were attempting to spread open a crack, or your feet (*stemming*), or you can produce a counterweight to help balance your body over your feet, or by leaning off holds as in underclinging, liebacking, and stemming.

Underclings and liebacks differ in the orientation of the holds used for opposition. Underclings involve using your hands palm up in an upward pull that you oppose by pushing downward with your feet (Figure 1-8). A pure undercling allows you to make a long reach from beneath a horizontal overhang or flake. With your feet smearing, edging, or frictioning, you push down with your feet and walk them higher, while pulling up with your arms. This produces forces in opposition that glue you onto the rock while you make that long reach to a high hold. Many undercling sequences last only one or two moves, although you can undercling rock flakes for long stretches.

Liebacks often follow vertical cracks for long distances between stances that allow you to rest. You can use lieback technique one move at a time, but you can also use continuous lieback technique

Figure 1-8. *The Undercling to a Long Reach: The climber uses the bottom of a rock flake as an undercling hold. His hands pull upward on the hold while his feet push downward onto a friction slab to create opposing forces. Then he can walk his feet up the slab, while maintaining opposition, and reach up with one hand to gain a high handhold. Small downward-pointing flakes can also be used to create opposition.*

to climb cracks in 90-degree corners or flakes on a wall. You climb lieback corners using your feet against one wall while your hands pull in the opposite direction to produce the counterforce, as shown in Figure 1-9. When the wall is smooth, your toe points directly up it, with the entire sole against the wall to maximize friction. Keep your feet as high as possible to prevent them from slipping off. This position strains fingers, hands, wrists, arms, shoulders, and back muscles and requires commitment to the technique, or you will fall off.

Falls most often occur in liebacking when your feet slip off because you lower them to lessen the stress on your arms and hands. Less frequently,

A

B

Figure 1-9. **Liebacking a Corner: A**—The climber pulls against the crack with a straight arm and pushes in the opposite direction with his feet against the flat wall. He needs to keep his feet high and close to his hands to generate enough counterforce to adhere to the rock. If he stands upright over his feet, they will slip off the rock and he will fall out of the lieback. Usually, liebacks fail when your feet slip as you attempt to relieve stress on your arms.

**B**—The climber has moved his right foot upward onto a small edge that allows him to stand up a little straighter without having his feet slip off. This position reduces the counterforce strength that he must generate with his arms. Small positive toeholds allow you to lessen your effort before continuing, but you must still lean back and cannot stay in this position for long before continuing.

your hands slip off a rounded edge that you are palming. Cracks with sharp edges afford a good grip and make liebacks easier. If there are positive edges or lower-angle spots to friction, then you can stand in a more upright position to relieve stress on your hands and arms. You can occasionally turn your foot at a right angle to insert your toe into a wide spot in the crack to give a foothold.

Because of the strenuous nature of liebacks, climbers usually inspect a lieback for potential rests before starting out. Then they move quickly

Figure 1-10. **Stemming on a Steep Face Using Counterforces**

along to a rest spot, such as a stemming position that has footholds on both sides of the corner. The most difficult part of the lieback in a corner often occurs where the crack becomes less vertical. This difficulty arises because your feet are still on the steep wall, demanding a strong counterforce that you have difficulty providing because your hands no longer have as positive an edge to grip.

Liebacking is often mixed with face climbing, stemming, and jamming.

### Stemming

Climbers often stem between flake edges on steep faces. The boulderer in Figure 1-10 stands on flake edges using the inside balls of her feet to bring her center of gravity closer to the wall, placing most of her weight over her feet. She establishes and maintains upper-body balance by pinch-gripping rock flakes as she pulls her hands toward each other. The opposition forces created between her two hands counter another set of opposition forces created by her feet, as shown by the arrows.

The classic stem takes place in a right-angle corner where both walls have positive edges or smear holds (Figure 1-11). Stemming in a corner has an advantage over stemming on a face. On a face you can only move your legs so far apart before your hips hurt and you lose balance. In a corner you can increase your stem span by turning and rotating your hip. In doing this you "backfoot" the holds behind you to provide counterforce.

Stemming is a type of face climbing, since upward progress depends on footwork combined with mantle-type moves and horizontal pull moves. Occasionally you can find a pull move for your hands to help stand over your feet. Beginners expecting abundant positive downward pull holds may have a very difficult time progressing, while an expert enjoys a relatively easy ascent.

Stemming can be useful even if the corners do not have walls at right angles. You can sometimes stem shallow grooves on steep faces. Rock climbers can ascend overhanging cracks more easily if there is any opportunity to stem on face holds on either side of the crack. Ice climbers can ascend overhanging shallow grooves in a relatively straightforward manner by stemming between walls with crampons. In all cases, stemming effectively brings your body position from leaning backward to vertical and allows you to get weight off your arms onto your feet.

*Figure 1-11. Stemming in a Corner*

### Weight Shifts

Climbing on a face involves smoothly shifting your center of gravity from one position to another. The climber in Figure 1-12 starts a traverse to the left by placing her leading foot onto a distant and slightly higher hold. At the end of this initial movement (A), her center of gravity is slightly left of her right foot, which supports most of her weight. She maintains balance by providing a counterforce off the distance foothold while gripping small finger holds. To move her right foot left at this time would place her center of gravity to the right of her feet and upset her balance. The small finger holds will not allow her to apply enough upper body strength to offset the resulting poor balance, and she would fall.

In a correct movement sequence, she moves her hips to the left (B), which shifts her center of gravity in the traverse direction. This allows her to stand in a stemming position with her center of gravity equally spaced between the two footholds, requiring very little upper body strength. To complete the movement, she moves her left hand and then her right hand in the traverse direction in preparation for the last weight shift. The final weight shift (D) moves her center of gravity first horizontally and then vertically in a smooth flow. She moves her center of gravity horizontally toward her left foot assisted by a pull from her left hand and a springing start from her right foot. She completes the sequence in a flowing manner by pushing upward with her left leg once her center of gravity is over this foot. To continue traversing she may have to change feet in one of the ways described below.

### Foot Sequences and Changing Feet

On a face, handholds and footholds, body position, and balance depend on each other. Often a sequence requires you to lead onto the next foothold with the left (or right) foot. If you use the other foot, your balance will be upset, your movement on the climb will falter, and you could even fall.

You have two options to put the correct foot forward. You can down-climb back to the last hold big enough to stand on with both feet and start out the second time with the other foot to gain the correct sequence. On a difficult climb you may have to go quite a distance, so a better option is to stay where you are and switch feet.

You can switch feet either statically or dynamically. You can switch statically if there is room on the hold for both feet; when the holds are relatively small, you hop. Figure 1-13 shows a static switch from right foot to left foot. The climber starts with

Figure 1-12. **Weight Shifts When Traversing a Steep Face from Right to Left**

D          C          B          A

*Figure 1-13. Static Foot Exchange*

*Figure 1-14. Hopping—Dynamic Foot Exchange*

A  B  C

A  B  C

her right toe on the hold (A). She sets her left toe down on the hold and gradually rotates her left foot downward to cover more of the hold (B) as she simultaneously removes her right foot by wiggling it off the hold (C). Notice that the position of her upper body does not alter during the foot exchange; her fingers maintain upper body balance.

The climber in Figure 1-14 also begins on her right foot and ends on her left. Since she only needs to have one foot on the hold at a time, she covers the hold with the ball of her foot (A). This foot placement requires less effort than that of the static sequence, where only the toe was on the hold. She sets up for the hop by gripping the positive finger holds well and then springing up or hopping off her right foot (B). Her upper body moves upward and downward during the hop; she moves both feet to the right and prepares to land on the inside ball of her left foot (C). The hop is quick and takes very little energy, but requires some coordination, and a couple of small positive finger holds.

### Barn Doors and Counterbalancing

When climbing on a steep face, you need to figure out how to keep your center of gravity, located somewhere around your navel, over your feet—or even one foot—as you move from hold to hold. As long as you grip two good handholds with vigor, you can offset poor balance, but you always have to let go of one hold to move on.

The climber in Figure 1-15 has a great handhold for his left hand and an adequate finger hold for his right. His right foot is on a small positive hold, and his left foot hangs in space (A). His balance point, somewhere around his navel, is to the left of his right foot, but he manages to compensate for this by pulling himself to the left using that good handhold. When he lets go of the left handhold, his center of gravity, indeed his entire body, rotates or *barn-doors* around the axis formed by his right foot and right hand (B). He is about to fall off unless he can pull off a most amazing save.

The climber could avoid the barn door by using his body as a counterweight to achieve balance. If

*Figure 1-15.* **The Barn Door—Counterbalancing on a Face**

the climber is to use the same foothold and finger hold as he did when he barn-doored in Figure 1-15, he has a couple of options. To make a high reach overhead (Figure 1-16A), he switches his left foot onto the small foothold and bends his torso to the left; his center of gravity is slightly left of his foot on the hold. He also places his right foot away from his body, using it as a counterweight to shift his center of gravity slightly to the right. He finishes up in balance over the foothold, assisted by gripping a small finger hold with his right hand.

The second option is to use these same holds to make a long reach to the left (Figure 1-16B). Here the climber begins in the position that previously led to the barn door. This time, however, he repositions his hanging left leg behind the right leg as a counterweight to move his center of gravity to the right. This use of a foot as a counterweight

Figure 1-16. *Using the Body as Counterweight for Long Reaches: A—The long reach overhead; B—The long reach to the side.*

This sequence seems complex, but it is a bit like learning how to ride a bike: you have to program your motor memory. After a few false starts and falls, you will find that very little effort is required. Climbing several grades below what you can just physically manage will allow you to acquire individual techniques and master putting them into sequence.

### Rest and Balance on a Steep Face

On steep climbs with sparse large holds, you usually want to move along as quickly as possible, but you occasionally need to rest to conserve energy. Move your midsection (and center of gravity) closer to the rock and over your feet (Figure 1-18). Hold your head back to see the next section of rock and hang your upper body off the bone structure of a straight arm. Placing one foot higher

gives him enough balance to cling to the finger hold while making the long reach left to a better hold.

### Combined Techniques

As you progress up any section of rock, you are likely to combine various climbing techniques. For example, the climber in Figure 1-17 edges with the outside of his left foot, smears with his right foot, mantles with his left hand, and starts an undercling with his right hand. He is using these holds to mantle and smear upward so that he can convert a relatively weak finger-grip undercling to a solid hand-grip undercling. After he has this solid hand undercling he will rotate his hip to the right so that he faces the rock. At that point he will move his left hand up to join his right in the undercling and work his left toe onto the mantle hold. Next, he moves his right hand around the right side of the flake so that he can lieback the flake and stand up.

Figure 1-17. *Combined Techniques*

than the other enhances the stability of this position by allowing your midsection to move closer to the rock. The tripod formed between your two feet and straight arm is a restful position.

### Foot Placement Under Overhangs

If you use the large, seductive foot placements often found deep under overhangs, you are likely to destroy your balance during a long reach to good holds above. If, like the climber in Figure 1-19A, you incorrectly place your foot deep under the overhang on a large placement and extend your body full-length to reach a positive handhold above, you will lean backward out of balance,

**A**
incorrect

**B**
correct

*Figure 1-19. Incorrect and Correct Foot Placements Under Overhangs*

*Figure 1-18. Rest Position: On a face the climber has one foot higher than the other, with hips swung into the cliff, and grips the higher hold with a straight arm.*

your elbows fully extended. You will reduce your ability to power up and you cannot see your next foothold. You will most likely fall if you attempt to move. Instead, return to your starting position and place your toe as far to the outside of the overhang as possible, using a small hold. Your foot will be beneath your center of gravity, enhancing your balance. By standing on your toe you also have a better reach: your elbows remain flexed and your arms can apply power. You can lean back to view your feet, step higher, and pull over the overhang (Figure 1-19B).

*Figure 1-20. **Null Moves and Pulling Over Overhangs:***
*A—Semirest position under an overhang; B—Last look;*
*C—The partial null move; D—Foot up and power up.*

### Semirest and Null Moves on Overhangs

Even when you cannot hang off a straight arm, if you rotate your hips into the wall you will place more weight over your feet and less on your fingers, hands, and arms. If you are underneath an overhang, swing your hips into the cliff (Figure 1-20A) in order to exert less effort. In this semiresting position you can get a good look at the holds above before continuing.

You can maintain balance in a static or dynamic manner, but if you move dynamically, passing through a series of small holds to arrive at a large one in a smooth flow, you will use less energy than if you do the moves statically, one at a time. The *null,* or *deadpoint,* move is a dynamic move that

requires good timing, courage, and bombproof protection nearby when you are in the learning phase. In its most dynamic form, the null move requires that your hands and feet completely leave the rock in an upward leap for higher holds. At the top of the leap, when you are no longer going upward and not yet started downward, you are momentarily weightless at the deadpoint. Pulling off a null move involves coordination to grip the higher hold in the fraction of a second that you have at the apex. There is the chance that you will miss the hold and fall, so only try this near good protection or with an overhead top-rope belay until you feel comfortable with the technique. Since the null move is so committing and easy to

C

D

miss, climbers more commonly use a partial null move to progress, as demonstrated by the climber in Figure 1-20.

The climber is doing a series of dynamic moves to surmount an overhang. He moves his feet up in opposition to the undercling holds and leans out on straightened arms for one last look before committing to the overhang (B). Between B and C he pivots into the wall over his feet, releases his right hand at the moment that he is no longer rotating forward and before he begins to rotate backward (the *deadpoint*), and reaches quickly but in control to grab the higher hold. During this move the climber's torso first moves into the wall and then upward. After grabbing the higher hold, he hangs from a straight arm to inspect his next move (C).

Leaning backward also leaves room between the rock and the climber's body to bring a foot up for pulling over the overhang. The climber sees another hold to the right of his body that will both give him room to bring his foot up and allow him to lever off a side pull to lift his body over the overhang. He puts a foot up and moves his hand to the right hold, shifts his center of gravity over the high foothold as he stands (D), and simultaneously brings his left hand up to the higher hold.

Common problems with dynamic technique are lack of commitment to the move, poor timing, and overshooting the hold.

In exiting from an overhang you need to maintain balance between footholds and handholds as handholds become smaller and the overhang hides footholds. Figure 1-21 shows a climber beginning

A         B         C         D

incorrect        correct

*Figure 1-21.* **Overhang Exits**

to exit from an overhang. She maintains balance between foot stemming and small finger holds (A). She needs additional holds to complete her exit, and B and C illustrate two options.

In the first option (B), the climber stretches full body length and reaches a high, large handhold with her fingers. Although the finger hold may be secure, the body position is not. Stretched out, the climber cannot see higher foot placements and does not have room to move her feet up. In this position she cannot use the upper body power required for the large handhold. Unbalanced, she is about to fall. This "flop" option is a poor choice.

The second option (C) allows the climber to maintain her balance. Starting from her initial position in A, she leans back on her finger holds. She can see her feet and has room to move them. With her right foot on a small edging hold, she moves her left foot on top of the overhang and then shifts her center of gravity forward to place her weight over this higher foot (D). The next step will take her up the final slab above the overhang to finish.

## Crack Climbing

On many cliffs, cracks offer natural lines of weakness that are used to produce climbs of the highest quality. Routes that follow natural crack systems, vertical lines along which a drop of water would fall, are the only flaw in an otherwise smooth face and have long been considered the classic and ideal route up the rock face. Crack climbing ability does not come naturally but requires experience, experimentation, and guidance. It can be strenuous and painful, and you may feel insecure until you have mastered the techniques. Why, then, do some climbers prefer crack climbing to all other forms? It provides good holds, good protection, and challenging routes up otherwise smooth and steep rock.

Crack climbing involves inserting your fingers, hands, feet, or even knees into the crack and camming them so that they lock. This process is *jamming*. Once you have jammed your feet and hands, you are secured to the rock and can remove one hand or foot at a time, move it upward, and jam it again. You repeat the process with the next hand or foot.

*Jam cracks* are classified by their width, since width determines which part of your body you jam. *Thin cracks* allow for finger jams, *hand cracks* allow for jamming the hand, and *fist cracks* allow for fist jams. Cracks that fall between these sizes require combining techniques. When cracks are larger than fist size, they are called *offwidth* and require specialized techniques.

Much of what has been said about balance and movement in face climbing also applies to crack climbing, with the addition of the specific crack techniques discussed below for handholds and footholds. In crack climbing you often use one foot or one hand on a face hold or on friction to maintain correct body position and upward movement.

### Thin Cracks

Thin cracks range from the width of the tip of a small pinkie finger to a size that allows the fingers to be inserted up to the knuckles. As with all cracks, you must choose to insert your fingers thumb up or thumb down. The thumb-down position allows the hand to rotate, or torque, which often makes the jam more secure.

If you can put only the tip of your pinkie into the crack, you usually hold the hand thumb up. (If

*Figure 1-22.* **The Pinkie Jam for a Thin Crack:** *Insert your pinkie and neighboring fingers into the crack and rotate your palm to lie against the left wall of the crack to secure the jam before moving on it.*

additional fingers fit into the crack, you *stack* them on top of your pinkie to increase the security of the jam.) A pinkie jam (Figure 1-22) is rather insecure, but you can strengthen it by leaning to one side or the other as in a lieback. If the crack leans to the left, for example, you might have a high pinkie jam with the right hand; your left hand will be low in the crack jamming, liebacking, or using a face hold on the left. Your left foot will usually be active out on the left face, edging any positive hold or smearing rounded holds. The inside edge of your right foot might well be stabilizing you by pushing against any protruding edge of the crack.

When a crack is wide enough to insert your fingers to the knuckle, new possibilities open up for jamming thumb down. You create a *finger lock* by inserting your fingers into the crack and rotating your thumb to create a cam (Figure 1-23A). If one edge of the crack offsets, you can use your thumb on the raised lip to create a counterforce to that created by your fingers (Figure 1-23B). When the crack is wide enough to insert your thumb, you can form a *ring jam* (Figure 1-23C). Your thumb closes upward, with your fingers pointing downward to form a ring. This works especially well if the crack has a narrow spot and flares out above

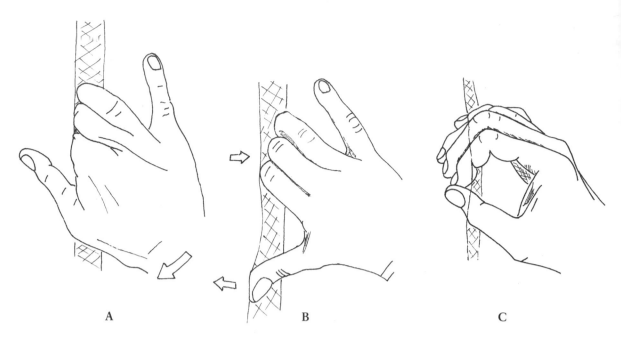

A                              B                              C

*Figure 1-23.* **Thin Crack Jams with the Thumb Down:**
*A—Finger lock; B—Finger lock with counterpressure by
the thumb; C—Ring jam.*

and below. The fingers stack in the taper above the narrows and the thumb pulls upward from below. When the ring closes, you have a kind of pinch grip that firmly welds you to the rock.

### Hand Cracks

Many climbers consider a crack that accepts the whole hand to be the perfect crack. You insert your hand with straight fingers, and your thumb is tucked in under your palm or placed on top of your index finger to help stabilize the jam. You create the hand jam by pressing your fingers against one side of the crack while the back of your hand presses against the other side. If your fingers can grip small knobs, cracks, or irregularities within the larger crack, your hand jam is all the more secure. Hand jams are shown in Figure 1-24A and B.

Hand jams are often tight, and you'll have to move your hand to find the most secure position. Some climbers find additional security by leaning to the left or right to lieback the crack off a jam. You can severely abrade the back of your hand or your wrist if you allow your hand to rotate in the

crack. To avoid these abrasions, insert your hand straight into the crack, rotating your wrist as you move upward. Most climbers also tape their hands or use commercially available Spider Mitts to prevent abrasions that result from hand rotation.

In jamming, you often use your upper hand in a thumb-down position while you use your lower hand thumb-up. You do this most often when the crack leans to one side or the other. When the crack is a straight-in vertical crack, you may be able to use both hands thumb up. If you are placing protection, a thumb-down jam overhead allows you to cam your hand for security.

If you use a thumb-down position above a constriction, you can mantle on the jam to make a long reach. Likewise, you can jam your lower hand, thumb up, against a constriction in a crack. As you make the high reach, move your feet up much as you would do when using an undercling.

A crack that readily accepts a hand jam will be the right size to jam a toe, so that you can move upward by using leg strength as you do in face climbing. Initiate a toe jam by rotating the sole of

Figure 1-24. **Hand and Toe Jams:** Λ—*Wide hand crack;* B—*Narrow hand crack;* C—*Toe jams.*

Figure 1-25. **Fist Jams:** A—*Fist jam with palm facing into the crack; B—View of the fist position with thumb over the fingers; C—Hand position for a narrow fist jam.*

your shoe to parallel the crack walls, insert it into the crack, and rotate your sole back to a horizontal position to cam it as you stand up (Figure 1-24C). In practice, you can focus on movement of your knee away from and toward the crack, since it controls the position of your foot and shoe sole. Toe jamming, like hand jamming, can be a painful process.

## Fist-size Cracks

In the classic fist jam, your thumb tucks in under your fingers with your palm facing into the crack (Figure 1-25A). In wider cracks you can place your thumb over your index finger to form a wider fist (Figure 1-25B), but this position produces a painful jam. In a narrow crack tuck your thumb under your palm, and fold your index finger and pinkie into your palm underneath the two middle fingers (Figure 1-25C).

A fist-size crack is more difficult to jam than a hand crack because you cannot expand your fist as much or with the same amount of force as you can expand your hand. The width of the fist jam is primarily determined by whether you place your thumb under your palm or over your index finger. As a result, fist jams work best just above a constriction and require conscious placement to find the best position.

When a large portion of your foot fits into the crack, you can use a foot jam, which is more secure when placed just above a constriction. Do not insert your foot too far, because the jam produced may be so good that you cannot extract it easily. If you should get stuck, you may have to climb back down a step to reverse the loading sequence.

### Offwidth Cracks

When a crack is too large for a fist or a foot, it is an offwidth crack. In narrow offwidths you use your entire arm in an arm bar (Figure 1-26A) to hold yourself in place. Your outside foot moves you up the crack in a heel-toe action, as sketched in Figure 1-26B. In a good heel-toe jam you keep your toes below and slightly outside your heel and smear the ball of your big toe. Your inside leg should be in a leg lock that you achieve by rotating your hip, knee, toe, and heel for maximum adhesion.

The arm bar, inside the crack, opposes the back of your upper arm and elbow against one wall of the crack while your hand pushes against the opposite wall. Arm bars work well if your arm and hand are diagonally down and away from your shoulder, allowing your shoulder to rotate in and over the elbow. The outside hand, on the edge of the crack, can often be low, pushing up on any lower-angle spot.

To make upward progress hold your body in place with the arm bar and inside leg lock while moving the heel-toe jam as high as possible. Then release the inside leg lock and stand up on the new

A
arm bar

B
heel-toe

*Figure 1-26.* **Narrow Offwidth Cracks:** *A—The arm bar in a narrow offwidth;* **B**—*The heel-toe sequence.*

heel-toe jam, with an outward motion of your hips. Finally, release your arms and move your upper body up to reestablish the arm bar. You have now arrived back at the starting body position and are a little higher in the crack.

As the offwidth becomes wider, you can use your arm inside the crack in a wide arm bar. Your outside hand uses whatever hold or friction is available on the edge of the crack (Figure 1-27A). If the crack becomes too wide to heel-toe, stack

**A**
arm bar

**B**
foot stacking

**C**
wide foot stacking

your feet at angles up to 90 degrees, as shown in Figure 1-27B and C.

Not everyone enjoys overhanging offwidth cracks, but a movement sequence created by Randy Leavitt and Tony Yaniro, called *Leavittation*, makes climbing them possible. You hang from a handstack and support your weight on one jammed knee as you move the handstack. For example, in a left-leaning crack that fits your knee, place your left palm against the left-hand crack wall and jam your right fist between your left hand and the right-hand crack wall, palm outward (palm inward for a vertical crack). To move the handstack, support your weight on your knee while palming and liebacking the crack and using

your abdominal muscles. After setting the handstack, release the jammed knee, and heal-toe and balance with the other leg as you move the right foot directly below the handstack. Then, jam your right knee as high as possible and remove your right foot from the crack, and hook your toe against the rock to lock the jam. Blue jeans are a good choice of clothing for this technique because they inhibit knee abrasion, do not stretch, and can be taped at the ankle to prevent bunching around the knees.

### Spreading the Crack

When cracks are hand or fist to offwidth in size, you can *spread the crack* by creating opposition

Figure 1-28. *Spreading a Crack*

Figure 1-29. **The Chimney Feetback Sequence**

Sit in a higher position and repeat the feet-back movement.

force with your hands on the sides of the crack (Figure 1-28). Spreading the crack works particularly well if there are small flakes inside the crack around which you can wrap your fingers, and if the crack is not vertical. Indeed, the technique works well in face climbing if you have opposing flakes as holds. Spreading a crack grows more strenuous as positive holds inside the crack and on its edge become fewer and as the crack becomes overhanging. On overhangs this technique may allow you to set up to move to the next and, you hope, better hold.

### Chimneys

Cracks wide enough to accept your entire body are called *narrow*, or *squeeze, chimneys*. These chimneys may also flare—they may be narrower on the inside than on the outside. There is a tendency to move back into a chimney because of the sense of security that comes from being firmly wedged in. However, it is as hard to move up as it is to slip down when you are securely wedged. Climb squeeze chimneys by using offwidth techniques involving heel-toe and foot stacking, or bridging if the chimney is just a bit wider. Meanwhile, use an arm in an arm bar. You can often bypass constrictions in a chimney by jam-

Push off with the hand at your waist and stand up.

One hand may be out for stability or on the rear wall to push up.

Begin with your foot back and move your hand(s) to waist height.

ming a hand or fist above the constriction and liebacking around it off the jam.

In wider chimneys your feet, knees, and hands bridge on opposite walls, providing counterforces to hold you in. You are, in effect, camming your entire body. In a wide chimney you unload, move, and then set the body cam—feet against one wall, back against the other. The *chimney feetback sequence* is shown in Figure 1-29. This technique can feel precarious, since you unload the cam by using your leg to push upward against gravity. You feel secure only when you are stationary after the cam is reloaded. If you ever have to down-climb a chimney, you will find that it is not as insecure as it might seem because gravity helps you move downward into a secure, cammed body position.

## Taping for Hand and Fist Jam Cracks

When you climb cracks, rotating a jammed hand on protruding crystals can quickly shred the back of your hand and wrist. Taping can save a lot of pain. Commercial Spider Mitts made of 5-10 rubber are an alternative that also works well.

*Figure 1-30. Palmless Glove Taping Pattern*

(Time will tell if these mitts become popular.) To tape your hands, use breathable athletic tape or medical cloth adhesive tape from a sporting or medical supply store. Before taping, clean your hands of dirt and skin oils with soap or alcohol. If your hands are hairy, you can shave the hair or burn it off, being careful not to cut or burn yourself. (If you do not mind pulling your hair out by its roots when you remove the tape, you may forgo this last step.)

The pattern of taping shown in Figure 1-30 forms a palmless glove that allows you to feel and grip the rock but protects the back of your hand and has the advantage of being reusable. It works extremely well for hand jams, though it does not protect the side of the hand well; use a wrap-around tape pattern or modification of the palmless glove with extended sides for pure fist jamming.

Loop a long strip of 1-inch-wide tape starting from the wrist, up the back of the hand, around a finger, and back down to the wrist (A). Pinch the strip in half where it passes around the finger. Repeat for each finger and the thumb (B). Tie the finger strips together by taping across the knuckles and the back of the hand and around the wrist (C), so that no skin remains exposed (D). (The tape for step C can be any width.) Be sure to flex your hand when taping to allow the hand to bend throughout its full range. Your wrists will swell in the course of a strenuous jamming session: do not wrap them too tightly. Additional strips of tape along the base of the thumb and across the knuckles help tie all of the strips together and close up any holes. Make sure no skin shows through.

At the end of the day, use scissors (rather than a knife) to cut the glove off at the inside of the wrist (E). Peel the tape up over the fingers. Reuse the glove by positioning it over the fingers and thumb and wrapping the wrist with new tape. After about a week of daily use, you may need to make a new glove as the wrist becomes so thickened with tape that its flexibility is limited.

You can tape your knuckles for climbing finger cracks, particularly when you anticipate doing a move involving a jam with one or two knuckles.

A simple wrap of the tape around the joint that allows the joint to bend seems to work.

## Rock-climbing Shoes

Most climbers do their first climbs in nothing more than a pair of running shoes, basketball shoes, or boots, and classic first ascents have been done in sneakers. But given a choice, most of us prefer to climb in shoes specially made for climbing. These shoes have evolved a great deal, particularly during the 1980s and 1990s.

Pioneer Victorian climbers led out in smooth-soled boots. To give these boots more friction they began adding soft iron nails to the soles and heels. These nails evolved into special patterns and types arranged around the edge and interior. On modern soles individual rubber lugs mimic the shapes of individual nails worn by the earlier climbers (Figure 1-31A). The pattern of a unique collection of these nails is preserved in the trademarked Vibram lug pattern. (The name Vibram derives from *Vitale Bram*ani, one of its inventors.) Nailed boots worked to some extent on granite and even helped climbers stand in cut steps on snow and ice. On dolomite rock, a rock similar to limestone, some climbers preferred hemp-soled boots, as frayed strands of rope would catch on sharp edges and protrusions to provide good traction.

During the 1950s shoes with Vibram-type soles predominated, evolving over the course of two decades, and culminating in Royal Robbins climbing shoes. Commonly called RRs, these had distinctive blue suede uppers and a special composition sole. Indeed, if you own a pair, they are still the preferred shoes for climbing Yosemite-type walls, and they work very well for alpine rock climbs. Unfortunately, they are no longer available.

Smooth-soled shoes similar to modern climbing shoes began to make their appearance in the 1960s. The shoes were named after the initials of famous climbers. The RD (René Desmaison), which had brown leather uppers, quickly became

*Figure 1-31. **Climbing Shoes Through Time:** A—The Royal Robbins shoe is still considered to be the best big-wall boot. The rubber sole pattern is that used by Galibier, the company that manufactured the shoes. B—The EB dominated climbing in the late 1960s and the 1970s. C—The Fire started the modern shoe revolution in 1982. D—The La Sportiva Tao, a modern low-cut anatomical shoe for steep edging, has a slingshot rand that limits lengthwise stretching.*

popular. Other climbers preferred the high top PA (Pierre Allain) for edging. The soles of both were made of a hard composition rubber. By the end of the 1960s, EBs came to dominate the climbing-shoe market and did so for the next decade. The EB (Edouard Bourdineau) had a softer composition sole that gripped the rock well by standards of the time, but a canvas upper that quickly became brittle from foot perspiration. Because the shoes were made on a narrow European last, some

climbers went around with tightly pinched toes. Those who wore small shoes to give them superior edging control suffered great pain and many lost their toenails to a malady called EB Toe or Black Toe.

In 1982, the Fire (pronounced *fee-ray*) climbing shoe, featuring a sticky Spanish rubber, was introduced to the climbing world. This shoe revolutionized both shoe designs and climbing. Wearing sticky rubber, climbers found that they could casually stand on rock slopes where they had slid down previously. A new world of extreme friction and face climbing opened up in the 1980s. Sticky rubber is a softer composition that deforms well over microcrystals, providing good holding power, but it is less durable than harder rubber when used for edging and therefore wears more quickly.

The 1980s saw an increase in the number of people climbing. Along with the Fires came new protection and greater numbers of fitness-minded individuals who took up climbing, leading in turn to increased interest by shoe manufacturers, who produced shoes that fit better and function better than earlier shoes. You now have your choice of shoes with soft or hard rubber, pointed shoes for steep faces with pockets, and stiff shoes for edging, supple sticky shoes for friction and slabs, high-top shoes with sticky rands (rubber around the edge) and flat toes for cracks, and low-cut shoes for ankle flexibility on overhangs. All of them have a close fit—they average one to one-and-a-half sizes smaller than street shoes—to fill the shoe and eliminate foot roll from small edges. At an extreme, some specialized and painful shoes curl your toes under to allow you to stand on micro-edges. When you choose climbing shoes, remember that they will stretch about one-half size sideways and perhaps lengthwise, depending on material and construction. Most climbing shoes have rubber rands that wrap completely around the bottom edge of the shoe to help grip in corners or cracks. Some newer shoes, like the La Sportiva Tao (Figure 1-31D), prevent lengthwise stretching with a non-stretching slingshot rand that extends from the upper heel to the toe. Remember that you will have to wear tight shoes, living with any pain, until they do stretch.

When buying shoes consider what kind of climbing you will be doing. Shoes for face climbing should be low cut for foot articulation, have an anatomical (close) fit, and allow you to feel the rock through the sole. The rubber should be relatively hard for edging. Shoes for multipitch climbs—climbs that extend for multiple rope lengths—should fit more loosely since you will be wearing them for long periods of time. Most shoe companies produce a relatively comfortable general-purpose shoe that will get you up most hard climbs.

As your skills advance, you can consult catalogs, reviews in climbing magazines, friends, people on the rock, and salespersons to learn the advantages of the latest models.

## Following the Leader

After you practice movement skills and gain initial proficiency, you need to learn how to put on a harness and tie into the rope to accompany an experienced team doing short lead climbs. Ideally, you should join two experienced climbers who will do the leading and belaying while you—climbing between them—learn about the process. If you read Part II you will gain an overview of how the climbing system works so that the instructions that you receive from the experienced team will be more understandable. After becoming skilled in belaying and rope handling, also covered in Part II, you will be ready to support the leader as the second in a party of two. If the leader uses established bolted protection, you can concentrate on movement techniques, since you only have to unclip carabiners from the bolts and hang them from your harness. If the leader places protection, you will need to understand more of how the leader thinks in order to communicate with and work well with her.

The leader initially solves physical movement puzzles and routefinding problems that confront the team in climbing sections of rock, or *pitches*, between belay points. When the leader arrives at the top of a pitch, and has set up a fail-safe belay, it becomes the second's turn to climb.

Many leaders store a map of the pitch in their head and use it to communicate with the second. The leader may tell the second how to overcome potential problems with removing protection, managing rope, or climbing difficult sections.

A leader might sketch out a *route topo,* such as

the one in Figure 1-32. It is important to remember that the symbols of the mental topo remain as an image in the leader's mind even if guidebooks to the area are written in a descriptive essay style. In this particular mental topo, standard guidebook symbols are used for face climbing, corners that face left or right, overhangs, straight-in cracks, liebacks, belay stations, degrees of difficulty, and so on. On the map in the leader's head, a piton or bolt becomes more than just a shaped bit of metal. These objects become landmarks of the climb, along with overhangs and other rock features that mark specific locations.

On the specific climb in Figure 1-32, the leader cannot see the second and might ask if the second is at the Tricam under the roof. The leader knows that beyond the Tricam is a particularly difficult section involving thin edging to the jam crack followed by a difficult pullover on a fist jam. If there is too much slack as the second climbs the lower face, the rope may well catch in the crack at the roof lip. The leader might ask the second, who stays in one spot a bit higher for a long time, if he is at the right-facing corner just below the fixed piton, or if he is at the fixed piton at the knob traverse. These are precise locations on the climb that give the leader specific information about the difficulties that the second is about to face. The experienced leader can also anticipate specific problems of rope management or protection removal and communicate these to the second.

Solving physical problems on your own is one of the most appealing aspects of rock climbing. In the initial stages of learning how to climb, you can carefully observe the leader's movement. Did the leader use a lieback at a particular place or stem? Was the left foot or right foot on the large hold, or was that large hold ignored because it might destroy balance? This type of observation requires you to focus carefully on the leader's movement.

flake belay

*climbing rope*

SLCD

hill route

potential rope drag

**Left-facing corner**

fixed piton

knobs

ght-facing corner

5.8+ lieback

5.7 hand crack

5.9 move

**Roof**

Rope may hang p in crack at lip

Tricam under roof

5.8 face climbing

bolt

two-bolt belay

*Figure 1-32. **Following the Leader***

---

## References for Future Reading

Graydon, Don, ed. 1992. *Mountaineering: The freedom of the hills.* Fifth edition. Seattle: The Mountaineers.

Kopischka, Layne. 1988. Wide-crack technique for intermediates: *Climbing.* 108:112–13.

Leavitt, Randy. 1988. Advanced offwidths: Leavittation makes them manageable. *Climbing.* 109:90–91.

Long, John. 1989. *How to rock climb!* Evergreen, Colorado: Chockstone Press.

Loughman, Michael. 1981. *Learning to rock climb.* San Francisco: Sierra Club Books.

Meyers, George, and Don Reid. 1987. *Yosemite climbs.* Evergreen, Colorado: Chockstone Press.

Peters, Ed, ed. 1982. *Mountaineering: The freedom of the hills.* Fourth edition. Seattle: The Mountaineers.

Raleigh, Duane. 1990. Testing the new soft shoes: 1990 climbing shoe review: *Climbing.* 120:86–103.

_____. 1990. Shoes, shoes, and more shoes: 1990 climbing shoe review: *Climbing.* 121:80–86.

CHAPTER

2

# *Special Techniques*

Climbers did not invent, overnight, the techniques described in this book. Rather, they developed them over time, experimenting with different holds and positions, reusing those that worked and discarding those that did not. In the same way, climbers with disabilities are now experimenting and developing special techniques suited to their individual needs.

The following narratives, featuring three individuals and two programs, illustrate some of the unusual methods that climbers with disabilities have developed to pursue the sport. Because of the individual nature of disabilities, what works for one person may not work well for another, so this chapter is not meant to be definitive. As climbers develop more systems and equipment to accommodate various disabilities, there will continue to be new information.

Two of the individuals featured here, Mark Wellman and Hugh Herr, have made exceptional achievements that few able-bodied or disabled climbers could duplicate, without similar single-

minded efforts. Their accomplishments are offered not as an example of how all people with disabilities should climb, but to highlight Mark's and Hugh's commitment to the sport, their willingness to experiment, and their honing of body and mind to reach their goals. Climbers, both able-bodied and disabled, may choose different goals, but everyone can learn about the process of climbing from these two individuals and the other climbers included in this chapter.

## Seven Thousand Chin-Ups

Mark Wellman awoke one morning four rope lengths below the summit of El Capitan after seven days and as many bivouacs spent climbing the 3,000-foot-high wall known as the Shield. His partner, Mike Corbett, led the last pitches and Mark followed by cranking off the last few hundred chin-ups without pausing to rest. When the severe angle of the wall dropped off, Mark finished the trip to the summit the way he had started—aboard Mike's back. Mark Wellman had just completed a vertical journey that would be an adventurous challenge to any person, able-bodied or not, but for Mark it was a milestone; years earlier a mountain scrambling accident left him without the use of both legs.[1] After a visit to the White House and congratulations from then-President Bush, Mark and Mike returned to the Valley and climbed a very challenging route on Yosemite's Half Dome. With these ascents, they joined other less heralded pioneers in expanding recreational opportunities for people with disabilities.

Mark's climb followed seven long years of rehabilitation plus a taxing training program that would leave most athletes gasping. El Capitan was Mark's first venture into big wall climbing, and he demanded excellence of himself to meet this challenge. Mark and Mike devised a new technique for ascending vertical walls, complete with a uniquely rigged harness and modified ascending devices. Designing and building adaptive equipment, or developing techniques to accommodate a personal disability, is common among climbers with disabilities.

On the climb, Mike led while Mark belayed. Once Mike finished the lead he tied off the lead rope as well as a second rope for Mark to ascend. Mark unclipped from the anchor, swung out from the wall when it was overhung, and began doing chin-ups using the modified ascender (Figure 2-1).

*Figure 2-1.* **Climbing El Capitan:** *The sketch is based on a photograph by Jay Mather of the* Sacramento Bee, *reproduced in* Climbing Back *by Mark Wellman and John Flinn.*

With each chin-up Mark gained 6 inches of upward movement, so that he cranked off 320 or so in a 160-foot pitch and about 7,000 chin-ups in all to ascend El Capitan. Mark described his comeback in a biography, *Climbing Back*, which he wrote with John Flinn.

---

## On Top Again

Hugh Herr is an exceptional climber. At age 12 Hugh tackled his first really difficult route, a 5.10 in the Shawangunks called Retribution. At 17 Hugh had distinguished himself by ascending Supercrack, then one of the hardest climbs in the country—and the world—with only one fall. This feat marked him as a rising star in the climbing world. Hugh went on that year and the next to establish new routes at this standard.

In the winter of 1981, Hugh and his partner Jeff Batzer did a technical ice climb on Mt. Washington, New Hampshire, that ended on the flat Alpine Garden. There they decided to sprint to the summit but found the weather disorienting. They turned back and began descending, but visibility was less than 30 feet and winds reached 64 four miles per hour, with faster gusts. They became lost and dropped into the Great Gulf Wilderness, far from safety. Mt. Washington is renowned for its fierce winter weather: daily temperatures (without windchill) are often well below freezing. With the windchill, the relative temperature can range from –50 to –100 degrees. To spend a night out in such an environment without suitable bivouac gear could only lead to tragedy. During the nights and days that followed, Hugh froze both his feet, and after being rescued he eventually lost both legs below the knees. His partner, Jeff, lost several fingers and toes and one foot.[2]

Even while in rehabilitation, Hugh began to climb rock again, and he made a dramatic and inspiring comeback from this debilitating accident. In the biography *Second Ascent*, Alison Osius describes the difficulties that Hugh faced and how he made a new life for himself.

Eventually, Hugh moved to North Conway, New Hampshire, where he became a part of the climbing community that had lost one of its members, Albert Dow, to an avalanche during the search for Hugh and Jeff. After reaching top climbing form again, Hugh was attracted by a supremely difficult and poorly protected route, Stage Fright. To do this climb Hugh had to learn to use his body in a new way, since he could no longer simply rock forward onto a hold as would most able-bodied climbers, and he had to train hard to become strong. His worst fear was that he would fail and require a rescue in a community that had rescued him once and lost one of its members in doing so. Finally, through careful training, dedication, and concentrated emotional and physical effort, he successfully climbed the route.

As part of his return to climbing, Hugh had begun experimenting with designing and making prosthetic devices, including artificial legs (Figure 2-2A). He developed sets of legs of different length; he improvised Lycra attachments for these

*Figure 2-2. **Bouldering with Self-Designed Legs:** The rock sketch is from a photograph by Anthony Herr, and the detail of the cramponed foot is after a photograph by S. Peter Lewis. Both photos appear in* Second Ascent *by Alison Osius.*

legs to his stumps; and he developed feet of different shapes, including a crampon foot (Figure 2-2B) that allowed him to ice climb.

The qualities that Hugh relied on to climb Stage Fright and re-emerge as a top climber served him well in the academic world. He was a mediocre student before losing his legs, but he graduated summa cum laude a few years later. He also pursued his interest in prosthetic devices. Hugh wanted to develop a cushioned socket to reduce the pain to his leg stumps as he climbed and went about life. Over time, working with engineers, he devised and shared in a patent for an artificial limb socket with inflatable bladders that can be adjusted as an amputee's stump swells and shrinks during the day. The dedication and intensity of effort that Hugh developed while climbing allowed him to succeed in other areas once he turned his attention to them.

## A Climber with One Arm

John Donlou was climbing Mt. Rainier when a block of ice, hurtling down the mountain, struck him and completely severed his arm just below the shoulder. His partners secured him on the mountain and descended to get help. Ten hours later, in the fading light of evening, a helicopter arrived to pick him up. That trip to the hospital began a long journey that was filled with support from his family and friends.

Encouraged by his friend and guide Bruce Brossman, John Donlou returned to rock climbing.[3] As with others who have disabilities, he has had to develop his own technique. In a profile for *Climbing* magazine Dick Dorworth wrote, "Donlou's balance is remarkably good and his sequence of movement is always the same: one foot carefully and precisely placed, followed by the other, and then a pause to study his options. The rhythm of the climb takes a full rest until his left hand goes for the next hold, not, like most climbers, with the smooth grace of a dancer, but instead with the swift strike of a snake."

John Donlou also returned to school to become a psychiatrist, since he no longer had the two hands required to do his former job as an anesthesiologist. Today he specializes in helping people cope with trauma, bringing to his clients a practiced personal understanding of how to do so.

## Climbing Blind

Up against vertical rock, our field of vision compresses to 6 inches. It narrows again as we feel for the microscopic holds of difficult face climbs, and ends as we feel around corners. Imagine, then, climbers without sight who feel their way up a cliff. Participants in the Blind Climbing Program, a combined effort of the National Sports Center for the Disabled and the International Alpine School, do just that.

Paul DiBello, who set up the program, believed that climbing is well suited to individuals who are blind. Paul himself is sighted, but he understands

*Figure 2-3. **A Climber Who Is Blind Sensing the Rock with Her Fingers:** Many climbers who are blind have partial but perhaps deteriorating eyesight. An eye mask helps prepare these individuals to live with total blindness. Sketch from the video* Reach for the Peak, *narrated by Paul DiBello and others, and produced by Victor Sieff for the American Cable Network.*

what it means to have a disability. He lost both legs as the result of a winter climbing accident, and went on to become a world champion skier. He still climbs with the beginners in the Climbing Blind Program.

Initially, Paul met with skepticism from organizations for the blind. He tried out his idea in pilot programs staged at climbing sites in New Hampshire and Colorado, working with athletic individuals who were blind. These individuals were not simply put through a one-day climbing experience, but learned the full range of basics—knot tying, belaying, and movement skills—that any beginner would learn. These aspects of the program continue as the program has expanded to include individuals of diverse abilities.

The rewards to program participants are the same types of rewards gained by able-bodied individuals who climb. Participants get exercise and gain skills in agility and problem solving, accomplishing things thought by many to be impossible, and in the process renew themselves and grow. People with disabilities must learn to take measured risks in life in order to survive, and climbing can encourage that process. People who find that they can move up a cliff may be able to meet other environmental challenges like walking down a sidewalk with a cane for guidance. This new way of experiencing the world helps individuals who are blind to live independently, just as it helps any novice deal with challenges outside of climbing.

## Rolling on a High Ropes Course

Many educational programs that offer climbing to promote personal growth also offer ropes courses for the same reason. Ropes courses and climbing differ in many respects but are similar in that they both require commitment and self-trust. High ropes courses also place participants in positions of exposure—space between your feet—similar to that experienced in climbing. A high ropes course is built of ropes strung as much as 40 feet above the ground between trees or telephone poles, and requires that participants traverse the ropes from one small platform to another. These crossings are challenging and can be frightening, even when you know that a belay safeguards you.

*Figure 2-4. **A Participant Challenges Himself Using a Wheelchair on a High Ropes Course**: The sketch is from a photo on the cover of Mark Haven's book,* Bridges to Accessibility: A Primer for Including Persons with Disabilities in Adventure Curricula.

Two programs, Project Adventure in Massachusetts and Breckenridge Outdoor Center in Colorado, have developed high ropes courses for people who use wheelchairs.

For a moment imagine yourself in a wheelchair. The chair's wheels are set on narrow boards, but there is a gap that reveals a drop of 40 feet. The instructor at your side and fellow participants below encourage you to cross to the next station. You propel yourself forward, trying to ignore the drop that you must face in order to keep the chair's wheels on track. Although you are securely tied into a safety system, the challenge demands total concentration and a steady hand, and you are euphoric when you reach the other side. Later, as you face a new challenge in new situations, you realize that those same skills of concentration and steadiness will serve you well there, too.

Ultimately, the rewards of accepting and meeting challenges, including those of climbing, are available to those of us who seek them in whatever way and at whatever level we choose. To learn to climb, able-bodied individuals can turn to wilderness-based experiential education programs like the National Outdoor Leadership School, Outward Bound, and the Wilderness Education Association; guide services associated with the American Mountain Guides Association; regional outing clubs like the Appalachian Mountain Club and Mazamas; and experienced friends with teaching skills. Suggestions for learning to lead climbs on rock are also given in Chapter 9.

There are many organizations that serve people with disabilities, including a growing number that offer climbing activities or climbing programs. A few of these are listed below:

The Breckenridge Outdoor Center
P.O. Box 697
Breckenridge, CO 80424
Scott Ingram, Director
(303) 453-6422

The National Sports Center for the Disabled
Blind Climbing Program
P.O. Box 36

Winter Park, CO 80482
Paul DiBello, Director
(303) 892-0961

Project Adventure
P.O. Box 100
Hamilton, MA 01936
(508) 468-7981

A more complete list of organizations that work with individuals with disabilities is given in *Sports and Recreation for the Disabled: A Resource Manual*. The complete reference is given at the end of this chapter.

Occasional newsworthy events and programs are covered in the following magazines:

*Palaestra: The Forum of Sport, Physical Education and Recreation for the Disabled*
P.O. Box 508
Macomb, IL 61455

*Sports 'N Spokes: The Magazine for Wheelchair Sports and Recreation*
2111 E. Highland, Suite 180
Phoenix, AZ 85016-4702

*Climbing*
P.O. Box 339
Carbondale, CO 81623
(303) 963-0372

As you continue reading this book and progressing in your climbing career, consider the words of Tom Anderson, an instructor at the Colorado School for the Blind who is himself blind.[4] "It's easy to sit back and take the path of least resistance and not do it, but if you have the inner strength . . . you will reach out and do it." Climbing requires knowledge, desire, and effort both to get started and, as you learn more, to accomplish the goals that you set for yourself. You can start by reading this book and by finding experienced climbers to show you the way.

## References for Future Reading

Dorworth, Dick. 1989. John Donlou, The one-armed climber. *Climbing*. Oct/Nov:136.

Havens, M. S. 1992. *Bridges to accessibility: A primer for including persons with disabilities in adventure curricula*. Dubuque, Iowa: Kendall/Hunt Publishing Co.

Osius, Alison. 1991. *Second ascent: The story of Hugh Herr*. Harrisburg, Pennsylvania: Stackpole Books.

Paciorek, Michael J., and Jeffery A. Jones. 1989. *Sports and recreation for the disabled: A resource manual*. Indianapolis, Indiana: Benchmark Press, Inc.

Plummer, William, and Vickie Bane. 1991. Never say grounded. *People Weekly*. 36(13):53.

Rivera, Margo, and Stacy Stefan. 1992. The metaphor of rock climbing in a psychiatric setting. *AEE 20th International Conference Proceedings Manual:* 135. Association for Experiential Education, Boulder, Colorado.

Roberts, David. 1986. The mechanical boy comes back. *Moments of doubt*. Seattle: The Mountaineers.

Wellman, Mark, and John Flinn. 1992. *Climbing back*. Waco, Texas: WRS Publishing: 254.

Yankovich, Joanne. 1986. Blind climbers open other's eyes. *Rock & Ice*. December:76.

_____. 1986. Climbing and the blind—a perfect marriage. *Palaestra*:32.

## Endnotes

1. A few people were afraid that the positive media coverage given to Mark would divert attention from the need to improve access for people with disabilities. Others say that Mark Wellman's climb deserves cheers—not jeers as reported in *Mainstream* (April 1992) 16 (7):38.

2. *People Weekly* (10/7/91) reported that Jeff Batzer was married and a student at Lancaster Bible College in Pennsylvania.

3. See *People Weekly* (3/20/89), page 93.

4. This quote is from the video *Reach for the Peak*, narrated by Paul DiBello, Tom Anderson, and climbing instructors of the International Alpine School, and produced by Victor Sieff for the American Cable Network.

# PART TWO

# Tools
# to
# Climb
# Rock

# 3

# Knots

## About Knots

Technical climbers use a handful of knots regularly and a few more for special situations. Poor knowledge of knots has contributed to some climbing accidents. It is important to be able to tie knots correctly and without delay. You should practice tying knots in fair weather with an experienced climber to check them, then practice them at home with a short piece of climbing rope or clothesline until they become second nature to you.

### Knot Characteristics

Laboratory tests show that tightening knots in a rope lowers the overall strength of the rope 20 to 40 percent. This dramatic reduction in strength does not seem to have any practical effect on rope strength in climbing situations. Ropes under stress fail either because they are cut or because a knot comes untied as a result of improper tying.

A knot is not finished until you dress and set it. *Dressing* means orienting all parts of the knot so that they are parallel to each other and do not overlap, making sharp bends. (When two different knots will serve the same purpose, the stronger knot is the one in which the rope has broader, more symmetrical bends.) Dressing a knot tied in webbing requires special attention because webbing easily folds over onto itself, preventing the smoothness you want in all parts of the knot. *Setting* a knot means tightening the parts of the knot so that they touch each other, creating friction that prevents the knot from untying. Some, but not all, knots are not considered complete until they are *backed up* with a second knot that prevents the load-bearing knot from untying. You jam the second knot tightly against the first (see Figure 3-10H, where an overhand knot backs up a bowline on a coil). A well-finished, set, and backed-up knot is a secure knot.

### Common Knot-tying Terms

Knot: A piece of rope tied or folded upon itself; used for fastening two ropes together or fastening a rope to something else. A knot consists of a *standing part* or end, a *bight* or *loop*, and a *running end* or tail.

Bight: A doubled section of rope, formed in the middle of the rope, that does not pass over itself.

Loop: A doubled section of rope that crosses over itself, leaving an opening between the parts.

Standing Part: The end of the rope that is stationary. Often a knot is formed by passing the rope around the standing part.

Tail or Free End: The short free end of the rope left over when a knot is tied in the end, as opposed to the standing part of the rope. The tail must not slip back through or the knot will untie.

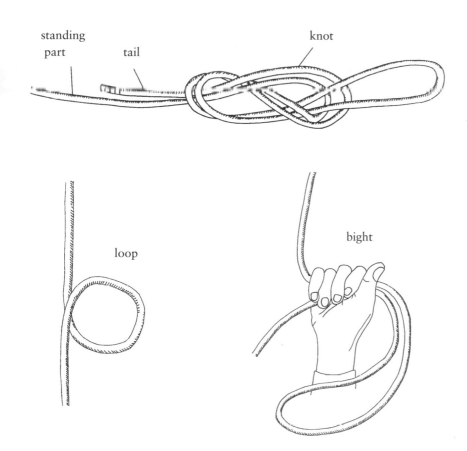

standing part    tail            knot

loop

bight

*Figure 3-1. **Parts of the Rope in Reference to a Knot***

## Common Knots

The following knots are those used most commonly in climbing. These knots are strong and do not tend to come untied. Notably missing from this group is the simple bowline knot. The two figure-eight knots that replace the potentially troublesome bowline are stronger, more easily inspected visually, and less susceptible to accidental untying. One form of bowline, the bowline on a coil, is included because it allows a climber to tie directly into the end of a rope.

### Overhand Knot

The overhand knot is the most basic knot and is frequently used to back up another knot. Figure 3-2 shows how the overhand knot is tied.

The water knot, illustrated in Chapter 4 (Figure 4-1D), is a retraced overhand knot tied in flat webbing. Due to the slippery nature of nylon webbing, the water knot requires a backup to ensure its security.

### Figure-eight Loop

The figure-eight loop is useful when you wish to tie into the middle of a rope. It is very secure and easy to inspect.

To tie this knot begin with a bight of rope and

Figure 3-3. *Figure-eight Loop*

make a loop of the bight (Figure 3-3A). Then twist this loop around the standing part of the rope and pass it back through the first loop formed (Figure 3-3B). Usually you clip a carabiner into the bight of the knot and attach it either to an anchor or to yourself.

### Figure-eight Retraced or Follow-through Knot

Figure-eight retraced knots (Figure 3-4) are used to tie around an object. You might use this knot to make an anchor around a tree or to connect the rope to your harness. The knot is tied by a retracing process, a technique used in tying many different knots.

### The Clove Hitch

The clove hitch is an adjustable knot that you can tie in the middle of the rope, and it is particularly useful when you set up a cliff-top belay stance near the edge. In laboratory tests, clove hitches slip at approximately 700 pounds, but in my experience this low value of slippage appears not to be a problem. (Indeed, on one occasion I have seen a carabiner broken by force transmitted from the rope to the carabiner by means of a clove hitch tie-in. The knot did not slip.) Given an adequate stance, clove hitches provide safe, easily adjustable tie-ins to anchor points for belaying. Back them up with a figure-eight knot to be absolutely safe.

You can tie a clove hitch by the method recommended here (Figure 3-5).

Figure 3-2. *Overhand Knot*

Figure 3-4. *Figure-eight Retraced:* **A**—*Tie a figure-eight knot on a single strand of rope, leaving a long tail. Wrap the tail around the object that you wish to tie around, such as a tree. Then retrace the tail, following the arrows.* **B**—*The completed knot. After you set the knot, there should be enough tail—normally 3 or 4 inches— to prevent accidental untying. Some climbers tie an additional backup knot that they jam up against the completed figure-eight. But if the figure-eight retraced is tied* properly, with sufficient tail, the backup knot is not essential. **C**—Adjust the length of the tail by hooking your thumb and finger around the knot to form a closed circle. To increase tail length, pull rope through the knot as indicated by the arrow labeled 1. Then pull the tail in the direction of the arrow at 2. If the tail is more than a few inches long, it will hang down where you might step on it as you are climbing. An overhand knot tied near the end of the tail will prevent this problem.

Figure 3-5. **The Clove Hitch—Hand Held Horizontally (Viewed from Above)**

Step 1. Cross hands with the right hand above the left, palms down and horizontal, thumbs along the rope, as shown in A.

Step 2. Hold the right hand steady and move the left hand beneath the right hand in an arc on the horizontal plane, as indicated by the arrow in A. This should result in two vertical loops (B). Make sure that the two vertical ends of the loop are touching the horizontal connecting strand between the loops.

Step 3. Hold the left hand steady and bend the right loop toward you. Then move it to the left, as shown by the arrow in B, and place it over the fingers of your left hand, on top of the left loop.

Step 4. Transfer these overlapping loops to the anchor point (C).

Step 5. The finished clove hitch in both loose and set forms (C). To set, simultaneously pull the two ends as shown by the arrows.

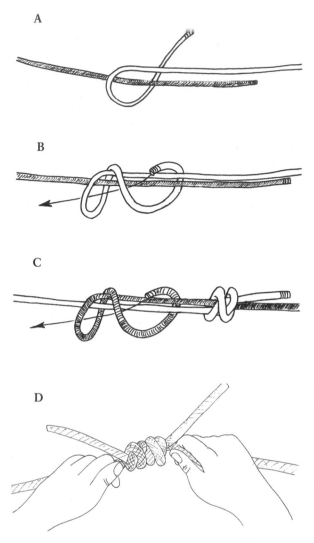

A

B

C

D

## Grapevine (Double Fisherman's) Knot

You can use the grapevine knot to tie two different ropes together. It is the knot of choice for tying rappel ropes together and tying cord or webbing slings on climbing protection (nuts). Grapevine knots tied in ropes containing Kevlar, a high-strength but slippery synthetic, are more secure with three wraps around the standing part of the rope rather than the two illustrated.

A method for tying the grapevine knot is described in Figure 3-6; Figure 3-7 shows how to take the knot apart. In this procedure you undo the right half of the knot first.

## Prusik Knot

Named for Dr. Karl Prusik, who invented this knot, the prusik is useful in everyday climbing and in search-and-rescue operations. Use it as a means of ascending a standing rope, as a tie-off for a rope, as a linkage in a pulley system, and as a rappel safety. The knot grips best if you use a small-diameter rope on a larger-diameter rope, but you can use slings of nylon tubular webbing normally carried while climbing. Avoid using Spectra webbing, which is susceptible to friction melting. Tie the knot, as shown in Figure 3-8, by wrapping the smaller-diameter sling around the standing rope. The prusik works by introducing friction that can be alternately set and released as needed. More wraps of the prusik around the standing rope produce more friction.

## Bachmann Knot

The Bachmann knot (Figure 3-9) is a friction knot like the prusik, but you insert a carabiner into the knot to provide a handle. Place the carabiner through a loop of small-diameter rope or sling material. Position the back of the carabiner against the rope and parallel to it. Now wrap the sling loop around the rope and through the carabiner, working from top to bottom. The free end of the loop at the bottom is the attachment point.

## Bowline on a Coil

Use the bowline on a coil to tie yourself into the end of the rope. If you are an alpine climber who

*Figure 3-6. **Grapevine (Double Fisherman's) Knot***
*Step 1. Place the two ends of the rope parallel to each other and loop the distant rope around the near rope and itself (A)*
*Step 2. Continue looping the rope about itself to form two loops. Pass the tail or free end of the looped rope through the inside of the doubled loop (B) and set the knot.*
*Step 3. Reorient the ropes so that the remaining untied tail is positioned as shown in C and repeat steps 1 and 2. This sequence helps ensure that the completed double knot is correct.*
*Step 4. When both knots are completed, visually check that the crossed part of each knot is on the same side and that each knot nestles into the other without a gap, as shown in D. If the crossed parts of the knots are on opposite sides or there is a gap, the knot should be retied.*

**A**

**D**

**B**

**E**

**C**

**F**

**Figure 3-7. Dismantling the Grapevine Knot**

Step 1. Examine the crossed "front" side of the knot labeled 1 in A. Then turn the knot over, following the arrow labeled 2.

Step 2. On the knot's "back" side, labeled 2 in B, move spot 3 to the right to new position 3 with your thumb. This takes effort.

Step 3. After moving spot 3, its new position is indicated in C. Now turn the knot to the front side (the arrow labeled 4).

Step 4. The front view, after turning, is labeled 4 in D. Move the spot labeled 5 to the right to new position 6 shown in D and E.

Step 5. Compress the knot from the sides as indicated by arrows labeled 7 in E. This loosens the knot enough to dismantle the right side so that it looks like drawing F.

Step 6. Now pull one end of the knot free as indicated by arrows labeled 8 in F. Dismantle the remaining knot to finish.

**Figure 3-8. Prusik Knot:** Hold the small-diameter loop so that the grapevine knot joining the ends of the loop will not interfere with the prusik knot when it is completed. The grapevine knot also should not be at the end of the loop, where it would interfere with a carabiner clipped into the loop. Wrap the small-diameter loop around the standing rope three or four times. Set the knot and check if that it holds in the use intended. If the knot slips, add another wrap of the loop to increase friction. To release tension in the prusik, loosen the part of the small-diameter loop, labeled 1, that is parallel and against the standing rope. Then loosen the wraps.

start

wrap

load

*Figure 3-9. Bachmann Knot*

mistakenly ventures into an exposed spot without having first put on your harness, you can quickly safeguard yourself by tying into the rope with this knot. Later, you can stop on a good ledge to put on your harness.

The bowline on a coil also provides the standard tie-in for a backup belay, independent of the rappel anchor and harness, to safeguard novice rappellers who might inadvertently release their controlling brake hand. In this system, one end of the belay rope goes to the rappeller's bowline tie-in, and the other end of the rope attaches to an independent anchor.

The sequence for tying the bowline on a coil is shown in Figure 3-10.

Check to ensure that the bowline on a coil is tied correctly. If the loop (Figure 3-10C) is twisted so that the standing part of the rope is away from your body, the bowline is not formed and the coil will slip dangerously when weighted. Visually inspect the loop at step C, and physically test it by attempting to make the knot slip at step G. Push on the bight while pulling on the standing part of the rope with as much force as possible. Remember that your body weight will be applied to this knot if you fall. If the knot slips, it will constrict your diaphragm and keep you from breathing.

Bowlines need to be backed up with a safety knot to prevent accidental untying. Figure 3-10H shows an overhand knot tied for this purpose. Physically test the knot before tying the backup knot.

**A**—Wrap the rope around your waist with a minimum of three wraps, working upward. The cross-hatched area will become a loop and the stippled area will become a bight in the finished knot.

**B**—Form a loop in the standing part of the rope and pull this loop up through the inside of the coil wrapped around your waist.

**C**—Make sure that the standing part of the rope is against your body. Turn the loop over the coil around your waist.

**D**—Weave the tail through the loop going over the near side, under the standing part, and over the far side of the loop.

**E**—The tail or free end of the rope now forms a bight (stippled) that weaves through the loop (crosshatched) formed in the standing part of the rope. This loop is passed over the bight in the next step.

**F**—Tighten the loop once the bight and loop are formed, as shown by the arrow.

**G**—After tightening, the loop holds a symmetrical bight in the free end. This is the completed bowline. The arrow shows the path of the free end to tie an overhand knot as a safety backup.

**H**—The completed bowline with an overhand knot tied tightly against the bowline to keep it from untying.

*Figure 3-10.* **Bowline on a Coil**

# References for Future Reading

Graydon, Don, ed. 1992. *Mountaineering: The freedom of the hills*. Fifth edition. Seattle: The Mountaineers.

Padgett, Allen, and Bruce Smith. 1987. *On rope*. Huntsville, Alabama: National Speleological Society.

Peters, Ed, ed. 1982. *Mountaineering: The freedom of the hills*. Fourth edition. Seattle: The Mountaineers.

Setnicka, Tim J. 1980. *Wilderness search and rescue*. Boston: Appalachian Mountain Club.

# 4

# *Harnesses*

## The Climbing Harness

A climbing harness is a system of nylon straps by which you secure yourself to the climbing rope. A harness that fastens only around your waist is a waist harness or swami belt. If it has attached leg loops meant to take your weight (during a fall, when rappelling, or when lowering), it is a sit harness or a waist harness with leg loops. There are several types of sit harnesses. The two discussed here include the tied swami belt with leg loops and the sewn harnesses with buckles and leg loops. If you fall backward, you can turn upside down. Most climbers use only a waist harness with leg loops in the belief that they can maintain an upright position during a fall.[1]

### *The Swami Belt with Leg Loops*

The swami belt with leg loops (Figure 4-1) is an inexpensive but safe harness for adults and small children. It is not as convenient as a sewn harness and is perhaps slightly less comfortable than a sewn harness. The advantage it offers is that with a single piece of webbing, you can custom-fit individuals of many different sizes and shapes.

Use a piece of tubular nylon webbing 17 feet long—long enough to make two or three passes of webbing around the waist. This allows you to fit the completed harness snugly without excessive tightening of any one strand. Any excess webbing that remains after you finish the harness can be taken up by tying it around all of the bands of the waist loop.

In tying the swami belt with leg loops you must observe four rules:

**1.** You should not be able to pull the crosspiece between the leg loops above the swami-belt waist loop, which would, in effect, make the harness a simple waist belt. In a fall, a simple waist belt keeps you from breathing by constricting the diaphragm movement that makes breathing possible, rather than transferring body weight to the legs.

**2.** For safety, back up a water knot. I prefer to tie an overhand knot through one strand of webbing (rather than all of the strands going around the waist) for this safety backup. After the tie-off you can tie an overhand knot around all the strands of the waist loop to keep them together. Some individuals prefer tying the water knot positioned on one of the leg-loop pieces to keep it from potential interference with knots used to tie into the rope.

**3.** The individual leg loops must be tight enough so they cannot slip down. If the leg loops slip, they can pinch you severely as your body weight comes onto the harness. If the webbing is long enough, you can hold up the leg loops by passing a strand of webbing first around the waist and then through the leg loop on the opposite side so the leg loops are held up by the waist loops (not pictured in Figure 4-1).

**4.** Tubular webbing has most of its strength in its surface. Therefore, when the surface of the webbing becomes frayed, its strength is seriously reduced. Replace the webbing when it is frayed.

C—Take the slack out of the waist portion of the harness and secure the harness with a water knot. Back it up with overhand knots pulled to jam against each side of the water knot.

*A—Tie the leg loops of the swami belt with an overhand knot in a bight of flat webbing. Size the leg loops to fit snugly. Tie the leg loops symmetrically about the marked center of a 17-foot-long piece of 1-inch-wide tubular nylon webbing.*

*B—Adjust the fit of the leg loops, pass the webbing behind your back, and wrap it around your waist two or three times. Leave enough free end of the waist loop to tie a water knot.*

Figure 4-1. **Tying a Swami Belt with Leg Loops**

*D—Close-up of the water knot and the securing overhand knots. The harness is not completely tied until you jam the two overhand knots against the water knot to prevent slippage in the tubular nylon webbing. If you have long tails in the sling, tie overhand knots through the waist loops.*

### Sewn Harness with Buckles

The sewn harness with buckles consists of a waist band of wide, flat webbing with leg loops that are either permanently attached or separate. The harness in Figure 4-2 has permanently attached leg loops. These harnesses are snug but comfortable for free climbing. In a fall, body weight comes onto the leg loops. The harness is put on as shown in the illustration.

harness buckle
waist loop
waist-loop ear
leg-loop tie
leg-loop buckle
leg-loop body
waist-loop extension
leg-loop slot

*A—The outside of the climbing harness with its parts labeled.*

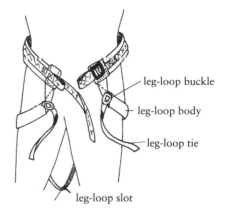

leg-loop buckle
leg-loop body
leg-loop tie
leg-loop slot

*B—Pass the waist loop behind your back with its buckle on your left, wrap it around your waist, and leave the leg-loop body hanging free.*

*D—Secure the buckle by doubling the waist-loop extension back around the waist-loop buckle and rethreading it through the other side of this buckle. This last step is critical.*

*C—Thread the waist-loop extension through the buckle. Complete the leg loops by threading the leg-loop ties through the leg loop slots to the leg-loop buckles.*

**Figure 4-2. Putting on a Sewn Harness with a Buckle**

*E—The secured waist-loop buckle.*

## Harness Tie-In

Attach the climbing rope directly to the harness using a figure-eight retraced. (Details of this knot are shown in Chapter 3, Figure 3-4). Note that you should not use a carabiner as an intermediate link for this connection in ordinary climbing situations because carabiners may open accidentally, which might result in injury.

To tie into the harness (as shown in Figure 4-3), pass the long tail through the tie-in loops or *ears* on the waist harness (points A and B), and through the leg-loop portion of the harness (point C). This way, the harness is held together by the rope, and the buckle backs up this primary attachment. In harnesses with ears, it is important to tie into both ears so that in the event of a fall, the impact forces will be distributed correctly.[2] Other types of harnesses depend more heavily on the buckle for primary security. No matter what type

Figure 4-3. *Tying into the Harness*

A—Tie a figure-eight knot and pass a long tail through ears A and B and then through the leg-loop strap at C. Finish the knot by following back through. Refer to Figure 3-4 for details of this knot.

B—Tighten the figure-eight knot to complete the tie-in. Leave a 3- or 4-inch tail or use an overhand as a backup.

of harness you are using, always check that the harness waist loop passes through and back through the buckle to secure it, as illustrated in Figure 4-2D and E.

On a climb that is of long duration, you may wish to remove the leg loops while staying tied into the waist loop of your harness to answer a call of nature or to remove or add clothing. In this case, you would tie in by connecting the tail of the figure-eight knot through the ears of the waist loop, but not through the leg-loop strap at point C. You then attach the leg-loop strap of point C to the completed knot with a locking carabiner, which can be opened for easy removal of the leg loops. This technique works for a number of harnesses of similar design.

Figure 4-4 **Rigging the Sewn Harness with Buckle for Rappelling:** *Pass a runner sling through the two ears of the harness and the leg loops and lock them all together with a locking carabiner, or two carabiners with opposed gates. This creates an attachment point for the rappel that does not rely on the harness buckle for safety.*

Figure 4-5. **Tie-in for the Swami Belt with Leg Loops Using a Figure-eight Knot**

When you rappel with a buckled harness, you can trace a runner sling through points A, B, and C. This sling will act like the rope in Figure 4-3 to hold the harness together, independent of the buckle. Attach rappel devices to the runner sling as shown in Figure 4-4.

### Tying into the Swami Belt with Leg Loops

Tie into the swami belt with leg loops directly with a figure-eight retraced knot (Figure 4-5). Tie off the tail of the retraced figure-eight knot with an overhand knot to prevent the loose end from dangling underfoot. The overhand knot is not absolutely required as a finishing knot as long as 3 or 4 inches of tail remain outside the knot after you tighten and dress the knot.

## Endnotes

1. If you fall backward, you can turn upside down. A chest harness connected to a waist harness may keep climbers upright and provide greater security during a fall. The UIAA's *(Union Internationale des Associations d'Alpinisme)* current recommendation to use a chest harness in combination with a seat harness is under review (personal communication from John E. Williamson, Chair of the American Alpine Club Safety Committee) and subject to change. Tests indicate that the chest harness itself may contribute to neck injuries in falls longer than 20 feet.

2. A 1993 letter from REI, Inc. reports an accident in which a climber was tied into a harness using only one ear. This changed the way in which the forces were distributed to the climber in a fall and resulted in severe injury.

# 5

# *Rope*

## Climbing Rope

The classic image of climbing is the climber starting up a slope, pack on back, festooned with hardware, with rope over a shoulder. Historically, climbing has been a "companionship of the rope," the roped leader guiding the way for the team. In the early days of climbing, the most skilled person always climbed first and did not expect—and could not afford—to fall, for fear the rope might break. The rope was used to safeguard the passage of the second, who was usually less skilled than the leader. Modern rope construction has changed this way of climbing. So reliable is climbing rope that we now expect leaders on the most difficult climbs to fall repeatedly in order to make progress, to improve their skills, and to have a day of fun. Ropes have come a long way.

### *Rope Construction*

The rope used for rock climbing today is *dynamic kernmantle* (core-jacket). *Dynamic* describes the ability of the rope to stretch as it absorbs the force of a fall. *Kernmantle* describes the construction of the rope, illustrated in Figure 5-1. The kern, a high-strength inner core of twisted nylon threads, is covered by an outer braided jacket or sheath, the mantle. The twisted strands of the core behave like miniature springs, lengthening as they absorb the energy of a fall. They provide most of the rope's strength; the jacket protects the core and determines most of the rope's handling characteristics and abrasion resistance.

Most modern climbing ropes are 45 to 50 or even 55 meters long (150, 165, or 180 feet, respectively), and 10 to 11 millimeters in diameter. The 50-meter length was first used extensively in Yosemite Valley where belays were protected by bolts, but this length is becoming essential in other areas where bolt-protected routes have been established. An 11-millimeter kernmantle rope is a good choice for general climbing, for climbing schools where the rope will experience heavy use, for working with groups, or for guiding. Many climbers prefer a 10.5-millimeter rope because it is slightly lighter; it combines good abrasion resistance with moderate weight. Some experienced climbers use an even lighter 10-millimeter rope. Climbers do not ordinarily use ropes of 9.0 or 8.8 millimeters as single strands. (They do use these ropes in *double-rope* or *twin-rope* techniques to help reduce the friction or rope drag that occurs when ropes turn right angles. Two ropes also allow easier rappelling.)

### *Rope Retirement*

It is important to know when to retire a climbing rope. You need to consider the number of hours of use, the number and severity of falls held, the presence of abrasion damage to the sheath, and accidental exposure to acids and other solvents.

The UIAA (*Union Internationale des Associations d'Alpinisme*) safety commission recommends retiring a rope after about five years of use or

*Figure 5-1. Kernmantle Rope Construction*

10,000 to 20,0000 meters of climbing. To use this method you need to keep a rope logbook to record the date and distance of each climb. Some rope manufacturers recommend a maximum of four years of use, even if use is occasional. With normal weekend use, two years is a reasonable working life for a rope. But if you are one of the fortunate individuals who climb daily, the life expectancy of your rope can be as little as three months to one year.

To be conservative, retire a rope when it experiences a single severe fall. A fall is severe when the fall distance exceeds the amount of rope between the belayer and the leader, a fall factor of one (the fall factor is very important to take into account in considering the seriousness of a fall on the serviceability of a rope; the subject is examined briefly at the end of this chapter and in detail in Chapter 11).

A number of lesser falls may also make the rope unsafe. Rope is not perfectly elastic: each fall takes some of the twist out of the twisted strands, reducing the spring of the rope, permanently elongating it a little more, and reducing its shock absorption for the next fall.

Remember that the rope is your lifeline. Replace it more often than you think is necessary: your life is worth more than the cost of a new rope.

After a fall and lowering to the ground or after

securing yourself to an anchor, untie and shake the rope out to allow the internal braid to reset and to reset the knot, which also absorbs energy in a fall. Another method of resetting the rope is to tie into the opposite end for the next attempt.

Kernmantle ropes may be damaged internally in a manner that requires close inspection to detect. One standard way to determine rope damage is to inspect the rope sheath with an 8- to 10-power hand lens. Puffs or strands of core sticking out of the sheath and limp or hard spots indicate damage. If you see sheath abrasion (more than 50 percent of the sheath fibers are damaged at any one spot) with a 10-power hand lens, retire the rope. Another way to test the rope is to tension it and check visually and by feel for irregularities.

If damage is confined to the end of the rope, you can cut the damaged part away. Often, enough will be left, particularly with a longer rope, to use for lead climbs or perhaps for top-roping. Cut the rope with a hot knife (the knife will probably lose its temper), so that the blade both cuts and melts through the rope, fusing the internal fibers of the core to the sheath. A piece of electrical tape around the rope adjacent to the cut completes the process and provides an identifying marker.

## Coiling Rope

The two common methods of coiling a rope are the *mountaineer's coil* and the *butterfly coil*. The mountaineer's coil creates a continuous circle that you can carry over your shoulder and neck and allows you to carry a number of ropes at one time.

On the other hand, for a single rope you can form the butterfly coil faster even if the rope is encrusted with ice, you can make it into a backpack, and it is less likely to tangle during uncoiling.

### The Mountaineer's Coil

Many people form the mountaineer's coil by wrapping the rope around their feet and knees when sitting, but this normally creates irregular-

*Figure 5-2.* **Forming the Mountaineering Coil While Standing, Using the Left Hand to Control Twist**

length coils. If the rope has been badly twisted, however, this may be the only way you can achieve the mountaineer's coil. Making the mountaineer's coil while standing—though possible only for people who have hands large enough to hold 165 feet of coiled rope in one hand—is faster and gives you greater control over the length of an individual loop once you master the technique. You can never satisfactorily untwist ropes that are badly kinked from a belay plate by this method and you must either form the mountaineer's coil while sitting or use the butterfly coil.

To form the mountaineer's coil while standing, hold an end of the rope in your *off hand* and with

*Figure 5-3.* ***Whipping the End of the Mountaineering Coil***

your *control hand* (normally the right hand for right-handed people) stretch out the standing part of the rope two arm lengths across your chest (Figure 5-2). The length of a loop is determined by the distance between your outstretched hands. With the rope stretched out, grasp the rope between the thumb and fingers of your control hand. To remove twist from the coil, give the rope a half-twist and bring the newly formed coil over to your off hand. Use your off hand to grasp and enclose all the loops formed by this process.

Finish the coil by whipping the ends tightly, as shown in Figure 5-3. You need to tighten each wrap of the whip to gain enough friction to keep the wrap from falling apart. If you do it properly, you will not need to wrap extremely long ends around the coil to secure it. Long ends are unnecessary and even undesirable if you need to use the rope quickly.

### The Butterfly Coil

To make the butterfly coil, take both ends in one hand and stretch the doubled rope full-length across your chest. Measure out two and a half or

Figure 5-4. **Forming the Butterfly Coil**

three lengths and drop them on the ground; you will use this rope to tie the coil together when you finish (or, if your rope has a middle mark, you can grab the middle mark and skip the step of dropping several lengths on the ground). Now you are ready to form the *butterfly wings*. Take an arm-to-arm length of rope, double it, and drape it over the palm of your hand, forming a loop on either the left or right side of the hand. You form the next wing by draping the next doubled length of rope across the same palm with the loop facing the opposite direction, as sketched in Figure 5-4A. Do this until all the remaining rope is in the palm of your hand. Now use the lengths of rope you dropped (or the ends of the rope, if you started with the middle mark) to make three or four wraps around both wings (Figure 5-4B). Form a bight in the standing part of the rope and pull it partway through the loop at the top of the wrapped coil (Figure 5-4C). Take the remaining end of the rope and place it over the body of the wrapped coil and through the last formed loop (Figure 5-4D). Tighten to finish the butterfly coil. Form a backpack from the coil by placing it on your back and passing the free ends over your shoulders. Wrap these ends across your chest and waist, and tie them together (Figure 5-4E).

## Uncoiling and Stacking

Organizing an uncoiled rope so that both ends of the rope are available and the rope will run freely without tangling or knotting is called *stacking* or *flaking*. The belayer stacks the rope at the beginning of a climb, before anyone ties into the ends. The leader usually makes last-minute preparations while the belayer stacks. Stacking properly allows the climber to progress smoothly while being belayed safely. This is especially critical for the leader, who should not have to hang on while the second deals with a tangle.

To uncoil and stack a mountaineering coil, free the lashed ends and hold the coil and one end in one hand. Do not uncoil two ends at the same time or the rope may knot. Put one end on the ground, slightly away from where you are stacking. (If you bury the first end with subsequent loops, you will have to lift the stack, which may tangle it so you have to untangle and restack it.) With the other hand, undo the coil one loop at a time, dropping it on the ground, out of the dirt (perhaps on a plastic sheet or in a rope bag) adjacent to the belay site. Be careful not to stack the rope where climbers from other teams will walk on the rope or have to step over it. The first end on the ground becomes the bottom end, which the belayer ties into. The leader ties into the top end, which remains in the belayer's hand until the stacking process is completed. If you stack the rope properly, you will be able to feed slack to the leader smoothly as needed.

Once the stack is organized, do not move it by pushing it or lifting it, because you can tangle the rope. Any time you move the belay, stack the rope at a new site to ensure that the leader does not get stuck in the middle of a pitch because the rope is tangled.

The butterfly coil is not as likely to tangle during uncoiling. To uncoil it, unfasten the finishing hitch, unwrap the coil, and drop the wings on the ground. You will have a doubled rope. To ensure that there will be no tangles, start at one end and stack half the rope; then start at the other end and restack the entire rope, making sure that both ends are available.

### Stacking on Multipitch Climbs

In a stack, the rope to the climber must always come off the top. This happens naturally when two people switch leads on multipitch climbs. The rope end passing to the original leader will automatically finish up on the bottom of the stack as the second climbs. The leader for the subsequent pitch, who was previously the second, now has the end of the rope on top of the stack and is ready to climb. This neat order of stacking changes, however, when one person leads two pitches in a row. The leader's rope will wind up on the bottom of the pile and must be stacked before the same leader can start up the next pitch. The stacking can be most efficiently done by the belayer, while the leader reorganizes the climbing protection on a gear sling.

On multipitch climbs, you sometimes belay on a stance directly above a crack or flake that may be a trap for a dangling rope. In this case, form butterfly loops with the rope across your feet, a convenient rock horn, or the belay tie-in to prevent the rope from catching on anything below as the leader attempts to make upward progress.

## Throwing Rope

To establish a rappel or top rope, you often need to throw rope directly down a less than vertical cliff or off to the side. A technique that allows you to aim your throw is shown in Figure 5-5. Starting from the rope tie-in at the anchor (see Chapter 10, Anchor Systems), form seven or eight butterfly or mountaineer's coil loops in the middle of the rope. Leave enough slack to allow the loops to reach over the edge of the cliff. Lay these loops down, out from underfoot, in a handy spot. Starting from the free end of the rope, form seven or eight more loops, leaving 10 to 15 feet of slack between the two sets of loops. This second set of loops will be a throwing weight that you can aim. Drop the first set of loops over the cliff edge while you hang on to the second set of loops that includes the free end of the rope. Throw the second set of loops and free end overhand or sidearm hard enough to hit the target. If you misdirect the first throw into a rope-eating tree, reorganize and try again.

Figure 5-5. *Throwing the Rope. Tie in before you do this.*

### Accidental Cutting

Climbing ropes are basically very reliable. Indeed, climbing ropes without prior damage have not been known to break from the impact of a simple fall. This fact can be misleading, however, because a rope tensioned over a rock edge is very susceptible to cutting. At cliff tops, you should pad the rope with clothing, packs, or custom-made sheaths of canvas or other heavy-duty material. Tie these pads into the anchor so they cannot be lost over the cliff edge. Partway up lead climbs, long runners often allow a rope to stand away from an edge where it might be cut in the event of a fall.

The rope can be cut in a more subtle manner if you step on it. This grinds dirt composed of small, sharp crystals, mostly quartz, into the rope where they cut the fibers of the mantle and core. *Never step on a climbing rope!*

## Properties of Climbing Ropes

Perhaps the most significant property of kern-mantle rope is that it stretches to absorb the shock of a fall. This property distinguishes the dynamic ropes used for rock climbing from the static ropes used for rope ascending and rappelling in caving. The amount of rope stretch under body weight is a rope's *working elongation*. Dynamic ropes have a working elongation of about 5 to 10 percent, while the working elongation of a static rope of the same diameter rope is less than 1 percent.

The *impact elongation* of a climbing rope is the amount of stretch suffered by the rope during a fall, measured in tests as approximately 20 percent of the rope length between the belayer and the climber. Impact elongation, belay method, rope slippage through the belay, and position and security of rock protection all determine the total distance of a fall. The impact force is the force felt by a falling climber when the rope stops a fall. For the rope to be effective, this force must be within the range that the human body can withstand without injury for short periods of time. Maximum impact force is about 2,000 pounds for the average 11-millimeter rope.

### Fall Factor

Dynamic ropes are given a fall rating—they are called 5-fall, 9-fall, or 11-fall ropes—on the basis of a test established by the UIAA. (Since the UIAA simply gives a pass-fail to this test, a 9-fall rope is the manufacturer's rating and not the UIAA's.) The nature of this test is described in Figure 5-6.

A weight of 80 kilograms (176 pounds), approximating body weight, is dropped over a simulated carabiner 10 millimeters in diameter. The weight falls 5 meters onto 2.8 meters of rope attached to a static anchor. This is a very severe fall—very near the maximum severity possible. It simulates a locked-off belay that does not allow rope to slip through a belay brake. The ratio between the length of rope (2.8 meters) and the distance fallen (5 meters) is the *fall factor* (here it is 1.78). If the weight were attached directly to the anchor with-

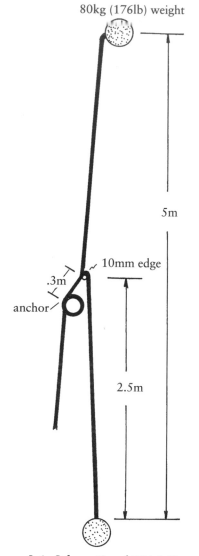

Figure 5-6. *Schematic of UIAA Drop Test. An 80-kilogram (176-pound) weight suspended 2.5 meters above a simulated carabiner (10-millimeter edge) drops 5 meters onto 2.8 meters of rope for a fall factor of 1.78. The distance between the anchor and simulated carabiner is .3 meter.*

out the carabiner, the fall factor would be 2.8 meters: 5.6 meters, or 2. A fall factor of 2 is the most severe fall possible. This is an important concept, which is examined in detail in Chapter 11. Before you launch out on your own as a leader, you must understand the fall factor, since it affects where you should place your first piece of protection, as well as the impact forces that you, the belayer, and the anchor experience in a fall.

To carry the UIAA approval, a rope must survive at least five severe falls of fall factor 1.78, and the first fall must have a landing or impact force not exceeding 2,640 pounds (15 times body weight). Since climbers do not normally experience real impact forces of this harshness in the field, a 5-fall rope would appear to be safe, indeed, though some ropes are made to withstand up to 11 falls.

Specific data for individual climbing ropes vary, but statistics for an "average" rope are given in Table 5-1.[1] Labels on ropes can underreport rope diameter up to 0.5 millimeter, and rope length by 10 percent. This means that climbers are better protected and get more for their money than they pay for.

To obtain information for specific ropes, ask at your local climbing store, look for annual comparisons in climbing magazines, or write to the manufacturer.

### Abrasion Resistance, Water Absorption, and Handling Characteristics

Abrasion resistance is another characteristic of interest to the climber. The higher the abrasion resistance, the longer the life of a rope and the less easily the rope can be cut over an edge.

A wet rope is heavier than a dry rope, ices quickly to the point of uselessness in cold conditions, and is weaker than a dry rope. Some ropes are coated to prevent water absorption either by coating individual threads before weaving them into the rope, or by coating the finished rope. In theory, coated dry ropes shed water more easily than uncoated standard ropes, and they may be more abrasion resistant. Tests indicate that ropes with tightly woven sheaths typically absorb less water than loosely woven ones irrespective of their coating.[2] Water absorption can vary between 10 and 50 percent of the rope's dry weight.

Besides damage from abrasion, ropes are susceptible to deterioration caused by ultraviolet waves in sunlight as well as the effects of acids. Climbers are usually concerned about "petroleum products such as gasoline, paint, oil, etc. All of the fiber producers state that no petroleum product will harm nylon, . . . but evidently the information is not being picked up by many climbers."[3] Periodically clean ropes in lukewarm water using a detergent and gentle action to remove dust and rock fragments, followed by a through rinsing.

How a rope feels in your hand—its handling characteristics—and its resistance to kinking are also important for daily climbing.

Table 5-1. "Average" Climbing Rope Statistics

| Manufacturer's stated diameter in millimeters | 11.0 | 10.5 | 10 | 9 |
|---|---|---|---|---|
| Impact force in pounds | 1850–2090 | 1958–2310 | 1760–1870 | 1320–1540 |
| Static elongation % 80kg load | 5–7.5 | 4.2–8 | 1.5–8 | 5.5–10 |
| UIAA Falls | 7–12 | 7–9 | 6–7 | 7–11* |
| Weight 165 feet in pounds | ≈ 8.5–9 | ≈ 8 | ≈ 7 | ≈ 6 |

*UIAA fall number for 9.0 millimeters is for a double rope.

## References for Future Reading

Newell, Dick. 1990. Product interview by Larry Coats. *Rock & Ice*: 36.

Robbins, Royal. 1979. Climbing rope myths. *Summit* (February–March).

Raleigh, Duane. 1991. Hanging by threads. *Climbing*. 126:82–92.

## Endnotes

1. This is a summary of data collected by Duane Raleigh for a 1991 rope review for *Climbing*.

2. *Ibid.*

3. Newell, 1990.

# CHAPTER

# 6

# Belaying

## Belaying Basics

While the rope provides a classic image of mountaineering, belaying is the reality behind the image. In belaying, two individuals form a team that is much stronger than the simple combination of two individuals' skills. Belaying provides forgiveness in the vertical world and safeguards the team so that a falling climber can be caught and held safely on the rope.

The basics of belaying are the belay chain, the rope-manipulation sequence, and the belay stance. A proper belay comprises many components, including anchors, harness, and tie-ins. We will start by examining the belay chain, rope-manipulation sequence, and the hand-manipulation sequence that holds the rope against a friction surface. The components of the belay are easiest to illustrate with a waist (body) belay, although belaying with a mechanical brake has certain advantages discussed later in this chapter.

### The Belay Chain and Rope Manipulation

Your job as a belayer is to pay out or take in rope as the climber moves, so as to catch the climber with as little slack as possible in case of a fall. To check a fall, you instantly pull the rope against an object (such as your waist or a belay device) to create friction. The principle is the same whether you are using a waist belay or a mechanical belay brake. In order to understand the sequence, look at the *belay chain* shown in Figure 6-1.

Focus on the climber at the tie-in point, and then follow the rope back to the belayer. The rope passes around the belayer's back, which will become the *braking friction surface* in a waist belay. To hold the rope against the braking friction surface, the back, you use the hand on the side opposite the climber as a brake. This hand is the *braking hand.* The other hand, which grasps the rope before it goes around the back, is the *helping hand*, sometimes called the *feeling hand*. Notice that if you tried to hold the climber with only the helping hand, there would be no friction between the climber and you. This means that you would be trying to hold a falling climber with only the strength of one hand, an impossible task.

Novice belayers often mistakenly belay the wrong end of the rope and confuse the braking with the helping hand. These mistakes occur because the novice does not consider the belay chain before concentrating on the hand-manipulation sequence that serves to hold the rope against the braking surface.

To be ready to apply friction instantly, you use your braking hand and your helping hand in a coordinated manner to move the rope past the braking friction surface. As shown in Figure 6-2A and B, which illustrate the hand-manipulation sequence without showing belay anchors or other essential components of the belay chain, you begin with the helping hand extended and take in (arrow 1a) rope from the climber. The braking hand starts next to your body and then pulls (arrow 1b) rope across the braking friction surface, your own back. Your helping hand winds up next to your body and your braking hand extends from your body.

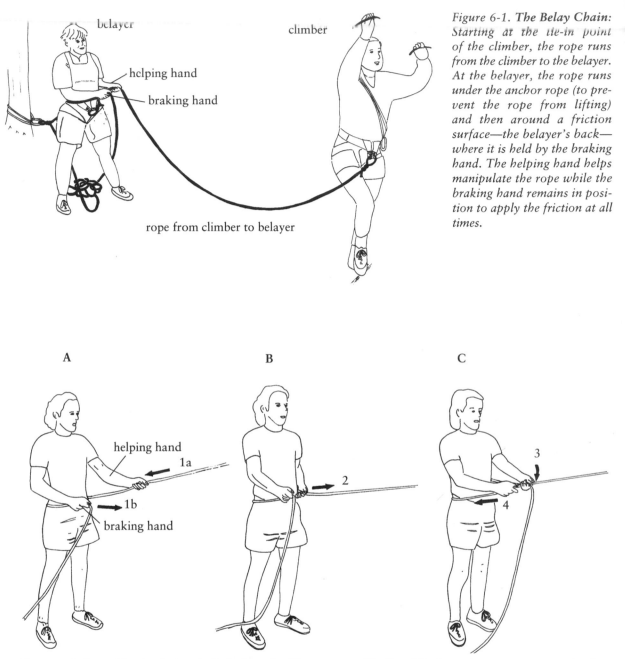

Figure 6-1. **The Belay Chain:** *Starting at the tie-in point of the climber, the rope runs from the climber to the belayer. At the belayer, the rope runs under the anchor rope (to prevent the rope from lifting) and then around a friction surface—the belayer's back—where it is held by the braking hand. The helping hand helps manipulate the rope while the braking hand remains in position to apply the friction at all times.*

belayer

climber

helping hand

braking hand

rope from climber to belayer

A

B

C

helping hand

1a

1b

braking hand

2

3

4

Figure 6-2. **Rope Manipulation in Belaying:** *A—The belayer pulls in the rope from the climber with the helping hand (1a) and pulls it around the friction braking surface with the braking hand (1b).*

*B—The end of this sequence, in which the helping hand is next to the hip and the braking hand is extended from the body. Holding the rope in the braking hand, the belayer extends the helping hand in the direction of the* arrow (2). C and D show the sequence to get back to the starting point.

*C—The belayer moves the braking hand and the helping hand together and grasps both ropes with the helping hand (arrow 3). The braking hand remains closed around the rope, and slides along the rope to a position next to the body (arrow 4).*

As shown in Figure 6-2C, extend your helping hand and grasp both strands of the rope with the helping hand (arrow 3) so that your braking hand remains on the rope between your helping hand and your back. Now slide the braking hand along the rope (arrow 4) to your body. Never let go of the rope with your braking hand. If you do, and the climber falls at that instant, you cannot hold the climber with only your helping hand. Release the braking side of the rope (arrow 5) with your helping hand. You are now (Figure 6-2E) in the starting position (Figure 6-2A), ready to repeat the cycle.

A common mistake occurs when you begin normally (Figure 6-3A) but bend at the waist and straighten the elbow on the braking arm in order to take up a maximum amount of rope. In this extended position, it is difficult to reach beyond the braking hand and you may use your helping hand to grasp the two ropes between the braking hand and the body (Figure 6-3B). Since you cannot slide your braking hand to the original position, you must remove it from the rope (Figure 6-3C) and you cannot apply effective, instantaneous braking action. To avoid this problem, leave the elbow of your braking arm bent, do not bend over at the waist, and take in a smaller amount of rope during each cycle.

## The Belay Stance

Body position and location of the belay, collectively termed the *stance*, is an important consideration. At stake is your ability to remain in control at all times to prevent injury to yourself and the

D—*The helping hand prepares to drop the rope on the braking hand side (arrow 5). This leads back to the starting position shown in E.*

E—*The belayer has dropped the braking side of the rope with the helping hand and is ready to repeat the belaying sequence.*

F—*If a fall should occur at any time during A–E, the belayer gains additional friction by wrapping the rope across the midsection with the braking hand (arrow 6).*

incorrect: reaching across with helping hand below braking hand

incorrect: straight elbow on braking arm

incorrect: removing the braking hand

A                                    B                                    C

*Figure 6-3. **A Common Mistake in Rope Manipulation:*** *A—The sequence begins normally with the braking hand next to the body and the helping hand extended. The braking hand is correctly extended with the elbow remaining bent.*

*B—In an incorrect belaying sequence, the belayer straightens the elbow of the braking hand and bends over*

*to maximize the amount of rope taken up in one cycle, positioning the helping hand between the braking hand and the body.*

*C—The belayer removes the braking hand from the rope. You cannot make an effective belay when you remove your braking hand from the rope.*

leader. During the belay, position your body relative to both the force of a falling climber and the anchor. You always need to examine the key points diagramed in Figures 6-4 through 6-7.

**1.** Make sure there is no slack in the belay anchor. If the climber falls and there is slack (Figure 6-4A), you will be abruptly pulled to the end of the anchor and experience shock forces as the anchor

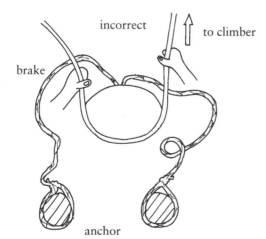

incorrect                to climber

brake

anchor

*Figure 6-4A. **A Slack Anchor Rope***

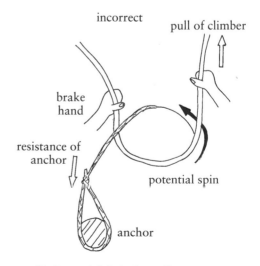

incorrect                pull of climber

brake hand

resistance of anchor

potential spin

anchor

*Figure 6-4B. **Potential Spin from Shear Forces***

rope suddenly stops your forward motion. You may even be pulled off the ledge. Besides causing injury, the shock of the sudden stop could cause you to drop the rope and lose control of the falling leader.

**2.** Safeguard against forces that might cause you to lose control of the belay. In Figure 6-4B, the tie-in point is at the midpoint of the belayer's harness, and the anchor is on the opposite side of the pull applied by a falling climber. This produces unaligned shear forces that will rotate the belayer. To eliminate these forces, pass the anchor rope around the same side as the rope leading to the climber (Figure 6-4C) or interchange braking and helping hands.

**3.** Couple natural terrain features with body position to brace against a potential fall. For example, you can brace against a low wall with a leg extended on the helping-hand side of the body to counteract the force of a falling leader, or sit in a well-braced position (Figure 6-5). Here you use your left hand as the brake hand and brace your right foot to counteract a pull in the direction of the climber. Even on a flat ledge, you can offset

*Figure 6-5. A Secure Body Position with Belayer's Right Leg Braced Against the Pull of a Falling Climber*

rotational forces by extending your leg on the helping-hand side of the body to counteract the pull of the falling leader. In alpine climbing, there are times when no artificial anchor can be set up and you have to depend on a strongly braced body position alone to hold a fall.

**4.** *Aim* the belay, so you do not swing during a fall. In Figure 6-6 the belayer can rotate and be pulled off the belay ledge. To prevent this situation, use the intermediate protection shown to aim the direction of pull. Sometimes, depending on the location of protection in relation to belay geography, you can aim a belay more effectively by using either your right or left hand as the braking hand. Learn to belay effectively with both hands. You can also reduce the potential rotation shown in Figure 6-6 by decreasing the distance to the anchor.

**5.** In a waist belay you must guard against the possibility that the belay rope will unwrap from your waist during a fall (Figure 6-7). You can use a carabiner safety, as shown in the enlarged detail of Figure 6-7, to hold the rope in place. If the leader falls, this carabiner also keeps the rope from abrading your armpit as the rope is pulled upward.

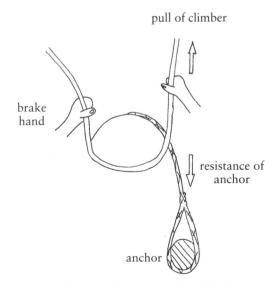

*Figure 6-4C. Correct Alignment of the Climbing Rope and Anchor Rope to Prevent Spin*

shorten tie-in

place intermediate protection and clip rope in

Figure 6-6. *Aiming the Belay*

(It is not necessary to take this step when you are using a belay device, since the device clips through a carabiner that will hold the rope in position.)

## Carabiners and Anchor Basics

Carabiners allow the belayer, who remains stationary, to attach quickly to a "bombproof" anchor before the climber moves. In this section we will examine common top-rope belay systems, the amount of slack that you need to provide, and the security of natural tree anchors. Chapter 10 covers belay anchors in greater detail.

Figure 6-7. *Preventing the Belay Rope from Unwrapping:* To prevent the rope from unwrapping in the event of a fall, clip the rope through a carabiner on the side opposite from the brake hand.

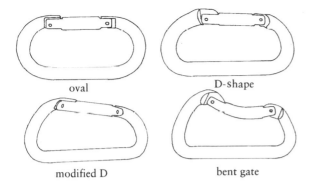

oval        D-shape

modified D        bent gate

*Figure 6-8.* **Carabiner Shapes**

## Carabiners

You commonly use carabiners to attach ropes to intermediate protection points and belay anchors, to assemble friction brakes for rappelling, and to connect aid climbers to aid points. Usually made of aluminum alloys, carabiners come in three basic shapes (Figure 6-8): the generally useful oval, the stronger D-shape, and the modified D with a large gate opening. The bent-gate carabiner is a modified D designed for quick rope clips in sport climbing. Almost any catalog of climbing equipment will show a wide range of variations of these shapes, some having specialized uses.

In all designs the load is intended to be applied along the long axis of the carabiner. With the gate closed, carabiners should have a minimum strength of about 2,000 kilograms, and a gate-open strength of 600 to 700 kilograms. The D-shape and modified D-shape apply more of the load on the body of the carabiner and hence are stronger, but the gate is the weakest part of the device.

Locking carabiners (Figure 6-9A) are generally stronger than nonlocking because the gate area is reinforced by a threaded screw lock. The threads are covered by the screw lock to prevent accidental fraying of webbing. Locking carabiners offer more security than nonlocking ones and are commonly used for belaying or for setting up top-rope climbs. Currently twist-lock carabiners that lock automatically are commercially available. When nonlocking carabiners are used for these purposes, two carabiners with the gates *opposed* and *reversed* (Figure 6-9C) should be used.

Carabiners treated with care are useful for many years. Retire carabiners that have been shock-loaded, dropped, or hammered upon, as well as ones that have wobbly gates or excessive scars from incidental contact with rock. Such carabiners develop microscopic internal cracks and can be expected to break under the stress of a fall. Hollow, lightweight carabiners are more susceptible to such damage than carabiners made of heavier stock.

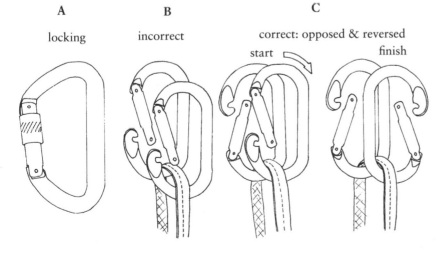

A      B          C

locking     incorrect       correct: opposed & reversed

start          finish

*Figure 6-9.* **Combining Nonlocking Carabiners to Replace a Locking Carabiner: A—***Locking carabiner with screw gate.* **B—***Incorrect way to combine two nonlocking carabiners. The carabiners can open accidentally when both gates point the same way.* **C—***The correct way to combine two nonlocking carabiners: reverse the gates (left) and then turn one carabiner so that the gates are on opposite sides (right).*

### Slinging Trees with Carabiners

When you use a sling around a tree, the sling can form either a girth hitch or, for want of a better name, a V-hitch (Figure 6-10). To form a girth hitch, pass the sling around the tree and through the loop formed by the distant end of the sling. To form a V-hitch, pass the sling around the tree and clip the two ends of the loop with a carabiner. Make sure that the V formed between the two sides of the hitch is 60 degrees or less to prevent problems (see Chapter 11, Fall Forces).

If a sling barely makes it around the tree and you use a carabiner to join the ends (Figure 6-10), you will be loading the carabiner along its axis as well as perpendicular to its axis. This *triaxial loading* is dangerous. If the load perpendicular to the axis pulls on the weak gate, the carabiner will probably break. To avoid this risky situation, lengthen the sling by adding a second sling and fasten the two slings together with a locking carabiner or gate-opposed carabiners.

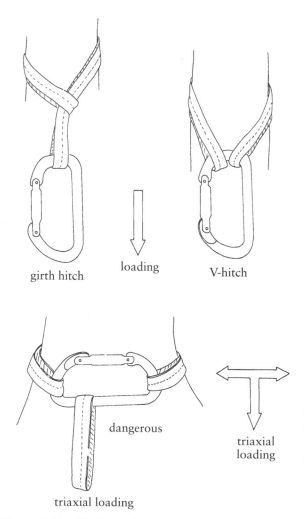

girth hitch    loading    V-hitch

dangerous

triaxial loading

triaxial loading

*Figure 6-10. **Girth Hitch, V-Hitch, and Dangerous Triaxial Loading***

## A Belay Tie-In

Whether you arrive at the top of a cliff after a lead or set up the anchor from above, you usually want to stand or sit at the edge to watch or talk to the climber below. Yet available anchor points—large trees or protectable cracks—may be many feet back from the edge. You can solve this problem quickly by tying yourself into a large loop of rope extending from your harness to the anchor and back, as shown in Figure 6-11. If you use this variable-length tie-in, you can still use many different belay brakes and assume many different stances anywhere on the cliff.

The tie-in sequence requires that you establish an anchor, assume a stance, and finally tie yourself to the anchor. First, create an anchor with its attachment carabiner and clip your rope through this carabiner so that it runs freely. A locking carabiner or two nonlocking carabiners with gates opposed here give added security. Next, return to the cliff edge, assume a stance that allows you to aim the belay, and finish tying yourself to the anchor. Notice that the rope goes from your harness tie-in point through the anchor carabiner and back over the cliff edge to the climber below. Tie a figure-eight knot into the rope that leads to the climber and clip it to your harness tie-in point with a locking carabiner or two carabiners with opposed and reversed gates. You are now secure at the edge of the cliff, ready to belay and observe the climber below.

*Figure 6-11. The Belay Tie-In Loop*

## Waist Belays for Top Roping

When you give a waist belay, as shown in Figure 6-12A, your stance determines the amount of friction available to hold the climber. All belayers on the top (or bottom) of a cliff should be tied into and at the end of a taut leash attached to the belay anchor. A standing belayer who is tight against the anchor leash and leaning over the cliff edge can exert almost 250 pounds of friction to control a fall. A short fall—as little as a few feet—can produce this much force, if there are no other sources of friction in the system. You cannot exert enough braking friction to stop the rope from slipping around your waist, and the climber will take an "elevator ride" down the climb. On the other hand, by sitting down (Figure 6-12B) you make a 90-degree bend in the rope where it passes over your leg. This bend increases friction by about 40 percent, so that you can hold a maximum of about 350 pounds of force before the rope begins to slip. Thus, a sitting belayer has more control over a short top-rope fall than a standing belayer.

### A High-Friction Waist Belay for Top Roping

In some situations, you may want more friction than a normal waist belay can provide. If you are at the top of a pitch and have only a couple of carabiners available, but you want to stand at the cliff's edge to observe the belayer, you prefer to be pulled away from the edge rather than toward the edge in the event that the climber falls. If there are good cliff-top anchors available, then use the setup shown in Figure 6-13.

At the cliff top, tie in with a clove hitch or figure-eight on a bight and adjust the length of your leash to stand near the edge. To belay, pass

incorrect: standing waist belay
with minimal friction

correct: sitting waist belay
with increased friction

Figure 6-12. *Friction on Top-Rope Belays*

possible counter
anchor

solid anchor

to climber

*Figure 6-13. A High-Friction Waist Belay for Top Roping*

the rope through a carabiner on the anchor tree to make a 180-degree turn. This configuration increases the maximum impact force by about 90 percent, to about 450 pounds, before the rope runs dynamically around your waist. You are in control at the edge and have as much belaying friction as a mechanical belay plate provides (an obvious advantage with icy ropes that will not work with the mechanical belay devices). To prevent being pulled toward the anchor and away from the edge during a fall, you would need to place a counter anchor at the cliff edge.

## The Slingshot or Social Belay

Slingshot or social belays allow you to belay at the base of a climb, gaining visual contact and casual conversation with the climber, yet use an overhead anchor. The rope runs from the climber at ground level, as shown in Figure 6-14, through a carabiner attached to an overhead anchor and back to the belayer at ground level. The completed system looks like a stretched slingshot with the V-shaped center of the system at the top of the cliff. A method of setting up a slingshot anchor is described in Chapter 10, Figure 10-1.

With a slingshot system, the climber usually starts at the base of a cliff and climbs to the top. Then you lower the climber to the ground. Both the waist-belay and the mechanical-belay systems described below give enough friction to control potential falls, but most people prefer that the friction of lowering be absorbed by the mechanical device rather than by their waist.

Belayers often employ a slingshot belay without being tied into a ground-level anchor. This system works as long as you are directly underneath the overhead anchor, have a tight rope on the

*Figure 6-14. **The Slingshot or Social Belay** (see chapter 10 for setup details)*

late under the climber's feet or bending knee; allow the climber to focus on climbing without constant concern about rope tension. At the same time, do not exert a distracting pull that destroys the climber's concentration or makes it seem as if you were winching the climber up the route.

Belaying a leader is somewhat different from giving a top-rope belay. You can pull the climber off balance with a rope that is too tight and provide for a fall that is unnecessarily long if the rope is too loose. Your job is to have the proper amount of slack, as shown in Figure 6-1. When the climber is climbing smoothly, there will be 1 to 3 feet of slack forming an arc that you constantly adjust as the leader moves upward.

At the *crux* (the most difficult section of a climb), the leader may experiment with a move two or three times before finally committing. The alert belayer reduces the amount of slack in anticipation of a fall. You can compensate for the leader's up and down movement by paying out and taking in slack as the leader works out the moves. (If the climber is leading and has overhead protection at the crux, you take rope in as the leader moves up and pay it out again after the leader passes the protection.)

### Limitations of Waist Belays

Use the waist belay in situations where other belay brakes do not work, such as when the rope ices up. The waist belay produces a lower impact force on the protection piece that would hold a fall; marginal protection pieces placed on a dicey lead are more likely to hold. On the other hand, the waist belay allows more rope to slip through the system. The leader will fall farther before stopping, with an increased possibility of hitting a ledge.

A waist belay may not provide enough braking friction to catch a fall for "normal" leads where there is little to moderate friction in the belay chain. A waist belay gives a very dynamic belay that can result in loss of control and friction burns to your waist and hands. Use gloves and heavy clothing to help control the waist belay and protect your body.

climber, and weigh more than the climber. The direction of pull on you, in this case, is upward. The force generated in a fall will be offset by your weight coupled with friction of the rope on the upper anchor. If you stand away from the bottom of the climb, however, a fall will jerk you toward the cliff and you may collide with either the cliff or the falling climber. Worse, you may become disoriented, stumble, and drop the climber. Use a tie-in when you belay.

### The Proper Amount of Slack

When you belay top-roped climbs, keep the rope tight enough to "feel" the climber. You want neither a tight nor a loose rope, but one that allows you to feel the slightest amount of resistance. Make sure that you belay smoothly, without jerking the climber. Do not let a loop of rope accumu-

Figure 6-15. *The Munter Hitch:* **A**—*Form two loops that touch a crosspiece.* **B**—*Bend both loops toward you.* **C**—*Place a carabiner through the loops and pull the tail of the rope toward your body. This completes the Munter hitch. To feed out the rope to a climber, pull as indicated.* **D**—*To take in rope, pull toward you. The action of taking rope in or letting it out reverses the position of the hitch, as shown by comparing C and D.*

## High-Friction Belay Brakes

Both the Munter hitch and mechanical belay plates give you greater holding power than a waist belay, and transfer the friction generated in a fall to a carabiner, the rope, or a mechanical plate rather than your waist. Some high-friction belay brakes incorporate tubes to dissipate the heat produced by the friction. As you use belay brakes, carry over your knowledge of the belay chain, friction surface, and helping and braking hands.

### The Munter Hitch Belay

The Munter hitch provides a quick, lightweight belay brake that you can use with a minimum of equipment. There are a number of ways to tie the Munter hitch. The method illustrated in Figure 6-15 is based on the clove hitch. Begin by forming two loops of rope that touch a crosspiece (A). Take the loop formed behind the crosspiece, here the left-hand one, and bend it forward (B), opening the loop. Now pass the carabiner through the resulting hitch, enclosing the two strands of rope at the top

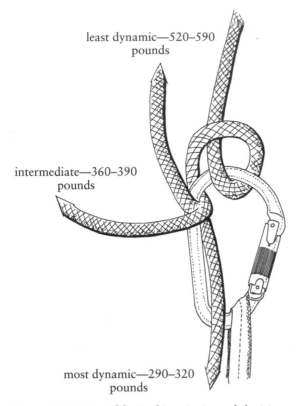

least dynamic—520–590
pounds

intermediate—360–390
pounds

most dynamic—290–320
pounds

Figure 6-16. *Variable Braking Action of the Munter Hitch: Data based on test by the Ontario Rock Climbing Association reported in* Rock Climbing Safety Manual *(1985).*

shown in Figure 6-16, from a dynamic, through an intermediate, to a nearly static position. These different braking positions allow the belay to apply between approximately 290 to 590 pounds of stopping force.[1] As a result, you can generate a more static belay with a Munter hitch than with a waist belay or many mechanical-belay brakes. Static belays can stress the protection system more than dynamic belays, as discussed in following pages.

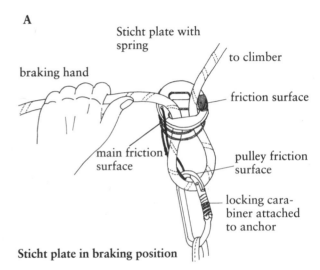

A

Sticht plate with
spring

to climber

braking hand

friction surface

main friction
surface

pulley friction
surface

locking cara-
biner attached
to anchor

**Sticht plate in braking position**

of the loop. You are now ready to belay (C). You reverse the hitch by pulling when you take in rope from the climber (D). Keep your fingers out of the hitch: if a fall occurs, the hitch could trap them.

The Munter hitch works best with a large-diameter carabiner that has a rounded end—the pear-shaped carabiner—fixed in position to your harness or other anchor point. The large, rounded carabiner allows the hitch to "turn over" or reverse without first taking up excess slack better than a smaller carabiner would, so you can change from feeding out to taking in or braking the rope. It can be difficult to reverse the Munter hitch if you do not use proper technique and a pear-shaped carabiner. You can vary the braking friction provided by the Munter hitch by moving your hand and altering the position of the brake, as

B

to climber

**figure-eight device in braking position**

Figure 6-17. *Sticht Plate and Figure-eight Device Showing Braking Position and Friction Surfaces*

### Mechanical Plates

Mechanical plates magnify the strength of your hand by passing the rope over a metal friction our face. Well-known mechanical brake plates include, among many others, the Sticht plate (Figure 6-17A), the Tuber, and the Air Traffic Controller. Figure-eight devices with rectangular holes and rounded corners, similar to a Sticht plate, are also available (Figure 6-17B). A figure-eight descender, normally used for rappelling, can be used in a manner similar to the Sticht plate, although this is recommended only for emergencies. For normal climbing situations mechanical plates are advantageous and widely used. Attach the plate to the carabiner with a retaining cord to prevent the device from slipping away from you, making you lose control of the belay.

### Using a Mechanical Plate

To use a Sticht plate, serving here as a prototype of slot-shaped mechanical plates, or a figure-eight device, extend a bight of rope through a hole and then clip a carabiner through the bight, as shown in Figure 6-17.

This figure shows how to hook up these devices and which surfaces provide friction. You can transfer the hand sequence that you learned for a waist belay to belay with these mechanical devices, as illustrated in Figure 6-18.

There is another popular hand sequence for mechanical belay plates that differs somewhat from that used for waist belays. This may be a confusing sequence and should only be attempted after you thoroughly understand the belay chain and the functions and locations of the brake hand, helping hand, and friction surface. The major difference from the waist-belay sequence arises from the use of the helping hand as both a helping hand and a second braking hand. The helping hand moves back and forth on the rope to both the climber's side and the braking side of the mechanical plate.

The sequence begins as for a waist belay: pull slack from the climber with your helping hand while your brake hand pulls the rope through the plate. Now the sequence departs from that of a waist belay. With your helping hand you release the rope leading to the climber and grasp the rope on the brake-hand side. In this position the helping hand becomes a second braking hand. You can now release the original braking hand and reposition it adjacent to the plate. Then drop the braking side of the rope and return your helping hand to the climber's side of the rope to help pull in slack from the climber. Now you can start the sequence over. What is important is that you always have a functional brake hand on the rope ready to apply braking action. Like a race driver careening around a curve on a cliff edge, you must always be ready to brake instantaneously, so always have a braking hand on the rope and be ready to use it.

In order to brake effectively with a mechanical plate or a Munter hitch, it is important to have the belay plate in front of you so you can pull back on the rope instantly. It is most comfortable about waist height. This occurs naturally when you belay from your harness, but may require planning when you belay directly from an anchor.

Because they provide lots of friction and dissipate heat, mechanical plates are useful to lower climbers from the top of a climb. The heat and friction is transferred to the metal plate rather than to your waist, or to the sheath of the rope in a Munter hitch. On a lead climb, the mechanical plate also allows you to hold a fall with less effort because it generates more braking friction—it is more static—and creates less discomfort than a waist belay. For a moderate fall, energy is absorbed mainly by rope stretch, together with deformation of tie-in knots and the climber's and belayer's bodies. The energy of a fall also places stress on the protection piece the leader counts on to catch the fall. As the belay brake provides increasing braking friction, the impact force on the protection piece increases twice as fast as it does on the rest of the system. The static or dynamic nature of different mechanical plates varies in degree.

### Choosing a Belay Brake

The art of belaying begins with the choice of belay brake. Belayer and leader together need to consider the needs of each different situation, and

to climber

helping hand

pull rope through

pull rope in

braking hand

brake plate

A—Pull in the rope with both hands until you extend your braking arm to its working extension.

B—Hold the rope with your braking hand, and slide your helping hand out along the rope.

C—Bring both hands together. The helping hand should be higher than the braking hand.

D—Hold both parts of the rope with the helping hand, and slide your braking hand toward the brake plate, keeping it ready in case of a fall.

E—Slide your helping hand toward the brake plate to return to the original position shown in A. The cycle starts over.

F—Holding a fall. Bring the braking hand down to produce a sharp bend in the rope. This creates friction at the brake plate. In order to do this quickly, you must stand immediately behind the brake plate.

Figure 6-18. **Hand Sequence for Belaying with a Brake Plate**

piece together the right system. You are a team, connected by a rope. Team work requires prolonged attention, positive verbal and nonverbal communication, and emphatic commitment to the project at hand, as well as to each other.

Both the design of belay brakes and the strategies for using them appear to be changing as climbing itself changes. At one end of the scale are the braking needs of social-belay novice climbers who work with bombproof protection and overhead anchors; at the other end are the needs of lead climbers who tremble through long run outs to marginal protection. For the first situation, a foolproof belay plate, such as the Grigri, allows novices to lock up the rope safely and prevents the loss of precious height during a fall. The run-out lead climber, however, desires a belay that does not lock up, but lets the rope slip through it to keep stress off the marginal protection. The sport leader working with beefy bolts and the adventurous climber placing good protection at reasonable intervals find themselves at the middle of the spectrum. All these different situations place radically different demands upon the belay brake and its effect on protection.

In an "average" lead climb there is little to moderate friction provided by ropes running over carabiners or around corners. An "average" fall on the lead is also likely to be moderate, onto closely spaced, good protection. For the average top-rope or lead climb many belay brakes are suitable and recommended,[2,3] as long as they do not permit the belayer to apply too little or too much braking force. Too little force will allow the leader to continue falling; too much force may cause the protection to pull and lengthen the fall distance. This subject is examined in greater detail in Chapter 11.

Belay techniques that provide too little braking force for lead climbs, and are not recommended even for top-roped sport climbs, include figure-eight descenders used in rappel or sport mode (Figure 6-19). In sport mode a bight of rope passes through the large hole in the descender directly to a belay carabiner. This generates even less friction—on the order of 200 pounds—than the waist belay, giving rise to the possibility that a belayer

sport mode—
not recommended

rappel mode—
not recommended

*Figure 6-19. **Incorrect Belay Techniques with a Figure-eight Descender:** A—The sport mode has too little friction to control reliably the fall of even a top-roped climber, and can lead to injury. B—The rappel mode also has too little friction to hold reliably a top-roped climber; this mode also kinks the rope. Do not belay a lead climber using either mode.*

may lose control of a falling climber even on a top rope. In the rappel mode you can generate a somewhat higher braking force—between 240 to 270 pounds—which is roughly equivalent to the waist belay. This is not enough braking force to hold the average leader fall when there is medium to low friction in the system. In addition, the figure-eight descender in the rappel mode tends to kink the rope, which may make it impossible for the belayer to pay out rope to the leader.

The Sticht plate is a useful and recommended

belay device, and serves as the model for discussion of slot belay devices because it was the first on the market. The Sticht plate with a spring provides a more dynamic belay than one without a spring, and may be better suited for moderate to severe falls on climbs with a medium amount of friction in the system. Sticht plates with springs also are suited for easy, low-fall-factor falls without much friction in the system. Other slot belay devices provide variable amounts of braking force, listed in pounds in Chapter 11.

Many climbers employ the figure-eight descender (see Figure 6-17B), as a springless slot plate, although this use is not officially recommended. Springless slot plates can lock up during a severe fall when there is little friction in the system, and may damage the rope, or even cut it. To prevent lockup, clip an extra carabiner onto the bight of rope between the plate and your locking carabiner. Tube-shaped plates, used with the large end against the belay carabiner, appear to prevent lockup, but make sure not to reverse them.

For slingshot belays, sport climbers have begun to use mechanical belay devices such as the Petzl Grigri, designed to lock up automatically if the climber falls. Since these devices produce a completely static belay, some climbers advocate that the belayer not be tied into a stance.[4] During a fall you will be lifted and your body deformed to absorb energy and make the belay more dynamic. Of course, you need to be careful that you are not dragged horizontally or hit by the falling climber, lest you lose control of the belay or be injured. Static belays should be avoided for lead climbs.

## Belaying on Glaciated Cliffs

The soils on cliffs in glaciated areas, covering much of the northern part of North America and northern Europe, are usually very thin glacial till soils that are often a few inches to a few feet thick, as sketched in Figure 6-20. These soils formed during the melting of a glacier. They are made up of the rock load pulled off and carried along at the base of glacial ice. Beneath these thin soils, the bedrock of the ledge is polished from the abrasive action of the glacier that occurred before the till was dropped. When exposed at the surface, this polish can produce mirrorlike smoothness and extremely slippery slab climbs. It should be obvious that tree roots do not penetrate this glacial polish, although the rare tree may send taproots into a crack.

Always be suspicious of trees growing in glacial

---

### Static Belays and Marginal Protection

Many belay brakes useful for well-protected sport or lead climbs are not suitable for adventure climbs with long run outs to marginal protection. For example, the Grigri is a device designed to lock off the rope during a fall to provide an absolutely static belay. A Munter hitch in its most static mode, as well as other highly static belay brakes, also effectively lock off the rope. A locked-off rope transmits elevated stresses to protection pieces. Beefy bolts found on sport climbs, and well-protected pieces placed on the lead might withstand these forces. The marginal small to tiny protection pieces, which may be the only protection found on some adventure climbs, probably will not be able to withstand these forces, particularly for a long fall.

If you lead on marginal protection, you may already have a good idea of what you are getting into. To have the best shot at success, place your belay point farther away from the marginally protected crux rather than closer, use dynamic slings (described in Chapter 7), and choose the belay brake that best combines the ability to stop the fall with the likelihood that it will not pull your protection. Stay away from high-friction devices.

A

small tree
with high
tie-off

fallen tree

till soil

rock

incorrect belay

B

nut backup

large tree tied off at
its base

till soil

rock

better belay

*B—A better belay. The tree used for the tie-off weighs as much as the shock force that will be produced in a fall. The tree is tied off at its base to prevent leverage, and a nut anchor is used to back up the tree anchor. By sitting, the belayer makes a 90-degree turn in the rope across the legs that increases braking force by up to 40 percent. Finally, the belayer will be pulled directly downward into the rock rather than outward if a fall occurs.*

*Figure 6-20. **Till Soils on Cliffs: A**—The belay is incorrect in three ways. First, the tree used for belaying connects poorly to the thin till soil through its spread-out roots. Second, the tie-off point is above the base of the tree and will produce leverage. Third, the belayer increases the effect of leverage by standing, and will rotate outward if a fall occurs.*

till soils on cliff ledges as belay stations for technical climbing. These trees usually have roots that spread out over the surface of the soil and are not deeply rooted or firmly attached to the ledge. Observe two rules of thumb when belaying from these trees: First, pick a tree that weighs more than the shock force that would be generated on the tree by a falling leader; second, tie off the tree as close to its base as possible to prevent leverage. Sit

rather than stand so that your body does not act as a lever, and to increase the friction of the belay. Back up the tree with artificial protection pieces, using nuts, if you have any doubt.

Shock forces are discussed in detail in Chapter 11. To summarize shock forces briefly: In falling you can generate a force many times your body weight when you stop at the end of the rope. To test this out experimentally, jump up and down on a bathroom scale and read the maximum instantaneous weight, or impact force, recorded on the scale. You jump a few inches, but the scale registers a couple of hundred pounds. Now consider the force if you take a screamer fall and come to an abrupt stop on the end of the rope. This shock force is transferred to the belayer and the belayer's anchor. To absorb a high-value shock force, choose a substantial tree weighing 2,000 to 3,000 pounds, with a girth of several feet. When large well-rooted trees are not available, back up small tree anchors with nuts, and use a braced body position.

## Communications

Good communication is required in climbing at all times, and becomes more critical when the situation is difficult. When climbers can converse easily, they talk normally and do not need special jargon. As you gain experience, you may find that you will climb under environmental conditions that make it difficult to communicate—in wind storms and other heavy weather, when separated from your companion by overhangs or bulges that muffle sound, or in situations of stress when you must get a request across quickly and unmistakably. Climbers have developed a shorthand communication system that relies on one- and two-word phrases to communicate fundamental requests for rope management. To prevent misunderstanding, these phrases include questioning signals that are always followed by a response acknowledging the original signal. In crowded areas, climbers may use each other's name to differentiate their signals from identical signals being used by other teams. The generally accepted terms used are listed below.

Climber: **"On belay?"** Question to belayer.

Belayer: **"Belay on!"** Response to climber.

Belayer: **"Climb"** or **"Climb when ready."** Tells the climber it is okay to climb.

Climber: **"Climbing."** Indicates that the climber is starting up; sometimes the belayer is not ready yet and tells the leader so. "Climbing" can also mean that the climber is moving again after stopping for an extended period of time.

Climber: **"Up rope."** There is loose rope in the system and the belayer should take in some of it. There is no spoken response, since it is obvious to the climber that the rope is being taken in. When you are at a top-rope site with several ropes of different colors, it is helpful to mention the rope color in the signal: "Up on blue."

Climber: **"Slack."** The rope is too tight and the climber wants slack. If the belayer pays out rope without the rope becoming slack at the climber (because of friction in the system), the belayer may tell the climber to pull out what is needed. Once the climber starts up again, the signals "Climbing again" and "Up rope" should be given if they are necessary.

Climber: **"Tension."** This signal urges the belayer to make the rope very tight because the climber is in danger of falling or because the climber needs to rest for some reason. A second might have difficulty getting out a piece of protection from a difficult stance, for example, and ask for tension.

Climber: **"Falling."** The climber is falling and the belayer should lock off the belay.

Belayer: **"[Number of] feet."** This tells the leader how much rope is left and gives the leader a chance to set up a belay. Break the number up into its components—such as "two-zero" instead of "twenty"—to make the communication clearer.

Climber or belayer: **"Rock, rock, rock . . . !"** Shouted at the top of your lungs, this tells anyone below to get out of the way of a falling rock, carabiner, nut, etc.

Climber: **"That's me."** This tells the belayer that the rope is not hung up in a crack or bush but has come tight on the climber. This situation often occurs just before the "Belay on" call, as the former leader initiates the belay out of sight of the second.

Climber: **"Watch me."** Not a traditional signal, this term is used now when climbers are doing a particularly hard move to warn the belayer to be especially attentive.

### Confusing the Signals

The Pipe Pitch of the Whitney-Gilman Ridge has two cruxes. First comes the Pipe Overhang followed by a platform, then a simple but very exposed mantle out of the void of the Black Dike. The first time I led off this pitch, I almost caused myself to be pulled backward into this void.

Still a bit wobbly after completing the Pipe overhang, I looked around the corner into the void of the Black Dike. There was no protection to minimize a fall during the mantle. I had almost completed the mantle when I said to myself, "I seem to have a lot of drag on this rope." My belayer, two right angles and an overhang below, heard the operational word *rope*. He began taking it in, exerting a slight tug that prevented further progress on my part. I was held in mid-mantle, firmly committed to completing it or suffering the consequences of going back down. Unthinkingly, I said in a firm but not loud voice, "Take up the rope." My belayer began to pull me backward with an effort that matched the firmness of my voice. Now panicked at what appeared to be an inevitable fall, I screamed at the top of my voice, "Rope!" I started to slide into the void, as my dutiful belayer complied by pulling with all his strength. Just before my foot, or was it a knee, popped off the out-sloping top of the mantle, I realized my error. Reversing my command, I emphatically shouted, "Slack," and my responsive belayer paid out slack. Adrenaline heightened, I clawed and crawled my way onto the ledge and then around the corner when I was able to stand up.

In the 18 years since, I have never confused these critical signals again!

---

Belayer: **"I am with you."** This response reassures the leader.

Climber: **"Off belay."** The climber is secure and tells the belayer to break the belay apart.

Belayer. **"Belay off."** Confirms that the belayer has broken the belay apart and tells the climber that the rope can be managed without interference from the belayer.

The question "Belay off?," with the word *off* accented, is not a good way for the belayer to ask the leader if the belay can be taken off, since it may be mistaken for a statement. It is usually posed by an impatient belayer whose leader is not setting up the upper belay anchor fast enough for the belayer. The belayer may be cold, hungry, or have other personal needs, and be impatient. If the leader has forgotten to tell the belayer "Off belay," however, the belayer is justified in the question.

Rappeller: **"Off rappel."** The rappeller has not only taken the rappel apart, but has walked away from the area to avoid rock fall that might be caused by the next rappeller.

---

### References for Future Reading

Chisnall, Robert. 1985. *Rock climbing safety manual*. Kingston, Ontario: Ontario Rock Climbing Association.
Gadd, Will. 1992. This ain't no trad weenie roast!: Safety in the sport climbing arena. *Rock & Ice*. 49:94–9.
_____. 1993. Toys: Belay and descending devices. *Rock & Ice*. 54:106–108.

# Endnotes

1. These figures are supplied by the Ontario Rock Climbing Association in its Safety Manual.

2. The Ontario Rock Climbing Association Safety Manual provides a summary of the results of extensive drop tests on different belaying techniques.

3. Gadd, 1993, lists properties and recommendations for belay devices in table form with a brief discussion.

4. Will Gadd's 1993 article describes problems and gives advice to novices involved in sport climbing.

# CHAPTER

# 7

# Protection

## The Development of Protection

Being roped to the belayer does not safeguard the leader unless there is a way of attaching the rope to the cliff. On a lead climb, the leader places protection in the rock, uses natural protection, or takes advantage of protection that has been fixed in place by a previous climber. (Modern protection, "pro," includes a wide range of metal devices that can be wedged, pounded, or even drilled into the rock.) The leader clips the rope through a carabiner attached to the pro so that the rope can slide as the leader moves upward. This running protection does not prevent a fall but minimizes potential fall distance.

At the top of the pitch, the leader places several pieces of protection or uses fixed or natural protection and then ties into it. This anchor—the protection at the end of a pitch—ensures that the leader will not be pulled off his or her stance while belaying the second.

Early climbers, with great ingenuity and boldness, used natural chockstones wedged between the walls of chimneys for protection. Arriving at the chockstone, the leader untied from the rope, passed the rope behind the stone, and retied. Of course, not all climbs had natural protection, and those that did might not have it when it was needed, before a difficult section of the climb. Thus, climbers had the incentive to experiment with artificial protection.

Protection developed along two parallel but different paths, which can be divided loosely into protection that was pounded into a crack (wedges and pitons) and protection that was placed in a crack (artificial chocks, including spring-loaded camming devices). Climbers in the United States, for example, drove hardwood wedges into cracks to build a ladder up the side of Devil's Tower in Wyoming, and drove a single wedge to protect a traverse across a blank section of the Old Cannon route on Cannon Mountain in New Hampshire.

Europeans also used wood wedges, but for thinner cracks developed soft iron spikes called *pitons* or *pins*. Climbers pounded pitons into cracks, where the soft iron molded to the shape of the crack. With pitons, leaders could protect themselves whenever they arrived at a stance with a suitable crack. *Aid climbing*—using the protection to support body weight—became possible and allowed climbers to ascend outrageously overhanging walls for the first time.

Robert Underhill, who apprenticed on European mountains, introduced pitons to the United States in the 1930s. The security of this artificial protection allowed people to climb at a new level and established routes such as Standard on Cathedral Ledge in the White Mountains of New Hampshire and the North Ridge of the Grand Teton in Wyoming.

The next step was rigid steel pitons, first forged from the axle of a Model-T Ford by John Salathé, who used them to pioneer climbs of the southwest face of Half Dome and Lost Arrow Spire in

Yosemite Valley, California. Unlike the soft iron pitons, Salathé's pitons could be removed and reused, so only a limited number were needed for a long climb.

In the 1950s, Chuck Wilts introduced rigid and durable pitons of a chrome-molybdenum steel alloy to Yosemite Valley. A decade later, equipment innovator and climber Yvon Chouinard began making and selling rigid pitons as a backyard industry. Eventually, he produced a range of piton sizes and shapes that are still state of the art today. Pitons became the dominant form of artificial protection, raising the standards of climbing. Using pitons, climbers scaled the big walls of Yosemite Valley with increasing frequency, and established difficult climbs across the United States. Rigid pitons were the protection of choice until the early 1970s.

Protection for modern *free climbing*—climbing in which the climber does not use protection as a hand or foothold—evolved separately from pitons. In England, climbers collected natural chockstones of various shapes while walking along railroad tracks to the climbing area. They carried the stones in their pockets until they found a likely looking spot to use them on the climb. With the introduction of flat nylon webbing and carabiners after World War II,[1] enterprising climbers began to sling large hexagonal machine nuts with their interior threads filed smooth. Leaders could place these artificial chocks quickly, and seconds could retrieve them for use on the next pitch. In addition, the nuts came in various sizes and could cover a great range of placements. Among the nuts or chocks later developed were cylindrical knurled Pecks, foxhead wedges, and symmetrical hexes.

Yvon Chouinard's introduction of tapered nuts called *stoppers* and passive camming nuts called *Hexcentrics* provided the next landmark. Passive cams allowed climbers to protect parallel-sided cracks for the first time. Greg Lowe experimented extensively with passive cams of all sizes and shapes, but Vitali Abalakov, a climber and engineer in the former U.S.S.R., widely introduced these ideas to the West. Ray Jardine developed a spring-loaded camming device, the Friend. Many types of passive and spring-loaded camming devices and tapers are now part of the modern climbing rack. Advances in metallurgy, too, have produced a range of extremely strong nuts sized to fit the smallest of cracks.

By the early 1970s, artificial nuts had almost entirely replaced pitons. Nuts were both quicker and easier to place, and provided the same, or greater, security. In popular climbing areas such as Yosemite Valley, cracks had been enlarged by the quarrying action of the repeated insertion and removal of pitons. Thoughtful climbers realized

---

**An Unusual Piece of Protection**

One unique example of the evolution of artificial protection that combined the durability of iron with a wedged placement occurred on what is now the Whitney-Gilman ridge of New Hampshire's Cannon Cliff. Bradley Gilman and his cousin Hassler Whitney climbed this prominent ridge with an extremely exposed crux without protection. This section was probably the hardest climb in the country in 1929. Even today the crux, although now considered to be of moderate difficulty at 5.7, prompts hesitation.

In 1931, Robert Underhill and Kenneth Henderson "improved" the route[2] by sliding a long pipe with an iron ring welded to one end into a crack beneath the crux. Subsequently, leaders could come to this spot, untie, pass the rope through the ring, and tie back in. Climbers were undoubtedly grateful to have this protection.

Unfortunately, climbers today cannot enjoy the pleasure of using Underhill's protection: the ring fell off the end of the pipe in the early 1970s, and the pipe itself disappeared after a half-century of use.

that their climbing resource, the rock itself, was being altered rapidly. Doug Robinson's article, "The Whole Natural Art of Protection," in the 1973 Chouinard Equipment catalog[3] and John Stannard writing in *The Eastern Trade* helped popularize this view, and by 1974 the climbing community had turned to pitonless climbing. Today, piton scars provide placements for nuts, fingers, and hands on older free climbs, but most climbers agree that the rock should be preserved in as natural a state as possible and deplore practices such as chipping holds or otherwise altering the rock.

During the 1980s climbers began to use *bolts* designed for industrial anchoring in masonry and concrete, placing them on blank walls that were otherwise without protection. This interest led manufacturers to produce bolts made expressly for rock climbing; whole new areas opened up and climbing standards rose to a higher level.

## Nuts

### Aluminum Nuts

A standard wedge-shaped nut made from aluminum is called a *taper*. Most have tapering sides that form faces of unequal width so that they will fit two different size ranges (Figure 7-1). The newest tapers have rounded corners and curve on one side, so that they offer passive camming action. Tapers that curve on both sides provide tremendous holding power—so much that they are often very difficult to remove.

Tapers are designed to slot above a constriction in a crack. To achieve a secure placement, obtain as much contact between the rock and the taper's faces as you can. An incorrect placement (Figure 7-1) illustrates two mistakes. First, do not place a

*Figure 7-1. Curved Tapers in a Crack*

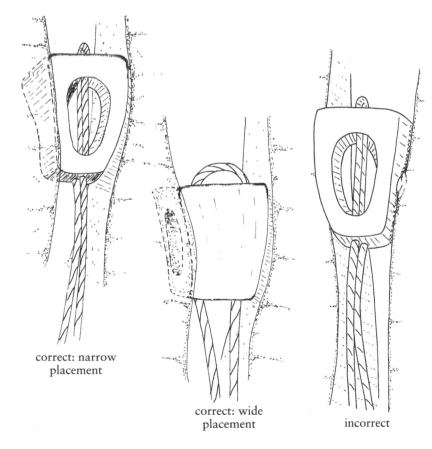

correct: narrow
placement

correct: wide
placement

incorrect

*Figure 7-2. Lifting, Rotation, and Failure of a Wired Taper*

placement                 lifting and rotation                              failure

taper so that one face rests on a protruding nubbin or crystal that may break or allow the nut to slip under the force of a fall. The nubbin may dig into the taper, requiring a vigorous one-handed effort on lead to remove and replace the nut properly, but it will not hold a fall. Second, be sure to place the nut entirely within the crack so that both faces completely contact rock surfaces.

Tapers usually come with a sling attached, and the sling influences the strength of the protection. Formerly, tapers were slung with small-diameter round nylon webbing called *perlon*. The larger the diameter, the greater was the strength of the perlon, and each 1-millimeter increase in perlon diameter added about 1,000 pounds of breaking strength to the sling.

Also, since a perlon sling has some flexibility, you could often use a carabiner to attach the rope directly to the sling without fear that the nut

would rotate out of the crack. If nuts rotate, they may fall out of the crack or slip deeper into it, becoming difficult to remove.

Most new small tapers come with wire slings, which are stronger than perlon. The stiff wire also acts as a handle that allows you to reach high to place the nut. Larger tapers come slung with 5.5-millimeter Kevlar threaded through drilled holes. Tapers with a wire sling are easily rotated by the movement of the climbing rope, causing the nut to dislodge (Figure 7-2). To prevent this problem, always use a short sling or *quickdraw,* making sure to attach the quickdraw to the wire with a carabiner (Figure 7-3A).

The holding power of a modern taper—one without obvious fraying of the wire sling— depends on how well the face of the nut makes contact with the rock. Nuts with small faces have little contact with the rock and are at best marginal

A
correct

B
incorrect

*Figure 7-3. **Slinging Tapers:** A—The correct method uses a carabiner to attach the nylon sling to the wired nut to prevent cutting. B—The incorrect method, without an intermediate carabiner, can lead to accidental cutting of the sling in a fall.*

protection. Always look for frayed slings and friable rock around cracks.

The weakest point on the wire sling of an aluminum taper is where the wire bends sharply as it passes through the head of the stopper to form a loop. This weakness determines the lower size limit for wired nuts of this design. Small nuts also have less surface contact with the rock than larger nuts,

so the force produced during a fall concentrates on a smaller area so that a small nut pulls more easily than a large one.

### Brass and Steel Nuts

To overcome the above problems, you can use brass nuts with silver-soldered cables, which come in a range of sizes and shapes, including an offset shape designed for the chipped area where a piton was removed. Brass nuts deform rather easily, adhering well to tiny nubbins and irregularities, but they fail by shearing out of the crack.

Small steel nuts have a higher shear strength, and represent a second strategy to overcome the problems of small nuts. Steel nuts are made by injecting powdered stainless steel into a die under extreme direct pressure. The nuts are then drilled and a steel cable is inserted and soldered in place.

Climbers commonly carry both brass nuts and steel nuts (Figure 7-4) and often use them with a dynamic sling that absorbs energy by ripping apart to minimize the load on the nut.

*Figure 7-4. **A Steel Nut in a Crack and an Offset Brass Nut Compared in Size to a Penny***

### Hexcentrics

Hexcentrics are larger nuts made of aluminum. They allow a number of placement possibilities, including camming and noncamming positions. They are desirable because they are effective, relatively inexpensive, and lighter than spring-loaded camming devices (discussed below).

You can place a Hex either lengthwise as a taper or sideways to cam in vertical cracks (Figure 7-5). The holding power of Hexes—and all nuts—is improved by having as much as possible of the surface of both faces in contact with the rock. You also enhance the placement of Hexcentrics, and all nuts, by slotting them as well as setting them in a camming position simultaneously. Use Hexcentrics as tapers in wide vertical cracks by placing them above a tapering section or as cams in a narrower parallel-sided crack. To achieve a good cam in a horizontal crack, place the sling so it leaves the nut near the roof of the crack.

### Setting and Removing Tapers and Other Nuts

The leader sets a nut with a slight tug. Setting causes small crystals to bite into the metal of the nut and hold it in place. If you do not set a nut, friction from the rope may rotate and slot it deeper into a crack, or allow it to fall out of the crack. Oversetting, however, may make it difficult to remove. To remove a taper or other nut, the second must generally reverse the placement sequence, looking at the relationship of the protection to the crack and deciding whether the nut was purpose-

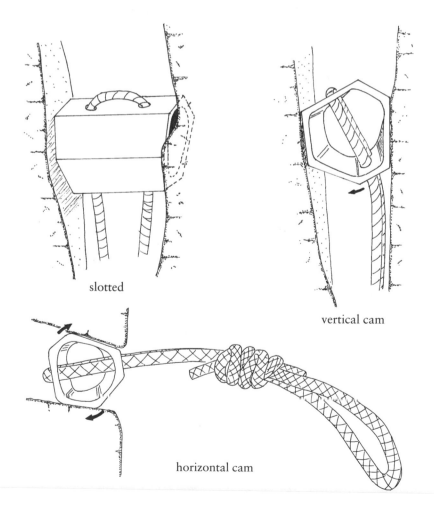

slotted

vertical cam

horizontal cam

*Figure 7-5. **Using a Hexcentric Nut as a Wide Wedge and as a Cam:** The Hexcentric, originally designed by Yvon Chouinard, is now made by Black Diamond. The arrows show camming direction of the Hex.*

*Figure 7-6.* **Two Cleaning Tools:** *One tool is shown hooking behind a taper.*

fully placed or accidentally rotated. The leader can call down the information about how the piece was placed from above. Do not grab the sling and blindly yank, since you may set the protection more firmly and bend and break the wire sling where it attaches to the nut.

Grasp larger nuts with your fingers and lift or rotate them from the placement. For smaller nuts, you may use a cleaning tool with a hook (Figure 7-6) that allows you to reach into a crack and behind the nut. The hook on cleaning tools should be narrow enough to fit behind the nut. You can grind hooks narrower on a grinder if the hook on your cleaning tool is too wide. Pad the palm end of the cleaning tool and hit it with your hand to free a sticky nut.

### Sliders and Lowe Balls

Sliders and Lowe Balls (Figure 7-7) are spring-loaded two-piece tapers that expand to wedge into varying sizes of thin cracks. Sliders evolved from the early practice of stacking or combining two single tapers, one upside down with respect to the other, as a single unit to wedge into odd-size

Sliders

Lowe Balls

*Figure 7-7.* **Combined Spring-loaded Wedging Nuts**

cracks. The Slider adds a spring to allow one-handed insertion.

The Lowe Ball is a logical and innovative combination of shapes to produce a wide range with firm holding power for a small nut. Its curved half-ball surface slides up a brass groove while its flat face orients itself to the rock surface and wedges. Place these small nuts in tapering slots so both faces are in full contact with the rock.

horizontal placement

vertical placement

*Figure 7-8. **Lowe Tricam Used as Cam:** In a horizontal crack you achieve a secure cam when the sling leaves the nut near the crack's roof, the nut is slotted, and a lip both prevents the beak from pulling directly outward and forces the Tricam to rotate forward and cam.*

### Lowe Tricam

A wonderful, innovative passive camming device, the *Lowe Tricam* (Figure 7-8) works in flares too small for most spring-loaded cams, piton scars, pockets, and horizontal cracks, as well as in places where spring-loaded camming devices also work. Tricams require attention and sometimes two hands to place properly. As a result, they are not as easy to place as a spring-loaded camming device when hanging on is difficult. You can use a Tricam as a passive nut or as a camming device, but you can usually cam it for additional protection any place that you can use it passively.

To prevent movement in the direction of pull, place the Tricam so that its beak rests in a depression or against a rock lip. Tricams work well in tapering or parallel-sided cracks. An outward or downward tug on the Tricam will start it rotating and produce the camming action. You get the best camming action in a horizontal crack when the Tricam's sling wraps around the top of the nut.

Tricam removal requires what is usually an obvious reversal of the camming direction, and perhaps some movement to the side. You may have to rotate Tricams placed in pockets with a large interior and a small opening 180 degrees inside the pocket before they come out.

## Spring-loaded Camming Devices

Spring-loaded camming devices, or SLCDs, work well in parallel-sided cracks, under down-pointing flakes, and in larger pockets. They come with either three or four cams and with one or two axes. Three-cam units, or TCUs, which are used for protecting thin cracks, are small. They provide less friction and reportedly rotate more easily than four-cam units. The tendency to rotate increases in TCUs whose cams are close together and provide more of a pivot point. Devices with two sets of cams on two axes allow for greater contraction and expansion than four cams can on a single axis. Hence, camming devices with two axes fit a larger range of crack sizes than those with just one axis.

When you insert this type of protection into a crack, orient the stem so that it points in the direction that it would rotate if subjected to a leader fall. For vertical cracks try to place the stem as vertically as possible. If you see a device with its stem protruding horizontally from a vertical crack, you know that the leader has made a bad placement that can be corrected by using the next size smaller piece.

Try to size a spring-loaded camming device so that the cams are halfway retracted after you have inserted the device into a crack (Figure 7-9A). A device that is too small for the crack will open too far and possibly invert under load (Figure 7-9B). A device that is too large will be fully retracted (Figure 7-9C). It will be hard to remove because

you cannot retract the cams any farther to make it smaller than the crack. Overcamming often occurs in the middle of a demanding lead, when you hastily pull an SLCD from the rack and shove it into the crack by pushing on the stem. In desperation you reason that the second can deal with the problem. Yes, but a crowbar may be required!

An SLCD with two axes is strong enough to use as a passive nut in an open position (Figure 7-9D). Do not use the single-axis SLCD with the cams open: the cams may accidentally invert and the placement will fail.

SLCDs are manufactured with flexible or rigid stems. The rigid stems are stronger but break when bent over edges, whereas the flexible stems can

| A | B | C | D |
| correct | use a larger SLCD | overcammed | correct for SLCD with 2 axes |
| | | | incorrect for SLCD with 1 axis |

*Figure 7-9. Spring-loaded Camming Devices: In each sketch the SLCD is located in the crack far enough from the edge to prevent the cams from popping out of the crack. A—The SLCD has a rigid stem oriented in the potential fall direction. Its cams are properly contracted into the midrange. B—The crack is wide for this SLCD.*

*The next larger size would be a better choice. C—The SLCD is overcammed and may be very difficult to remove because you cannot make it smaller than the crack. D—You can use SLCDs with two axes (shafts) fully open as passive nuts, but do not use a one-axis SLCD in this manner: it can fail if the cam inverts.*

A

B

Figure 7-10. *Two Ways to Safeguard SLCDs in Horizontal Cracks: A—Tie a loop of Spectra cord through the hole in front of the trigger bar to prevent leverage. A safer placement for this crack would be a Tricam or B—an SLCD with a flexible stem.*

bend over edges but tend to fray and need replacing sooner.

A potentially dangerous placement occurs when the rigid stem of an SLCD protrudes from a horizontal crack. If the clip-in point of the device is at the end of a stem, a fall will turn the stem into a lever and the stem may snap. There are two ways to overcome this problem. Tie a small loop of Spectra cord (the current material of choice for slinging) through the stem holes forward of the trigger bar (Figure 7-10A). When the rope loads this sling, no levering action occurs on the stem.

Alternatively, you can use an SLCD with a flexible stem (Figure 7-10B). These stems are made of woven wire and may be single or doubled in a U-shape. The potential weakness of this design is that wire can fray and break strand by strand. Some manufacturers cover the wire with a stiff plastic

nut remover

Friend of a Friend

Figure 7-11. *Tools for Removing Deeply Placed SLCDs*

designed to help shield the wire from abrasion. The wires controlling trigger bars also require routine replacement, which the manufacturer can do inexpensively.

### Removing Spring-loaded Camming Devices

Pressure from the climbing rope trailing behind the leader can make the device work—or walk—its way into the crack. The second may find it difficult to pull the trigger bar while pushing with the thumb in order to remove the protection. This situation is almost certain to happen when the leader places the SLCD in a crack at an overhang lip and the rope runs over it as the leader ascends. The easiest way to prevent this problem is to place a passive nut rather than an SLCD at the lip.

Special tools and ordinary nut-removers such as those sketched in Figure 7-11 may help extract protection from these problem placements. The best special tool is an extended SLCD trigger bar called *Friend of a Friend*, designed by Ed Leeper. This device has hooks on one end to grip the SLCD trigger bar, and a trigger on the other end.

In an emergency, you can slip small wired nuts over both sides of the trigger bar and link them together with a carabiner (Figure 7-12). The cara-

biner allows you to pull on the trigger bar while you push with a nut remover on the stem. Executing this maneuver almost always requires you to hang from a rappel rope, a piece of protection, or a belayed rope from above, but usually results in success.

### Camming Devices Placed Behind Flakes, in Parallel Cracks, and Slotted

Camming nuts create outward forces that translate into friction to oppose the force of a fall. For a spring-loaded camming device the outward forces are generated as the stem is pulled in the direction of the fall. Belayed falls with a body belay or mechanical plate create maximums of approximately 1,000 to 2,000 pounds of force, respectively, parallel to the stem of a camming nut. Cams may double this force as they transfer it to the walls of a crack. Because the energy of a fall is doubled and transferred to the rock, camming nuts placed behind flakes or loose blocks will push out and may break off the flake or block.

In general, SLCDs placed in parallel cracks hold as long as friction of the cams against the wall equals or is greater than the force on the cams in the direction of the fall.

*Figure 7-12. Emergency Removal of SLCD Using Wire Tapers*

basic connection

in operation

SLCDs should hold in solid granite, but they may not hold in weakly cemented sandstone or highly weathered rock. When the force of a fall does overcome friction of the cams, the SLCD slides, sometimes leaving behind grooves like ski tracks.

In irregular cracks you can improve the placement strength of a camming nut by slotting and camming the nut. In order for a slotted and cammed nut to come out, the nut would have to pull through the narrows of the slot in addition to overcoming the friction of the cam against the wall.

## Nuts for Offwidths

Protection for wide cracks has always been something of a problem. Climbers used large pitons called *bong-bongs* in the 1960s. More recently, they used hollow aluminum tube chocks, and most recently very large homemade spring-loaded camming devices that are now commercially available as Big Dudes (Figure 7-13A). A recent addition to the large-crack arsenal is the BigBro (Figure 7-13B), which features two tubes, one inside the other, that lengthen under spring pressure and lock open by means of a threaded ring. One-handed placement is possible for all of BigBro's four sizes, which fit fist-size to arm-bar-size cracks. A sling attaches to one end of the tube to help wedge or cam it into position above a slight constriction. The weight and bulkiness of large-crack protection usually means that most climbers go without unless they know ahead of time that they will absolutely require it.

## Pitons

With the advent of nuts, many climbers are no longer familiar with the use of pitons. Pitons, however, are often fixed at belay stations on free routes, and are still used for aid climbs and for winter climbs (when cracks are often partially filled with ice, preventing nut placements). As a result, there is still good reason to learn how to place pitons.

*Figure 7-13.* **A Big Dude and BigBro Placement**

A
Big Dude

B
BigBro

### Trusting Fixed Protection

The move to all-nut free climbing in the early 1970s inadvertently created dangerous pitons. When nuts became the norm, any piton placed on a free climb was usually left in place as fixed, or *resident*, protection. Over the years, a layer of rust formed on the outer surface of the pins and in some cases the rock itself slowly weathered, resulting in loose pitons. Climbers cannot be certain of the quality of a resident pin placement without personally removing and replacing it. Always doubt the holding power of any pin found in place unless you have reason to believe it safe. Often, there are good nut placements nearby so you can set up an independent belay or at least back up fixed pins.

In densely populated climbing areas, local rescue groups often replace resident pins to protect climbers who have too much faith in pins. Check with the rescue group in your local area for its replacement policy.

There are two types of pitons: *blades* and *angles* (Figure 7-14). Since the holding power of a blade comes from friction between the rock and the piton, you must drive these pins tightly into a crack. The holding power of an angle comes from compression between the back and front of the piton, as well as friction.

### *Placing and Removing Pitons*

Placing a piton requires the use of a heavy (20- to 25-ounce) hammer with a large, flat face (Figure 7-15) and a pick to help pry pitons during removal. You normally carry the hammer in a holster. Attach a keeper sling from your harness to the hammer's shaft so you will not lose the hammer if

**A**
Lost Arrow

**B**
Bugaboo

**C**
Angle

*Figure 7-14.* **Piton Types:** *Pitons may be blades (A and B) or angles (C).*

*Figure 7-15.* **Piton Hammer and Holster**

Figure 7-16. **Good and Bad Placements of Pitons:**
A—A good blade placement with the blade horizontal or downward and with high friction between the rock and piton. B—Hollow and poor. C—Good: upward but high friction. D—Good friction with eye upward but poor placement of carabiner, which will both break the carabiner and lever the piton. E—A sling corrects this placement. F—Good if tied off with hero loop. G—Good angle with the back and front wedging opposite sides of the crack. H—Poor angle with the sides of the piton in contact with the rock.

you drop it. The sling should be long enough to allow you to extend your arm fully.

Pitons should fit about three-quarters of the way into a crack to start, and should produce a ringing sound that rises in pitch as the pin is driven. If the crack quickly bottoms out, the pin cannot be driven. If the crack widens inside, you will not hear the rising ringing sound, and the placement will be poor. While piton placements in cracks at all angles can be excellent, horizontal cracks provide an advantage in leverage over a pin in a vertical crack. Examine both the good and the bad placements in Figure 7-16. Tie off pitons that are not driven (to the eye) with narrow half-inch nylon loops, called *hero loops*, to prevent leverage.

To remove a piton, drive it back and forth several times as far as it will travel (Figure 7-17). Pull the pin out in the middle of its travel, using your hand or the pick on the hammer. Climbers often attach an old carabiner with a keeper sling to the

Figure 7-17. **A Worm's Eye View of Piton Removal:** With the hammer drive the piton, in position at site 1, back and forth in the crack as far as possible, to sites 2 and 3. Then, when it is back at site 4, use the pick to lever the piton out of the crack.

pin so they do not drop the pin and lose it. You will invariably pound upon and weaken the carabiner, so mark it and dedicate it to piton removal.

Aid climbs often require piton placements that are tied off using hero loops to prevent leverage. In advanced aid techniques you can stack pitons to fit larger cracks, although large camming nuts lessen the necessity of stacking of pitons. Small wired tapers, Tricams, and three-cam units have lessened the need to use hero loops on pitons that do not go into the crack fully.

## Bolts

Bolts have been around for a couple of generations. Climbers accept bolts as long as the bolts allow them to maintain the adventure and challenge of climbing. On Yosemite-size walls a few bolts linking short blank rock sections maintain the challenge, whereas massive numbers guarantee the climb. On adventure climbs, a single bolt might turn a series of dangerously unprotected moves into a long climb of exciting adventures. On sport climbs, bolts allow climbers to create gymnastic routes at the limits of their physical abilities on otherwise unleadable rock.

Bolting was self-regulating as long as climbers tediously placed the bolts by hand, but the introduction of the power drill has changed the situation. The rate of placement has risen sharply, numerous new cliffs have been developed, thousands of new climbers have entered the sport, and gymnastic ability has increased dramatically for practitioners of bolted sport routes.

Another advantage of power drilling is that the ¼-inch bolt has given way to the stronger ⅜-inch bolt. Falls on bolts produce stress fractures, temperature swings weather bolt holes, and chemical reactions attack bolt metal, so examine the quality of bolts and their placements carefully. Never hit a bolt with a hammer and do not trust a bolt showing signs of hammer damage. Old bolts may hold a fall, but they may not, so never trust these bolts alone for protection.

### Bolt Types

Climbing bolts fall into three functional classes. A hammer-in bolt is pounded into the hole; a torque bolt is placed in the hole and torqued with a wrench; and a glue-in bolt is a threaded rod glued into an oversize hole.[4] This discussion covers only the hammer-in bolt because it is frequently used and the problems it presents are representative.

The Rawldrive is a common hammer-in bolt for hard rock, such as granite. As the bolt is pounded into place, the split and slightly bowed shank is compressed, exerting an outward spring force against the walls of the hole. Rawldrives depend on lots of friction between the bolt and the rock, so they only work in very hard rock. The screw-top Rawldrive is weaker, because of the threads, than the buttonhead design.

Wedge-type hammer-in bolts include stud drives, machine bolts used as aid rivets (a scary technique used for some big-wall climbs), and ½-inch baby angles pounded into ⅜-inch holes that are used for anchors in soft sandstone. For soft rock, glue-in bolts are probably stronger and safer than ½-inch baby angles or Rawldrive bolts. The drilling required to place these bolts has become possible with the advent of power drills.

### Placing Bolts

Place a bolt on a smooth rock face free from flakes, hollows, or natural drainage where freeze-thaw cycles will promote rock weathering. Bolts placed in natural drainage may be solid when placed but fall out when touched the following season. Gently chip any protruding crystals away so that the hanger can sit flush with the rock. Do not hit the area hard enough to fracture the rock.

The hole for a hammer-in bolt should be perpendicular to the rock surface and about ¼ inch longer than the bolt shank. This space allows the bolt to lengthen as the split shank compresses. Orient the split shank perpendicular to the direction of pull when the bolt is inserted into the hole to maximize resisting friction.

Overdriving a Rawldrive bolt or torquing a threaded anchor into a rock depression too hard

Figure 7-18. **Distorted Rawldrive Hanger:** *The base plate of the bolt has been distorted, weakening the metal. After Ed Leeper.*

will distort and may crack the base plate (Figure 7-18). Bolts that have been pounded upon after placement are susceptible to internal failure and are time bombs waiting to go off. You can recognize a bolt that bottoms out in the hole because the hanger spins freely or you can see the shank behind the hanger. Do not trust these bolts.

During the 1980s, many bolts were sealed with epoxy to prevent water infiltration. John Middendorf IV, reporting on research in *Machine Design Trade Magazine,* says that epoxy can corrode steel[5] and concludes that polyester resins are better in all respects for sealing bolts.

Figure 7-19. **Forces Applied to a Bolt by Hanger Design:** *A—Perspective and cross-section views of a Rawldrive placement. The cross section indicates correct and incorrect loading directions; B—Perspective and cross-section views of a poor homemade bolt design. This design creates an outward pull on the bolt shaft when a downward pull occurs on the bolt hanger. This bolt should not be used; it needs to be replaced.*

Commercial hangers for bolts made from stainless steel or chrome-moly steel come in various sizes. All rate at strengths of more than 4,000 pounds. These hangers apply force placed on the bolt perpendicular to the shaft—downward along the surface of the rock for a properly placed bolt (Figure 7-19A). Try not to pull a bolt outward along its axis (Figure 7-19B), since outward pulls work directly against the relatively smaller frictional resistance of the bolt shaft to the rock.

Outward pulls, such as those created by a fall under an overhang, produce torquing forces on many types of bolt hangers. Thus, when underneath overhangs you should use bolts that are beefy and designed, if possible, with nontorquing hangers. A belayer leaning off a bolt at waist level at a belay station may also create outward pull.

Note that the principles that govern loading bolts are the same as those that govern loading ice screws, discussed in Chapter 13 under "Loading Ice Screws."

Homemade anchors are often made from aluminum, angle iron, and strap steel. You can guess their strength by evaluating how much material supports the load and to what degree leverage occurs. A poorly designed hanger will act to exert a pull away from the rock, as shown in Figure 7-19B. The worst possible design places the force parallel to the shaft of the bolt, which is the direction required to pull the bolt straight out of its hole.

### Bolt Anchors

A bolt anchor consists of bolts, the webbing that links the bolts together, and an attachment point such as a rappel ring. Many of the webbing slings at rappel routes show signs of melting caused by friction produced as a rappel rope is pulled across the sling material. You can recognize friction melting in a smooth, blackened surface stripe on the nylon sling, corresponding to the position of the rappel rope. Do not rely just on such slings, which are reduced in strength. At frequently used rappel stations a multitude of slings accumulates. Consider carrying a knife to cut away the oldest of these slings when they pile up;

you may even want to leave behind a rappel ring to prevent friction melting of new sling material. Make sure that you rappel from the equalization point of the slings.

When you secure yourself to the webbing or chain, make sure that you will remain attached to the anchor even if one bolt fails. This usually means that you must clip the attachment carabiner through a loop and not around two strands of webbing or a length of chain stretching between two bolts. Since undetectable structure and placement problems may exist with bolts, always insist on two or more bolts for an anchor. Three-bolt anchors are not uncommon. For the first person down a rappel, back up a bolt anchor with chocks where possible.

There are excellent and poor webbing or chain patterns to attach bolts together. Analyze webbing patterns to determine the loading sequence and directions of the bolts that make up the anchor: you want to see if the pull on the bolts is chiefly downward, as occurs when bolts are above each other, or whether rotational forces are applied to individual bolts. Before rappelling, check the entire rappel system, including the anchor. If you do not like it, change it until you are satisfied.

Figure 7-20 represents various configurations in which webbing can connect bolts. Diagram A is a common pattern of connecting two bolts with sling material that produces a complex and high-stress pattern on the sling, multiplying the load on both bolts and sling. This setup also produces rotation that turns the bolt away from a favorable downward pull. (Details of the stresses involved in this configuration are described in Chapter 10; see the section explaining Figure 10-7.)

Diagram B shows that by placing one bolt almost in a vertical line with the other you form a two-sling anchor that will bear the load of the anchor equally. B and C represent patterns of *pseudo-equalization* in which both bolts are loaded only in one direction or in a limited range of directions (indicated by the arc drawn below C). A *self-equalized* anchor pattern that directs the forces equally to both bolts through a wide range of arc is shown in D. Keep the angle Ø between the

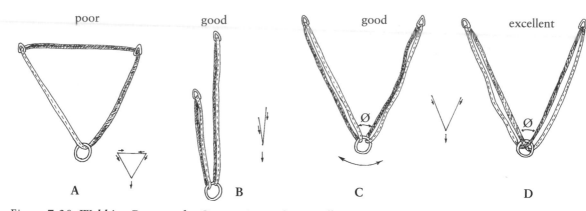

| poor | good | good | excellent |

| A | B | C | D |

Figure 7-20. *Webbing Patterns for Connecting Bolts:* *A*—*A poor pattern for connecting two bolts;* *B*—*A good pseudo-equalized pattern;* *C*—*Good for a downward* pull; *D*—*An excellent self-equalizing pattern. The best choice is to do both C and D, using three slings. The angle Ø should be 60 degrees or less.*

slings for all of these anchor patterns to 60 degrees or less to maximize the advantage of having two bolts. This placement will prevent load multiplication on the bolts and slings. (Load multiplication is also discussed in Chapter 10.)

Allen Sanderson suggests that using three slings in a combination of patterns C and D is perhaps the best for connecting two bolts.[6] The one long sling of pattern D forms the primary load-bearing anchor because it is self-equalizing. The weakness of the pattern is that the entire anchor fails if this sling fails. To overcome this problem, use two slightly longer slings connected in pattern C to act as a backup that will not load the rappel point unless the primary sling fails.

If you anticipate establishing bolt anchors, you should be familiar with the simple physical principles discussed in Chapter 10, and refer to the references listed at the end of this chapter.

### Using Bolts with Missing Hangers

You may often find Rawldrive bolts with missing hangers on older routes. You need not pass these up, since you can use them by slipping a small wired taper over the nut and sliding the nut head tightly against the bolt shaft, as illustrated in Figure 7-21. This protection is at best insecure, since it may fail if the wire taper rotates during a fall and the nut slips over the bolt's threads. Safeguard this marginal protection by using a dynamic sling, and by carrying a bolt hanger with you.

## Slings on Horns

Slings around natural rock horns (sometimes called *chickenheads*), flakes, knobs, and similar features need to be snug at the base of the projec-

Figure 7-21. *Using a Wire Taper to Replace a Bolt Hanger*

tion to prevent leverage and lifting by rope drag. You can secure slings on horns with a slip knot snugged up against the rock (Figure 7-22), and you can keep slings on flakes from lifting by jamming a knot, or the doubled sewn area, between the flake and rock wall.

## Bent-Gate Concerns and Enchaining Carabiners

A carabiner used to clip into running protection normally has its gate turned out from the rock and downward to prevent accidental opening. Having the gate out and down on bent-gate carabiners designed for fast, easy clip-ins of bolted sport climbs can lead to accidental unclipping of the rope during a fall. Tests reported by Recreational Equipment, Inc. in 1990 show that "it is not the shape of the gate that presents this problem, but rather how far a carabiner's nose sticks out to 'catch' the rope, holding it against the gate and causing that gate—whether straight or bent—to open." REI recommends avoiding

Figure 7-23. *Enchaining Carabiners: Beware of passing the rope through the lower carabiner (backclipping) so that rope friction causes the lower carabiner to rotate against the upper one and unclip from it.*

*Figure 7-22. **A Slip Knot Used to Tie Off a Rock Horn***

"situations where the rope may cross back over any carabiner."[7] This is good advice if you can plan your falls ahead of time. But it would be better to avoid using these carabiners unless they provide a decided advantage for a specific climb. You might also remember that once you are clipped in, you may find it easier to stand in position, and you can place a second carabiner with reversed gate through the rope end of the quickdraw.

Enchained carabiners (Figure 7-23) are sometimes used to allow the rope to run freely through the protection where use of a full-length sling simply lengthens the distance of a potential fall. Enchaining is used most often on fixed pitons when climbs follow vertical lines. Always avoid enchaining where the rope produces a twisting force on the carabiners to produce a *backclip*, since the carabiners can unclip from one another during the twisting. While enchaining may work in some situations, the use of a short quickdraw sling between carabiners avoids the disadvantages of enchaining and still keeps additional fall distances to a minimum.

## Quickdraw Slings

Quickdraw slings are useful when you want a short sling to prevent nut rotation. You can fashion quickdraws out of a full-length sling or you can purchase quickdraws. Figure 7-24 shows a technique for making a quickdraw from a full-

A   B   C   D

*Figure 7-24. Quickdraw Slings: The sequence A–C shows how to make a quickdraw sling from a full-length sling. You can return the quickdraw to full-length by unclipping one carabiner from C and placing it in one of the free loops in B. D is a commercial quickdraw.*

length sling. This technique allows you to revert quickly to the full-length runner. Unclip a carabiner from one end of the quickdraw (C), clip this carabiner into one of the three released loops (B), and pull. Diagram D shows a commercially made quickdraw for comparison.

## Dynamic Slings for Marginal Placements

Until recently, forces created by the acceleration of gravity and friction in a fall have been absorbed by the rope, deformation of the climber's body, and the tightening of knots. The force experienced by a piece of protection is approximately twice the force experienced by the belay or the falling climber. Steel and brass micronuts are marginal placements that resist pulling out of a crack by means of the small amount of friction between their faces and the rock. They can pull in a fall because a well-placed micronut may have a resistance as low as 800 pounds, while the force tugging on the piece can easily be 1,000 to 2,000 pounds or higher. (Other marginal placements include most ice protection because of the uncertain quality of the ice, and perhaps fixed pitons and ¼-inch bolts.)

A *dynamic sling* (Figure 7-25) absorbs energy as its stitches rip apart, so all of the energy of the fall is not transmitted to a marginal placement.

Bill Forest introduced the Fall Arrest, the first commercially available dynamic sling. It was rather complex and expensive, and is no longer available. John Bouchard introduced a simpler design, the Air Voyager, made of folded and cross-stitched 1-inch webbing. These are also no longer available, but many are still in use. In the Yates Screamer, the latest type of dynamic sling, folded webbing is stitched along the length of the sling.

Yates Screamers and Air Voyagers are ordinary sling material doubled over and sewn with thread. In the Air Voyager, bar tacks run perpendicular to the sling, and each bar tack absorbs energy once

A          B

*Figures 7-25. Dynamic Slings: A—The stitches of the Yates Screamer are parallel to the length of the sling to reduce carabiner gate vibration. The Yates Screamer is shown without the protective Lycra sheath supplied with it. B—An Air Voyager used on a ¼-inch bolt. After clipping in, rotate the carabiner so that the gate is down and facing out, like the bottom carabiner. Always use full-strength carabiners with dynamic slings and place them only on running protection, never belays.*

the process is activated at 700 pounds. Ripping apart one bar tack simply lowers the number available to rip, and the sling remains functional as a dynamic sling as long as there are other bar tacks. Once all bar tacks are ripped, it becomes an ordinary sling.

A potential problem with this design is that the periodic ripping of bar tacks may cause the carabiner that connects the sling to your rope to vibrate, and the gate may open and close. When the gate is open, the carabiner is weakened and could fail.

The lengthwise stitching pattern of the Yates Screamer, which activates at 550 pounds, minimizes gate vibration, but to ensure security you should use only full-strength carabiners; adding a lightweight locking carabiner on the rope end of a dynamic sling adds extra assurance against the gate opening. If you use the latter option, you will need to develop the habit of making sure that the gates are unlocked before starting off on a lead. Do not use lightweight hollow carabiners on dynamic slings.

## References for Future Reading

Cannon, Neil. 1985. Air voyagers. *Climbing*. 88:54.

Chouinard, Yvon. 1989. *Great Pacific/Chouinard equipment catalog*. Ventura, California.

Graydon, Don, ed. 1992. *Mountaineering: The freedom of the hills*. Fifth edition. Seattle: The Mountaineers.

Jones, Chris. 1976. *Climbing in North America*. Berkeley, California: University of California Press for the American Alpine Club.

Leeper, Ed. 1980. *Alloy steel climbing hardware*. Boulder, Colorado: Ed Leeper.

Long, John. 1989. *How to rock climb*. Evergreen, Colorado: Chockstone Press.

Lubben, Craig. 1989. Understanding your Friends. *Rock & Ice*. 33:76.

Middendorf IV, John. 1988. Drills, hangers, bolts: The dope for doing it right. *Climbing*. 106:103–108.

Peters, Ed, ed. 1982. *Mountaineering: The freedom of the hills*. Fourth edition. Seattle: The Mountaineers.

Piana, Paul. 1988. Salathé wall. *Climbing*. 110:50–60.

Raleigh, Duane. 1989. Soft rock: The glue-in bolt solution. *Climbing*. 115:106–107.

———. 1992. Anchors away: The nuts of bolts, part 1. *Climbing*. 134:101–110.

———. 1992. Sticky business: The nuts of bolts, part 2: glue-in bolts. *Climbing*. 135:125–128.

Recreational Equipment, Inc. 1990. *Climbing 1990*. Seattle.

Robbins, Royal. 1973. *Advanced rockcraft*. Glendale, California: La Siesta Press.

Robinson, Doug. 1973. The whole natural art of protection. In *Chouinard equipment catalog*.

Sanderson, Allen. 1989. Rapper's delight: A safer method. *Climbing*. 116:122–125.

———. 1990. Chain rappel anchors: The non-degradable choice. *Climbing*. 121:94–97.

Stannard, John. 1973. Nuts in the Shawangunks. *The eastern trade*. Tillson, New York.

Webster, Ed. 1987. *Rock climbs in the White Mountains of New Hampshire*. Second edition. Eldorado Springs, Colorado: Mountain Imagery.

## Endnotes

1. Carabiners were developed before World War II, but aluminum carabiners came after the war.

2. Webster, 1987.

3. Robinson, 1973.

4. See Raleigh, 1992, on glue-in bolts.

5. Middendorf, 1988.

6. Sanderson, 1989.

7. Recreational Equipment, Inc., 1990, page 10.

# CHAPTER

# 8

# Rappelling

## Introduction

When you rappel, you run the rope around your body or a mechanical device to create friction, and this friction against the rope allows you to make a controlled descent. In a wider sense, rappelling includes the whole process of setting up an anchor, throwing the rope, setting up the brake, descending, and retrieving the rope. Many of these subjects are discussed elsewhere in this book, so this chapter will concentrate on rappel brakes and descending.

Rappelling takes little skill, but it calls for great vigilance. You must concentrate on setting up the system and double-check it—and have your partner double-check it—before you back over the void. When you are fresh, concentration comes easily, but climbers often find themselves rappelling at the end of the day when they are tired and ready to head home. It is important to learn

to rappel correctly and to practice the skill so it comes easily when you need it.

The brake should provide enough friction so that you can control your descent. When you choose a brake, you should consider how steep the slope is and how much you weigh.

**Impact Forces and Rappelling**

When I was 17, I horrified a group of matrons as I jumped off a bridge that spanned an almost-dry creek. I went into free-fall, wild with ecstasy, until I saw the creek coming up. I braked so hard that my body slid completely around in the rappel formed by wrapping the rope through my legs and over my shoulder. My descent abruptly arrested, I came to a stop in a fetal position, hanging completely upside down, in the creek's last remaining puddle. My embarrassment was offset by the expressions of wonder on the faces of the women on the bridge. On another occasion, I rappelled off a 40-foot-high pyramid-shaped training tower so fast that I swung back into its base and braked instantly when I reached the ground. Not once did I wonder about the safety of the anchor. Wiser now, I understand the errors that I survived.

Rappelling rapidly followed by rapid braking has something in common with a lead fall caught by a belayer. In both situations *dynamic impact forces* have a shock effect on the gravity-accelerated rappeller or climber, belayer, anchors, and other elements in the system as you come to a stop. In a free-fall of 15 feet followed by a sharp braking action, impact forces greater than 1,500 pounds, or far more than body weight, are transferred directly to the anchors on the tied-off end of the rappel rope, which more than likely is a tree or climbing protection in a crack. You may have seen this style of rappelling in old commercial advertisements that suggest that

*continued on page 106*

you only go around once in life. How true! The anchors had better be good or you are in for a ground fall.

Descending smoothly will keep impact forces nearer to your body weight, which can be held by a very small anchor (although most people want a beefy anchor for a large margin of safety). Look closely at that supposedly macho man in the old-time advertisements. You will see that he is tied in at the cliff edge and doesn't intend to go anywhere on rappel.

A rappeller on the way to disaster.

## Rappel Brakes

A rappel brake should provide the proper amount of friction required for you to use the force of gravity to control your descent. You need to match the amount of friction between the rope and

rappel brake to your body weight and the steepness of the slope. The friction will produce heat as a by-product, so you need to take precautions to protect yourself and the rope from abrasion wounds or friction burns.

### The Body Rappel

In a body rappel or *dulfersitz* you wrap the rope around your body to provide friction (Figure 8-1). This rappel is useful on short descents on gentle slopes. I use it, for example, to safeguard myself when I am setting up top ropes and need to clear ropes that have tangled in brush. Each time the discomfort reminds me that I would not want to body rappel a full-length climb except in an emergency. That day has come and may come again, however, so it is worthwhile to know the technique.

To rappel using your right hand as your braking hand, straddle the rope, then pass it around your right hip, across your chest, over your left shoulder, and down your back to your right hand. To rappel left-handed, reverse the hip, shoulders, and braking hand. Do not make the error of braking with the hand that is on the same side as the rope as it goes around the shoulder (Figure 8-1B).

Both the body rappel and the arm rappel (following) are potentially dangerous because you are not tied directly to the rope. If you were to lose your balance during the descent, you could fall out of the rappel and get hurt. It is especially easy to fall out of an arm rappel.

An arm rappel is useful on exposed but low-angle slopes such as slabs that you can walk down (Figure 8-2). Twist the rope around your arms so that it passes just below your shoulders. A small amount of friction is generated, which makes this technique more secure than walking down the rope hand over hand.

### Figure-eight Brakes

When you use a mechanical rappel device, you allow the metal surfaces to dissipate heat. They also allow for sharper bends in the rope, making it easier to lock off the rope during the rappel. The figure-eight descender (Figure 8-3) has long been used for general climbing. Several versions of the figure-eight are available. A figure-eight with an enlarged

Figure 8-1. **Body Rappel:** Correct and incorrect body rappels for a left-handed brake. Having your shoulder wrap on the same side as the hip wrap, as in B, is potentially dangerous, since the shoulder wrap can come undone and you can fall out of the rappel. The danger is increased if you also brake with the hand on the same side as the hip and shoulder wrap. Instead, wrap the rope around the opposite shoulder (here the right) from the hip wrap, as shown in A, and brake with the hand on the opposite side as the shoulder wrap.

oblong attachment hole, for example, can double as a belaying device, and figure-eights with other modifications allow the brake to be used for rescue work.

To rappel, form a bight in the rope and slip it through the large hole of the device and over the outside of the smaller opening (rather than through it), as sketched in Figure 8-4. Use a locking carabiner to clip through both the smaller hole and an attachment point on your harness (see Chapter 4, Figure 4-4), to prevent the rope from coming off the brake accidentally.

### Carabiner Brake

Many rappellers use a carabiner brake because it is effective and requires no gear other than the cara-biners used as a normal part of protection-anchor systems. Oval and D-shaped carabiners work best; the shapes of offset D-shaped and bent-gate carabiners make it difficult to use them for this purpose. The brake can require up to six nonlocking carabiners (Figure 8-5); the labels in Figure 8-5 help explain how to form the brake in Figure 8-6.

First, compare a cross section of the completed brake in Figure 8-6E with the perspective view of Figure 8-5B. The completed brake has two carabiners with opposed and reversed gates that form a platform that serves as a base for the brake. These platform carabiners are attached to the harness by means of a sling and two attachment carabiners (not illustrated in Figure 8-6E). Friction in the

Figure 8-2. *Arm Rappel*

Figure 8-3. **Figure-eight Brakes**

connect to harness

Figure 8-4. **Connecting the Rope to the Figure-eight Brake**

brake is created by the solid backs of two opposed braking carabiners in contact with the bights of the doubled rappel rope, or of a single rappel-rope bight for a single-rope rappel.

To set up the brake, follow the sequence illustrated in figures 8-5 and 8-6. Attach two carabiners with gates opposed or a single locking carabiner to your harness, then attach two carabiners (to form a platform) with gates opposed and reversed perpendicular to the first carabiners. The opposed gates prevent accidental opening of the carabiners through side-loading of the gates. Next, form a bight in the doubled rappel rope and push it up through the platform carabiners. Weave one or two carabiners—the braking carabiners—across so that the doubled rappel rope comes to rest on the solid back of the brake carabiners when tight-

ened. Whether you use one or two brake carabiners depends on the amount of friction required to control your rate of descent. You usually use two brake carabiners when rappelling with a single rope or when using a doubled rope on a steep drop. Rappels on gentler slopes may work with one brake carabiner.

## Body Position

A number of body positions are useful in rappelling when you are moving off the lip of a shelf, over overhangs, down slabs and faces, or down free drops. On most rappels, the most difficult physical (and mental) part is moving from a horizontal plat-

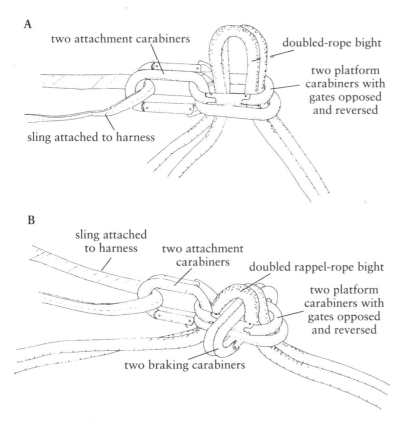

Figure 8-5. *The Carabiner Brake in Perspective*

**A**

two attachment carabiners

doubled-rope bight

two platform carabiners with gates opposed and reversed

sling attached to harness

**B**

sling attached to harness

two attachment carabiners

doubled rappel-rope bight

two platform carabiners with gates opposed and reversed

two braking carabiners

form to a steep wall. Once on the steep wall, rappelling is usually easy and straightforward.

Before you rappel, tuck in all loose articles of clothing, hair, and equipment that could be accidentally drawn into the friction brake. To hook up the friction brake, face up-slope, the direction that you will face during the rappel. This position prevents the rope from twisting as you attach it to the friction brake. For exposed starting positions use a safety sling running from the anchor to your harness while you prepare to rappel. Unclip from the anchor only after you are attached to the rappel rope and begin the descent.

When you start backward on the horizontal platform, the brake usually provides too much friction, and it may be necessary to lift the rope to reduce friction. Walk backward toward the edge, continu-

ing to lift the rope until you go over the edge and need the additional friction to offset gravity.

### The Edge Stance

At the edge, spread your feet widely to form a platform that keeps you stable (Figure 8-7). Use this legs-apart position during the rappel to avoid swinging sideways across the cliff face. Push your midsection outward, tensioning the rope, so your legs are at an angle to the cliff face. This angle becomes greater as the cliff face becomes steeper and reaches an extreme on overhangs (Figure 8-9A). This position forces your feet against the wall and prevents them from slipping. Lean your upper body slightly backwards, but stay upright enough to see foot placements clearly. This is the basic *edge stance.*

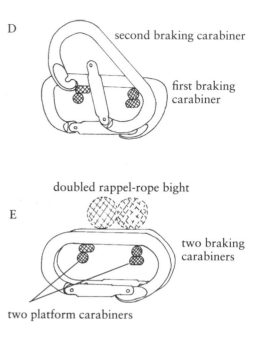

Figure 8-6. **Weaving the Carabiner Brake in Cross Section:** *The completed brake shown in perspective view in Figure 8-5B is also shown in cross-section view in Figure 8-6E. The two attachment carabiners and attachment sling are shown in Figure 8-5. For clarity, in Figure 8-6 the doubled rappel-rope bight is not illustrated except in E.*

*A—Pass the first brake carabiner over the near side of the platform carabiners (cross-hatched) with the gate open and the carabiner's back angled at 45 degrees to the plane of the platform carabiners. Rotate the back of the first brake carabiner parallel to the plane of the platform carabiners, and the gate closes.*

*B—To pass over the far side of the platform carabiners, open the gate and again rotate the back of the first*

*brake carabiner to a 45-degree angle to the plane of the platform carabiners.*

*C, D—Once across the far side of the platform carabiners, the back of the first brake carabiner rotates parallel to the plane of the platform carabiners and the gate closes again. If you use a second brake carabiner, start it from the opposite side so that you oppose the gates. The back of the second brake carabiner will be on the same side as the first to provide friction against the rope (C, D, and E).*

*E—This cross-sectional view of the complete carabiner brake is the same as the perspective view of Figure 6-5B. When you finish this sequence, tighten the doubled-rope bight against the brake carabiners.*

From this position, walk your feet down the cliff face, using whatever footholds are available, while maintaining the edge stance. You can maintain this stance to the bottom of the cliff or assume one of the other stances described below, as the terrain and friction dictate.

Place one hand, the *guide hand*, above the friction

brake, and the other hand, the *brake hand*, below the device (Figure 8-7). The guide hand is usually the off hand (left hand for a right-handed person), which helps you balance. The rope passes smoothly through this hand during the rappel. You can also take your guide hand off the rope and use it to help push away from the rock or adjust your clothing.

guide hand

braking hand

*Figure 8-7.* **Edge Stance**

as parts of the friction brake gives more control for rappelling.

### The Face Stance

Once you have descended far enough for the rappel rope to contact the cliff edge, you can assume a *face stance* if the cliff is about 70 degrees or less. This position requires less effort. Rotate your body out of the edge stance so that an imaginary line connecting both hips is parallel to the rope and is in the fall line of the cliff. On lower-angle cliffs or on cliffs where there are abundant face holds, you can even rotate far enough to face down the cliff (Figure 8-8B).

The face stance may take a bit of adjustment, but it has some advantages. First, you can see where you are going and step from hold to hold as you descend, as though you were walking. You sacrifice lateral stability, so it is important to stay directly beneath the point where the rope passes over the edge of the cliff. This point marks the top of the fall line of the rappel and is the point underneath which you will swing if you slip. You can be out of the fall line and counteract the tendency to swing by pushing against face holds with your legs, but if you do slip you will swing back and forth like a pendulum before coming to rest in the fall line.

A second advantage of this position is that you can rest your braking hand against your hip, taking stress off your biceps. The face stance is definitely a faster and easier way to descend on less than vertical faces provided that you do not have too much or too little friction. You can quickly move back into an edge stance if you must pass over another lip during the rappel.

### Steep Faces and Free Rappels

When descending a steep face, you usually stay in an edge stance with your feet almost perpendicular to the face. If the rappel is free, so that you hang directly on the rope and require additional friction for braking, you can obtain that friction by passing the rope from the brake down through your crotch and back up to your braking hand. This change in rope position adds the friction of the underside of your pant leg to the brake system.

The rappel braking hand acts like the belay braking hand, holding the rope against the friction brake. If you accidentally release the rope from your braking hand while rappelling, you will lose most of the friction it provided and lose control of your descent. For this reason, it is important to belay novice rappellers until they demonstrate competence. Even experienced climbers sometimes use safety backups, as discussed below.

You usually keep your braking hand below your body, wrapping the rope around your hip for friction. The most comfortable position is to hold the braking hand against the crest of your hip bone. If you hold your braking hand high and away from your body, you increase the work that your biceps must do.

When you rappel on a single rope, pass the rope coming from the friction brake around your far hip and then around your back to your braking hand. Including the back of your hip and buttock

A
modified edge stance

B
face stance oriented to
the fall line

*Figure 8-8. **Face Stance**: A—A climber is in a modified edge stance. B—He swings into the rope's fall line, assuming the face stance to gain a better view and ease of rappelling.*

A

B

*Figure 8-9. **Overhangs***

You can brace your braking hand against the bone structure of the upper outside surface of your leg to relieve the stress placed on your biceps.

As in all rappelling, you should descend smoothly and slowly. Avoid rapid acceleration followed by rapid deceleration, since this motion produces forces that far exceed body weight alone and shock-loads your anchor.

### Overhangs

To rappel an overhang, descend using the edge stance until the balls of both feet are on the lip of the overhang (Figure 8-9A). Then slowly lower your buttocks well below the level of the lip until you can see the wall directly beneath the overhang. If the overhang is small, you can take one foot from the lip and brace against the wall underneath (Figure 8-9B), following with the second foot. Once both feet are on the wall, continue descending in the conventional manner.

If the overhang is wide enough to prevent bracing below the lip with your legs, your upper body and hands will swing back into the face above the lip. You want this to happen in the least painful manner. One method is to place your hip against the upper face of the overhang and descend slowly, being careful not to trap the fingers of your guide hand between the face and the rope. Another method is to push off and descend rapidly, trying to clear the overhang before you swing back in. Again you must be careful not to injure your guide hand. This method stresses your anchor more than descending smoothly.

---

## Working in Midrappel

In order to stop in midrappel on lower-angle slabs to free a piece of protection, you can wrap the rope around your leg two to four times (Figure 8-10A). This position usually gives enough friction to allow the release of your braking hand so you can work. To add to the security of the leg wrap, you can also have someone on the ground tug lightly on the free end of the rope to give you a *ground belay*. (The ground belay is shown in Figure 8-11, where it is employed as an emergency

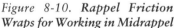

*Figure 8-10.* **Rappel Friction Wraps for Working in Midrappel**

A

B

tie-off

leg wrap

belay.) On steep rappels, where you feel insecure about simply leaving the rope hanging as a source of friction, tie the free end of the rope around the standing end above the rappel brake (Figure 8-10B) or use a prusik safety. Prusik safeties present their own problems, however, as you will see in the following section.

---

## Safety Backups

There are four common ways to safeguard a rappel: double-check the entire system before you back over the edge, belay the rappeller, have the rappeller use a prusik safety, and set up a ground belay. As noted at the beginning of this chapter, it is often desirable to safeguard rappellers, and safeguarding novices with a belay is mandatory (see "A Belaying System for Beginning Rappellers" in Chapter 17).

To set up a prusik safety, place a prusik knot on the rappel rope above the belay brake and attach it to your harness at the rappel attachment point. (The technique of tying a prusik is explained in Chapter 3, if you need a review.) The prusik is useful for stopping in midrappel for extended periods, and—in theory—you can move the prusik as you descend and it will catch you if you slip on rappel. However, a number of problems make this system's use doubtful in an emergency.

The first problem involves overhangs. If the prusik loop is too long, you can rappel below the overhang while the knot can tighten out of reach above it. Usually, the only solution is to use a pocket knife to cut the safety without cutting the tautly stretched rappel rope. The second problem is that the prusik fails to tighten in many emergencies, and the friction of sliding down the rope partially melts the knot. It is easy to understand why this happens. The prusik knot must be loose enough to slide, but tight enough to stop a fall. The knot will not tighten automatically: it needs to be set (tightened and deformed) by the rappeller. In an emergency, rappellers hold the knot in a death-grip, and prevent it from deforming and catching.

Figure 8-11. *A Ground-Belay Safety Backup*

As a result, many prusik safeties used on rappel fail.

If you set a prusik knot to stop in midrappel—perhaps to remove a piece of protection that is stuck—you must loosen the knot before you can move on. First take your weight off the knot. Standing on a rock edge makes loosening simpler, but the stretched rope will tend to rebound when unweighted, carrying the prusik knot upward and away from you. You can also bring your foot up fairly high and wrap the rappel rope around it a couple of times. Then bring the free end of the rappel rope up to your hand. Stand up and loosen the prusik, allowing the rappel rope's free end to slip through your hand until the rappel brake loads fully and you can descend normally.

The ground belay is an emergency safety backup to use with injured rappellers and is controlled by a ground belayer who puts tension on the rappel rope (Figure 8-11). This tension increases the friction at the rappel brake. Do not use this belay routinely with beginners, who should be belayed with a top rope. The ground belayer can produce varying amounts of tension either by gripping the rope loosely or by sitting comfortably in a loop of rope. The belayer must be attentive in order to exercise control of the belay.

---

## Rappelling Summary

Since you usually rappel at the end of a hard day of climbing when you are tired, hungry, and dehydrated and have already spent physical and mental energy in the intense concentration of climbing, you are more likely to make mistakes than when you are fresh. Like all climbers, you tend to relax once you get to a large shelf that serves as a rappel station. As noted above, rappel anchors can be slings around marginal natural anchors, old fixed pitons with a tangle of rope-burned slings, or some other piece of gear that is not entirely safe. Add to this the fact that climbers do not wish to leave their personal gear behind, and the conditions are ripe for an accident. Gravity is a powerful force ready to accelerate the unwary to the ground.

Secure yourself at the rappel station, independent of the rappel rope and even the rappel anchor. Avoid being unfastened from anchors and establish a backup anchor that will not be weighted unless the primary anchor fails. Examine the rappel anchors. Tie ropes together and have someone else check your knots before throwing the rope down and also check the attachment of the rappel brake to you and your harness. Make sure your harness buckle is secure, and that clothing and long hair are tucked in away from the rappel brake. Visually recheck the entire rappel system at the edge just before you lean back.

Set up a backup anchor and send down the heaviest person to test the system; then remove the backup and have the lightest person come last, descending as smoothly as possible. If you are not sure that the rope will reach the bottom of the cliff, tie a very large knot in both ropes—a double figure-eight (Figure 8-12), or a single figure-eight with a carabiner through it that cannot possibly pass through a rappel device, even under impact force, so that you cannot rappel off the end. More than one climber has rappelled off the rope end at the close of the day. The first person down should have prusik slings available to ascend the rope if needed. Good habits can prevent accidents.

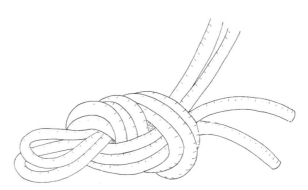

*Figure 8-12. **Double Figure-eight Safety Knot to Prevent Rappelling Off the End of the Rope***

## Rappel-Rope Retrieval

Climbers usually rappel on a single rope doubled around an anchor (for a half-length rappel) or two ropes tied together with a grapevine knot (for a full-length rappel). If you are rappelling the route you climbed, there should be no problem reaching each belay station with two ropes. The grapevine knot can, however, get stuck when you pull the rope, unless you take precautions. When you set up the rappel rope, place the knot on one side of the anchor. Later, you will pull that side of the rope; if you don't, the knot may hang up in the anchor. Climbers routinely quiz each other about which rope to pull to focus their attention and impress the information on their mind. On multi-pitch rappels, you pull one rope after the first rappel, pull the second rope after the second rappel, and alternate thereafter. This system allows you to thread the lower rope (the end being pulled) through the lower anchor to expedite the process.

A second problem is that the knot joining two ropes can hang up at the edge of the rappel platform if the edge is a sharp lip. When there is a platform just below the lip, begin the rappel as usual, step down to the platform, and readjust the position of the knot so that it hangs over the lip. If you are rappelling on a red rope and a purple rope, for example, and you will be pulling purple, then feed red through the brake until the knot moves to where you want it. Remain attached to the rappel at all times, or attach yourself to protection pieces placed at the stance as you remove the rappel brake and adjust the knot position.

You can also prevent a knot from hanging up at the lip by changing the angle from which you pull it. If you are on the ground, seize the rope and walk directly away from the cliff, decreasing the 90-degree bend in the rope at the lip and thus reducing friction. (Some climbers rig up the rappel rope high in a cliff-side tree to reduce the angle. This procedure is not recommended, even with a large tree, because it produces a levering action that could pull the shallow root systems out of cliff-top soils and cause the anchor to fail.)

The rope itself can get caught if there are trees in the fall line of the rappel. To prevent this situation, walk away from the trees, parallel to the cliff base, to change the area in which the rope will fall. Just as the rope goes over the edge, give the rope a good jerk to pull it away from the trees. This technique is also useful if it appears that the rappel rope might hang up in a crack directly under the rappel point.

If the rappel rope does catch on a tree or in a crack, try pulling on the opposite rope to free the stuck point. You can also try walking away from the cliff or along the cliff to change the direction of pull.

To take a seemingly welded grapevine knot apart, see Chapter 3, Figure 3-7. Once one of the loops of the knot is loose, the knot comes apart easily.

## When the Rope Gets Stuck

Sometimes, no matter what you do, the rope gets stuck firmly, and you must reascend the cliff to retrieve it. If you have a second rope, simply reclimb the pitch. If the rope is taut from the anchor to the ground and both ends of the rope are available, you can climb the rope safely with ascenders, prusik knots, or Bachmann knots. If there is a lot of slack, you may be able to lead the pitch on aid using the slack as a lead rope. If one of these strategies does not work, call for help and remember that in most environmental conditions, a night out on the cliff will not harm you. On the contrary, it provides fodder for colorful stories you can tell your friends.

What remains are the desperate options that arise as you climb a stuck rope that can come unstuck under your weight.

If you cannot secure help and if the weather or other conditions dictate that you must get off the route, your options are limited to potentially dangerous techniques. If only one end of the rappel rope reaches you, you might tie it off and prusik up, frequently placing nuts below you in case the rope suddenly comes unstuck. Tie into any slack below you with a knot attached to your harness by means of a carabiner. As you ascend, attach yourself to higher and higher knots in the rope and keep putting in the protection. Should the stuck end free itself, you will fall onto the rope that you are ascending, protected by the pieces that you placed, the prusik, and the backup knot.

As a last resort, alpine climbers high on the mountain sometimes stretch a stuck rope as much as possible before cutting it, using the length salvaged for further descent. After the descent, these short lengths make great tie-downs.

## Memorable Rappels

With experience, rappels from small cliffs blend together and slip gently into recesses of memory. Memorable rappels are usually scary. I remember one from atop Mt. Asgard, just north of the Arctic Circle on Baffin Island. Topping out after a midnight-sun ascent, we saw clouds rolling in from Cumberland Sound. Realizing that our predicted 24-hour window of good weather was about up, we quickly started back down. Tom went last on the outrageous rappel from the top, but from then on it was my duty. Going last gave me time to reflect on just how far north and how isolated we were. By the ninth rappel my mind began playing tricks. Fears that I had been holding at bay grew until another friend, Chris, took over the somber duty until we reached the exit snow fields below. Mental and physical fatigue arrived with the darkest period of the 24-hour day and forced us to stop for a few hours before descending to our tents, euphoric with our success.

Another memorable rappel was done from poor anchors, established as though by Braille in the dark, and used only because there appeared to be little other choice. Then, there was a long free rappel from the Maiden, high above Colorado's Eldorado Canyon, where I could overcome vertigo, induced by slowly twisting in the wind, only by closing my eyes.

I remember only one rappel with pleasure and a smile. When Gene and I climbed the North Face of the Grand Teton we reached the summit just before dark and descended to a bivouac above the rappel station on the Owen-Spalding route. We snuggled deep into our lightweight, cold sleeping bags, counting on the first guided party to appear with a second rope needed for the rappel. When the party appeared, I brazenly asked if we could "have a ride down your rope." The guide, who I recognized as a famous climber, agreed but told us to be careful because there were "loose rocks at the edge." Not wanting him to think that we came up an easy route, I answered that we had come up the North Face and had found plenty of loose rocks both underfoot and overhead. The guide's eyes opened wide and he extended his hand and introduced himself, explaining in friendly fashion and evident respect that he himself had not yet done the North Face. He spoke loudly to his clients: "Make way! Make way! These men have come up the North Face." With that wonderful proclamation in our ears, we backed out over the void.

# CHAPTER 9

# *Leading Rock*

## Introduction

This chapter explores leading, from getting started to getting down. It discusses ways to prepare for your first lead, outlines information you need to lead climbs on sight (without having climbed them before), and provides suggestions for racking gear, placing protection, and traversing. Even if you do not lead now, it is worth reading this material because you will better understand what goes on at the other end of the rope. This chapter also covers tying off a fallen climber, climbing with style, and getting down from a climb—information of use to both leaders and seconds.

## Starting Out

While climbing on a top rope can be physically demanding and give much satisfaction, there can be an even greater challenge and satisfaction in leading. The leader not only has to climb, but he or she also has to figure out where the route goes, place the protection, and risk a fall. These activities can demand great mental and physical effort. The second, on the other hand, follows the route and takes out the protection while having an overhead belay.

Many climbers refer to leading as being on the *sharp end* of the rope because it can be dangerous to climb above protection. Making a major mistake can lead to serious injury. Once you start leading, however, it is hard to top-rope or follow exclusively. To lead well, you need solid movement skills, a high degree of concentration, and a realistic grasp of your ability to solve problems while on the climb. Given the penalties of making a mistake, how do you learn to lead safely?

Most people learn to lead by climbing with fellow climbers. This system works well if the other climbers are experienced, have empathy, and impart good safety habits. You can assess your friends' technical expertise by reading climbing books and watching other climbers. Also pay attention to how they talk about climbing, treat equipment, and relate to other people. But climbers may move well, treat their equipment well, and be considerate of others, yet be unable to teach you how to climb safely. Where does this leave you?

Many clubs provide instruction by experienced climbers. Indeed, the Sierra Club, Appalachian Mountain Club, Mazamas, and other organizations played an important role in the early development of the sport. College outing clubs also have a time-honored role in educating fledgling leaders. More and more colleges and universities offer semester-length climbing courses for credit as part of professional outdoor leadership programs (this book is to a large extent the outgrowth of one of these programs), and others offer climbing courses of shorter duration as a student activity.

Guide services offer basic, intermediate, and advanced climbing lessons. Guides generally are dedicated individuals who enjoy the sport so much that they climb for recreation as well as employment. Experienced guides who have worked with fledgling leaders can anticipate mistakes well before you make them. The American Mountain Guides Association accredits many guide services and individual guides in the United States. In Canada, the Canadian Guide Association is the accrediting body.

## Learning to Lead Adventure Climbs

To experience the sharp end of the rope, you may want to begin leading on bolt-protected "sport" climbs, where movement skills are more important than knowing how to protect. Indeed, a handful of short quickdraw slings with carabiners and a few longer slings for a bolted belay anchor are all that you need to protect yourself. *Adventure climbs* emphasize skills in route finding and protecting as well as skills in movement.

Before leading, you should have developed good movement skills by bouldering and following experienced leaders on roped climbs. You can learn a lot by placing protection and arranging anchors while standing at the bottom of the cliff. Start by experimenting with passive nuts such as tapers and Hexcentrics, testing each piece in a variety of placements, learning to slot, cam, and set to develop an "eye" for a crack. Then practice with spring-loaded camming devices (SLCDs). You will find that you can slot an SLCD and improve placements over simple camming alone.

When you have mastered placing protection at ground level, try the following strategies to prepare for leading a first pitch.

• Climb and down-climb a short pitch on a top rope. You can even climb with a small- to moderate-size pack as a handicap; when you climb without it, you will feel even more secure. If you can down-climb the pitch smoothly, you will be able to lead it.

• Ask an experienced friend to lead an easily protected climb and then pull the rope, leaving the protection in place; your friend then rappels or walks and belays you from below. Now you lead the pitch, clipping into the protection as you go: your aim is to learn the moves. Climb a second time, concentrating on becoming familiar with the size, placement, and kind of the protection. Next, strip the protection from the climb, and lead the climb using only these protection pieces on the rack. Finally, take a complete rack and lead the climb.

• To learn how to place dependable protection, lead a short crack on aid that takes nut protection easily. Choose a vertical crack that widens and narrows frequently, so that it is easy to place well-seated protection. After you place each piece, attach an *etrier* (a special short ladder made of flat webbing) and stand in it. The reality of putting your weight on the protection (*aiding*) will help you think carefully about whether each piece is well placed. You will also find out which placements actually work. Keep the climb short—20 to 30 feet—since aiding takes time. You normally will only drop 2 to 3 feet in an easy aid crack if you do not commit gross errors that lead to pulling out all of the pieces. Oppose the lowermost nuts, as discussed later in this chapter, to counter this possibility.

Another advantage of aiding a crack is that you will get in the habit of placing protection at regular, close intervals. Some new leaders have a tendency to skip protection on easy sections because they "know" they will not fall. Protecting easy sections, however, develops your skills and also helps protect hard sections, since protection is the total of all pieces.

Not everyone will want to follow these strategies. Some climbers want to jump on challenging climbs right from the start. But because there is the potential for accident (and even death) in adventure leading, you are well advised to learn step by step and develop solid skills in placing protection before you lead climbs that are at the limit of your climbing ability.

When you start leading, choose climbs that you have climbed before as a second, or top-roped, so you know what to expect. A good first adventure lead is many grades beneath what you can follow or what you can lead when clipping bolts. Choose a climb that protects well, one with good cracks or flakes and one that has good stances so you can take the time necessary to sort through your gear rack to get just the right size nut to fit into a crack. Novice adventure leaders who are able to race up difficult climbs on a top rope or with bolted protection need to adopt a different pace in order to learn how to place protection on easy to moderate climbs. You should not be anywhere near your physical ability when learning to place protection. These early climbs should build a solid base for more difficult leads to come. An experienced leader can direct a novice leader to climbs that fit these requirements, and can give helpful hints while on the climb.

### Choosing On-Sight Leads

Leading a climb with which you are unfamiliar is called an *on-sight lead*. Unless you are a very good climber, you will probably want to consult a guidebook to find climbs that are the right level of physical difficulty for you and that promise to be well protected. There are two types of guides: the descriptive and the topographic (topo) style. Both commonly use photographs to help describe the major rock features on a route. The descriptive guides are written as narrative, detailing the general characteristics of a climb, such as its length, rating, and main features. For example:

> Pitch 1. 120 feet, 5.8. Follow an overhang that diagonals up to the left for about 20 feet and then forms an inside corner. Climb this section with a delicate combination of lieback and friction. Above follow a crack with a small pine tree up to a birch. Reach a second birch and a belay stance after a short friction pitch.

The descriptive guide is useful if there are a limited number of climbs in an area, but becomes cumbersome if you want to get information about, for example, the 34-pitch Nose Route on El Capitan, or the thousands of pitches in Yosemite

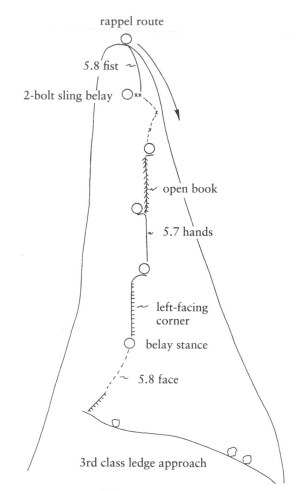

*Figure 9-1. A Guidebook Topo*

Valley. The topo-style guidebook uses symbols as climbing shorthand, so that multipitch climbs can be described on a single page. Figure 9-1 is a topo of a typical climb. Topos contain notes about special features: for example, that a pitch is 180 feet long and sustained at its grade. The author may add comments, based on opinion or other sources of information about the climb—for instance, that the pitch is ugly.

## Rating Rock

When you choose a climb, you may well ask: How hard is it? What techniques does it require—

lieback, face, mantling, or crack? How long will the climb take? How difficult is it to protect? Is it a high-quality climb?

### Yosemite Decimal System

The difficulty level of a climb is given as a *rating*. The initial rating system used in the United States was adopted by the Sierra Club from an early European system. At that time, the Sierra Club rated climbs from easy to very severe, the latter being a category that was undefined at the time. In the 1950s a different system was introduced. Climbs were rated according to difficulty, ranging from class 1 (a scramble where hands are not needed) to class 5 (a climb that requires both rope and protection for safety). There was, however, no way to distinguish very easy from very hard class 5 climbs, a problem that showed up at Tahquitz Rock in Southern California, where most of the climbs were class 5. Climbers added decimals to subdivide the class, with 5.0 (read "five-o") being the easiest and 5.9 (read "five-nine") being the hardest.

For many years, the decimal subdivision system was closed; that is, no climb could be rated higher than 5.9. Then class 5.10 was added to represent what was considered to be the hardest possible free climb at the time. (Aided climbs are rated differently, A1 to A5, based on the difficulty of placing aid, the security of the aid once placed, and potential fall distance. Some aid climbs might later go free, thus changing the rating; e.g., an A2 crack might go free at 5.10.) The system, with modifications, was accepted for use in Yosemite, and has become known as the *Yosemite Decimal System*, or *YDS*. It has come to be the standard within the United States.

Usually, each area has a number of well-established climbs that serve as the standard of their grade. The best way to discover the nature of a 5.6 climb is, of course, to climb one. The problem is that cracks, faces, liebacks, mantles, or climbs requiring stemming may all be rated 5.6, but one will seem harder or easier than another to a specific climber because of the climber's particular skills. For this reason, climbers often classify climbs both as to their level of difficulty and their type—for example, a 5.6 crack. This gives information about the difficulty of applying specific techniques to the climb.

When you gain enough experience on different levels and types of climbs, the rating serves as a short description of each climb. If you have the skills to lead cracks where you must jam and protect at grades up to 5.8, but you can lead bolt-protected face climbs up to 5.10, you can easily choose climbs that are appropriate to your level.

Eventually, the YDS 5.10 grade contained climbs that were as different from one another as the original 5.7 was from 5.10. To accommodate new climbs that are harder than those previously established, the system currently uses the letters *a*, *b*, *c*, and *d*. A 5.10a is significantly easier than a 5.10d, though you may find 5.10b moves on a climb that is generally a 5.10a.

Some guidebooks use a three-tier system, grading difficult climbs as normal, plus, or minus: 5.10, $5.10^-$ or $5.10^+$, but this system appears to be slowly being replaced by the four-tier letter system (a through d).

The 1970s saw a dramatic increase in hard free-climbing, which provided the stimulus to open up the grading system beyond 5.10, so some climbs are now rated at 5.11, 5.12, 5.13, and even 5.14 grades, each of which is in turn subdivided into a, b, c, and d levels. Further evaluation and definition of the grading system are possible and even probable, since climbing is demonstrably not a static sport.

The original YDS rating system graded the crux of a climb, but in Yosemite, where climbs followed long cracks that demanded endurance as well as the ability to do a crux move, the rating became that of the entire climb. You might grade a crack 5.7 if there is a moderately difficult move or sequence of moves with easier climbing before and after. A nearby crack could have a succession of moves of the same difficulty as the crux of the 5.7 crack for the length of the climb. The second crack would receive a much higher grade—5.9, perhaps. Face climbs, on the other hand, are sometimes graded by their hardest move. Route topos often specify the individual grades of difficult sections, whether in a crack or on a face. There are many subtle variables in rating. One 5.9 may have moves that favor a short person, while another 5.9 may favor someone with a long reach. You will always find some climbs that are harder at their grade than others. Although they may be frustrating, savor these climbs: you can weave them into tales that you tell around the campfire.

Because climbers travel from area to area, the YDS has been applied in a relatively standard manner within the United States, with allowance for local peculiarities in the rock.

### Commitment Grades

Commitment grades, denoted in roman numerals I through VI, describe the time that experienced competent climbers can expect to spend on a route, excluding the approach and descent. A grade III route in the mountains will take far longer to approach, climb, and descend than a grade III on a big roadside cliff. Expert climbers may be able to climb very much faster than even experienced competent climbers. Indeed, expert climbers have climbed two grade VI climbs on El Capitan in a single day; experienced competent climbers expect to spend two or more days on each of these climbs.

Table 9-1 shows the normal length of time required to climb various grades as well as the characteristic length of these grades.

### Table 9-1. Table of Commitment Grades

| Grade | Normal Time | Characteristic Length |
|-------|-------------|----------------------|
| I | 1 to 3 hours | A few pitches |
| II | 3 to 4 hours | 2 to 4 pitches |
| III | 4 to 7 hours ("short day") | 3 to 8 pitches |
| IV | 7 to 10 hours ("full day") | 6 to 12 pitches |
| V | 1 to 2 days | 10 to 18 pitches |
| VI | 2 days or more | 15+ ("big wall") |

### Quality and Danger Ratings

Some climbing guides use quality and danger ratings to give more information about specific climbs. Quality ratings commonly use one to four

stars (*). A one-star route has at least one characteristic, such as a short sustained section with good rock, that makes it a better than average climb. Routes with the highest number of stars indicate that the route is one of the best in the area. Since quality is rated by the author of the guidebook, the determination is not standardized, but you will find it a generally good recommendation if you are new to an area.

Danger ratings, representing the author's opinion or local consensus, tell you how difficult it is to place protection on a climb. If a guidebook uses this rating system, the absence of a rating usually indicates that the route contains the normal protection possibilities for the area. An R rating indicates that protection is difficult to place, or that little protection is available.

The most dangerous pitches are usually X-rated, and you should be extremely cautious; they are not suitable for an inexperienced leader. If you must climb one of these routes, try to find a local climber who has done it many times to guide you, but don't be surprised if you cannot. Many climbers take on X-rated routes once in a lifetime, if at all.

## Racking Gear

It is the leader's responsibility to decide what to take on a climb. The collection of protection and slings that you take makes up the rack. Most climbers carry a general rack containing gear that will fit a range of possibilities, from thin to fist-size cracks. This gear can be racked on a runner-strength sling designed to slip over the climber's head and one shoulder, or it can be racked on harness loops, depending on both the climber's preference and the nature of the climb. The rack sketched in Figure 9-2, a shoulder rack, contains three quickdraw slings for clipping fixed protection, a complete set of small wired steel or brass micronuts, three small wired tapers, four or five larger wired tapers, two three-cam units (TCUs), the four smallest Tricams, SLCDs to fit a crack range, and a large Hexcentric; eight full-length

*Figure 9-2.* **Organized Gear Rack:** *This shoulder sling has gear organized by type and size. A few free carabiners are also on the rack.*

slings to lessen rope drag, and one double sling for setting up an anchor. The micronuts fit on one carabiner and the wired tapers on another; generally each of the other pieces should have its own carabiner for ease of access. Three to five additional carabiners are on the rack to be used as needed.

If you know from inspection, a guidebook, or word of mouth that your climb is in an offwidth crack, you can leave behind the micronuts and add large crack protection (or be prepared to go without). If your route is a bolted face climb, you can leave behind most of the rack, taking only quickdraws and a few longer slings, plus perhaps a few Tricams to fit small pockets or micronuts for anticipated cracks. You would take quickdraws and a few longer slings.

How you place individual pieces on a rack, and their order, is determined by your need to take them off quickly with one hand. Most climbers consider nut size and type as well as the kind of climb in organizing their racks.

A single nut on a carabiner goes onto the gear sling with the gate up and against your body. When you rack a number of small nuts on a single carabiner, you may leave the carabiner on the rack, gate facing outward, to make individual nut removal easier, or you may remove the carabiner with all of the small nuts still attached and attempt to place one of the nuts. If you need the next-size nut, it is already in your hand and you can insert it directly into the crack. You would then put the carabiner and remaining nuts back on the rack and use a free carabiner to attach the nut placed in the rock to the rope.

During a climb, you may stop on a stance and estimate what gear you will need for the next few moves or section, then move this gear to an accessible position on the rack.

Tension can arise when two climbers organize their racks differently and swap the rack as they alternate leads. To avoid this problem, carry your own gear sling. When you are the second, as you climb you can put gear from the climb on your rack the way you want it and obtain the unused gear at the belay stance. If you are not going to lead the next pitch, you can make the leader's job much simpler by reracking systematically, using the leader's arrangement.

When following, place each nut on a single

carabiner and all nuts on a single shoulder-length gear sling. Take apart each sling created by the leader as you go, reducing complex configurations to single slings whenever stances permit. Shoulder-length slings will usually have one carabiner on them and quickdraws will usually have two carabiners. In this way, when you arrive at the belay stance you can reorganize the gear rack quickly with less likelihood of dropping gear.

If you climb overhanging rock or mainly use quickdraws on bolted climbs, you may find it more convenient to rack gear on the waist loops of your climbing harness, since a shoulder-length gear sling would swing backward. You may find that it is easier to clip carabiner gates out at the waist rather than in. Specialized chest harnesses are also commercially available to rack gear for big wall and overhanging free climbs.

To avoid dropping gear in the process of switching it from one person to another, make sure that both climbers are clipped to the anchor (to free up their hands). Remove one basic unit of gear at a time, such as a nut with attached carabiner, and pass that unit to the other person. Make eye con-

tact: do not rely on a tug to tell you that the gear is secured. This process is similar to how a nurse hands a doctor a scalpel in the operating room over the table: like a knife plunging into the patient, a Hex plunging into the void will create problems. Often, you need only turn to one side so the other person can remove the gear from your rack, thus limiting the number of hands involved in the operation. You can hand all shoulder-length slings to the other person at one time.

If you are alternating leads and you led the last pitch, the rope is stacked properly and your partner is ready to climb. If you are to continue, the rope must be restacked. Your partner can restack as you finish racking.

## Protecting the Belay

When you start a lead, place the first piece of protection to aim the belay and prevent the belay anchor from having to absorb high impact force if you fall. You place the first piece of protection

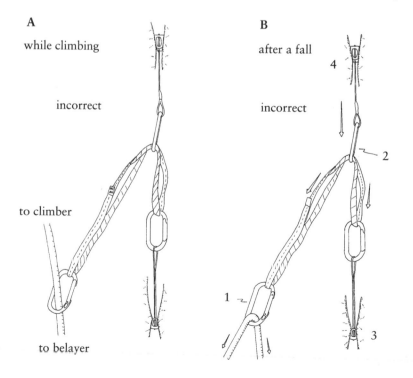

A
while climbing

incorrect

to climber

to belayer

B
after a fall

incorrect

*Figure 9-3. Creating Pulley Systems with Opposed Nuts: Both A and B are incorrect procedures.*

early to protect the primary anchor, the belayer, and ultimately yourself. Additional pieces of protection also protect the belay by reducing potential fall forces on the system as well as shortening fall distances.

### When the Belayer Is to the Side

When the belayer is not directly at the base of a climb, there is always the danger that the climbing rope may cause the first piece of protection to rotate so that it pulls out. Should this happen, subsequent pieces may fail, creating a domino effect that destroys, or *unzips*, all your protection. As a result, you need to make sure the first piece of protection is nondirectional so it will not pull out. The way to do this, if you are using nuts, is to oppose them.

### Forces on Opposed Nuts

Use opposed nuts to prevent a nut from pulling out whenever there is potential for both downward and upward pulls. Situations where this might occur are at a belay and at the end of a traverse followed by a vertical section. Wired nuts in particular are prone to rotating out of the crack with even slight amounts of traversing. Do not create a pulley system that multiplies the load on the anchor, as illustrated in Figure 9-3. If the climber falls, the resulting force is applied on the climbing rope in the vicinity of the first carabiner (Figure 9-3B), resulting in a doubling of the force. (This assumes that there is no friction in the system, including that of the rope sliding through the carabiner.)

The force on the upper nut will be approximately four times the force experienced by the falling leader because the whole nut-sling system acts as a pulley. First, the falling leader exerts a force that the belayer resists; the sum of these two forces tugs on carabiner 1 in Figure 9-3B. Carabiner 1 then exerts a pull on carabiner 2 that is resisted by the lower nut (3); the forces of carabiner 1 and 3 tug on carabiner 2. As a result, carabiner 2 experiences a force twice that experienced

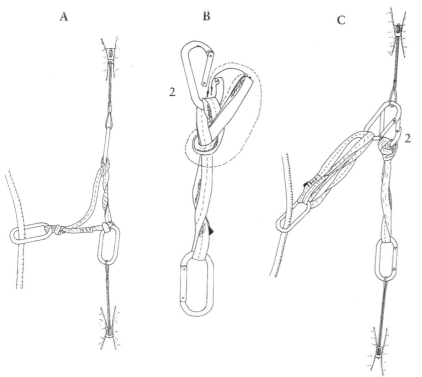

A    B    C

2

2

*Figure 9-4. Avoiding Pulley Systems by Tying Off Nuts in Opposition: A—Clove hitches were used to connect the two nuts and join the opposed nuts to the rope. B—The trial-and-error method was used to make a taut connection between the nuts. A sling was wrapped around the carabiner twice in the process of doubling the sling. A separate sling was doubled and used to connect the protection to the rope.*

by carabiner 1, which was already double that of the falling leader. As a result, carabiner 2 and the upper nut (4) attached to it experience an undesirable *load multiplication* of four times the impact force on the falling leader. The topic of load multiplication is covered in detail in Chapter 10.

Avoid the pulley effect by fastening the sling of the lower nut directly to the carabiner (2 in Figure 9-3B) attached to the upper nut without slack, as shown in Figure 9-4. Intermediate slings from the lower nut to carabiner 2 can be single, double, or triple. They can be wrapped one or more times around carabiner 2, in combination with doubling.

The clove hitch shown is hard to do in the field—you will need to use trial and error to some extent—because setting up opposed nuts must often be done one-handed while you are hanging on or in a precarious state of balance. If you can stand at the placement, use the clove hitch. If you need a simpler method, you can extend a sling from the lower nut through carabiner 2 as though you were going to create a pulley system. Then tie an overhand knot snugly against carabiner 2, and slip the free end of this sling over the gate end of carabiner two, as illustrated. This is not the ideal solution because shock in the knot may allow it to slip. But if you are hanging on with one hand, it presents a quickly realized solution of greater merit than the pulley system.

---

## Placing Protection

Place protection often enough to keep yourself from hitting a ledge. With slack and rope stretch, you might easily fall twice as far below your last piece of protection as you were above it. You usually set protection, to prevent movement, by giving it a tug that causes rock crystals to bite into the nut faces. Be careful not to tug so hard as to make it difficult for your second to remove the nut. Sometimes you will place a piece of protection that you know is hung up on tiny crystals but would not catch a fall. Consider ahead of time what you will do when you are "maxed out." You may not

fall, but if you leave inadequate protection, the thought of a long fall may inhibit your climbing—as well as keep you awake at night thinking about what might have been. Placing protection correctly can allow you to relax, giving you renewed energy that you did not expect, and you may find that you are not at your limit after all. And if you do rest on aid, you can always come back another day.

### Clipping In with One Hand

When you lead free climbs where you can stand on two feet, you usually place protection as high as possible to give yourself a top rope for a short distance. The belayer pays out slack while you pull it overhead with one hand and clip into a carabiner that you stabilize with the other hand. This procedure requires two free hands. On difficult, or sustained, climbs you hang on with one hand and clip the rope with the other; sometimes (as suggested by the name of a slab climb in Tuolumne Meadows, Too Thin to Clip In) you do not want to let go with either hand. Clipping in can be the crux of a climb. As a last resort to prevent a fall on a sustained climb, hang onto your protection with one hand (using it as aid) while you clip with the other.

In a typical example of what you want to avoid when leading a sustained crack climb, you place protection overhead and start to pull up the rope to clip it in. In the process, the carabiner swings, inaccessible, into the crack. You sigh, drop the rope, move the carabiner out of the crack, and start anew. On the second attempt you get closer. You hold the carabiner out of the crack as you lift the rope to the gate. The gate does not open and the carabiner rotates against the rope to a position where clipping is impossible. In the meantime, you are trying not to fall off the climb.

How does a leader clip in? On sustained climbs, many leaders use bent-gate carabiners on the lower end of a quickdraw or on the sling of a protection piece. Bent-gate carabiners are easier to clip than straight-gate carabiners because they help channel the rope into the gate, and their gate spring may be less stiff than that of a straight-gate carabiner. (On the other hand, straight-gate carabiners give added security that the rope will stay clipped.)

*Figure 9-5.* **One-handed Clip Using the Ring-Finger Pad:** *Stabilize the carabiner with the pad. Do not put your entire finger through the carabiner lest you fall.*

If you are using straight-gate carabiners with stiff springs, use the following method to clip in. Place the tip of your ring finger through the bottom of the carabiner and pull downward to stabilize it. The carabiner gate must face your thumb. If you use your middle finger, which is larger, you will find that it is more difficult to slip the rope through the gate (Figure 9-5). Do not insert your entire finger into the carabiner, lest you fall and leave the finger behind. Finally, push the rope through the gate with your thumb and relax—you are clipped.

In another technique of one-handed clipping, you clip the rope near your harness tie in point with a quickdraw, ask the belayer for slack, and then lift both the rope and quickdraw to clip the upper quickdraw carabiner to the protection.

You should learn to clip in with either hand. Practice clipping one-handed while sitting in your living room, and on easy climbs, so you can do it quickly when you arrive at the "moment of truth" on a hard climb.

As a general rule on sustained climbs, place your protection low, somewhere between your waist and head. You will find it easier to clip and get positive protection, even if you do not get the security of protection above your head.

## Using Two Ropes

In *double-rope technique,* you use two ropes that are approximately 9 millimeters in diameter. This technique has several advantages, offset to some degree by the difficulty of managing two ropes. First, you can reduce rope drag by arranging both ropes in paths without sharp bends, and, second, you can reduce potential fall distance as you clip in (Figure 9-6). This system takes forethought as well as cooperation with the belayer. It helps if you use two different-color ropes. You use the left-hand rope, say, red, for protection on the left, and the right-hand rope, perhaps blue, for the right-hand protection. When you arrive at a piece of protection on the right, the belayer pays out slack in the blue rope without changing the tension of the red rope. If your belayer is out of sight, you may have to ask for slack on blue. This process is tricky with either a waist belay or belay device, but can be mastered with experience. It is important that you not negate the advantages of the double rope by twisting the two ropes together, producing sharp bends, friction, and rope drag. A watchful belayer will help keep the ropes straight.

There is a second advantage to climbing on double ropes. In Figure 9-6, the leader is clipping the right-hand rope into protection and has pulled up slack for this purpose. There is no additional slack in the left-hand rope. Should the leader fall while clipping in the right-hand rope, the fall length would be twice the distance from the leader to the last piece of protection for the left-hand rope, plus rope stretch. In contrast, when you use a single rope, you pull up slack in the rope that will catch the fall, lengthening the potential fall distance. The fall length will be twice the distance to the last piece of protection, plus rope stretch, plus the amount of slack needed to clip in, as well as the stretch of the rope at the bottom of the fall. Thus, if you fall while clipping using a single rope, you can go quite a bit farther than with a double rope.

A double rope is an advantage when you rappel: it gives you two ropes at all times with only a slight increase in weight over a single rope. You do have to manage the additional rope, and bear the cost of buying it, but these disadvantages do not outweigh the advantages of the added strength.

In the UIAA test for double ropes, only one of the two ropes is tested using a 50-kilogram weight instead of the 80-kilogram weight for ropes meant to be used alone.

As distinguished from double ropes, the evolving *twin-rope* technique employs two small-diameter ropes that are clipped through the same protection pieces on separate carabiners, at least for the first few pieces where potential impact forces are high. (These ropes may also have a wider diameter for the first few feet and taper to a smaller diameter farther along on the rope.) Higher on the climb, where potential impact forces are lower, you can clip the rope through separate protection pieces as you would a double rope. The light weight of these ropes is suited to extremely difficult gymnastic climbs where you need the lightest possible rope that has the advantages of a double rope.

## Rope Drag

It is important to place protection so that it will not create undue drag on the rope. An inexperienced leader inadvertently may create a problem of rope drag, as shown in Figure 9-7, where the leader placed two pieces of protection beneath an overhang and then climbed up to the right.

The climber has produced two sharp turns in the rope, dramatically increasing the amount of

*Figure 9-6. Double-Rope Technique*

friction in the system. Rope drag will cause him to spend almost as much energy tugging on the rope as climbing. In addition to causing balance problems and possibly a fall, rope drag can rotate and lift nuts from their placements.

You can easily keep the path of the rope straight by using full-length slings (Figure 9-7B). In some situations, it is appropriate to use double-length slings to prevent rope drag. The long sling could lengthen a fall, but it reduces rope drag and prevents an unopposed nut from rotating free of the rock.

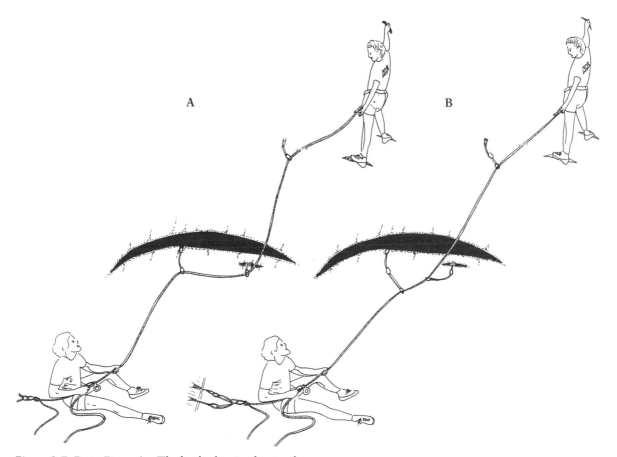

*Figure 9-7. **Rope Drag:** A—The leader has inadvertently formed two nearly right angles in the rope, creating significant rope drag. B—Using longer slings, the leader straightens out the rope path to decrease rope drag.*

## Traversing

Traversing (climbing laterally) presents problems for both the leader and the second. The general rule for a traverse is: *Always place protection before and after a hard move.* Protection before the move is for you; protection after the move is for the second.

In Figure 9-8, the leader on the traverse has placed protection before doing a hard move across a steep slab. Because the remainder of the traverse was easy, he put in no more protection. The second has arrived at the difficult move and is removing the protection before attempting the move. If the second were to fall, there would be no more protection and the second would swing across the slab and hang beneath the leader. The leader should have placed protection just after the difficult move.

In practice, of course, you cannot always place protection both before and after a hard move. For this reason, both leader and second should be able

to lead the pitch, and perhaps be prepared, with knowledge and ascending equipment, to climb the rope after a fall. When protection is placed before a hard move but not after, the second should be the better climber of the team, or at least the person more willing to accept risk. The leader can also minimize danger to the second by choosing a higher belay stance, giving the second more of a top rope during the traverse.

### Three Climbers on a Rope—A Problem for Seconds

Figure 9-9 adds a third climber to the situation. The leader has led up a vertical crack and then followed a horizontal crack to the right. Should the second remove the protection on the vertical part of the climb? On the traverse?

If the second is inexperienced, the leader must anticipate this situation and, before starting out (especially if the second's progress is not within view), instruct the second as to what protection to remove or leave in place. Removing the protection

*Figure 9-8. An Improperly Protected Traverse: After the second removes the protection, he can swing a long way if he falls. The leader should have placed protection before and after the crux to protect the second.*

Figure 9-10. *Protecting Vertical Cracks at the End of a Traverse*

Figure 9-9. *Three Climbers on a Traverse*

on the vertical crack will not endanger the third climber, who will have a rope directly overhead. Clearly, the second should leave the protection on the traverse, unclipping the lead rope and clipping into the protection the rope that trails to the third climber. If the third climber falls on the traverse, the remaining protection limits the fall to a short pendulum.

In addition to the belay provided by the leader, the third climber can *back-belay* the second while on the traverse to prevent a swinging fall. To do this, the second ties into both ropes through the appropriate harness tie-in points, and receives a belay from both the first and third climbers. This

system prevents the second from swinging during a fall.

If the protection were removed from the traverse by the second, the rope would stretch diagonally from the climber on the ground to the leader on the belay stance. With no protection between the third climber and the leader, the third climber could pendulum across the cliff any time during the climb.

### An Easy Traverse Followed by a Hard Crack

You often traverse from a belay ledge to a vertical crack. Figure 9-10 shows how an inexperienced leader can create a problem.

Here the leader has face-climbed horizontally 30 feet from the belay to the base of a crack. At the crack, the leader protects with a taper directed against a downward pull and then climbs the crack, protecting the ascent with additional tapers. After ascending the crack for 20 feet, the leader puts in the last piece of protection, climbs 2 more feet, and falls off. How far will the leader fall? Think out this problem, which is a matter of reasoning as well as mathematics, as if you were leading the pitch. The answer is presented on the following page.

*The Answer:* In a traverse followed by a vertical crack, the lowest taper or other piece of protection tends to rotate toward 180 degrees and may pull out, causing the pieces above it to pull, and so on. Climbers refer to this sequential failure of protection as *unzipping*, because it resembles the action of a zipper opening.

In this situation, the top piece has the best chance of holding because the force pulling on it still has a downward component. If the top protection piece holds in a fall that unzips all other pieces, the leader will still fall nearly 20 feet, plus rope stretch (see box). This situation is shown in Figure 9-11. (I have seen scared leaders trying to put nuts in a crack overhead faster than the nuts below them could lift out.) If the last piece pulls out, the leader will fall twice as far as the amount of rope out, or 104 feet (two times 52 feet) plus rope stretch.

There are ways, of course, to prevent tapers or other protection pieces from rotating and unzipping. At the end of a traverse you have three safe choices before starting upward. First, you may break the traverse and vertical section into different pitches. Second, you can place opposed nuts at the end of the traverse to resist both upward and downward pulls. Third, you can use double ropes to minimize rope drag, although opposing nuts will still be necessary at the end of the traverse.

### Increased Potential Fall Distance on Traverses

Recently, while leading the second pitch of a climb called Solid Gold in Joshua Tree National Monument, a friend of mine took a fall. He was not more than 6 feet from a good bolt that held, but three onlookers were surprised when he went several body lengths and broke his foot as he collided with an upsweeping friction ramp. The belayer wondered if she had made a mistake and was responsible for the injury.

The answer is no. When a climbing leader ascends vertically directly above the belayer, gravity directs the climbing rope downward. As a result, the total amount of slack in the climbing rope amounts to a couple of feet. The belayer attempts to provide just enough slack for the leader to move without belayer-applied tension, and no more. The leader will have to contend with

*Figure 9-11. **Unzipping Protection***

2 ft

20 ft

30 ft

## A Surprisingly Long Fall

When the leader falls (Figure 9-11) and unzips all but the last piece of protection, the fall is almost 20 feet. How can this happen when the leader was only 2 feet above the last piece? Before the fall, the leader had 52 feet of rope out—30 horizontal feet plus 20 vertical feet—plus the 2 feet above the protection. The leader essentially climbed the two legs of a right triangle with a 90-degree angle formed between the horizontal traverse line and the vertical crack. To find the length of the rope between the belayer and the remaining piece of protection (the hypotenuse), use the Pythagorean formula:

$$[c(belayer\ to\ piece)]^2 = [a(traverse)]^2 + [b(crack)]^2.$$

$$c^2 = (30\ ft)^2 + (20\ ft)^2 = 900\ ft^2 + 400\ ft^2 = 1,300\ feet^2$$

We need the square root of 1,300 feet, so

$$\sqrt{c^2} = \sqrt{1,300\ feet^2},\ and$$

$$c = 36\ feet\ (distance\ from\ belayer\ to\ the\ remaining\ nut).$$

Before the fall there were 50 feet of rope from the belayer to the nut that held the fall. Unzipping the protection contributed 14 feet (50–36 feet) to the fall. In addition, the leader was 2 feet above the last piece of protection that held, making the total fall 16 feet (14 feet + 2 feet). Rope stretch due to 7 percent impact elongation might add about 3.5 feet (50 feet x .07) for a total of 19.5 feet. The leader thought that the fall would be only about 4 to 5 feet.

*Figure 9-12. Gravitational Loops on a Traverse: Gravity on the climbing rope produces loops in the slack, which is greater than that produced when the climber ascends vertically directly above the belayer. The belayer can limit the amount of rope in the loops to some extent at the expense of increased tension on the leader.*

*The three positions of the fallen climber represent the distance from the last piece of protection to the leader (1–2), the amount of gravitational slack involved in the fall (2–3), and rope stretch (3–4).*

loop

the weight of the rope between himself and the belayer, plus whatever friction exists in the system.

Traverses present an additional problem to the belayer. The belayer still gives slack for the leader, but hanging loops form in the rope due to the pull of gravity on the rope itself (Figure 9-12). These loops represent additional slack that the belayer cannot completely control. The belayer cannot eliminate these loops, because to do so would produce unacceptable tension on the leader. This situation is severe when there is a long, easy traverse at the level of the belay followed by a rising traverse. If the belayer can see the leader and loops, he normally pulls some of the slack out of the loops at the expense of slightly increased tension on the leader, but if the leader is out of sight of the belayer this slack tends to accumulate. My friend had moved horizontally away from the belay for quite a distance on easy ground. He was most of the way through the rising traverse and was attempting the crux when he fell.

You need to understand that fall distances on a traverse are likely to be larger than you might suppose because of the gravitational slack in the loops. Three factors influence fall distance in a fall from a traverse. First is the distance from the nearest protection. The leader will swing directly underneath the last piece of protection for a distance equal to the amount of rope back to the last protection piece. The second component of fall distance is the slack accumulated in the loops, and the third component is rope stretch. When the leader is out about 100 feet on a traverse, gravitational slack will normally be about 4 to 6 feet compared to the 1 to 2 feet of slack that the belayer provides for a vertical pitch. The amount of gravitational slack can be considerably larger if the belayer is not concentrating or if the leader is out of sight. As a result, total fall distance for a traverse is potentially greater than for a fall from a vertical pitch directly over the belayer's head.

A partial solution to reducing fall distance on a traverse is to protect more often than you would on a vertical climb. This reduces the distance back to the last piece of protection. Certainly this is important near cruxes. In retrospect, my friend's fall would have been considerably lessened had he placed protection in the thin crack at the crux. In addition, belayers need to be especially attentive to balancing the amount of rope in the gravitational loops with an acceptable tension on the leader.

---

## Climbing Unroped

Spur-of-the-moment unroped climbing is always dangerous.[1] Some climbers solo because they lose their way or because they attempt an exposed approach unroped. Climbers who do not intend to solo a route often unrope for convenience: At the top of a difficult lead climb, they might wish to cover quickly the low-grade third-, fourth-, or fifth-class terrain quickly, where a fall over the exposure would be fatal. Other experienced climbers unrope near belay or rappel anchors without clipping in and fall to their death when they slip, or when a ledge collapses. This spur-of-the-moment unroped climbing is dangerous, but most climbers have done it at one time or another.

Purposeful soloing is attractive to some leaders after they gain experience leading difficult climbs, even though doing so is clearly dangerous. One famous early soloist was Paul Preuss, who had reached more than 1,200 summits at the time of his death from a fall at age 27.[2] He had done major climbs solo, and advocated never climbing a route without being able to down-climb it. Nevertheless, he died in an accidental fall when a hold betrayed him. Soloing has come into the forefront recently, and has been practiced by increasingly experienced, skilled, and trained climbers. In some regards, soloing takes climbing out of the realm of sport because each move is a life-or-death situation. Staying on the rock becomes life itself. If you are experienced enough to solo and can make a mature judgment concerning the safety of your own person, do not forget to consider family and friends affected by your loss. Make sure that you are soloing for yourself and not the envy of others.

## Getting Down from a Climb

Many climbing areas have one or more descent routes, which may range from walking down a gentle trail to negotiating a steep gully, to rappelling. In alpine climbs, descending is often the second half of a climb and just as technical as getting up. Give as much if not more attention to studying the descent line as you give to the ascent line. Picking the right descent gully from the top can be a difficult problem.

Gullies are often filled with loose rock. Although it might not seem possible at first, you can learn to scramble down the gullies without starting an avalanche of rocks at each step. When two people descending encounter a particularly loose section, only one person should move at a time. The lower person takes cover around a bend from the fall line or behind a protecting rock.

Rappel descents on established multipitch climbs are often fixed and marked by a trail of old slings. One problem that occurs is that many climbers start down the wrong way, leaving entic-

*Figure 9-13. Improvised Rope Climbing System Using Runner Slings and Carabiners*

ing footprints and rappel slings marking a false path. Be prepared to backtrack.

When you can see that both ends of a rappel rope reach the bottom of a rappel, your descent is assured. If you cannot see the bottom of the rappel, tie one or more knots in the rope end to prevent the rope from slipping through the rappel brake. A prusik safety can be use to safeguard a very slow rate of descent should the rope not reach. You must know how and have the gear necessary to reclimb the rope.

---

## Climbing the Rope

Most free climbers do not set out to climb the rope, but may find themselves in a situation where this is necessary at least for a short distance. If you do set out to climb the rope, as you might on a big wall, you will probably take along specialized gear, including mechanical rope ascenders and special rope slings called *etriers* to stand in as you climb. While you will not have this specialized equipment on a free climb, in an emergency you can climb the rope with slings and carabiners that you are likely to have with you (Figure 9-13).

Place two Bachmann or prusik knots on the rope (these knots are described in Chapter 3). The upper knot attaches directly to the climbing harness, and the lower knot attaches to slings, formed from shoulder-length slings commonly used for running belays, that make stirrups for your feet. These are fastened together to the proper length for your body proportions. Making these slings the proper length is one of the most critical steps in setting up an efficient ascending system. You can adjust the length of foot stirrups by tying overhand knots in individual slings near the foot (Figure 9-13A). The climber is secured to the lower Bachmann ascending system with a short (dark) sling as a safety backup.

One of the advantages of the system shown is that you can comfortably rest for as long as desired in a sitting position. To stand, place your feet

beneath yourself and pull up on the rope (Figure 9-13B). While standing, move the upper Bachmann knot up the rope and sit back down on your harness, which returns you to the position of A. Take your weight off the lower Bachmann knot and move it up the climbing rope as high as possible. The sequence starts over.

### *The Improvised Baudrier Chest Harness*

If you plan ahead to climb a rope, you may want to take along a sewn chest harness of wide comfortable webbing, available from a number of manufacturers. If the need to climb the rope occurs unexpectedly, as when your partner leads a 5.14 pitch, you can improvise a *Baudrier chest harness* in the field with runner slings that you have along for free climbing.[3] For short climbing distances most people forego improvised chest harnesses at the expense of added effort with their arms. However, during a full-length climb the chest harness will help keep you upright and conserve strength and endurance.

You can make a Baudrier chest harness from a double-length runner sling by passing one arm through the runner and then behind your back. Now pull the doubled runner around to the opposite side of your body and bring it up under your armpit (Figure 9-14A). Tie a knot by passing the doubled runner around a bight in the far side of the sling to form a loop which is passed through the original bight (Figure 9-14B). Tighten the knot to complete the chest harness (Figure 9-14C).

Since this harness is improvised, it is probably not long enough to fasten to your seat harness. You make this connection using a doubled single-length runner and a carabiner (Figure 9-14C). An additional carabiner passed around both the completed Baudrier chest harness and the freestanding rope will allow you to lean back with some support as you proceed upward. A chest harness must not tighten enough to constrict your breathing, so always check it or any other harness before committing to the rope.

*Figure 9-14. An Improvised Baudrier Chest Harness Tied with a Standard Double-Length Sling*

## Tying Off a Fallen Leader

A belayer may need to hold a fallen leader in the position of a fall if weather and other conditions permit and if lowering the leader would seriously aggravate injuries. Subsequent actions then depend on the belayer's ability to reach the climber or get help, but first the belayer must have some method of relieving the climber's weight from the belay brake, tying off the belay rope, and extracting himself or herself from the belay system. A prusik tie-off (Figure 9-15) can be used in this situation. In 20 years of climbing I have never needed to do this, but it is wise to be prepared if the situation should arise.

If you use a body belay, you can wrap the climbing rope a number of turns around your leg and even step on the rope to lock the wraps in place to free both hands. Then fix a prusik knot around the climbing rope leading to the fallen leader and attach the prusik sling to the primary anchor using a carabiner. Once you connect the prusik, allow the belay rope to slip to the point where the prusik grips and holds the weight of the fallen climber. Then you can unwrap the belay rope from yourself and tie it directly into the anchor with a figure-eight knot on a bight. Ordinary shoulder-length slings can serve as the prusik sling for this emergency situation. It is important to make sure that your anchor system can counteract an upward pull, since transferring the leader's weight directly to the anchor will exert a direct upward pull.

If the belayer is using a mechanical plate, the extraction procedure is much the same as with a body belay. If the mechanical belay is being used directly off a primary anchor, then extraction is even easier. The belayer simply ties a knot in the belay rope adjacent to the belay device on the braking-hand side. This knot attaches to the primary anchor by means of a carabiner. The tie-off is completed. The belayer can then unclip from the anchor and help the fallen climber.

*Figure 9-15. Prusik Tie-off of a Fallen Climber from a Waist Belay*

## Confidence

Fear is very healthy—it keeps us alive. You need to judge whether your fear arises from real danger or from fear of the unknown. In climbing, the former is associated with getting hurt. It can come from a poorly protected climb, loose rock, or other environmental dangers. But fear also comes from normal self-doubts related to taking on challenges.

Even experienced climbers know that they will have to face fear, and controlling it can be one of the major challenges of climbing. Use guidebooks to help you avoid climbs that are too hard or unprotected; choose a climb at a level with which you are comfortable. Stretch your abilities on short climbs near the ground or by bouldering before attempting to stretch your abilities when far off the ground. Choose climbs that protect well and make sure that cruxes protect well. You can do those long run outs on difficult terrain when you are an expert. Stretch and do a warm-up climb so that your body is functioning smoothly. Do that hard pitch soon afterward, before you get tired. Take rest days. As Winston Churchill said, "All men are cowards when they are fatigued." For backcountry climbs, be in excellent physical condition so that you will be fresh after a heroic approach. Being properly trained for both strength and endurance will go a long way toward increasing your confidence.

One of the pieces of advice often given climbers is to relax. If you use energy in shaking, that is energy taken away from the concentration needed to climb. If you find yourself shaking, speak quietly to yourself and visualize your movements in the next section to focus your mind on climbing instead of falling off. This usually works when you are on climbs that are within your physical ability and experience. If, in desperation, you need to hang off protection, do so. With experience, you will wean yourself away from this aid. Climbing is a self-imposed sport with internal rewards. If you do not make false claims about the style in which you climb, or alter the environment, most people do not really care about your style of climbing. They may have some fun with one-upping you, but you can handle that. People will respect you for your integrity far longer than they will remember a claim that you make about getting up some hard climb. If it is a false claim, they will remember that.

After picking a route that you can do, do not try to climb it all at once in your mind. Consider short segments of rock, from stance to stance or pitch to pitch. Take a second rope for rappelling, so that you are not committed to doing the entire route. You will be pleasantly surprised by getting up most of the routes that you attempt if you start with a positive attitude. Of course, on some routes you will retreat. When you do retreat, do it off secure anchors even if that means leaving gear behind. You will leave less gear if you have a few tied, as opposed to sewn, slings along that can be untied and retied around chockstones or trees.

Get an early start on longer climbs. Be ahead of the crowd or choose an alternate route so you will not spend time worrying about someone dropping loose rocks on you. Be careful not to drop rocks on the party below. Consult the guidebook to see how long it should take you to do the climb. Giving yourself not only enough time to climb but to retreat or descend without bivouac will give you an extra measure of confidence.

## Style

Style refers to how you do the route. Style is concerned with preserving the spirit of adventure. Getting up the climb by any means may be initially satisfying, but with experience you will care about how you did it. The best style is usually total free climbing without the direct aid of gear, such as nuts or slings. Using a piton or bolt for a hold, or even holding on to these while clipping in, is not considered to be in the best style. Pitons, bolts, and nuts are part of a system meant to safeguard a fall, not to make upward progress possible.

An ideal pure style would do away with shoes, chalk for your hands, ropes, and other gear, leaving you to progress smoothly up the climb in total control. But climbers have universally accepted ropes and gear as safety items. A few have come closer to realizing the ideal by doing away with chalk and even climbing without shoes. Certainly, how you move your body is part of your style. There is an immense difference in how you feel getting up a climb in a jerking, hesitant manner as opposed to a smooth ascent in which you flow up the climb.[4] Obtaining this sense of flow where body and mind work in meditative harmony to solve problems presented by rock can even be a primary reason to climb.

In the final analysis, style is up to you so long as you do not alter the rock and are honest about the style in which you did the climb. This is doubly important for first ascents. The safety of subsequent parties is at stake, since they will be attempting to do the climb in as good or better style than the first ascent party. If you need to grab a piton or rest on a nut to keep from falling off, do so. No one should get hurt to live up to a sporting standard, but come back later when you can do the climb totally free, and you will feel better about the climb and about yourself.

---

## References for Future Reading

Csikszentmihalyi, Mihaly, and Isabella Selega Csikszentmihalyi. 1990. Adventure and the flow experience. In *Adventure education,* edited by John C. Miles and Simon Priest. State College, Pennsylvania: Venture Publishing.

Gervasutti, Giusto. 1957. *Gervasutti's climbs.* Translated by Nea Morin and Janet Adam Smith. Seattle: The Mountaineers.

Graydon, Don, ed. 1992. *Mountaineering: The freedom of the hills.* Fifth edition. Seattle: The Mountaineers.

Horst, J. Eric. 1989. Happiness is a pair of big guns. *Climbing.* 116:118.

Long, John. 1989. *How to rock climb.* Evergreen, Colorado: Chockstone Press.

Meyer, George, and Don Reid. 1987. *Yosemite climbs.* Denver, Colorado: Evergreen Press.

Peters, Ed, ed. 1982. *Mountaineering: The freedom of the hills.* Fourth edition. Seattle: The Mountaineers.

Setnicka, Tim. J. 1980. Ascending techniques. Chapter 13 in *Wilderness search and rescue.* Boston: Appalachian Mountain Club.

Smutek, Ray. 1978. Crevasse self rescue. *Off-Belay.* 40:2–8.

---

## Endnotes

1. Meyer and Reid, 1987. Refer to pages 4 through 16 for a discussion of accidents in Yosemite.

2. Gervasutti, 1957.

3. Setnicka, 1980, page 217, and Graydon, 1992, page 105. You can tie this harness with custom-length slings that allow a direct clip into the waist harness.

4. The concept of flow has been examined extensively by Csikszentmihalyi, who worked with many athletes, including climbers. Flow is a creative state in which a climber is totally involved with the challenge, using appropriate skills and receiving immediate feedback. The climber does not stop, however, to evaluate the feedback. "Action and reaction have become so well-synchronized that the resulting behavior is automatic," says Csikszentmihalyi. In a more mystical sense flow occurs when you are "one with the rock." Flow is one of the primary reasons that people engage in an activity such as climbing that is without obvious external reward.

# 10

# *Anchor Systems*

## Anchor Basics

At a belay stance, a climber places two or more protection pieces to form an anchor, and then uses slings to fasten or *tie into* the anchor against any potential pull. The ideal anchor system will distribute the load equally to all anchor points so as not to stress any single anchor point unduly. If one of the anchor points fails, the system as a whole should not fail.

There are two types of anchor systems: *self-equalizing* and *pseudo-equalizing*. Self-equaliz–ing systems adjust automatically to share the load equally over a range of directions; pseudo-equalizing systems are those that share the load equally in only one direction. Self-equalizing systems apply more readily and for a larger number of situations than pseudo-equalizing systems, although climbers use both systems routinely.

The principles that guide the safe creation of anchor systems are relatively few. Systems that appear to be complex are made up of simple subsystems linked together. It is important that these subsystems and linkages be done correctly, since climbing safely and stopping falls ultimately depend on a safe anchor. Once you gain an understanding of these principles, you can rapidly establish safe anchor systems, in familiar as well as new situations, with a wide variety of available slings and ropes.

## Self-equalizing Systems

The basic self-equalizing anchor system is illustrated in Figure 10-1. Twist a climbing sling and pass a carabiner, parallel to the axis of the sling, through the two loops formed and around the crossed section of the sling. In this way, each of the two loops of the crossed sling in the drawing on the top, labeled A and B, forms a complete circle around the carabiner. When you climb, these loops

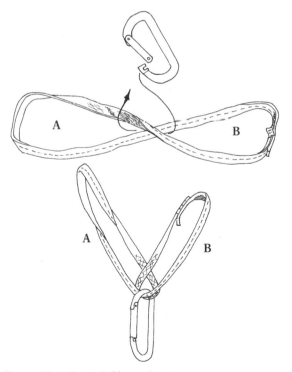

*Figure 10-1. Basic Self-equalization*

attach to anchor points such as pitons or nuts.

Trace the path of the two sling loops around the carabiner in the drawing on the bottom, noting how each loop encircles the carabiner independently. If you pull the left-hand end of loop A to the left, sling material will continuously travel around the carabiner and loop B will get smaller as loop A enlarges, until loop B is wrapped tightly around the carabiner and loop A cannot get any larger. Since loop B wraps around the carabiner, the system as a whole will not fail if the anchor point that loop B attaches to pulls out.

If you incorrectly rig this system, as shown in Figure 10-2, it can fail if one anchor point fails. Here the load-bearing carabiner encircles the crossed sling perpendicular, rather than parallel, to its axis. It does not enclose the two loops of the crossed sling: if the sling pulls to the left, loops A and B will slide through the carabiner. If either of the anchor points fails, the system fails. Experiment with both the correct and incorrect attachments to see the difference in action.

In Figure 10-3, a basic self-equalizing sling connects two anchor points, a piton and a nut. Because the anchor points are at different heights, a second sling is needed to complete the system. The load-bearing carabiner is at the equalized position of the system. It can rotate through the equalization arc and still equally distribute the load on the two anchor points.

equalization arc

Figure 10-3. **Two Self-equalized Anchor Points:** *The load-bearing carabiner can travel through an arc and remain equalized. This carabiner is physically limited in its arc of travel by the length of the sling to which it is attached. Angle A determines load multiplication of the system and should be less than 60 degrees; if necessary, add slings to one or both anchor points to reduce the angle.*

## Load Multiplication

You have seen why it is desirable to connect two anchor points so that they share a load equally. You can offset the advantages of this sharing, however, if you do not understand the principles involved.

The angle, A, between the two sides of the equalized anchor, shown in Figure 10-3, is very important in determining how the anchor points share the load. This angle should be no greater than 60 degrees because of a factor called *load multiplication,* which comes into play at larger angles. When the included angle between sides is 60 degrees or less, each side of the equalized anchor holds approximately half of the total load. As the included angle increases, each side of the anchor carries an increasing load; combining

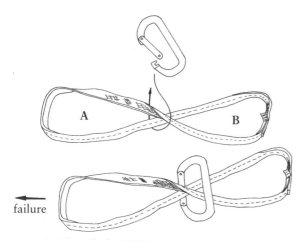

failure

Figure 10-2. *Incorrect Attachment*

anchors improperly can convert a potentially safe anchor into one that might fail.

Figure 10-4 shows an experiment that illustrates load multiplication. In A, the climber holds a 25-pound weight from an equalized sling. A spring scale like those found in an angler's tackle box is placed in one side of the equalized anchor system to record how much tension the weight exerts on this side and its anchor point.

With the ends of the equalized sling held together, the spring scale reads 12.5 pounds; that is, the weight is taken up equally by both sides of the sling. When the climber pulls the equalized sling apart to increase the angle between the sides, he applies force with his hands and arms. As demonstrated in Figure 10-4B, the increased tension is recorded on the spring scale. When the sides of the sling are held at an angle of 90 degrees, nearly 18 pounds of force is exerted on one side of the sling (and therefore on the anchor point): an increase of nearly 50 percent. This result is somewhat unexpected, and the force grows as the angle between the sides of the equalized anchor becomes greater. Thus at an angle of 120 degrees the spring scale will record 25 pounds of tension in

one side of the equalized sling, a total of 50 pounds of tensional force on both sides. (If you actually perform this experiment, you will find that your results will not be perfect because of friction and varying spring tension within the scale, but it is accurate enough to demonstrate the principle.)

Now imagine replacing the climber's arms with real anchor points. As you increase the angle between the slings, the load multiplies. The effects are summarized in Table 10-1, with load multiplication plotted as the tension, $T_1$ and $T_2$, on anchor slings as a percentage of an applied load of a 150-pound climber. Load multiplication is divided into zones: None to Moderate, Moderate to High, and High to Extreme, based on the angle between slings. The desirable zone—None to Moderate—occurs when the angle between slings is between 0 and 60 degrees. Each sling in this zone bears approximately half the applied load. At the 120-degree end of the Moderate to High zone a tensional force equal to the applied load is transferred directly to *each* of the anchor points, and the total anchor has to hold twice the applied load. This result negates one of the advantages of using two anchor points, which is to share the tensional force

A

parallel slings

B

90°

90-degree angle

*Figure 10-4. **Tension in Anchor Systems***

Table 10-1. *Table of Load Multiplication:* Calculated for a static load of a 150-pound climber and expressed as a percentage (%) of the applied load. Zones of load multiplication are indicated. $T_1$ and $T_2$ are the tensional forces in each side of the anchor separated by the angle A.[1]

| A° | $T_1$(150 lb) | $(T_1 + T_2)$ | % Applied Load | Load Multiplication Zones |
|---|---|---|---|---|
| 0 | 75 | 150 | 100 | None |
| 15 | 75.8 | 154.3 | 103 | |
| 30 | 77.6 | 155.2 | 104 | to |
| 45 | 81.3 | 162.6 | 108 | |
| 60 | 86.6 | 173.2 | 116 | Moderate |
| 75 | 94.6 | 189.2 | 126 | Moderate |
| 90 | 106.1 | 212.2 | 142 | |
| 105 | 123.2 | 246.4 | 164 | to |
| 120 | 150.0 | 300.0 | 200 | High |
| 135 | 195.8 | 391.6 | 261 | High |
| 150 | 289.6 | 579.2 | 386 | to |
| 175 | 1704.6 | 3409.2 | 2272 | |
| 180 | ∞ | ∞ | ∞ | Extreme |

of the applied load between anchor points. In the High to Extreme zone the anchor points would have to hold almost 12 times the applied load at 175 degrees and an infinite amount at 180 degrees. Such load multiplication is clearly undesirable and dangerous to the safety of your anchor points:

Figure 10-5. *Load Multiplication Caused by Using a Triangular Sling Pattern. The lower angle between slings is 90 degrees.*

attempt to keep the angle between anchor points to 60 degrees or less for nut or fixed anchor slings.

### Static Load Multiplication on a Common Rappel Anchor

When two anchor points are connected in a triangle, as commonly happens with the two bolts of a fixed rappel anchor, you can inadvertently increase load multiplication even further[2] (Figure 10-5). The climber holds aloft a 25-pound weight with slings connected to a single sling, forming a 90-degree triangle. Now the spring scale connected directly to one anchor point measures the force applied to it at 32.5 pounds, or 130 percent of the applied load. This reading sharply exceeds the 18 pounds measured in Figure 10-4B, where the angle was approximately the same. The triangular pattern not only increases load multiplication drastically, but in addition the applied load attempts to rotate the anchor points. Alternative desirable sling patterns for connecting anchors are described in Chapter 7 under "Bolt Anchors."

## Extending the Basic Self-equalizing System

You can use the basic self-equalizing system to distribute forces to three or more anchor points

Figure 10-6. *Equalizing Three Anchor Points*

25-pound forces are applied directly to anchor points F and G.

Combining self-equalization systems for three anchors always causes two of the anchor points to share half of the applied force, while the third anchor point bears the remaining half of the applied force. You might use this system if one of your three anchor points is a large well-placed nut and the two other anchor points are small well-placed nuts.

Three anchor points can share the applied force equally, as described below in the section "Equalizing Three Equally Strong Anchor Points."

### Connecting Four Self-equalizing Anchor Points

An anchor system formed by connecting four anchor points using the basic system is illustrated in Figure 10-7. To test your understanding of the system, there are blank underlined spaces for you to fill in the force applied at each point. Assume an initial force of 100 pounds. (Answers are on the next page.)

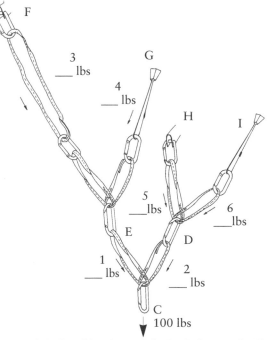

Figure 10-7. *Combinations of the Basic System for Four Anchor Points*

(Figure 10-6). Here, two of the anchor points are equalized as described above, and a second equalized system is integrated with the first. To analyze the force distribution, begin at the bottom carabiner, point C. This is the load-bearing carabiner for the system: the belayer connects to the anchor system through it. If you place a force of 100 pounds on this carabiner and the included angle A is 60 degrees or less, the two sides of the system, 1 and 2, share the 100 pounds approximately equally—each holds 50 pounds. On side 2 this 50 pounds of force is transmitted directly to anchor point D.

On side 1 the 50-pound force is applied to carabiner E, the load-bearing carabiner of a subsystem that equalizes anchor points F and G. At E the 50 pounds is divided into forces of approximately 25 pounds each on sides 3 and 4. These

If you apply a 100-pound force at carabiner C, the equalizing system distributes approximately 50 pounds of force along sling 1, on the left side of the system, to carabiner E, and an identical force along sling 2, on the right side of the system, to carabiner D.

Carabiner E is the load-bearing carabiner for a subsystem that distributes forces to anchor points F and G. The 50 pounds of force applied at carabiner E is distributed equally along slings 3 and 4 to anchor points F and G, which are therefore loaded with 25 pounds of force each.

Carabiner D is the load-bearing carabiner for the second subsystem, which distributes forces to anchor points H and I. The 50 pounds of force applied to carabiner D is distributed equally along slings 5 and 6 to anchor points H and I. Therefore, anchor points H and I are also loaded with 25 pounds each of the original 100 pounds of force applied at carabiner C.

### Linking Basic Self-equalizing Systems

To generalize the results of linking basic self-equalizing systems: When three or an odd number of anchor points are equalized in an asymmetrical manner, using combinations of the basic equalization technique, forces apply unequally to the anchor points. When two or an even number of anchor points are equalized in a symmetrical manner using combinations of the basic equalization technique, forces apply equally to all the anchor points.

At the end of a lead you can quickly equalize two or even three anchor points using the techniques discussed above to make a very secure anchor. The three-anchor system is especially useful when you have three anchor points and one of them is significantly stronger than the other two, since the two weaker anchor points can be combined into one anchor point with a greater combined strength that you then equalize with the remaining strong point.

When you set up top-rope anchors using combinations of the basic self-equalizing system, you will need a lot of slings and carabiners, especially since a fail-safe system for a top-rope anchor calls for locking carabiners or doubled carabiners with gates opposed and reversed. It is recommended, therefore, that you use longer slings in pseudo-equalized systems (see page 148), which can be made of sections of a retired climbing rope.

## Equalizing the Load on Three Equally Strong Anchor Points

To distribute the load equally to three anchor points of the same strength, use a double-length sling or a longer custom-length small-diameter rope (*cordelette*). Pass the sling through carabiners attached to all three anchor points, as shown in Figure 10-8. Pull the sling between the carabiners down to form Vs, twist them, and pass the load-

*Figure 10-8. **Connecting Three Equally Strong Anchor Points***

bearing carabiner through the loops they form and around the lower portion of the sling, as indicated by the arrow. The twists ensure that the sling is around the carabiner; if one anchor point fails, the carabiner will still be attached to the sling. Try failing each anchor point in turn to see how the remaining anchor points are affected in this setup. The method demonstrated is a general technique for connecting multipoint anchors if you have slings that are long enough.

An alternative method of fastening together multipoint anchors is shown in Figure 10-9. Connect the two outside anchor points by a long sling or a number of shorter slings fastened together with carabiners, and cross the middle of the sling (A). Pass a carabiner connected to the middle anchor point around the crossed point, parallel to the axis of the sling (B). As before, connecting the carabiner to the sling in this manner provides a backup if one of the anchor points fails. Now cross the sling again halfway between two of the anchor points (B), and connect two additional carabiners to the sling. Hold these two carabiners together with a third carabiner (C) to complete the system. Any load applied to the bottom carabiner of the system distributes equally to each of the anchor points. In addition, if any anchor point fails, the remaining two anchor points automatically share the force between them equally.

### Shock-loading Equalized Anchors

The reason for creating self-equalizing systems is to share the load equally between anchor points. You begin with the assumption that individual anchor points will not fail, but that self-equalization will provide a measure of security if one of the anchor points should pull out of the rock. If one of the anchor points does pull, however, the remaining anchor points may *shock-load* as the anchor-sling accelerates forward from the pulled anchor point to catch on remaining anchor points. The magnitude of shock loading is proportional to the distance the sling slides before it catches, in relation to the acceleration of the falling climber.

You can prevent shock loading by keeping the anchor sling from sliding. First create a self-

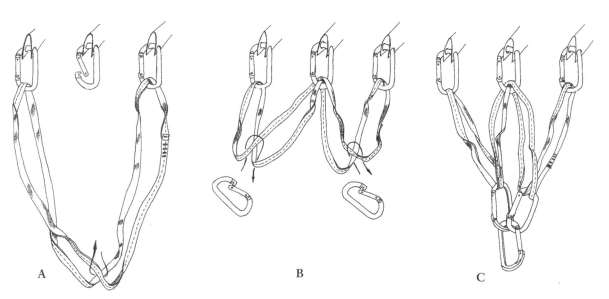

Figure 10-9. *An Alternative Method of Connecting Three Anchor Points:* To ensure staying clipped, you can use two opposed and reversed carabiners (instead of one as shown here and in other figures in this chapter) when clipping your harness to the anchor.

Figure 10-11. *A Simple Pseudo-equalizing Anchor*

Figure 10-10. **Preventing Shock Loading on a Multi-anchor System**

equalizing anchor system, and then aim the carabiner from which you belay toward the expected pull on the system. Take this belay carabiner and use it to tie an overhand knot around all of the slings of the system (Figure 10-10). You have created a pseudo-equalized anchor system that will prevent shock loading while equally sharing the load in only one direction.

---

## Pseudo-equalized Systems

A pseudo-equalized system distributes a load equally onto two or more anchor points, but in one direction only. An example of a pseudo-equalized system is shown in Figure 10-11, where two slings tie two anchor points into a single carabiner.

### Anchors for Slingshot (Social Belay) Systems

A *slingshot system* allows a belayer to give a climber a rope from above while remaining on the ground where it is easy to monitor the climber's progress. (To use this system on very difficult climbs, set up the anchor by walking to the climb's top along a trail, or lead an easier adjacent climb.) The climbing rope now runs from the belayer to an anchor set at the top of the climb—"top roping"—and back down to the climber, who is starting from ground level. Hence the climbing rope forms an upward-pointing V, somewhat resembling the elastic band of a loaded slingshot.

In top-roping situations climbers often fall, either because they are attempting routes that are difficult for their ability or because they are trying climbs of a high standard. Once climbers reach the top, they are often lowered (instead of downclimbing) back to the ground.

Falling and lowering subjects the anchor slings to repeated stretching and contraction, as well as

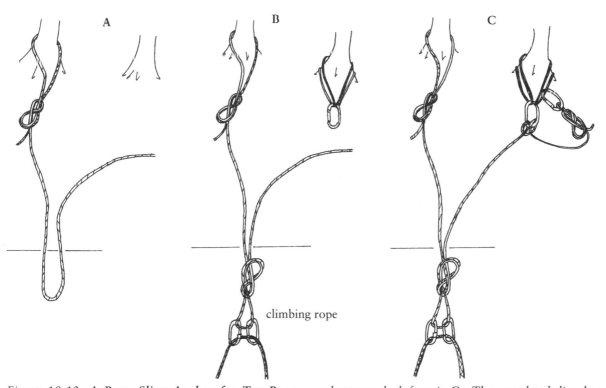

Figure 10-12. *A Rope Sling Anchor for Top-Rope Climbing: A—Tie a length of rope sling to an anchor with a figure-eight follow-through knot, place a bight in the rope, and position it over the edge to measure length. B—Tie a figure-eight knot into the bight that is hanging over the edge. Place the climbing rope through two locking carabiners to produce tension on the anchor sling* and remove slack from it. *C—The completed slingshot anchor system. Equal tension in the second anchor is achieved by using an easily adjustable clove hitch. Back this knot up with a figure-eight knot on a bight clipped into the anchor with a locking carabiner. You can use a single carabiner for both the clove hitch and figure-eight backup knot.*

abrasion where the rope passes over the edge of the cliff. You can pad the anchor sling, but you should also use two anchor slings over the side of a cliff to provide a safety backup if one of the slings is cut. A quick system for setting up two independent anchors that bear the load equally is illustrated in Figure 10-12. (A tensionless anchor, used for setting up rappel systems for groups, is described in Chapter 17.)

Tie a sling made of rope to an anchor (tree) with a figure-eight follow-through knot. Secure yourself at the edge, drape the sling over the edge, and make a bight that hangs just below where you would like the knot to be when you have finished (A).

Next, pull up the sling and tie a figure-eight knot in the bight that was hanging over the edge (B). Place two carabiners, at least one locking, on the figure-eight knot; thread the climbing rope through the carabiners; and drop both ends of the climbing rope over the edge to provide tension on the tied-off anchor sling. This tension is essential. (You use two carabiners so that the rope does not bend as sharply as it would over one carabiner.)

Now, working at the second anchor, adjust the tension of the free end of the anchor so both ropes will bear the load equally. Place a webbing sling with a locking carabiner around a second anchor tree, as shown in C. Tie the free end of the anchor sling into this carabiner with a clove hitch, which can be easily adjusted, and adjust the tension on this sling so that both anchor slings are equally tight. Set the clove hitch as tightly as possible and back it up with a figure-eight on a bight that is clipped into a carabiner on the second anchor sling. Place the figure-eight backup knot as close as possible to the clove hitch without loosening the clove hitch.

*Figure 10-13.* **Using the Climbing Rope to Pseudo-equalize Anchor Points:** *A—Connecting the first two anchor points. B—The two upper arrows show connections made using a carabiner, while the lower arrow points toward the second.*

This system allows you to adjust the tension on the two rope slings well away from the edge of the cliff, where it is easy to work in a relaxed manner.

### Pseudo-equalized Anchors with Rope Slings

A leader normally carries eight to ten slings on a climb and sometimes must use these up on the intermediate protection pieces, leaving none for the anchor. Equalizing two or three protection pieces for an anchor without slings sounds impossible until you realize that you can use the rope itself as a sling. If the pitch was less than a full rope length, the remaining length of 10 to 30 feet can be used to set up a pseudo-equalized anchor (Figure 10-13).

**Step 1: Connecting Two Anchor Pieces with a Rope Sling:** After completing the lead, clip to a temporary anchor, leaving room to maneuver. Go off belay and pull up as much slack as possible to use as a sling. Sometimes this means that the second needs to stand at the very start of the pitch, rather than away from it, to give all the slack possible. Place two pieces of protection in the rock and, taking enough rope to reach from the eventual belay position to the right-hand (or left-hand) piece of protection, tie into it with a clove hitch. Then make a V in the rope sling to create an equalizing subsystem and tie the rope sling into the second piece of protection, also using a clove hitch. The angle between the sides of this subsystem should be less than 60 degrees to minimize load multiplication. Tie a figure-eight loop knot at the end of the V formed by the sides of the subsystem.

**Step 2: Connecting the Third Piece of Protection:** After forming the first subsystem, tie the rope sling directly into the carabiner on the third piece of protection. Use a clove-hitch with a bit of slack between the two pieces of protection. If all three protection pieces are equal in size and placement, extend this last segment of rope sling directly to the V in the apex of the first subsytem and connect it there with a figure-eight loop knot and a carabiner. This will be the belay tie-in point. If the third piece is larger and better placed than the first two, a

more general situation, form a second subsystem and tie another figure-eight knot. Note that the figure-eight knot at the apex of the second subsystem extends beyond that of the first subsystem.

**Step 3: Tying the System Together:** Now fasten together the subsystems of the rope sling, using a carabiner to connect the figure-eight knots. The belayer attaches to the load-bearing figure-eight knot of the system with a carabiner. The free end of the rope leading to the second is used to belay.

**Solving Problems:** If there is not enough rope to set up a three-point anchor when you use the climbing rope as a sling, an anchor based on two pieces of protection may be sufficient. You can use a carabiner to connect directly to the first V of Step 1 (Figure 10-13A).

Alternatively, you may have one or two slings at the end of the pitch. Use these to self-equalize the first two protection pieces. Then pseudo-equalize the anchor to the third protection piece if you use the rope as a sling in a manner similar to that described in Step 2. The first subsystem of Step 2 (in Figure 10-13B) would then be formed by self-equalized slings rather than the rope sling shown.

Then again, in the real world of climbing there may be no slings left at the end of a lead to hook up the anchor. Indeed, there may only be enough rope left to tie into one protection piece. Presuming that you are committed to the climb and cannot just walk off, this is a serious situation, since one anchor point is not satisfactory to safeguard against a fall. However, you can temporarily strengthen one anchor with an aimed and braced body stance while the second climbs. After enough slack has accumulated and the second has gained a secure resting place, set up a rope-sling anchor system (Figure 10-13A and B).

There might even be a piece of protection on the ledge that the second can fasten to while the leader uses the accumulated slack to complete the rope-sling anchor. You will have to solve this kind of real-life problem using your judgment—neither this nor any other book can do it for you.

## References for Future Reading

Denise, Garet. 1987. Rappel stations—a bum rap:
How safe are those slings. *Climbing.* 102:92–93.
Setnicka, Tim J. 1980. *Wilderness search and rescue.*
Boston: Appalachian Mountain Club.

## Endnotes

1. Load multiplication on anchor systems can be explored with some simple calculations that use static loads, simple geometry, and the trigonometric cosine function, which is defined below. Figure 10-14 shows the general setup of a basic anchor system and how loading stresses it. In A, the rappeller, who represents the load, is sitting quietly on

*Figure 10-14. **Static Forces on Anchor Systems.** Modified from Setnicka, 1980.*

the rappel rope. The anchors are connected by slings, and the rappeller's body weight pulls the slings downward to form angle A. (The forces are similar to those visualized in the illustration of the climber holding a weight with a spring scale, Figure 10-5.) Let us estimate the magnitude of load multiplication without direct, and possibly disastrous, experience.

When the system is at rest, the downward force due to gravity $F_1$ equals the opposing force $F_2$, which is an upward force. (If this were not so, the rappeller would continue down to the ground or, more unlikely, fly up into the sky.) The upward force is provided by the rope under tension, which in turn pulls on the nut anchors. How much tension is there in the rope and on the anchor system? For this calculation, we will work with one half of the system (as we did in Figure 10-5). When we have calculated $T_1$, the tensional force in the left-hand side of the rope, or half the total tension, we can double that force to get the tensional force for the entire system.

Solve for $T_1$ using the vector Y, which is the horizontal component of $T_1$. The vertical component of $T_1$ is the force $F_2/2$ and the angle concerned is (A/2). To simplify, use F/2 since $F_1/2 = F_2/2$.

$$\cos (A/2) = \frac{F/2}{T_1}$$ by definition of a cosine = adjacent side of a right triangle F/2 divided by the hypotenuse $T_1$ of the triangle; and then

$$T_1 = \frac{F/2}{\cos(A/2)}$$ by transposing

For example: a 150-pound person sits quietly on the rope and makes an angle A of 30 degrees.

$$T_1 = \frac{150 \text{ lb}/2}{\cos (30°/2)} = 75 \text{ lb/cos } 15°$$
$$= 75 \text{ lb}/.966$$
$$= 77.6 \text{ lb}$$

Since $T_1$ is one-half the total tension on the rope, or the individual protection point, the total tension on the rope and anchor points is twice this amount, or 155.2 pounds. This represents a load multiplication of 103.5 percent and demonstrates that total rope tension is greater than the downward force $(F_1)$ of the climber sitting on the rope.

2. The increase in tensional force is directly proportional to the reciprocal of the sine function of the angle at the bolt. At 90 degrees this increase is zero. It becomes infinite at zero degrees. For the plot of these angles see Denise, 1987.

# CHAPTER

# 11

# *Fall Forces*

## Forces and Safety in Climbing Systems

A popular T-shirt motto admonishes climbers to "Fight Gravity." This is good advice, because gravity is very powerful, and it accelerates a fall earthward. To stop a falling climber we construct an elaborate belay system that includes an anchor, a belayer, a belay brake, the rope, and protection for the leader. The anchor ties the belayer to the cliff; the belayer assumes a stance and tensions the rope; the belay brake provides enhanced tension; and the rope stretches to absorb energy. Advanced designs can make low-stretch ropes absorb energy equally as well as high-stretch ropes do. Additional energy can be absorbed as the rope slides through the belay brake and slides over carabiners on protection in the system. Since energy can be transformed but not destroyed, some fall energy is converted to heat and some goes into tightening knots, and deforming bodies and harnesses. This chapter

examines how the forces of a fall are absorbed and distributed starting with simple concepts and ending with real systems.

## The Fall Factor

Climbers rarely want to fall, but for obvious reasons we must be prepared to fall. This is especially true because climbers recently have learned how to climb harder by repeatedly attempting difficult moves and falling, to the point that they have turned the rope into an active tool.

The *fall factor (f),* which tells us something about the force that the rope experiences, is the ratio between the distance of the fall and the amount of rope out. It is calculated by the following formula:

$$f = \frac{\text{distance fallen}}{\text{amount of rope out}}$$

When the fall factor is large, we expect rope damage. If the fall factor is small, the rope does not experience much stress or damage.

### A Roped Fall with No Fall Factor

Fall factor has no meaning if the climber is stopped by a ledge or the ground before coming onto the rope. An extreme case, and probable injury, occurs when there is no protection between the belayer and the leader, and the climber hits the ground. This fall produces no effect on the rope; the fall factor in this situation is the same as if there were no fall. In other words, the fall factor is a simplified way to think about potential rope damage.

### Simple Falls

We will examine a number of situations to see what each one means in terms of placing protection and strategies for leading.

In the simple but long fall shown in Figure 11-1, the climber was 15 feet above his protection and then fell 30 feet:

*Fall Forces* 153

$$f = \frac{\text{distance of fall}}{\text{amount of rope out}} = \frac{30 \text{ ft}}{30 \text{ ft}} = 1$$

A fall factor of 1 is a severe fall for the rope, the belay system, and the climber's body. Your rope is suspect for future use after taking such a fall.

If the leader had placed protection more frequently, the fall factor could have been reduced. For example, if a second piece of protection were placed 7.5 feet above the first, the fall would have been twice 7.5 feet, or 15 feet onto 30 feet of rope:

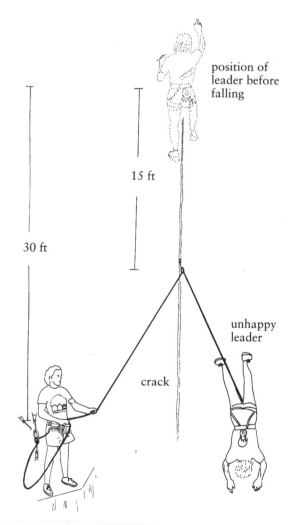

position of leader before falling

15 ft

30 ft

crack

unhappy leader

*Figure 11-1. A Simple Fall from Above Protection*

$$f = \frac{\text{distance of fall}}{\text{amount of rope out}} = \frac{15 \text{ ft}}{30 \text{ ft}} = 0.5$$

This fall would have been easier on the rope, the falling leader, the belayer, the protection pieces, and everything else related to the climbing system. By placing protection often, you minimize the fall factor and safeguard yourself as well as the belay chain.

### Falls in the Middle and End of a Lead with Intermediate Protection

A fall at the end of a lead is easier on the rope, protection, leader, and belayer than a fall of the same distance in the beginning or the middle of the same lead, as Figure 11-2 shows. Consider two potential falls, each with a fall distance of 6 feet, onto different lengths of rope as indicated by the two sets of numbers in the illustration. For the first 6-foot fall, with distances indicated by number in boldface type, the leader climbs 10 feet above the belayer, places protection, and then continues upward 3 feet to the crux. At the crux he falls the 3 feet back to the protection and then 3 feet below it, for a total fall of 6 feet, with the 13 feet of rope between him and the belayer. The fall factor is .46 (f = 6 ft/13 ft) and is of moderate size. This produces moderate stress on the protection pieces, belay system, and leader.

If, however, the climber gets past the lower crux and falls at a higher crux on the climb (the distances indicated by the italic numbers in parentheses), the fall factor will be lower. In this higher fall, assume that the leader climbs 20 feet above the belayer, puts in protection, and climbs 3 feet higher before falling. There is now a total of 23 feet of rope to absorb the energy of the 6-foot fall, compared to 13 feet of rope in the fall at the lower crux. The fall factor for the second fall is f = 6 ft/23 ft = .26. This is a less severe fall.

These two examples demonstrate that it is safer to fall higher on the climb than lower because as you near the end of a pitch there is more rope to absorb the fall energy. In general, to minimize the fall factor, do not set up a belay just before the crux even though you might desire the psycholog-

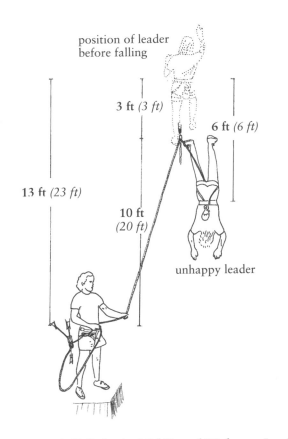

position of leader
before falling

3 ft *(3 ft)*

6 ft *(6 ft)*

13 ft *(23 ft)*

10 ft
*(20 ft)*

unhappy leader

Figure 11-2. **Falls in the Middle and High on a Lead with Intermediate Protection:** *Distances for the separate falls are indicated by boldface numbers for the first fall and italics in parentheses for the second fall.*

position of leader
before falling

30 ft

30 ft

unhappy leader

Figure 11-3. **The Maximum Fall**

ical satisfaction of having your belayer close at hand. To put it in a rule of thumb, *belay after cruxes rather than before them.*

### The Maximum Fall Factor

The maximum fall factor of 2 experienced by the rope and climbing system occurs when the leader falls an equal distance below the belayer as he or she was above the belayer. This might happen as illustrated in Figure 11-3, where the climber steps from a belay ledge to an exposed vertical climb with a lot of exposure. He climbs 30 feet without placing protection and then falls off, stopping 30 feet below the belayer.

The is a fall of 60 feet, or twice the length of rope between the leader and belayer; thus, $f$ = 60 ft/30 ft = 2. The rope should be retired, and the leader should be suspect for failing to put in protection or putting it in badly so that it pulled out.

This example illustrates how important it is to prevent a fall directly onto the belay and why the most important piece of protection to safeguard the belay is the first piece. This first piece protects the belay anchor, the belayer, and the leader. Think of your belayer and your anchor and protect early.

### Safety Tips for Minimizing Impact Forces

#### *Harnesses*

• Double webbing back through any harness buckle to prevent accidental slippage, unbuckling, and resulting falls. Keep in mind the climber who did not have his buckle doubled back and told his guide that this was not a problem, since the buckle would slip at about 350 pounds of force and he only weighed 150 pounds. Remember that your 150 pounds will produce a significantly higher impact force when you jerk onto the end of the rope in a fall.

#### *Rappels*

• Descend smoothly from anchors strong enough to hold potential impact forces. When you descend in a jerky or bouncing motion, you produce impact loading (it is like jumping up and down on scales). The impact force produced in a rappel, however, can rip out your life-saving anchor.

#### *Anchors*

• Use two or more anchor points and an equalizing system, with the angle between slings at 60 degrees or less, to minimize load multiplication on individual anchors related to the geometry of the setup. Three anchor points provide greater assurance.

#### *Running Protection*

• Place the first piece of protection early to safeguard the anchor system and belayer. Since this piece is not designed to safeguard the leader, you should place it no matter how you feel about the difficulty of the climb. Additional protection safeguards lower pieces, limits fall distance, and reduces the length of time that an individual piece must sustain maximum impact force.

• Do not create pulley systems when hooking two nuts together, as they promote high impact forces and failure of the protection points.

#### *Belaying*

• Tie into the anchor and belay from your harness (see Chapter 6, Figure 6-11), rather than belaying straight off the anchor system. You will lessen the impact load on the anchor and help minimize the force on the protection pieces that catch the fall. Practice tying off a fallen leader and extracting yourself from the belay. (If you top-rope with a slingshot or social belay, then little impact force is expected and belaying directly from the anchor system is more acceptable.)

• A fall at the end of a well-protected pitch is easier on the rope, the climber, the belayer, and protection pieces than a fall of the same distance at the beginning because there is more rope to absorb the force of the fall.

• Belay after rather than before cruxes to minimize impact forces, and keep the belay as far as possible from the crux.

#### *Fall Factor and Rope Retirement*

You should consider retiring a rope whenever it experiences a fall factor of 1 or more. As explained in Chapter 5, many short falls have a cumulative effect on rope performance. The effect will be greatest if the climber repeatedly falls from the same point, falling on one segment of rope. The interior of a dynamic rope is made of braided strands that act like coiled springs to absorb energy. A fall will permanently stretch them, making them less capable of absorbing the energy of the next fall. In addition, a fall may abrade, cut, or otherwise damage the sheath.

## Impact Force

When you fall, the energy of your falling body—the product of your mass and velocity at the time of braking—must be absorbed to bring you to a stop. Your velocity must be returned to zero. Your velocity at the start of braking depends on how long you have been falling. This, of course, means that the longer the fall, the more force is required to decelerate. The size of stopping force required to absorb the energy that you have acquired at the time of braking depends on the time during which you brake. A small force will do the job if you come to a stop over a long period. On the other hand, a large force will be necessary to stop the fall quickly. Most climbers want to stop quickly, but also want to experience minimum impact force on their bodies. These opposing desires create problems for people who design the dynamic ropes that we use.

### Impact Force and Rope Stretch

Ropes stretch to absorb energy. As the rope stretches, it exerts a continually increasing force until all of the energy of the fall is absorbed or until sufficient force is transmitted to the belay brake to overcome the friction of the brake and the rope slips. All belays are static, allowing the rope to stretch until they reach a certain limit determined by the belay technique and brake used, and then they allow the rope to slip and become dynamic. Once the rope slips through the belay brake, the amount of energy absorbed by rope stretch cannot get any higher; it levels off. Additional energy of the fall is absorbed by the friction of the rope slipping through the brake, around carabiners, and so forth.

The UIAA tests rope stretch or impact elongation in a totally static, nonslip belay using a procedure done on an engineered structure (see Chapter 5, Figure 5-6). Rope stretch under these conditions usually measures approximately 20 percent of the rope length between the anchor and falling weight. In a real rock-climbing fall, however, impact elongation has been measured at only one-third of the rated percentage; during a fall a rope with a UIAA impact elongation of 21 percent was measured at only 7 percent.[1]

### Static Impact Forces

If a belay is locked off (static), the belayer exerts a force that reaches a maximum when rope stretch reaches a maximum. This maximum force is the impact force given by the equation:[2]

$$I = mg + mg \sqrt{\left(1 + \frac{2fM}{mg}\right)}$$

I can be expressed in ft-lb/sec[2] or in pound-force (lbf) by dividing ft-lb/sec[2] by the value of g, which is 32 ft/sec[2]. We will use lbf because it seems the simplest to understand intuitively:

I = impact force in ft-lb/sec[2]

M = rope modulus in ft-lb/sec[2]. Material constant depending on cross-sectional area of rope, fiber content, etc.

f = fall factor (distance fallen/amount of rope paid out)

m = mass

g = acceleration constant of gravity (32 ft/sec[2])

Since the rope modulus, mass, and effect of gravity will be constant for any one climber, the maximum force depends on the fall factor. Since fall factor is a ratio of the height fallen to the amount of rope out, this means that the impact force is independent of absolute height of a fall.

A second interesting result is discovered when the fall factor is zero (f = 0). This is the most gentle fall possible when a climber's weight settles onto a top rope with no slack between the climber and the belayer. The equation for impact force becomes:

$$I = mg + mg \ \sqrt{(1 + \frac{2fM}{mg})}; \ or$$

$$I = mg + mg \ \sqrt{1 + 0}$$

$$I = 2 \ mg$$

This says that a 180-pound climber falling onto a top rope with no slack generates 360 pounds of force, which is perhaps twice what is expected. If the fall factor is 0.4, 0.8, 1.0, 1.4, 1.6, or 2.0, this climber generates an impact force of 1,137; 1,521; 1,676; 1,947; 2,067; or 2,288 pounds of force, respectively.

---

### A "Shocking" Near Miss

Todd led the crux pitch on Symmetry Spire and established a belay on a small shelf. His partner, Tom, fell while following. Expecting a 2- or 3-foot fall, instead he found himself plunging down the cliff, windmilling his arms as he dropped past holds that he could not grasp. When he stopped, he was back at the anchor point from which he began the pitch. He hastily clipped into the fixed anchor pitons now at his waist, and began to collect his wits.

Todd, the errant belayer, had been pulled off the belay ledge and was hanging sideways—confused and disoriented—just below the ledge. He had partially lost control of the belay rope, so that it whipped around his waist during Tom's plunge down the cliff face. Todd's anchor slings had been attached with too much slack, so the fall pulled him off the ledge and the impact force of the team's fall shock-loaded his three anchor nuts so hard that it broke a crack edge, allowing one nut to pull out. He was hanging over the void from two rather small nuts. Needless to say, these nerve-shattered climbers rappelled off the climb without completing the route.

## Fall Severity

The severity of a fall is determined by the duration of time that impact forces must be resisted. While a long fall and a short fall may have the same fall factor and resulting impact force, the longer fall will be more severe on the falling climber's body and the protection system because the impact force must be resisted for a longer period. While the leader's body, the protection piece holding the fall, and the belay anchor may sustain impact forces for short periods without damage, they may not be able to endure these impact forces for greater lengths of time. It makes sense to place intermediate protection pieces to limit fall distance.

---

## Impact Forces, the Belayer, and the Belay

Above, we looked at impact forces for static belays, but for leader falls it is desirable to have the dynamic belays that are provided by most belay devices. This section examines the role of the belayer and belay technique. If you simply grip the leader's rope in your hand without an additional friction surface, such as your waist, you might be able to hold a maximum of 50 pounds before the rope was pulled through your hand. You could also hold the rope loosely, so that it would run through your hand at a tensional force of less than 50 pounds. But as we have seen, a falling climber generates forces of hundreds and even thousands of pounds.

No matter how strong you are, you cannot hold a fall statically—without the rope running—above limits imposed by the friction of the belay brake as magnified by hand strength. Once the force of a fall exceeds these static limits, the rope will begin to run dynamically through the belay brake. A few belay devices purposely lock the rope while other designs lock up accidentally; these lockups place maximum stress on protection and should not be used on climbs without bombproof protection.

The energy of the fall is absorbed first by rope stretch during the static portion of the belay and then by friction as the rope runs through the brake or over protection-system carabiners during the dynamic part of the belay. The impact force of a fall will reach a maximum when the rope stretches to its limit at the end of the static portion of the belay, and will remain there until the fall is arrested.

What is the effect of the combined belay brake and hand strength on the maximum impact force that you can hold with different belay brakes? Many belayers use a Sticht plate without a spring with the belayed rope passing around a single carabiner. This combination has a braking force of about 440 to 500 pounds when used with a dry rope. If a fall produces a greater tensional force, the rope will run dynamically through the plate until friction over carabiners in the rope system absorbs the excess force. Other belay devices work in a similar manner although they have different maximum braking forces.

If you use a belay plate differently than described above, you can hold a larger maximum impact force. For example, the Sticht plate without a spring can hold a maximum of about 730 pounds statically if you belay using the plate with a dry rope, one carabiner, and a body belay. If you add a second carabiner, the additional friction increases the maximum force that you can hold to about 1,100 pounds. (In practice, there is little reason to use any belay plate in these combined modes since it creates too static a brake.) Note that if the rope is wet, the belay brake can hold about 200 pounds of force less for each of the belay methods described above before becoming dynamic.[3]

The maximum tensional force possible to hold, neglecting other sources of friction in the belay chain, is given below for a number of belay brakes.[4]

Figure-eight descender in sport mode: 200 pounds

Waist belay: 180 to 240 pounds

Sticht plate with spring: 340 to 400 pounds

Sticht plate without spring: 440 to 500 pounds

Munter hitch: 290 to 590 pounds

Air Traffic Controller: 600 pounds

Of course, the leader usually puts in intermediate protection, which increases the amount of friction in the system. This additional friction, along with the tensional force provided by the belay brake, determines the maximum impact force experienced by a falling leader and the protection piece catching a fall. The running protection limits fall distance for the leader, and works with the

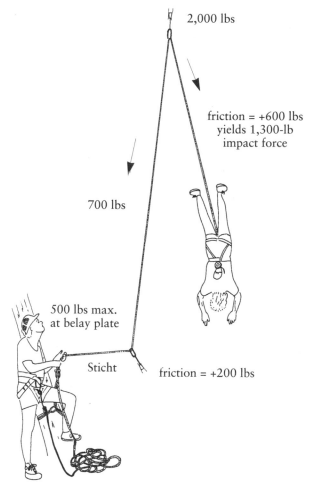

2,000 lbs

friction = +600 lbs yields 1,300-lb impact force

700 lbs

500 lbs max. at belay plate

Sticht

friction = +200 lbs

*Figure 11-4. Tensional Forces in the Belay Chain:* Starting at the belayer, each time the rope turns through a carabiner or runs over a corner of rock, the tension in the rope is higher on the far side. After Ed Leeper, 1980.

entire length of the rope and the entire protection system to absorb the energy of a fall.

### Magnified Impact Forces in the Belay Protection System

If you use a mechanical belay plate, you might be able to hold a maximal tensional force of about 500 pounds before the rope begins to slip through the brake. This maximal tensional force supplied by the belay brake is magnified throughout the belay system by friction of the rope over carabiners and perhaps around rock corners. For example, as shown in Figure 11-4, the initial 500-pound tensional force increases by about 40 percent, or 200 pounds, due to friction at the 90-degree turn in the rope at the first protection piece. By addition, this creates a 700-pound maximal force on the far side of the 90-degree turn. At the 180-degree turn, friction almost doubles the tension in the rope and adds 600 pounds of force, to make a 1,300-pound maximal impact force on the climber.

It is important to consider the tensional forces on the protection point that holds the fall. The belayer produces a tensional force on the protection piece directed back toward the belay, whereas the falling leader produces a tensional force on this same protection piece directed toward the falling leader. The sum of tensional forces on the protection piece holding the fall is approximately twice the force experienced by the falling climber. Thus, in Figure 11-4, the protection piece holding the fall experiences maximal forces of 1,300 pounds + 700 pounds = 2,000 pounds.

A similar analysis, using this simplified protection system, shows that the impact force on this protection piece varies widely for three common belay brakes. It reaches a maximum of approximately 1,000 pounds for a waist belay, 2,000 pounds for a slot plate such as a Sticht plate, and about 2,400 pounds for the Munter hitch brake in its most static mode.

### Implications of Belay Technique

The lower impact force of the waist belay results from the fact that first rope stretch and then sliding friction absorb the energy of a fall. The

falling climber travels farther down the cliff, however, before this energy is absorbed, with the added danger of hitting a ledge. If you use a belay that locks up in a severe fall, rope stretch without rope slippage is called on to absorb the energy of the fall. This force may rip out the protection piece holding the fall. Belay brakes that produce essentially static belays may also create obvious or hidden rope damage in a severe fall. For example, use of the Munter hitch has caused burned rope sheaths in test falls as short as 4 feet[5], and some belay plates can cut or damage the rope in a severe fall. On the other hand, most of the time our belaying techniques and rope systems work and let us down gently. Belay plates such the Sticht plate with a spring prevent lockup by design. You can prevent most belay plates from locking up by placing two carabiners on the rope between the plate and the belay carabiner. A clear advantage of the Munter hitch and belay plates is that they allow the belayer to control the rope easily during a fall.

The holding power of a nut used for protection depends on the area of contact between the nut and the rock, the breaking strength of the nut, the mechanical strength of the rock, and how well you place the nut. If the nut pulls out, fall length will be farther. With "average" protection we do not expect it to pull out because of the belay plate, but the potential is there if you use marginal protection and take a big fall. Smaller pieces of protection used in competent rock or larger pieces of protection in less competent rock should always be considered marginal. Marginal protection should also be considered in reference to the maximal tensional force that you can apply at the belay. If you switch from a belay brake with a low static limit to one with a high static limit, you also need to reconsider your definition of what is marginal. You can use dynamic slings on marginal protection to limit the tensional force experienced by the protection piece holding a fall, as described in Chapter 7. The Yates Screamer activates at 550 pounds of force as bar tacks rip, and no force applied to it can reach higher levels until all bar tacks are ripped out. This means that if you use a dynamic sling with a marginal piece of protection, the protection itself will not experience higher tensional forces as long as there are bar tacks to rip. Once all bar tacks are ripped, the sling behaves like an ordinary runner and directly passes tensional forces to the protection piece.

## Energy Absorption in Real Protection Systems

So far we have looked at the belay brake and friction around system carabiners as absorbers of energy in climbing systems. There are more ways in which energy gets absorbed in a real fall. Some of the energy gets absorbed in deforming the belayer's body and some of the energy goes into tightening the knot. In a simple system, without inter-mediate friction points and a static belay, the amount of energy that goes into knot tightening can be as much as 50 percent of the total.[6] This is why knots get so tight in a real fall that the leader needs help untying, or in extreme cases has to cut the knot away. It also explains why you should untie and retie your knots after a fall, if it is safe to do so, to reconstitute this part of the shock-absorption system.

Undesirable accidental circumstances some-times change the distribution of the energy absorption of the rope, belay brake, and protection system during a fall. For example, if the rope gets caught behind a rock flake or in a crack during a fall (Figure 11-5), this new point serves as the brake; the original belay brake is no longer effective. The force of the fall is taken up by rope stretch and protection between the point where the

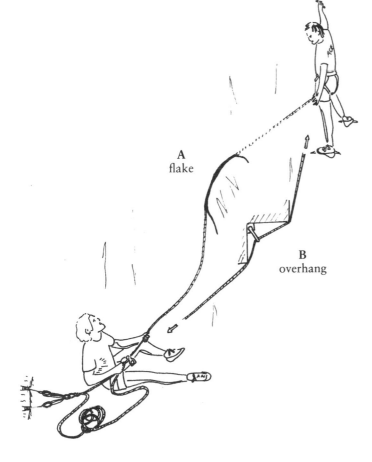

A
flake

B
overhang

*Figure 11-5. **Rope Drag and Tension**: At A the rope is stuck behind a flake; at B the rope catches on the edges of an overhang, creating friction that can be eliminated by using a longer sling on the carabiner. The rope on the climber's side of the obstructions must absorb most of the energy of a fall.*

rope is caught and the fallen climber, rather than the belayer and the climber. Since there is now less rope involved, impact forces are correspondingly higher. The protection pieces may fail and the rope may be cut. Rope drag on overhangs or corners produces a similar but less dramatic effect than a stuck rope. Rope drag adds friction to the system and concentrates the force of the fall in the rope and protection system on the side of the leader—clearly an undesirable situation.

## References for Future Reading

Cannon, Neil. 1985. Air voyagers. *Climbing.* 88:54.

Coats, Larry. 1990. Product interview with Dick Newell. *Rock & Ice.* 36.

Gadd, Will. 1993. Toys: Belay and descending devices. *Rock & Ice.* 54:106–108.

Graydon, Don, ed. 1992. *Mountaineering: The freedom of the hills.* Fifth edition. Seattle: The Mountaineers.

Leeper, Ed. 1980. Belaying: Forces and stopping distances. *Summit.* 25(6):6–12.

Loughman, Michael. 1981. *Learning to rock climb.* San Francisco: Sierra Club.

May, W. G. 1973. *Mountain search and rescue techniques.* Boulder, Colorado: Rocky Mountain Rescue Group, Inc.

March, Bill. 1977. The Sticht belay plate. *Summit.* 28–31.

Microys, Helmut F. 1977. Climbing ropes. *American Alpine Journal.* 21(51):130–147.

_____. 1984. A short course in rope physics—a rebuttal. *Climbing.* 85:61–62.

Peters, Ed, ed. 1982. *Mountaineering: The freedom of the hills.* Fourth edition. Seattle: The Mountaineers.

Robbins, Royal. 1979. Climbing rope myths. *Summit.* 25(1):12–17, 23–25.

---

## Endnotes

1. See Microys, 1984. The belay for this measured fall was a firm one and held up to 700 to 800 pounds of force before slipping. In a longer version of this article obtained from the author, the author quotes an example from Schubert (P. Schubert, "Zwillingsseile-Seiltechnik der Zukunft," *Der Bergsteiger,* October, 1982, pp. 77–79), involving the most severe fall possible—15 meters of rope and a 30-meter fall. Rope slippage measured 5.5 meters. When combined with a 7 percent impact elongation (15 meters x .07 = 1.05 meters), the distance added to the fall by rope slippage and impact elongation was 5.5 + 1.05 = 6.55 meters. The total distance fallen was 36.55 meters.

2. The discussion here and in the section headed "Fall Severity" follows the work of Microys, 1977. Any errors of interpretation are mine.

3. See March, 1977, for Sticht-plate braking values.

4. Many of these values are taken from the Ontario Rock Climbing Association's *Rock Climbing Safety Manual* and are based on drop tests conducted by the association. Values for the figure-eight descender come from Gadd, 1993.

5. See Leeper, 1980.

6. See Cannon, 1985.

# PART THREE

# Ice, Mountains, and Climbers

# Movement on Snow and Ice

## Snow and Ice Climbing Basics

The part of this book devoted to ice climbing assumes that you know the basics presented in the previous chapters on knots, harnesses, belaying, and rappelling. Although skills learned in rock climbing are generally helpful, specific movement and leading skills on snow and ice differ from those on rock. In rock climbing you adapt your body to the rock by using available holds, whereas in snow and ice climbing you can use an axe to create holds where you want them. Snow and ice climbing takes place in a colder environment and requires greater attention to protective clothing. Snow and ice climbing protection differs from rock-climbing protection, but linking protection into anchor systems and understanding the forces on these systems remains the same. If you take the time to master new snow and ice climbing skills, you will be able to move quickly through multi-pitch long sections of easy technical terrain. Later on, mastery of these same basics will make climbing steep ice and even thin ice easier and will enable you to make a safe descent.

## Dressing for Snow and Ice Climbing

Snow and ice climbing take place under environmental conditions that vary from very warm and moist to very cold and dry. What you wear is important because it can hinder or promote heat retention. You can adapt to the range of conditions by wearing layers of clothing. For the layer next to your skin choose synthetic underwear tops and bottoms made of polypropylene or newer synthetic fabrics that do not absorb odors as much as polypropylene does. These fabrics wick perspiration generated in even the coldest weather to the next layer and eventually to the outside air. Cotton is a poor fabric for winter underwear because it absorbs moisture easily, cooling as it conducts body heat away from your skin. Even wool, an old standby, conducts more body heat away from your skin than modern synthetics. The second layer can be synthetic or wool: synthetic pile is popular. Wear one or two layers of sweaters and a pair of pants. The outer layer should always be a wind shell, since wind makes you feel colder.

Because snow and ice climbing require active movement, three layers of clothing will keep you warm—and possibly even hot—at winter temperatures of 20 degrees Fahrenheit and below. To avoid overheating during the hike to the climb, wear only two layers. When you stop, you might even take off another layer for a few minutes to vent excess moisture before you cool down. Then dress warmly for the climb. You will feel colder while you stand around to belay, and it is difficult and can be dangerous to put on more clothes while on small stances. In very cold conditions consider taking along a sleeveless vest that you can put on over your wind shell when you stop.

Most snow and ice climbers wear a hat and add a balaclava made of synthetic fabric when it is cold. If you plan to go above the tree line, purchase a face mask that you can don without removing

your climbing helmet. These masks cover the lower part of your face and fasten behind your head with Velcro, rather than going under your helmet and hat. Carry the mask in an outside pocket of your pack for those few but desperate times when you pop up into wind from a sheltered climb.

On long climbs take along food to provide fuel for your body to keep producing heat. Do not expect to be able to sit down to a leisurely lunch in the dead of winter, or even to stop to get into your pack during the climb. Carry food with a high fat content—such as a peanut-butter sandwich, nuts, or cheese—in your pockets so you can eat while belaying. You might also want something like candy, chocolate, or a granola bar to supply immediate calories. Do not forget to drink water: you will lose two to six quarts of water by normal respiration and sweating during a day of activity. If you do not replace this water, expect to experience dehydration, muscle soreness, fatigue, and general lassitude.

### Helmets

Helmets (Figure 12-1) help protect your head if you fall or are hit by falling rock, ice, or equipment dropped by parties overhead. Helmets can keep your head from directly striking ice or rock in a fall and suffering injury, but they can also be responsible for injuries suffered in certain accidents, such as might happen in a backward fall.[1] In the end it is your individual responsibility to decide if wearing a helmet makes sense for you. A quick look at popular rock-climbing areas shows that most rock climbers today forgo helmets. They may understand that this is not absolutely safe. They choose not to wear a helmet when rock climbing because a bare head is cooler and less cumbersome, and to a certain extent because that is how everyone else climbs. On difficult gymnastic climbs, helmets can make balance difficult because they push you away from the rock. Many climbers believe that they can remain upright and protect their head in a fall. In contrast, a similar survey of winter climbing areas indicates that alpine rock and snow and ice

## A Clothing List for Snow and Ice Climbing

### Head

• Balaclava—These hoods cover the head and neck. A thin polypropylene balaclava is useful as a liner.

• Wool hat.

• Helmet—UIAA-approved for climbing, to protect yourself if you fall or are hit by falling ice.

• Face mask—The Masque brand has a Velcro fastener and goes on quickly in emergencies.

• Contact lenses—If you need corrective lenses, contacts give you better vision in a snowstorm (you do not want fogged glasses at a crux). In pleasant winter conditions, antifogging coatings keep eyeglasses from misting.

### Upper Body

• Foundation undergarment—Underwear of synthetic fiber such as polypropylene or of wool for your upper body.

• Wool or polypro shirts or sweaters—One lightweight and one heavy, to wear over your underwear.

• Synthetic pile jacket or parka—To wear over the shirt or sweater.

• Windbreaker—To wear as outer layer. It should have zipper vents to regulate heat.

### Hands

• Thin gloves (polypro)—These allow you manual dexterity in cold weather.

• Two pairs of light- to medium-weight wool or synthetic mittens—Wear one pair inside shells and keep the other pair as a spare.

• Shell mittens—Medium weight mittens keep your hands warm in most conditions as long as they are dry; shells help keep them dry. Wearing mittens and shells together, you should be able to grip an axe comfortably, and your hands will be protected if they strike the ice. Instead of mittens, you can use:

• High-tech gloves and liners—Made of synthetic material, designed for ice climbing.

### Lower Body

• Long underwear—Made of wool or polypropylene, as a foundation garment.

• Wool or synthetic pile pants.

• Windproof pants—To wear over all. A full-length zipper allows you to don or shed them easily even when you are wearing crampons.

### Feet

• Stiff-soled double boots—Designed for ice climbing, these are expensive but you probably should consider the $300 to $400 spent toward safeguarding your toes from frostbite a good buy.

• Gaiters—These keep snow out of your boots, insulate your lower legs, and hold in the bottoms of your pants so that you do not catch them with crampon points.

### Packs

• Medium-size alpine climbing pack—Allows you to carry personal and team gear as you approach the climb and on the climb itself. The pack should be small enough not to inhibit climbing but large enough to store the gear that you need for a day without requiring a lot of time to tie it on. Many packs are designed specifically for ice climbing.

Figure 12-1. **Helmets: A**—The Face Nord, a lightweight polyamid plastic helmet. **B**—The hand-laid fiberglass Joe Brown, used by many outdoor programs.

climbers accept the advantages of wearing a helmet.

It is almost impossible to avoid being hit by ice falling from above, either knocked off accidentally by a climber or naturally. If you knock ice off from the climb, yell "Ice!" to warn those below. If you hear the call, look down, not up, so that the ice hits the top of your helmet and not your face. After you have been hit a few times, you will learn not to belay or stand underneath other climbers.

Helmets used for rock, ice, and snow climbing should carry a UIAA certification that indicates that they are designed and tested for climbing.

Heavyweight helmets are made of hand-laid fiberglass; lightweight designs use molded polyamid plastics, Kevlar, and carbon fiber. Schools and outdoor programs usually choose heavyweight helmets, which offer maximum head coverage. Lightweight models are a good choice for the climber who would rather not wear a helmet. All helmets have adjustable headbands that allow you to wear a wool hat or go bareheaded underneath. Many models have ventilation holes to help make the helmet cooler.

### Mitts

Climbing snow and ice can be hard on the hands because of the cold and dampness, and the tools have at least some metal parts that conduct

heat away from your hands. Consider that on steep ice you are pumped with adrenaline and swing the axe with all of your strength. Your hand overgrips the tool and your fingers and knuckles get smashed between the axe shaft and the ice. The water in the damp glove conducts heat away from your hand, and your wrist leash cuts off circulation. At the top of the climb, in a state of incipient frostbite, both blood and feeling painfully return to your hands. How do you avoid this unpleasant side effect of ice climbing?

Mitts must not only protect your hands from cold and damp, they must also serve as a cushion when you inadvertently smash your hands into the ice. Most climbers use a mitten shell with a liner mitt. There are a number of commercially available "dry" shells. Shells should be durable and preferably inexpensive, although technologically advanced shells, which work well, may be worth the money. Canadian Army leather shells are the best of the army surplus; after being broken in, they have a palm that grips the axe well. Liner mitts need not be very thick to protect you from the cold, but they do need to be dry. Wet liners conduct heat much more rapidly than dry liners. Carry spare dry hand coverings in an accessible place, such as the kangaroo pouch of a cagoule, and change liners when they are damp. This precaution is especially important for steep ice, where you might grip the axe tightly and accentuate heat loss by conduction. Belaying often squeezes water out of the climbing rope and into your mitt. Try belaying with a second set of liners or gloves to keep the mitt combination dry during belays and give you added dexterity. You can switch hand coverings quickly and keep belaying gloves in the kangaroo pouch along with the spare dry pair of mitten liners.

---

## Crampons

English climbers began following snow climbs in lines of steps cut in the ice by guides with their ice axes while wearing nailed boots. By the end of the 1800s, climbers were using flexible four-point crampons, and in 1908 the Englishman Oskar Eckenstein designed a flexible ten-point crampon, which evoked protests that it gave an unfair advantage to the climber. Once Eckenstein worked out the technique of flat-footing, there was no longer a need to cut steps. Today flat-footing is called the *Eckenstein technique*, after its originator, or the *French technique*, after climbers who adapted it well to climbing.

Laurent Grivel, in the early 1930s, added two front points projecting forward, producing the flexible twelve-point crampon. This innovation gave rise to the front-pointing technique that became identified with Austrian climbers, who adapted it to the hard ice of the eastern Alps. Climbers today can have the most fun and move most efficiently by using each of these techniques alone and in combination where appropriate. On any given climb, the technique used can change frequently, allowing the climber to move in a more efficient manner in keeping with the terrain.

In the United States Yvon Chouinard developed a rigid crampon to replace the flexible crampon. Rigid crampons, which underwent yearly refinement, reduced front-point vibration that shatters ice. However, to prevent breaking these crampons it was necessary to wear them on boots that did not flex. In 1976, an ascent by Mike Lowe began an evolution of the Foot-Fang. There were "bolted to the bottom of his ski boots several jagged strips of chrome moly having needle-like front points that resembled nothing so much as the fangs of a pit-viper."[2] The Foot-Fang is an absolutely rigid crampon used by many to climb steep ice. Crampons continue to evolve, and current modular designs offer interchangeable monopoints and vertically oriented front-points.

When you start to climb on snow and ice, you have to learn to trust your crampons to provide security on ice. Just as you learn that rock-climbing shoes stick when you smear on a friction slab or edge on small footholds, so you learn how to use crampons for different kinds of footholds in flat, sloping, or steep ice. Figure 12-2 illustrates

SMC rigid

Foot-Fang

Salewa flexible

*Figure 12-2. **Rigid and Flexible Crampons***

three crampons: SMC rigid, Lowe Foot-Fang, and Salewa flexible. Most crampons have ten points perpendicular to the sole of the foot; some have shorter points in between for added security in snow. The ten points are used in *flat-footing*, the technique used to walk and climb on flat to gently sloping inclines. The two points directed forward in the plane of the boot sole plus the two frontmost of the ten points perpendicular to the sole are used in *front-pointing*, the technique used on steep ice.

SMC and Foot-Fang crampons represent two different approaches to crampon design. Both are rigid crampons especially suitable for climbing steep ice. You must wear the SMC rigid design on a very stiff boot because any flexing of the boot will work-harden the crampon and break it. The Foot-Fang is very strong and rigid in itself and does not depend on the boot for its rigidity or strength. The frontmost points of the Foot-Fang are vertical (similar to the points of ice hand tools). In contrast, the frontmost points on the SMC crampon are horizontal. Some climbers prefer the horizontal orientation for mixed climbing—they place the front points on small positive edges of rock. Both kinds of crampons work well; try both, and choose the one that suits you best.

Think about weight as well as rigidity in choosing crampons. If you intend to climb alpine snow or ice, you might consider using a lightweight flexible crampon on a mountaineering boot that will flex as you walk. In alpine settings approaches are often long, climbs are usually not as steep as modern roadside test pieces, and a lightweight flexible crampon and boot work well together.

Crampons are attached to your boots with straps that come in sets of two or four. They are commonly made of reinforced neoprene, which resists water rot. When the toe strap is one continuous piece, it begins on the outside of the instep, crosses the forefoot to the inside toe post, passes to the outside toe post, crosses to the inside instep post, and returns to the outside instep post (Figure 12-3A).

When you pass a strap through the toe posts, do so from the outside to the inside. After going through the post, pass the strap forward of itself. This technique will help prevent the strap from slipping forward over the toe when you frontpoint. If the strap slips, the slack can allow the crampon to fall off. This happened in the middle of my first ice lead and need not happen to you.

Feeding the crampon straps in such a complicated manner can be difficult at the best of times, but is particularly difficult when it is cold and your hands lose the required manual dexterity. Wear thin polypropylene gloves to protect your hands without sacrificing dexterity. Better yet, use speed straps with prethreaded toe straps (Figure 12-3B). One long strap passes through a ring or plate in the middle of the toe segment, to the instep post, where it fastens. This system significantly cuts time

and reduces the effort required to put on crampons. The Foot-Fang shown in Figure 12-2 has the quickest strap system. Toe and heel bails attach to solid boot flanges and act as step-in bindings.

Adjust new front points, as illustrated in Figure 12-3, so that they extend in front of the boot approximately half their length—that is, half the distance between the end of the front point and the base of the first vertical point. This position should be correct for normal ice. You can make the front points longer for honeycombed ice and shorter for thin ice.

As the forward-directed front points wear, file them—on their upper surface only—to their original shape. Do not file the lower surface of these front points. Do not use a grinding wheel, which can easily destroy the temper of the metal. You

Figure 12-3. Adjusting Crampon Straps: A—One continuous toe strap; B—Speed straps.

cannot climb hard ice with dull points, so you should keep the points sharp. On the other hand, if you dull your crampons by walking on rocks and climb frequently, you will soon file them away if you sharpen for every climb. With a bit of experience you will soon learn when it is critical to have freshly sharpened points. You can also file the ten bottom points to their original shape.

### Footwear

Modern ice-climbing boots largely prevent the cold-related injuries of previous generations, but the potential for cold injury remains. The boots have evolved from ski-boot technology and usually feature a hard nylon outer boot with a woolen or foam inner boot. Use the woolen inner boot in normal winter ice-climbing temperatures. A foam inner boot is very warm and used for extreme cold conditions such as climbing at high altitude. Most ice-climbing boots are stiff, so as to form a stable platform for the foot as you climb steep ice or kick a step in snow. They are relatively high, to support the lower leg. The very features that make boots work well for climbing steep ice make them somewhat difficult to walk in: their stiff soles have only a small amount of curvature, preventing the foot from rolling forward with each step. Some ice boots hinge to allow greater flexibility for walking.

Avoid walking directly on a climbing-hut floor in inner boots because water and abrasion will quickly damage them, and they are expensive. Take pile booties or sneakers for lounging in the hut or quick runs to the outhouse.

One of the chief dangers for snow and ice climbers is frostbite to the feet. Frostbite can be caused by cutting off the blood supply, for instance by wearing too many socks under boots with flexible uppers or by tightening crampon straps too much. If the boot flexes while you are front-pointing, the straps dig into the soft upper with each placement and cut off blood to your toes. Crampons that do not use strap systems, such as Foot-Fangs, do not cause this problem. In extreme cold, you need to take care even with modern double boots. The microclimate surrounding your feet is more important than ambient air temperature—

your feet can be at risk when you do not consider it to be excessively cold at the level of your face and hands.

Conduction—heat loss produced by touching cold objects such as metal—also causes frostbite. Crampons will conduct heat away from the foot just as steel-toed boots do. In very cold weather, insert a sole-shaped piece of Ensolite between boot and crampon to prevent some heat loss. Some crampons have a nylon plate for the same purpose; this plate also helps prevent wet snow from balling under the foot. Modern boot liners, particularly those of Aveolite foam, and overboots also prevent heat loss by conduction.

In otherwise fit individuals, there are two relatively common conditions, among others, that may contribute to frostbite. Cardiovascular circulatory problems, either organic or drug-related, can produce reduced blood circulation in the feet and toes. Twenty percent of the population has the condition called *Morton's Foot*, when the second toe of the foot is longer than the big toe. If the second toe touches the end of an otherwise well-fitting boot, it will get cold and may be frostbitten. If you have Morton's Foot, choose boots made on a pattern that gives your toe plenty of room. Be aware of your feet: loosen crampon straps, stamp your feet, and take aggressive action whenever they begin to feel cold.

### Flat-footing (Eckenstein or French Technique)

To walk in crampons you need to walk deliberately, picking up and putting down each foot carefully, even on flat ground. You can never shuffle because you may catch a point and fall. You cannot run in crampons without risking a broken ankle if a point sticks unexpectedly. I once saw a climber break into a run on flat ground, relieved at having successfully descended an exposed gully. A crampon point stuck into a tree root and I heard his ankle snap as his body raced forward of his stuck foot. Do not let this happen to you.

Novice ice climbers always begin flat-footing sessions hesitantly, but in the course of a day become very comfortable moving around on the

Most ice climbers sometime in their climbing career find that their hands turn cold and numb, followed by a flood of pain upon rewarming. Once you have experienced this miserable condition you will try everything that you can think of to keep your extremities warm: wearing dry gloves, warm boots, and a hat; drinking lots of water to avoid dehydration; eating high-calorie foods; and hanging from your wrist leash to avoid overgripping your axe on steep climbs, since overgripping cuts off the circulation to your hands. Perhaps none of these measures will keep your hands warm. A few unlucky people experience cold-induced agony whenever they go ice climbing.

When most of us get cold hands, our sympathetic nervous system sends out a message to open up more capillaries and send more warm blood to the fingers. The capillaries of people with Raynaud's (pronounced "ray nose") never get this message and remain clamped down. Their extremities turn white, bluish, and numb; when the extremities warm up, they tingle, burn, and throb. If you have experienced this problem while your climbing partners show no sign of distress, you may have Raynaud's Disease.

Raynaud's affects 5 to 10 percent of the total population, but women are five times as likely as men to suffer from it. People who subject their hands to stress—pocket-pulling rock climbers and knuckle-bashing ice climbers could certainly qualify—are more likely to develop the condition.

There is hope for long-time sufferers. The United States Army has done research on the subject and developed a 13-step program by which you can recondition blood vessels subject to Raynaud's. You will find further information in an article by Dorcas Miller in the October/November 1990 issue of *Climbing*. Dorcas explains the reconditioning program and describes how she treated herself successfully.

ice. So confident are they that they forget ice is slippery when they take crampons off.

Begin by walking on a nearly flat stream with a few gentle bulges or slopes. Flat-foot by placing all ten crampon points perpendicular to the ice (Figure 12-4A). Stamp your feet to get the points in. Do not try edging, with only the uphill-side points in actual contact with the ice (Figure 12-4B): the points probably will not hold, the crampon will skate, and you will fall. If you use crampons with parallel sides, such as Foot-Fangs, it may be possible to *hedge* (Jeff Lowe's term) by backing off from the traditional flat-foot stance by about 15 degrees. The idea is to get the uphill row of points all the way in while the downhill row rests on the ice. This position does not torture the ankles as much, but you can still skate. As you flat-foot on ice, your feet are farther apart than when you walk in street shoes on a rug. As

you go up slight inclines, splay your feet outward like a duck (*en canard*).

There are two techniques for flat-footing on slopes. First, place your foot on contour, or parallel to the slope, so both the toe and heel of your foot are at the same level and your body is sideways to the slope. Second, roll your ankle away from the slope. This movement rotates the bottom crampon points into proper position. In practice, consciously think about hip movement away from the slope, since your leg, ankle, and foot are attached and must follow hip movement (Figure 12-4C). Flat-footing is similar both in body position and movement to traversing friction slabs.

You need *dynamic balance* for flat-footing, just as you need it for ordinary walking. When you flat-foot and when you walk, you ordinarily begin in a position of balance, move dynamically through a position of imbalance, and return to a

A
correct

B
incorrect

*Figure 12-4. Flat-footing: A— Ten points in contact. B— Trying to edge. C—Body posture while flat-footing on a slope. The climber is rolling his hip out to get all ten points on each crampon into the ice.*

C

position of balance. It is possible, as many beginners can attest, to stand on one leg, but this stance requires much effort on the part of your leg muscles. Moving through the imbalance position requires commitment so that there is enough momentum to get to the other side. The more commitment, the less leg energy required.

It is customary for beginners to have someone spot them with an outstretched arm, to try to protect the head in case of a fall. Spotters should beware of getting caught by the points of the crampons. (If you are spotting, stay off to the side or ready to leap away from those crampon points. The best way to assist is to give feedback concerning whether the crampon is on contour. Remind climbers to roll their hips out in order to get all ten points into the ice.)

The basic movement sequence of flat-footing on gentle slopes is to move directly up or down the slope duck-foot fashion (Figure 12-5), a movement termed *pied en canard.* On water ice (see Chapter 14), pure flat-foot technique—incorporating the use of an axe for balance—is most useful for moving efficiently over long stretches of low-angle ice.

### Front-pointing (Austrian Technique)

Front-pointing is the technique of moving with crampons on steeper ice. Although we often speak

*Figure 12-5. Duck-Foot Walking on Gentle Snow and Ice Slopes*

*Figure 12-6. **The Four Front Points:** Hold the crampon horizontally by focusing on heel elevation in relation to the front points. Chip small platforms for the two forward-directed points; the two frontmost bottom points contact the ice.*

of two front points on each crampon, there are actually four points on each crampon involved in front-pointing, as you can see in Figure 12-6: the two forward-directed points parallel to the boot sole, and the two frontmost points most nearly perpendicular to the boot sole. When all four of these points are well planted in the ice, they will not shear out, and they form a stable platform on which to stand. In order to keep these points in the ice, you must keep your heel down so the sole of a rigid boot is horizontal.

Front-pointing involves short, gentle swinging kicks in a motion that chips small platforms for each of the front points. To kick a platform, swing your leg normally directly in front of you, at a

selected target. If there is a natural foothold, use it as long as it does not pull you out of balance. Do not choose the platform position at random. Take advantage of any ripple in the ice, even one as small as a fraction of an inch, to enlarge as a front-point platform. Hard swings tend to work-harden, or embrittle, the crampon points as they bounce off the ice, and to break away the small front-point ice platforms formed by a previous swing. When you climb on thin, iced-over rock, delicately attached ice columns, or steep ice, the ability to chip platforms for the front points becomes critical. These platforms allow you to get weight onto your legs and off your arms. Find a gentle bulge that is not too high and see how much force you need to form these platforms.

When climbing on front points, balance is important. If you boulder without hand tools, you will need to take small steps in order to stay in balance. This movement is very similar to the balance and small steps required on rock when only small holds are available. If you have large handholds on rock, or use hand tools on ice, you can always

Figure 12-7. *Front-pointing on Moderately Angled Ice.* **A**—*Push your upper body away from the ice and hold the bottom of your boot and crampon horizontal. Arrows show that rotation of the knee causes the boot heel and crampon to lift or drop.* **B**—*The front points and crampons positioned correctly in a horizontal plane.* **C**—*Front-directed horizontal points shear out of the ice when the heel lifts, and the climber falls.* **D**—*The horizontal front points leave the ice, and the frontmost bottom points shear when you drop your heel. The climber can fall again, but this rarely happens in practice.*

incorrect

incorrect

lean back on these and take larger steps. The analogies with rock climbing go further. You must keep your body upright and away from the ice. On low-angle ice, push your upper body away from the ice much as on a low-angle slab climb on rock (Figure 12-7A).

Knee position helps keep the sole of the foot and crampon horizontal (heel-down position) because your knee is connected to the top of the lower leg and in turn to the ankle and foot. Bend the knee slightly toward the ice surface to keep the foot horizontal (Figure 12-7A, B). If you consciously focus on your knee to gain the heel-down position, your foot, ankle, leg, and knee rotate in a natural way to keep the front points in proper position.

Climbing with a lifted heel may produce a fall (Figure 12-7C). Initially, the two frontmost bottom points on each crampon lift from the ice, reducing the stable platform. With further rotation, the two

forward-directed points of each crampon will shear away the small ice platform on which you are standing (Figure 12-7C), and you will fall. Alternatively, if your heel is too far below the front points, the two forward-directed points can lose contact with the ice and the two frontmost perpendicular points will shear from the ice (Figure 12-7D). In practice, it is somewhat difficult to lower your heels this far. Experiment with the various positions—heel-up, heel-down, and heel very low—to get an idea of when your points will shear and when they won't. Of course, practice only a few inches above the ground so that you will not get hurt when the points shear.

To down-climb with front points you extend your leg and kick, stiff-legged, as though you were kicking a football. If you want to move your right foot downward, extend the entire right leg and swing the leg as a unit without flexing the knee too much. At the same time, keep your upper body upright so you can see what is happening to your foot.

Climbing with front points requires what at first may seem to be strange body positions. The two forward-directed front points of many crampons follow the curve of the boot, making it necessary to angle your feet to place the front points perpendicular to the ice. Even parallel-sided crampons require similar, but less extreme, positions.

How you hold your feet varies with the geometry of the ice surface. For flat vertical surfaces, you must move your heels apart and assume a slightly duck-footed stance; this stance brings the knees together. This strange knock-kneed position becomes pronounced when you climb steep, sharply curved convex bulges, which are among the most strenuous ice climbs. It is harder to stand in balance on front points, and more effort has to go into hand-tool placements and upper-body strength.

On concave surfaces, bring your heels together to maintain the proper front-point angle with the ice; this position will seem relatively natural. The heel-together stance becomes more pronounced as slight concave surfaces turn into right-angle corners, which are climbed by stemming from wall to wall. Stemming allows you to get more weight over your feet, and generally makes these climbs less strenuous.

The next time you approach an ice climb, look for a surface that curves inward. Only a few degrees of curvature make a line up this surface less strenuous than a dead-vertical wall. Avoid surfaces that curve outward unless your objective is to pump-out on ice. Indeed, top-roping outward curving bulges is a good workout.

Front-pointing, once mastered, feels very secure. However, it has some drawbacks. In the front-pointing position, the points act as a fulcrum around which the body rotates. If the crampons are flexible ones on flexible boots, you resist this rotation largely with your calf muscles and to a lesser extent with your foot muscles. The more rigid the boot-crampon combination, the less muscular effort required to resist rotation, but if the crampons are absolutely rigid, they will be heavier, calling for more work by your upper leg muscles. Thus, although manufacturers have attempted to close this gap, you must choose among boot-crampon combinations that emphasize low weight versus high rigidity. Your decision may be influenced by whether you climb steep ice by the roadside or hike long distances to do alpine climbs.

Whether you are learning to front-point or helping someone also to master the technique, here is a checklist of principles to remember:

• Kick the ice with short, not overly hard, swings to form front-point platforms.

• Take short steps.

• Form a horizontal platform by keeping your boot heel down. Keep your upper body away from the ice. This position will help prevent front-point rotation in a vertical plane and allow you to see the position of your heel in relation to the front points.

• Bring your heels together or push them apart. The front points need to be perpendicular to the ice surface in a horizontal plane. An insecure placement results if only the front points on the inside or outside of each crampon are in the ice.

• Down-climb with a rigid leg and an upright body position that allows you to see all four front points and heel.

### Combined Technique (Pied Troisième)

Combining flat-footing and front-pointing takes advantage of the strengths of both techniques. Figure 12-8 shows a climber using the combined technique. His right foot is in the flat-foot position; his left foot is front-pointing. His arms are pushing his upper body away from the ice to keep his weight over his foot. On his next step, he can alternate and flat-foot with his left foot to give his left calf muscle a rest.

You can flat-foot when the incline of the ice varies from low angle to near vertical, and when there are one-step bulges. On low-angle ice, alternating flat-foot technique with one foot and front-

*Figure 12-8. **Combined Technique:** Flat-footing and front-pointing simultaneously.*

pointing with the other is efficient. You accomplish changes of direction by going onto front points with one or both feet. On moderate ground, the combined technique allows you to move fast with security and without tiring the calf muscles. On steep ice, you can rest calf muscles by flat-footing on the top of small bulges. You can overcome short walls (those slightly taller than one step) with the following sequence. Stand flat-footed at the base of the wall. Front-point with one foot halfway up the vertical section, and finish by picking up your lower foot and placing it on top in a flat-foot position.

## The Ice Axe

The ice axe has long been the hallmark of the mountaineer. The axe, along with the skill to use it and a pair of good boots, make up most of what you need to climb long snow slopes. During the

late 1960s and the 1970s the axe underwent a radical evolution that enables climbers to climb even steep frozen waterfalls with a sense of security.

The parts of the ice axe are shaft, spike, and head (Figure 12-9). The spike and shaft connect at the ferrule. The head has a pick on one end and an adze on the other. Use the adze for cutting steps in snow and ice. Use the pick to provide traction in hard steep snow and ice, and for self-arrest on snow. Use the shaft for snow belays.

The shaft of the axe was originally made of wood, a natural material that was lightweight but not very strong and susceptible to dry rot. I have seen at least one wooden-shafted ice axe, left outside a tent overnight, that suffered the ignoble death of being consumed by porcupines. (Presumably the animals wanted the salt left from the climber's hands.) Metal-shafted axes were stronger but cold to the touch and devoid of aesthetic appeal, even when the metal was wrapped. Yvon Chouinard introduced laminated bamboo shafts to

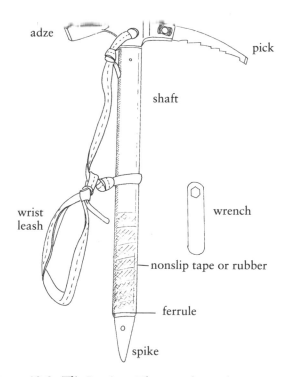

*Figure 12-9. **The Ice Axe:** The axe shown has interchangeable picks.*

provide strength and low weight combined with good looks. The best modern axes use high-tech carbon-fiber compounds, which are strong, lightweight, and well crafted.

The proper length of the ice-axe shaft depends on your height and its intended use. Traditionally, a 70-centimeter axe is the traditional choice for general alpine climbing. The alpine axe is often the single tool that aids movement on low-angle ice and snow as well as provides direct aid, termed *piolet traction* (*piolet* is French for axe), on steeper climbs. For steep climbs, a long shaft actually interferes with climbing because the spike hits the ice at the start of a swing. The increased leverage of the longer shaft also makes it more difficult to wield the axe high overhead. Generally, therefore, a 45- to 55-centimeter axe is recommended for steep climbing. On the steepest of climbs some climbers prefer shafts of hammer length, which can be as short as 20 to 30 centimeters. In sum, there is no rule about length, and climbers have used axes of every size to ascend the steepest of climbs.

## Droop Angle and Pick Angle

Pick *droop* refers to the angle between the pick blade and the axe shaft (Figure 12-10B), and is determined by the manufacturer. A pick with its blade perpendicular to the shaft has no droop. Droop increases as the pick blade bends (droops) toward the axe shaft. The pick blade can either be straight or curved. Modern ice climbing began with the introduction of radically drooped pick blades that hold well on steep ice.

Pick angle is the angle formed between the end of the pick blade and a snow or ice surface. Although picks on new axes come with a fixed angle, you can change this angle with a file. Pick angles can be positive, neutral, or negative (Figure 12-10). A positive pick angle produces a sharp point that penetrates snow and ice easily, which is an advantage when climbing hard ice, but may penetrate too rapidly during a self-arrest on snow. Axes dedicated to snow are often ground with a negative pick angle to slow penetration and give greater control during self-arrest.

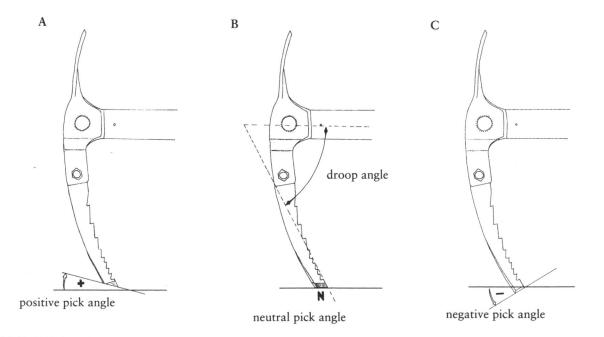

*Figure 12-10. Droop Angle and Pick Angle*

*On a rainy summer day in 1966, I went onto a glacier in the Alps with the purpose of testing every different type of ice axe available at the time. My plan was to see which one worked best for* piolet ancre, *which one was better at step-cutting, and why. After I found a few answers, it took the intervention of Donald Snell to convince the very reluctant and conservative Charlet factory to make a 55-centimeter axe with a curved pick for the crazy American. In those days a 55-centimeter axe was crazy enough—but a curved pick! I had the feeling that modifying the standard straight pick into a curve compatible with the arc of the axe's swing would allow the pick to stay put better in the ice. I had noticed that a standard pick would pop out when I placed my weight on it. My idea worked, and a few years later Rob Collister wrote in* Mountain, *"The development of a curved pick for axes and hammers was an event in ice climbing history comparable to the introduction of crampons in the 1890s, or the use of front points and ice pitons in the thirties. It could prove more revolutionary than either. Since it makes for both greater speed and greater security, it will encourage those who have previously been deterred by the need to choose between the two."*

—Yvon Chouinard in *Climbing Ice*

### Hammers

Ice hammers (Figure 12-11) are shorter and heavier than axes. You commonly use them in your off hand when climbing steep ice. Hammers have an anvil head in place of the axe's adze. The added weight of the anvil and short length give you additional momentum and control that result in more penetrating power, compensating for any lack of strength or coordination present in the off hand.

Hammers commonly have a reverse-curve pick that droops at an angle of 55 degrees. The reverse curve evolved from the straight pick of the Terrordactyl developed by Hamish MacInnes. You place Terrordactyl picks with a chopping motion, and you can even hook them onto rock ledges or into preexisting hand-tool placements. These radically drooped straight picks work extremely well when in place. However, they encourage smashing your knuckles into the ice; "Terrordactyl knuckle" has become a term to describe enlarged, deformed knuckles. The reverse-curve pick overcomes this problem to a certain extent as do newer designs with curved shafts. Reverse-curve picks allow a more natural swinging motion that spares the knuckles somewhat, and are just as secure.

One of the problems with striking the pick of an ice axe is that the pick tends to shatter the ice. You get around this complication by striking repeated targeted blows to remove brittle ice from the surface and to get at more plastic ice underneath.

Figure 12-11. **Hammers**

Lowe Alpine Systems introduced a hollow tube called a *Hummingbird pick* that allows ice to expand inside the pick and minimizes external ice shattering. Axes with hollow picks probably work better than other designs in very brittle ice. Interestingly, the tube can both be secure and rotate, simultaneously allowing the climber to move up or down in a lieback off the axe. Most other axe designs require the axe to be more directly overhead to remain secure, since the flat pick cannot rotate.

## Ice-Axe Techniques

### The Cane (Piolet Canne)

If you climb low-angle snow or ice slopes, you can use your ice axe as a cane. Grip the head of the axe with your hand, covering the adze with your palm (Figure 12-12). Direct the point forward in the line of travel. Place the spike into the ice with the shaft held vertically. As you step up, push down on the axe head with your palm to get an upward assist from your arm muscles.

It is important that when you supplement crampons with hand tools, you continue to use the crampons properly. In the cane position, the ice axe is simply an aid to balance: almost all your balance and progress come from proper use of your feet. Each new technique introduced here requires

greater concentration, when first added to crampon technique, than the one discussed before.

### Stepkicking

To climb snow, you kick steps with a stiff boot. The best boot for kicking steps is one designed for general mountaineering that has a relatively flat sole. You usually kick steps straight uphill on soft snow that is not too steep. As the snow hardens and the angle increases, you kick steps on a rising diagonal.

In soft snow, a good step will be the size of your forefoot. As snow hardens you may only be capable of using the edge of your boot to kick a narrow platform. Then you will reach a point where you will either have to cut steps or put on crampons.

You usually kick steps with an ice axe in hand.

Figure 12-13. *Stepkicking and Piolet Canne*

Figure 12-12. *Hand Position for Using the Axe as a Cane (Piolet Canne)*

Begin by using the ice axe as a cane to assist in walking (Figure 12-13). Always hold the axe on the uphill side when traversing. When you change directions, you switch the axe to the new uphill hand.

### Piolet Manche

On steeper snow slopes, you can gain security by using the axe as a self-belay by plunging it in the snow and using it as a stake; this technique is called *piolet manche*. Grip the head of the axe, oriented parallel to the snow slope, with both hands, palms on top of the pick and adze (Figure 12-14A). Plunge the axe shaft vertically into the snow. To progress upward, you bend and place the axe forward and then kick steps up to the axe. Gain balance in the step, remove the axe, and start the process over again. In the stake position, the axe provides a secure handhold. This handhold, which gives added security at the turn, can replace that provided by *piolet canne* when you change direction while traversing in zigzags (Figure 12-14B).

### Cutting Steps

You will need to cut steps when the snow becomes too hard to kick steps efficiently. In the evolution of winter climbing, the earliest climbs on low-angle slopes were done entirely without the use of crampons by cutting steps. With ten-point crampons (no front points), cut steps allowed ascents of slopes greater than 40 to 50 degrees. With the advent of front points, rigid boots, wrist leashes, and modern technique, stepcutting has become mostly a lost art. But lines of steps are still useful on short alpine slopes where it is faster to cross in steps than to put on crampons.

You normally cut steps in snow with the adze. A flat sharp adze will do a better job than a curved dull one. The classic pattern of stepcutting is an ascending diagonal, but as the slope gets steeper, the line of steps turns uphill. On low-angle firm slopes only the inner edge of your boot need be on a flat surface. In this situation, a step cut with a single slashing blow might be all that you need. As you cut the *slash step*, swing the axe at an angle so that it neither bounces nor sticks in the snow

A

plunging the axe

B

changing direction

*Figure 12-14. The Stake (Piolet Manche)*

too shallow—axe bounces

correct angle—axe cuts step

too steep—axe lodges in place

*Figure 12-15.* **Slash Step:** *Cut in hard snow for the inside edge of the boot.*

*Figure 12-16.* **Side Step:** *Cut in steep hard snow to hold the entire foot.*

(Figure 12-15). Instead, the axe should continue the arc of the swing to remove enough snow to allow your inside boot edge to rest on a cut platform.

As the firm snow slope becomes steeper or harder, you use more effort to remove snow for a *side step* (Figure 12-16). The side step is large enough to hold your entire foot. Swing the axe in a near vertical plane, using the inside corner of the adze. As you remove the axe, flick the axe to remove the cut section. Begin cutting the step near the end of the step that will be closest to you, and make the next cuts away from yourself. In general, you can cut a side step with three blows. If you cut the bottom of the step so that it slopes inward, you will gain an added sense of security as you stand in it. Stand in the next to last step and use the last step as a handhold while you cut a new step. You can also cut a parallel line of steps to use as footholds and handholds. These will not only enhance

security on the way up, but make descents by this line of steps secure as well. Instead of cutting a second line of steps, you can plunge a second axe shaft into the snow above the step and use it as a handhold.

### Pigeonhole Steps

As the slope of hard snow becomes steeper, you can cut *pigeonhole steps* directly up the slope (Figure 12-17). Since you use these holds for positive handholds as well as footholds, you cut a lip on the inward-sloping hold. You cut these steps with the axe adze, but in hard ice you will have to shape the interior of the hold with the pick. Cut a line of holds for each foot. The overall pattern will be a uniform zigzag of holds going up the slope, spaced a step apart, rather than a series of paired left and right steps. Since you place only the toe of

Figure 12-18. *The Slab Step: Make cuts 1 and 2, then pull off a piece of slab with the adze, 3.*

the foot in a pigeonhole, your calf muscles may begin to fatigue. To rest, cut an occasional long horizontal platform that you can stand on with both feet.

### Stepcutting on Windslab Snow

When you encounter snow that breaks off in slabs, you cut steps in a different fashion than in hard snow. First, make a horizontal slit in the snow with the axe pick held vertically (Figure 12-18). Second, make a slit starting up-slope with the pick held vertically. This second slit should cross the first slit at an angle of 45 degrees. Third, cut out the snow between the two slits with the adze.

### Stepcutting in Ice

You will need the pick to cut steps on ice. Cut a series of vertical incisions into the ice and then cut horizontally with the pick. You can level the bottom of the step using blows of a sharp adze. Cutting steps in ice is hard work, so you will probably only want to cut the occasional step as a rest, or to place protection while climbing in crampons. When cutting ice steps, use whatever natural platforms exist to save energy. You can find natural handholds and footholds where ice separates from rock, at the top of a bulge where snow sits on the ice, or at the base of ice columns.

Cutting the occasional step can turn an otherwise desperate ice climb into an interesting prob-

Figure 12-17. **Pigeonhole Steps**

lem. For example, when you leave a platform beneath a vertical or overhanging section, cut one or more front-point-size steps overhead. This maneuver will allow you to use more balance and less arm strength as you climb. On climbs where ice is at foot level and rock overhead, small steps cut to the side in the ice allow a balanced traverse. On thin or fragile ice, a series of light chipping blows will do the job while preserving the ice.

## More Ice-Axe Techniques

### Bracing with the Axe (Piolet Ramasse)

*Piolet ramasse* is the technique of using the ice axe as a counterbalancing or bracing tool on moderate slopes to assist balance while flat-footing (Figure 12-19).

Place the axe across your body about shoulder height. Hold it by the head with the adze under your palm and the pick directed away from your body. Your other hand holds the axe on the fer-

rule just above the spike. You can lean into the axe, pressing with shoulder and arm muscles on the head in a direction parallel to the shaft. This pressure helps keep the axe in the ice so that it will not pull out, and provides a third point of contact, in addition to each foot, for resting. When you move from this position you can use the axe as a handhold by pulling downward with the second hand at the top of the ferrule. Having this hand close to or touching the ice prevents leverage and allows you pull fairly strongly.

This bracing technique is commonly used with *pied troisième* (discussed earlier in this chapter), in which you flat-foot with one foot and front-point with the other in order to change direction.

### Resting in Balance on a Steep Slope (Pied Assis):
You can rest on relatively steep slopes of hard snow or ice by sitting in balance over your crampons, in the position called *pied assis* (Figure 12-20). Stabilize this rest position by using the axe in the cross-body brace (see Figure 12-19). *Pied assis* is

Figure 12-20. **Resting in Balance (Pied Assis):** *To stabilize this position, use the axe in a cross-body brace.*

Figure 12-19. **Cross-Body Bracing (Piolet Ramasse)**

one of many positions that you can assume during the course of a day of moving about on snow. It is the fluid and appropriate use of each of these techniques that makes an accomplished ice climber.

### Piolet Ancre

*Piolet ancre* is a technique in which you use the pick as an anchor. How you place the pick depends on axe design and your own physical limitations. Hold the axe above the ferrule at a point that seems natural for swinging—it will vary depending on the length of the axe. When you swing an axe with an alpine pick, the axe head should follow the arc or droop of the pick—that is, the curved line extending from the shaft to the pick (Figure 12-21). This means that you swing the axe from your shoulder using the upper as well as the lower arm. One common mistake novices make is that they swing with only the lower arm. Do not bend your wrist during the swing, or when the pick strikes the ice. Some expert climbers claim that they flick their wrist as the axe point enters the ice, but this is not necessary or even desirable for most of us. The length and strength of the swing vary somewhat, but start with the shaft angled away from the ice, nearly vertical. You can use considerable strength in swinging, but not at the expense of control. Begin with swings of modest strength.

If you examine the axe swing in the lower right drawing of Figure 12-21, you see that the upper arm pivots about the shoulder joint through an angle of about 35 degrees, whereas the lower arm

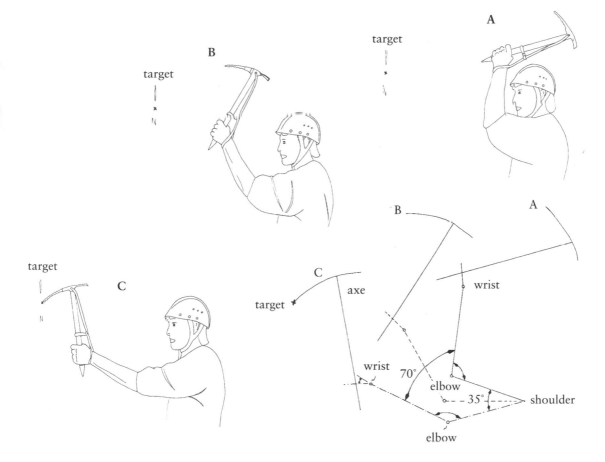

*Figure 12-21. **The Axe Swing from Upper Right to Lower Left***

pivots twice as far, or about 70 degrees. The elbow joint opens up as the arm swings forward, but wrist and hand position relative to the lower arm does not change throughout the swing. If you are using a reverse-curve pick, modify the swing to a chopping motion.

Swing the axe so that the pick strikes the ice perpendicular to the surface. In water ice, do not expect the axe to stick on the first swing. Instead, pick a target and hit it repeatedly, expecting the axe to stick on the second to fourth blow, depending on ice quality and your technique. You will observe experienced climbers, even on very steep ice, looking the ice over to pick a specific target. (This process relates to the nature of the ice, discussed in Chapter 14.) Place the axe directly above your shoulder so that you can balance underneath it.

The actual penetration of the ice surface presents difficulties to the novice. If the axe turns in your hand or you flex your wrist, when the axe strikes the ice surface the ice will shatter and placements will not be secure. At first it seems that your hand and wrist are not strong enough to control the forces of impact of the axe pick against the ice. Strength may not be the problem, however, as most climbers learn to control the wobbly axe after a number of hours or perhaps on the second day.

There are a couple of things to look for if you encounter this problem. First, choose an axe that has a shaft diameter that fits your gloved hand. Some axes have a very large cross section that requires a large hand to control. Also, the glove combination must not be so thick that you cannot grip the shaft. Second, smooth-shafted axes are designed to be slippery so that they penetrate the snow pack, giving security. This slipperiness makes it difficult to keep the axe from rotating in your hand when you hit hard ice. Wrap the lower part of the shaft with the nonslip tape sold in hardware stores for bathtubs. Third, as noted above, the length and weight of the axe have an effect on your ability to control it. Long axes with heavy shafts require more hand-wrist-arm strength.

Shorter tools, northwall hammers, or axes with added weight concentrated in the tool's head build up momentum during the swing. This momentum carries the moving axe into the ice at the angle directed and requires less hand-wrist strength. When climbing steep ice with two hand tools, you normally use a tool with added head weight in your weaker, off hand to gain added momentum.

When placed, the axe should be capable of holding at least a short fall. First-time climbers often want to move up on axes that wobble. You might be able to do so if you are on a moderate slope, if you are top-roping, or if you are balanced well on your crampons. On steeper ground or when leading, it becomes more critical to have good placements. These placements require perseverance, and you should never move up without a solid placement unless you are prepared to fall. With a bit of experience, you learn to *hear* good placements even from a distance as well as *feel* them.

*Figure 12-22. **Using the Axe to Anchor (Piolet Ancre)***

*Figure 12-23. **Mantling on the Axe***

The design of the curved pick locks the blade in place by lifting the shaft away from the ice. (This design seems to go against your natural desire to rest the spike against the ice.) Releasing a well-placed tool is sometimes difficult. First, push the spike against the ice and try lifting the shaft. If this does not work, try lifting the pick out of its hole by the head. You might try enlarging the pick hole by pulling out on the shaft, and then releasing by pushing in and lifting the head. This process may succeed, but done forcefully will torque the pick and may break it.

***The Ice-Axe Anchor:*** A climber moving across a slope with one axe can use it in the anchor position (*piolet ancre*) as an aid to balance, as shown in Figure 12-22. You place the axe pick and use it as a counterforce to your body to move across the slope; pull up on the handle to lock the pick and then lean from the axe to move. After moving, balance over your crampons, remove the axe, and place it again to continue.

***Mantling on the Axe:*** On a steep slope of hard snow or ice, you can mantle on the axe to push yourself upward. Place the axe well overhead and front-point up on crampons while holding onto the axe shaft with one hand (bottom of Figure 12-23). Place your other hand on top of the axe and then begin to mantle onto the axe top (center). At the top of the mantle, balance over your front points, remove the axe, and place it higher (top). In this way, you can move quite high in one placement. Balance during axe removal is easier if you can use a natural handhold or finger hold as an aid.

***Piolet Panne:*** *Piolet panne*, or daggering, is a technique using two axes that works well on long alpine gullies that have the consistency of Styrofoam. Grip each axe with a palm on top of an adze, as shown in Figure 12-24. Place the picks by thrusting them like a dagger. You usually dagger on moderately angled slopes of about 45 degrees, in combination with front-pointing and the odd flat-foot move to change directions. When conditions are right, daggering is a very enjoyable way to gain height quickly.

Figure 12-24. Daggering
(Piolet Panne)

*Piolet Rampe:* You can use the axe as a banister in the *piolet rampe* technique to descend short bulges or sections of ice to 45 degrees by a single axe placement (Figure 12-25). Place the axe well in front of you and duck-walk down the slope using the axe as a railing. Pull up on the axe shaft to lock it in position and allow your hand to slide along the shaft until it comes to the head. At this point move your feet and body well down-slope of the axe head, so that you reach back to hold onto it. Then, gain balance over your crampons and remove the axe. Repeat the sequence as necessary.

## Descending Snow Slopes

Descending snow can be fun, but it also can be dangerous. In ranges where rock climbing is the prominent technique used for ascending, such as the Grand Teton Range of Wyoming, many accidents occur when climbers descend on snow. An initial slip turns into a runaway toboggan ride that ends with a crash into rocks below. Low- to mod-erate-angle snow slopes require specific, practiced techniques to descend. Practice slopes require a good runout, free of rocks, at the bottom. J-lines, described on page 191, are used to safeguard self-arrest practice.

### Glissading

Glissading is a method of sliding down a moderate snow slope without crampons. You need a slope with soft surface snow and harder snow underneath. These conditions often occur on summer afternoons at elevation, in alpine areas, as long as the sun is on the slope. When the slope is in shadow, the snow quickly turns to ice, and you may need crampons for descent.

Done properly, glissading may be one of the most exhilarating aspects of mountaineering. You can cover great distances quickly. I once descended almost 3,000 feet with a heavy backpack taking only a few minutes for each 1,000-foot section. This descent was the reward for all the effort required to get that weight uphill.

You can glissade in either a standing, crouching, or sitting position, as shown in Figure 12-26. The

Figure 12-25. *Descending a Short Ice Slope (Piolet Rampe) from Right to Left*

standing position is similar to skiing and requires practice to learn. Stand crouched forward in balance, with your feet flat to the slope and pointing downhill. Hold the axe as a cane with the pick pointing away from you. Bend your legs at the knees and balance over the balls of your feet. If you wish to slow down, you can shift weight back onto your heels or turn to traverse the slope.

By crouching lower you can use the ice axe as a rudder and emergency brake. Hold the axe with one hand on its head and the other well down the shaft, with the pick pointing away from you. Digging the spike into the snow on your side acts as a brake when combined with a weight shift onto your heels. This is a slower method of descent. Your center of gravity is closer to the snow and not far away from the self-arrest position.

The sitting glissade places your heels and lower body on the snow, increasing the surface area of contact. It is useful when you cannot maintain

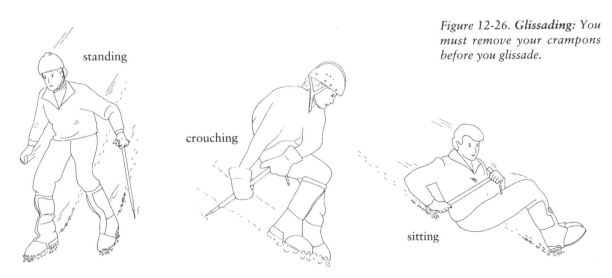

standing

crouching

sitting

Figure 12-26. *Glissading: You must remove your crampons before you glissade.*

your balance in a standing or crouching glissade, or when you would descend too rapidly. If the surface is soft, sitting will keep you on the surface and allow you to slide. Sliding in rough wool pants can slow you. Slick nylon wind pants or a full-length cagoule decreases surface friction and will speed your descent. You can still use the ice axe as a brake, and you will be ready to roll over into a self-arrest. Remember to remove your crampons for the sitting glissade, or you will probably end up with a sprained or broken ankle or punctured leg.

### Plunge Steps and Hand Grips

If you do not feel good about sliding down a slope, the plunge step is a workable alternative. Plunge-stepping uses body weight to produce a step. You descend facing outward, as shown in Figure 12-27; step off with a stiff leg and land on your heel, driving your heel down into the snow. This technique requires boldness, since it takes the

weight of your body to drive the step. Your "falling" weight decelerates as the snow compacts in the step, so you may feel more secure if you make your own steps rather than using someone else's steps.

While plunge-stepping, hold the axe in a modified cane position, ready to plunge into the snow below your foot should you lose balance. Instead of holding the axe with the pick forward (Figure 12-12), turn the adze forward. Hold the axe with your thumb around the adze and your fingers wrapped around the pick adjacent to the shaft. This position allows you to self-arrest almost immediately without reorienting the axe.

If plunge-stepping makes you feel insecure, descend by turning around so that you are facing uphill. Kick steps while using the axe in the stake position.

### Self-arrest

Self-arrest provides an emergency brake if you lose control while descending. You can self-arrest with or without crampons and, although the technique is usually done with a hand tool, it is possible to self-arrest without one. You need to practice the technique to learn it and should practice it periodically to keep the skill sharp. Practicing on slopes with safe run outs or using a J-line (as described on page 191) will provide a safeguard and allow you to have fun while learning or renewing the skills.

The aim of self-arrest with an ice axe is get your body weight over the pick, forcing it into the snow to act as a brake. In the arrest position, hold the axe across your chest so that the pick is about shoulder high and the spike somewhat lower (Figure 12-28). Arch your back between your shoulders and toes if you are not wearing crampons; arch between shoulders and knees if you are wearing crampons. There is a real danger of breaking your ankles and lower legs if crampons catch on brush or snow during a fall.

To enter the arrest position, roll onto the pick (Figure 12-29A). If you roll toward the spike you may lose the axe, pole-vault it, or—worse—force the pick into your body.

Since you usually self-arrest when you are slid-

*Figure 12-27. **Plunge Steps and the Self-arrest Grip***

Figure 12-28. *The Final Position in Self-arrest, with and Without Crampons*

Figure 12-29. *Roll Toward the Axe Pick, Not the Spike*

A
correct

B
incorrect

ing unexpectedly, your body may not be in the best position for the arrest, and you may have to obtain and maintain the arrest position. This movement requires practice, thought, and coordination. It is easiest to do quickly, before momentum builds up and carries your body down the fall line of the slope and away from the dug-in axe. To prevent the axe from being pulled above your shoulder where it cannot arrest the slide, aggressively arch your back and use your muscles to pull yourself back over the axe.

*Arrest Sequences:* There are four basic starting body positions for a fall. You can be on your front or back, with your feet downhill or uphill. If you fall face down, with your feet downhill, you are

*Figure 12-30.* **Arresting with Feet Downhill on Your Back**

*Figure 12-31.* **Arresting Face Down with Head Downhill**

*Figure 12-32. **Arresting Face Up with Head Downhill***

almost in the arrest position, and simply need to put the axe across your chest and arch your back. If you fall face up, with your feet downhill, roll toward the pick and arch your back to get the shoulder-high pick firmly dug into the snow (Figure 12-30).

If you are headfirst and face down, plant the pick out in front of you down-slope and across your body (Figure 12-31). The axe pick acts as a pivot, allowing your body to rotate around it until both feet are below the axe. You must pull yourself over the axe with an arched body to come to an effective stop.

If you are headfirst, on your back, you plant the pick out to the side, as in Figure 12-32. The pick again acts as a pivot point for your body, so your

feet will soon be below the axe. Again you pull your shoulders over the axe and you arch your back. This position seems very strange at first, but you will soon see that is effective.

You can also self-arrest without an ice axe or crampons by radically arching your back and digging in with well-gloved hands and toes. This technique is more effective than you might first think possible, but you must do it immediately or it will not work.

*J-lines:* Whether you are a novice or an experienced climber, you should practice self-arrest, preferably on a slope that has a clear run-out zone at the bottom, void of rocks and other obstacles. When this is not possible, you can use a J-line.

*Figure 12-33. Climber Attached to J-line*

ing your safety leash to the J-line, your assistants hold you by the legs, in the head-down position, until you give the signal to let go. After a bit of practice and a gain in confidence, you can launch yourself with vigor and success from this unlikely position.

## References for Future Reading

Blackshaw, Alan. 1973. *Mountaineering: From hill walking to alpine climbing.* London: Penguin Books.

Chouinard, Yvon. 1978. *Climbing ice.* San Francisco: Sierra Club Books, in association with the American Alpine Club.

Harrer, Heinrich. 1976. *The white spider.* London: Hart-Davis, MacGibbon.

Lowe, Jeff. 1979. *The ice experience.* Chicago: Contemporary Books, Inc.

_____. 1981. *Technical manual.* Lowe Alpine Systems, Inc.: Broomfield, Colorado.

March, Bill. 1973. *Modern snow & ice techniques.* Cumbria, England: Cicerone Press.

Miller, Dorcas. 1990. Raynaud's Disease: Can it be controlled? *Climbing.* 122:109.

Williamson, John E., and J. Whitteker, eds. 1989. Statistical tables, in *Accidents in North American mountaineering.* New York: The American Alpine Club, and Banff: The Alpine Club of Canada.

Construct the J-line with a climbing rope attached to solid snow anchors (described in Chapter 13) offset from each other so that the rope takes the shape of the letter J (Figure 12-33). Position anchors at both ends of the J and fasten the rope so that it hangs in a loop below the lower anchor. Use a nylon sling and carabiners to attach yourself. Should you lose control during practice, the J-line stops downward progress with an abrupt deceleration applied by rope stretch. Before using the J-line, make sure to test each anchor individually, using the efforts of a number of people to pull on it.

It is best not to have a leash of any kind attached to your ice axe so that it will not bounce wildly about should you lose control of it.

You can make the practice of headfirst self-arresting easier by cutting one or more large steps or platforms at the top of the J-line. These platforms are for you and two assistants. After attach-

## Endnotes

1. The 1989 *Accidents in North American Mountaineering* (Table III) indicates that lack of a hard hat was a contributing cause in ten to thirteen accidents per year between 1951 and 1988. However, John E. Williamson, editor of that publication, states in a 1993 personal communication, "Helmets are *primarily* to protect against falling rocks or objects. Leader falls *with* helmets can result in basal skull fractures *because* of the helmet."

2. Lowe, 1981.

# 13

# Protection on Snow and Ice

## Snow Protection

Snow and ice continually form, change character, and melt, requiring climbers to be alert to current conditions. Over the years, climbers have developed a variety of techniques and tools suited to particular conditions. There are ice screws and ice pitons, which are screwed or pounded, respectively, into the ice. Climbers can cut posts, called *bollards*, drill holes for an hourglass anchor, or bury axes or special plates called *deadmen* to form stable anchors. There are also many ways to use an ice axe to contribute to safety.

When you climb snow, you can protect on a step-by-step basis by using the ice axe. If you take a wobbly step, use the ice axe to regain balance by quickly plunging it and hanging onto it as a stake. If you do lose your balance completely, use the techniques of self-arrest described in Chapter 12 to come to a stop. These techniques are for individu-

als and do not safeguard a team. A team requires some type of anchor that works effectively on snow for belaying.

You cannot self-arrest on water ice. At the beginning of a fall, a quick, desperate, and lucky swing might lodge a pick and prevent a fall. Once the fall begins, however, you need bombproof anchors to stop it.

### Ice-Axe Belays

You can belay on your ice axe. Plunge the axe into the snow, shaft vertical, all the way to the axe head, as indicated by the arrow in Figure 13-1. Orient the pick blade perpendicular to the fall line and use it as an anchor. Stand in a kicked platform downhill of the axe and attach yourself to it by a sling clipped through the carabiner hole. Then, push the axe shaft into the snow until you bury the

plunge

*Figure 13-1.* **Ice-Axe Belay:** *Plunge the axe to its head and orient the axe blade across the fall line.*

head, to prevent leverage on the shaft. This belay anchor is only as strong as the weakest layer of the snow, which is usually at the surface. When the force of a fall applied perpendicular to the axe shaft causes the axe to rotate through the upper weak snow layer, it fails as an anchor.

*Boot-Axe and Hip-Axe Belays:* On moderate slopes the boot-axe belay overcomes some of the problems of the ice-axe belay. Drive the ice axe into the snow, shaft vertical, up-slope and adjacent to your uphill foot. Orient the head of the axe perpendicular to the fall line. Push it into the slope, stopping just above boot level, so that you can wrap the climbing rope around the axe shaft. The rope passes from you around the up-slope side of the axe shaft underneath both the pick and adze, and then around the down-slope side of the boot. The downhill side of the boot provides most of the friction to arrest a fall; the axe acts to reverse the direction of the rope. During the belay, keep the axe in place in the snowpack by pushing downward on the head. You can prevent the shaft from rotating by bracing it against your boot just in front of your ankle. Stamp down the snow beneath

*Figure 13-3.* **Hip-Axe Belay**

the axe and your boot to make this brace more effective.

When the snow slope gets steeper or softer, it is no longer possible to use a boot-axe belay. A hip-axe belay (Figure 13-3) may serve. You form a platform in the snow with your body weight and stamp out foot placements to use as a brace for your legs. Drive the axe in next to your hip and hold it with downward pressure from your hand and arm. Then pass the rope around the axe shaft and around your body to your braking hand. Since your glove and the rope are down in the snow, both are likely to be snowy and slippery. If you need more friction, wrap the rope around your wrist.

### Snow-Picket Belays

A snow picket (Figure 13-4) has a T-shaped cross section that resists shearing out of hard-packed snow much better than the oval shape of an ice axe. Larger in cross section, the snow picket can make a more effective belay anchor than the ice axe . You can purchase pickets or make them from stock T shaped aluminum. Under consolidated snow conditions, individual pickets can be

*Figure 13-2.* **Boot-Axe Belay**

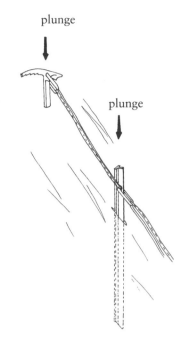

plunge

plunge

*Figure 13-4. Snow Pickets: Design and Linkages*

used as running protection for moderate-angle snow slopes. When you tightly link snow pickets or ice axes with connecting slings placed through carabiner holes in the picket tops, they make excellent anchors in firm snowpack.

Linked in this fashion, the lower picket serves as the primary anchor and the upper picket, or axe, as its safeguard. To pull out, the lower picket would have to rotate through a large arc in the snow. It is prevented from doing so because it is linked to the upper picket, so the upper picket must rotate and fail before the lower picket does. You can substitute long snow axes for snow pickets, but axes have less holding power because of their smaller cross section.

### Bollard Belays

*Bollard* is a nautical term for the mushroom-shaped post used when tying a ship to a dock. You can use an ice axe to cut a similar post in snow to serve as an anchor for belaying or rappelling. Use the adze of the axe and cut a symmetrical trench into the snow slope with a circular arc on the uphill side, coming to a point on the downhill end (Figure 13-5). Cut the bottom of the trench about 1½ feet deep on the uphill end. Allow this trench to rise to the undisturbed snow surface at the lower point. This excavation leaves a raised island of snow in the center of the trench. The uphill end of this island should have a little overhang to prevent the rope from slipping out of the trench; the remaining sides are vertical. Pass a rope around the island. Position yourself well downhill of the bollard to ensure a downward pull and sit in a braced stance composed of a kicked seat and foot braces that will absorb much of the energy of a fall. As in rock climbing, the stance safeguards the anchor by limiting the energy that the anchor must absorb.

The strength of a bollard depends on its size in relation to the consolidation and structure of the

4'–10'

*Figure 13-5. Bollard Construction and Stance*

snowpack. Bollards in firm snow with well-bonded layers may be as little as 3 to 4 feet across but in less firm snow may be up to 10 feet wide. It is a good idea to make and test a bollard on the slope that you intend to climb before starting out, where there is a safe run-out zone. Get several people to pull statically on the rope to duplicate the dynamic impact forces that can come onto the bollard.

You can strengthen a bollard by driving your ice axe into the trench on the uphill side, between the anchor rope and the snow island, where shearing forces are greatest. Line the trench with sweaters and jackets to distribute shearing forces over a wider surface. If you rappel from the bollard, use twigs, branches, and flat rocks rather than leave your gear behind, and do not multiply the load by bouncing when you descend. It is best to practice cutting bollards and test them before you try to rappel on them.

### Snow Flukes

A *snow fluke*, which is an aluminum plate with a steel cable (Figure 13-6), is designed to be inserted in a T-shaped slot in the snow. Snow flukes provide belays on hard, homogeneous snow, typical of summer alpine or glacier ice.

*Figure 13-6. Snow Fluke*

You must place the fluke in the T-slot (Figure 13-7A) at an angle of 40 degrees to the snow surface. To find this angle, place your ice axe perpendicular to the snow surface (Figure 13-7B). If you bisect the angle between the axe and the snow surface you will have a 45-degree angle; if you lean the snow fluke slightly—5 degrees—toward the upper snow surface and insert the fluke, it will be at a 40-degree angle to the snow. (Many flukes have a cable stop that sets the angle between the plate and the cable at 50 degrees, the desired angle.)

Hammer the fluke plate a foot or so into the crossbar of the T-slot and place the fluke cable into

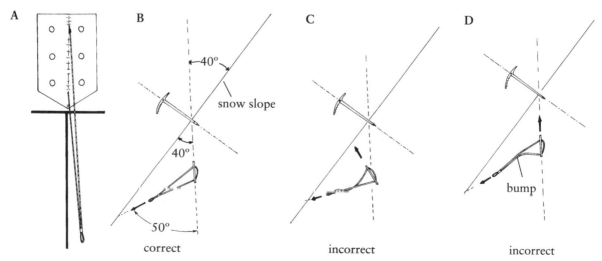

*Figure 13-7. Snow-Fluke Placements: A—The T placement (front view); B—Estimation of the 40-degree angle (cross-section view with axe indicating direction perpendicular to snow slope); C—Incorrect angle (cross-section view); D—A bump along the cable path (cross-section view).*

cross-sectional view with undisturbed snow layers

perspective view with girth-hitched axe

the cut-out stem of the T-slot, taking a direct line downhill to the belayer.

The snow fluke may fail if you place it at the wrong angle or dig the cable slot incorrectly. As the drawing of a snow fluke at an incorrect angle shows (Figure 13-7C), a pull on its cable will cause the fluke to pop up through the snow, and the belay will fail. If the fluke cable rides over a bump in the cable slot, an upward pull on the fluke occurs and again the fluke pops out of the snow (Figure 13-7D).

The belay stance you assume with the snow fluke is critical. On steep slopes, you need to sit well downhill of the fluke to ensure that the fluke and its cable pull at the proper angle. You can use snow flukes to belay on horizontal surfaces above steep slopes. Here you need to sit well in front of the fluke, but also back from the edge; you should not sit on a *cornice*, an unsupported overhang of snow.

### Ice Axes as Deadmen

Snow flukes belong to a general category of buried objects used for belaying called *deadmen*. You often need to belay on snow without having specialty items such as snow flukes along. Ice axes placed in horizontal trenches make improvised

deadmen, as shown in Figure 13-8. Girth-hitch a sling around the center of the horizontal axe and pass it to the surface through a vertical slot you have dug perpendicular to the trench. It is important that the T-shaped trench and slot disturb the natural snow structure as little as possible, retaining the snow's original strength. Placing the axe forward in the trench against the undisturbed front wall maximizes the strength of the placement. Take a stance well down-slope of the deadman to ensure the proper angle of pull on the attached sling and deadman.

You can strengthen the axe-deadman belay by inserting a second axe into the trench vertically through the sling and in front of the horizontal axe (Figure 13-9). Penetrating deeper as well as surface layers of the snow, this axe resists forward motion of the horizontal axe.

Under special circumstances you can even use a short hammer as a deadman. I once needed to safeguard bridging a deep and wide moat, or *randcleft*, between a glacier and a rock wall. I buried a short hammer while I was braced in a sitting position and attached the hammer to my climbing harness with a tight sling. The hammer itself became frozen in, as I later discovered when I attempted to retrieve it. This is an example of

Figure 13-9. *An Enhanced Ice-Axe Deadman*

successful improvisation, based on sound principles, that is often necessary in real climbing situations.

## Ice Protection

With the advent of modern tools and experience, climbers are tackling steeper ice with minimum amounts of intermediate protection. As a result, the old saying that the leader must not fall is still good advice. On the other hand, modern ice protection that is properly placed in good ice should catch a fall. The tubular, hollow-core ice screw, such as those manufactured by Black Diamond (formerly Chouinard-Great Pacific) or Lowe Alpine Systems, is the strongest design. This design, shown in Figure 13-10, minimizes fracturing of the ice because the displaced ice moves up into the core of the screw. A good example of ice-screw design, it has four cutting teeth and a conical interior. The tip of the cone is the toothed end of the screw. As ice enters the cone it can expand. The core fills with ice chips that are easy to clean out by

tapping the screw against a hammer or axe head. The outside diameter of the screw, which is the load-bearing surface, is larger than that of an older Salewa ice screw and should be harder to pull out of the ice. The older Salewa design had two cutting teeth and a interior with parallel walls that produced a solid ice core. To remove the core you had to melt it with body heat and ream the partially melted core with a stiff wire. Since cleaning the screw was the second's job, there was good reason to lead. Possibly this duty was the mother of invention that lead to modern ice screws. Salewa has designed a newer tubular screw along the lines of the Black Diamond model.

Lowe Alpine Systems produces a hollow, pound-in ice piton with small threads called the *Snarg*. The small threads allow the Snarg to be screwed out after a bit of initial chopping. The pound-in design was developed so that the protection could be placed from small or precarious stances. Snargs have replaced an older solid pound-in design typified by the warthog. Once the leader has started a pound-in, he or she can hang onto it for balance while driving it. For this reason,

ice screw          Snarg          warthog

Figure 13-10. *Ice-Protection Designs*

Snargs play an important part in safeguarding modern steep ice climbs. (While warthogs are discussed here, they are largely of historic interest and do not belong on a modern climbing rack. They shatter the ice excessively and are not strong. Snargs, which are almost as strong as ice screws, have replaced these primitive pound-ins.)

Snargs have a much larger load-bearing surface than solid pound-ins and they displace the ice core inward. As a result, there is very little shattering of the ice surrounding the screw. The Snarg gives reasonable protection at minimal stances on steep climbs, a compelling reason to have them on your rack. They are also useful to safeguard you when you are tired at the end of a long run out before you chop out a stance and set up a belay with screws.

Establish your belays with tubular ice screws to take advantage of their design strengths. The tubular ice screw with an uninterrupted cylindrical shape fails by bending. In water ice, it must first bend approximately 45 degrees across the length of the screw before it begins to pull out of the ice. The Snarg pound-in is not a complete cylinder; it has a slot in its side to allow for ice expansion and removal. The Snarg fails by breaking at this slot.

It is important to place both screws and Snargs all the way into the ice, so that they rest against the eye flange to resist bending.

The older warthog pound-ins, which are not as strong as tubular screws or Snargs, have to be hammered in all the way. Since they shatter ice extensively, they had to be placed well away from other pieces of protection.

Another disadvantage of the warthog is that it is difficult to remove. You may need to chop a warthog out for at least a third or half of its length. This is an exasperating and tiring experience for the second. The Snarg, on the other hand, might need a little chopping in the beginning but turns rather easily once started, because of the threads milled on its exterior. After a few turns you usually can pull it straight out. Tubular screws screw out for most of their length. This is normally not difficult. The leader puts the screw in originally and does most of the work of setting the screw and providing a space to turn it. The newest tubular

> ## The Birth of the Snarg
>
> *In the first years of the last decade, Mike Weis and I had long contemplated doing an extended climb of a steep frozen waterfall. But from experience on short routes we had discovered just how difficult it is to stop on a vertical pitch and place a tube screw. We also had found that solid-shafted pitons would most often completely destroy the ice of these climbs. My brother, Greg Lowe, provided us with the solution to the problem. He had made half a dozen chrome-molly tubes, about 9 or 10 inches long with the tips beveled to the inside. These tubes gave Mike and [me] the confidence to lead out on pitches of brittle, vertical, and bulging ice. A new world had been opened to us. . . . These ancestors to the Snarg were crude beasts. . . .*
>
> —Jeff Lowe on the Origin of the Snarg, Lowe Alpine Systems, Inc. *Technical Manual*

screws have flanges with some movement separate from the screw shaft, which simplifies removal as well as placement.

Ice protection placed optimally in high-quality ice is relatively secure. You can improve the margin of safety by placing a dynamic sling on each ice screw or pound-in used as an intermediate protection point. Dynamic slings, discussed in Chapter 7, rip apart and lengthen fall distance as they absorb the force of the fall. Most ice climbers use between one and four intermediate protection points per pitch. You can easily carry four dynamic slings on an ice-climbing rack.

### Starting Ice Screws

Placing an ice screw requires attention to detail. Once you select good ice, clear away especially brittle or rotten surface ice with a few axe blows and start a hole in the ice underneath with the axe pick. It is recommended that ice screws be placed at an angle of 45 to 60 degrees to the ice surface

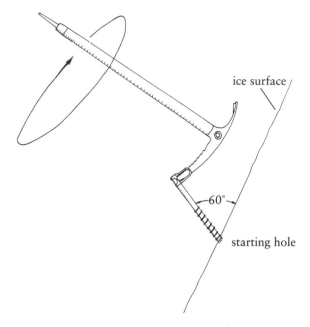

ice surface

60°

starting hole

*Figure 13-11. **Starting an Ice Screw***

*above* the screw. Initially, to catch the screw threads, tap the screw in the hole with a light hammer blow. Once the threads catch, insert the axe or hammer into the carabiner hole of the screw to get leverage for turning (Figure 13-11). Repeat the process of half-turns and pounding a few times

until the screw teeth catch. You may find that you can start screws with very sharp teeth simply by turning them, even in the hardest and coldest ice.

The pressure of the screw melts the surrounding ice, providing lubrication and allowing the screw to turn easily. (In the same way, when you ice skate, the ice beneath your blades melts and you are able to glide.) In extremely cold weather, the pressure of the lever-turned screw is not sufficient to melt the ice. Without lubrication, the screw will be hard to turn and will make disturbing chattering noises.

Lowe and Black Diamond now manufacture ice screws with large diameters, which resist shearing through the ice. They have more and sharper cutting teeth that cut more easily, and built-in ratchet eyes that allow easier placement. Placement entirely by hand is now possible in some ice conditions.

### Placing Ice Screws

Ice screws tend to shatter the ice as they enter it. The surface ice, in contact with very cold air, shatters more readily than the ice beneath the surface, which is more plastic (Figure 13-12A). If you do not remove the shattered surface ice, it easily breaks away when loaded, leaving the ice screw vulnerable to being bent at the point where the

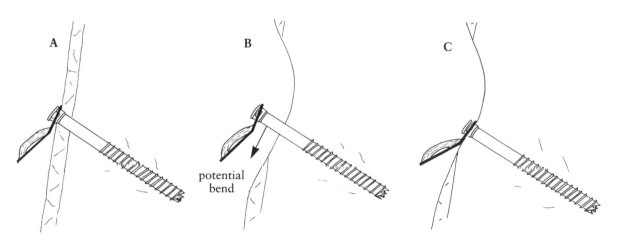

A

B

potential bend

C

*Figure 13-12. **Ice-Screw Placement (Cross-Section View):** A—The brittle surface ice will not support the ice screw and allows the screw to bend in the fall line and* *fail. B—The brittle surface layer is removed. C—The flange comes to rest on the solid ice interior. The placement will resist fall-line bending and failure.*

screw protrudes from the ice. When you place the ice screw, remove the surface ice and turn the ice screw into the bottom of the prepared hole until the flange of the carabiner clip-in rests against the ice (Figures 13-12B and C).

### Loading Ice Screws

Imagine an ice screw without threads. Such a screw should do an adequate job of protecting you if placed in good ice and loaded correctly, because of the way in which screws are intended to bear a load. You might not want to trust such a screw, but nevertheless it should work. The load-bearing surfaces on the screw are the outside surface of the screw and the bottom of the carabiner flange (Figure 13-13A). The screw threads should play a minor part in holding the load.

Therefore, we need to pay attention to the flanges of the ice screw. The flange, to which you clip, is an important part of the load-bearing surface. It needs to rest against the ice and point down-slope. There should be no clearance between the flange and the ice; clearance might allow the screw to rotate in a vertical plane and reduce the ultimate holding power of the screw. For this rea-

son, screw length is important: a screw should be short enough to allow the flange to rest against the ice. Therefore, tied-off ice screws will never hold as well as fully placed screws. Some commercial ice screws have a movable flange to aid in placement, and ice-screw hangers are sometimes available commercially as accessories.

The position of screw placement above a belay stance is also important. If you place the screw at waist to chest height and then pull on it, you will be applying force along the shaft, as shown by the arrow in Figure 13-13B, and it may pull out. When you belay, therefore, you should place the belay screws well above your chest so that the load will be applied parallel to the screw flange and perpendicular to the shaft of the screw (Figure 13-13A). Cut an adequate stance well below the screw anchor to stand on, so you need not lean on waist-high screws for the duration of the belay.

Also, chip away any ice bumps left beneath the attachment carabiner until the carabiner lies flat and produces a pull perpendicular to the screw axis. If the carabiner is not flat, it can lever the screw, forcing it out (Figure 13-13C).

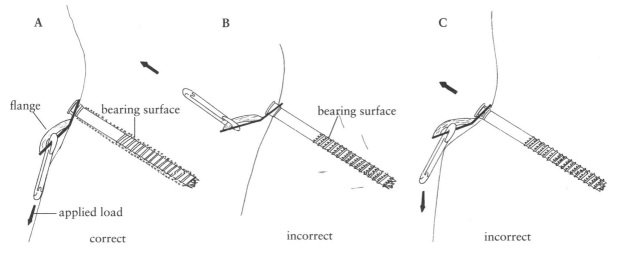

Figure 13-13. **Loading an Ice Screw:** A—The screw is loaded correctly (marked by Xs on the shaft surface) in a direction perpendicular to the main load-bearing surface. B—The screw is incorrectly loaded parallel to the screw shaft and only the small screw threads (Xs) bear the load. C—An ice bump beneath the attachment carabiner produces leverage and an outward force along the screw axis. This position incorrectly loads the small screw threads (Xs). The bump should be chipped away until the carabiner lies as in A.

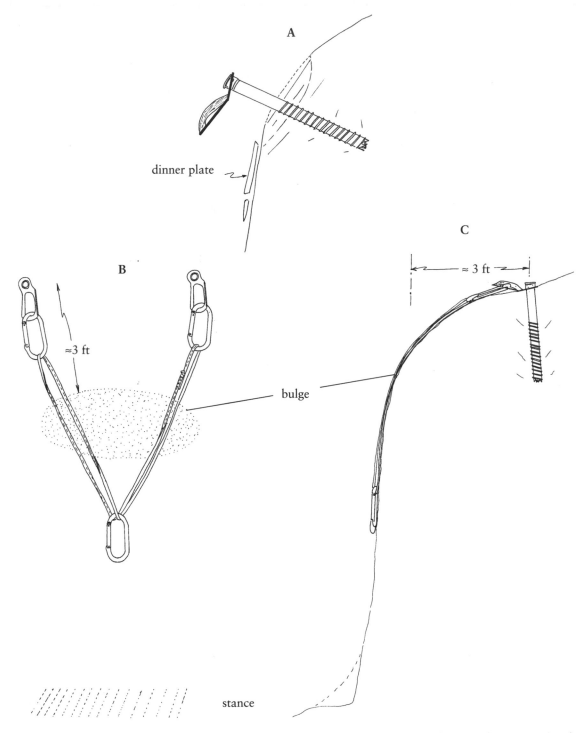

A

dinner plate

C

≈ 3 ft

B

≈3 ft

bulge

stance

*Figure 13-14.* **Ice Screws and Waist-High Bulges: A**—*A screw placed in the apex of a bulge will cause the bulge to dinner-plate.* **B**—*Front view of a naturally formed belay stance just below a bulge. The screws are placed well above the bulge and far enough apart so that fractures from one screw do not intersect those of the other screw.* **C**—*Side view of screws behind the bulge far enough to prevent shattering of the bulge.*

## Ice Screws and Bulges on Water Ice

Note that to be effective, screw placements described in this section require firmly frozen and structurally sound winter water ice. Screw placements that work better in softer ice at warmer temperatures are described in the next section.

Bulges on water-ice climbs present problems when you are placing ice screws. You naturally want to place a screw before attempting to climb the bulge. If the bulge is waist to chest height, you will most likely place the screw in the convex part of the bulge. In doing so, you will create large fractures in the brittle surface and you may break off large *dinner plates* (Figure 13-14A). If this happens, courtesy and safety demand that you trap the plates between the ice and your body and methodically break them up into small pieces before allowing them to fall.

If you place screws above a bulge for an anchor, you must place them far enough apart so that their fractures do not intersect, totally shattering the ice (Figure 13-14B). Usually, at temperatures below freezing in water ice, a 3-foot separation is sufficient. The screws also need to be far enough behind the bulge to prevent fracture in the bulge (Figure 13-14C). Again, the specific distance depends on ice conditions, but 3 feet is usually sufficient.

### Optimum Screw Placement

On softer alpine ice, or on steeper water ice, loading the screw (as in a hanging belay) might cause pressure melting. To strengthen placements and counteract this melting, place screws one above the other, as shown in Figure 13-15. When done correctly, this configuration is the most secure screw placement possible. The top screw connects to the bottom screw by a tight sling, and you clip into the lower screw. The lower screw must rotate downward through the ice to fail, but the upper screw resists this rotation. A force applied to the lower screw transfers directly to the upper screw, which must rotate through the ice before the lower screw can move. With this type of anchor, a friend of mine successfully caught a 300-foot fall when the leader was pushed down

*Figure 13-15. **Belay for Steep Ice:** The upper screw must rotate from its position before the lower screw can bend and fail. The belay anchors to the lower screw.*

a steep Canadian glacier by a falling cornice. The top screw pulled out about a quarter of an inch during the fall, but the bottom screw holding the fall did not move. (This is a good recommendation for the anchor, but not for climbing under a cornice.)

An independent screw placed slightly above and off to the side of the belay as a first protection point for the next pitch will prevent a fall directly onto the anchor and help safeguard it. Use a dynamic sling on this protection point.

### Ice-Screw Placements in Thin Ice

Placing screw anchors in thin ice is never satisfactory, but if you run out of rope and have a few inches of ice, you can set up screws as shown in Figure 13-16. Turn each screw in its hole until it

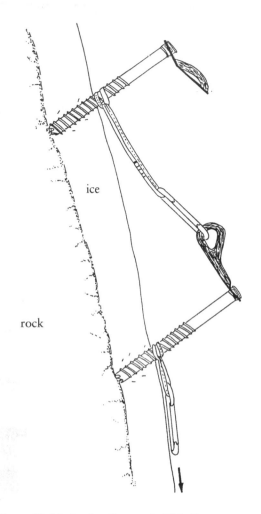

*Figure 13-16. Anchor Screws in Thin Ice*

a good idea to take along pitons and nuts to use in cracks that have been cleaned of ice. Tied-off tools, as discussed in Chapter 15, and a good stance can also enhance your belay.

## Bollard and Hourglass Rappels from Ice

You can usually have confidence in rappel anchors placed in rock walls bordering climbs. However, you may sometimes be forced by circumstance to rappel from ice. If you leave screws behind, you will leave behind a small fortune, assuming you happen to have enough screws available when you need them. Climbers have faced this problem before and come up with a number of solutions.

Ice bollards are identical in shape to snow bollards, but can be smaller because of the greater structural integrity of ice. On well-consolidated glacier ice, a bollard can be roughly 18 inches across and 6 inches deep on the upper side, which you in-cut slightly to prevent the rope from popping off. You can cut bollards in water ice, but this requires laborious controlled chipping with the axe pick to keep the bollard intact. Less chipping is required if you drape a double sling over the bollard as a rappel anchor rather than cutting deeper grooves to accept the thicker rope. Because of the work involved, most rappellers will seek a different anchor.

The Abalakov hourglass provides a secure rappel anchor that you can construct relatively quickly. To form this anchor, place two ice screws 22 centimeters or longer in a horizontal plane so that they point toward each other and intersect inside the ice (Figure 13-17). The optimal distance between screw entrance holes is 8 inches, and each screw is angled at 60 degrees from perpendicular to the ice. Next, remove the screws and clean the holes. Pass a 7-millimeter cord into one empty screw hole and catch it with the end of a flexible cable inserted into the second screw hole to pull it through. Finally, tie off the cord or use it to pull a sewn sling to form a rappel anchor. The plastic

hits rock, and promptly stop turning. If you turn any farther you will either bend the teeth of the screw, or strip the small ice ridges formed by the screw threads. Tie off the upper screw with a loop of small-diameter webbing (a hero loop) next to the ice to prevent levering, and tension the hero loop to the top of the lower screw. Next, tie off the lower screw with a hero loop next to the ice surface. Clip into the lower hero loop for your belay. The lower tie-off minimizes leverage on the lower screw. This lower screw must rotate to fail, but the tight sling attached from the top of the lower screw to the upper screw prevents rotation.

If you are climbing and belaying on thin ice, it is

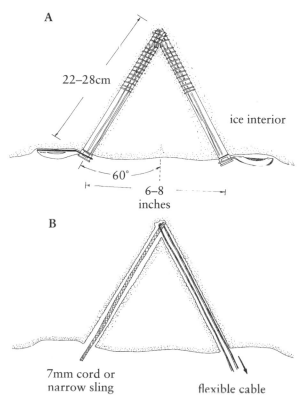

**A**

22–28cm

ice interior

60°

6–8 inches

**B**

7mm cord or narrow sling

flexible cable

*Figure 13-17. Cutaway of the Abalakov Hourglass Rappel Anchor (Viewed from Above)*

son, Canadian ice climbers, conducted tests in water ice, first in moist plastic ice and later in colder brittle ice. They found that the best placements, obtained by placing entrance holes 8 inches apart, failed at 2,900 pounds of force in moist ice at above-freezing air temperatures of 41 degrees Fahrenheit (5 degrees Celsius). In warmer ice, the 7-millimeter rappel sling failed by slowly shearing through the ice. In cold brittle ice at 14 degrees Fahrenheit (–10 degrees Celsius), with entrance holes 8 inches apart, the 7-millimeter sling failed at 3,250 pounds of force without the ice breaking. In the moist 41-degree Fahrenheit conditions, failure rates were lower when the entrance holes were placed at 6 inches, but still were an impressive 2,250 pounds of force. Clearly, the hourglass creates a strong rappel anchor.

You will want to practice and test this technique, as I have, using a mechanical-advantage system powered by three climbers, to gain confidence in it and to be efficient in creating, cleaning, and threading before you need to use it. As in any rappel, back up your anchor as you send the heaviest member of your party down first to test the need for the backup. When you become confident in the rappel anchor, you can remove the backup. The lightest member of the party should rappel last and slip as smoothly as possible down the rope.

## References for Future Reading

Lowe, Jeff. 1981. *Technical manual.* Lowe Alpine Systems: Broomfield, Colorado.
Toft, Murray. 1991. Getting down on a shoestring. *Climbing.* 124:100–101.

string used in weed-whackers or plastic-coated wire makes a very light cable loop. For emergencies, you may be able to improvise a threading cable using small wired tapers. Tie the cord to one wire stopper and push it headfirst into a clean screw hole. Use the back end of the second stopper to grip the head of the first to pull it through.

Abalakov hourglass rappel anchors, tested in glacier ice by the German Alpine Club, were found to fail at about 2,000 pounds with a 6-inch span between holes. Murray Toft and Joe Joseph-

# 14

# The Nature of Ice

## Introduction

There are many kinds of ice, and their environmental characteristics influence the season, or even time of day, that a climb may be attempted reasonably safely; differences in local ice properties affect the safety of anchors and tool placement once you have begun a climb. The expert climber on a steep water-ice climb will hang from one tensed arm while aiming the second ice tool to a specific ice patch that will take tools better than the ice immediately adjacent. You need to know the types of ice, their behavior during tool and anchor placement, and seasonal transformations for greater safety, enjoyment, and skill at the sport.

The four major varieties of ice are *glacier ice*, *alpine* or *couloir ice*, *rime ice*, and *water ice*. *Freezing rain*, supercooled water drops that freeze when they contact cold surfaces, occasionally produces unique ice climbs.

## Glacier Ice

New snow can be dry or wet. Dry, or powder, snow is made of well-formed hexagonal crystals (Figure 14-1). If the wind blows hard enough to transport the snow, the arms of these crystals break and a densely packed *windslab*, prone to avalanching, may form on lee slopes. If the new snow crystals settle with arms intact, and if the snowpack has the same temperature at top and

new snow crystal

$H_2O$ molecules migrate

granular snow

firn

glacier ice

*Figure 14-1. **Metamorphism of Snow to Glacier Ice:** New snow crystals become rounded as water molecules migrate from their pointed extremities to concavities, eventually forming grains. These grains connect to each other and, by eliminating most of the entrapped air, crystallize into glacier ice.*

bottom, then water molecules migrate from the pointed tips to concave areas between the arms.

The snowpack undergoes transformation as a result of heat exchange. Heat moves from the ground to the atmosphere during the coldest parts of the winter, and from the surface down during the summer when the sun is warmer than the ground. After the snows of winter collect, the warming days cause the snow to melt during the day and freeze at night. This melt-freeze cycle produces *corn snow,* the loose, granular snow so often encountered during the spring.

By the end of a season, individual grains bond firmly together through repeated melting and freezing to form a complex network. This processed snow forms a dense snow structure, or *firn,* that becomes part of the permanent snowpack. It can be very hard at night or in shadow, and turn into slush when the sun strikes it during the hottest part of the day.

Eventually the firn becomes compressed under subsequent layers of firn and undergoes further changes, forming glacier ice in layers that may represent hundreds to thousands of years of accumulating and metamorphosing snow.

Glaciers gain snow and ice during the winter and lose it during the summer both by melting and evaporation as the ice turns directly into water vapor. As the glacier loses snow and ice (ablation), *ablation surfaces* form: these areas are marked by accumulations of dirt (Figure 14-2) present in the snowpack but diluted enough during the winter that the snow appears white. Thus, glaciers take on a structure of white winter accumulation layers separated by summer ablation surfaces. If a summer or series of summers is warm enough for the glacier to melt intensely, an *unconformity structure* of ablation layers truncated by more recent ablation layers forms. This situation often produces an angular contact between older and more recent accumulation layers.

## Alpine Ice

Alpine ice forms in gullies, or couloirs, high on the side of mountain peaks, such as the Enclosure Ice Couloir (Figure 14-3). In shadowed alpine gullies, surface water percolates down through the snowpack and can transform it. By late summer to early autumn, the gully may become packed

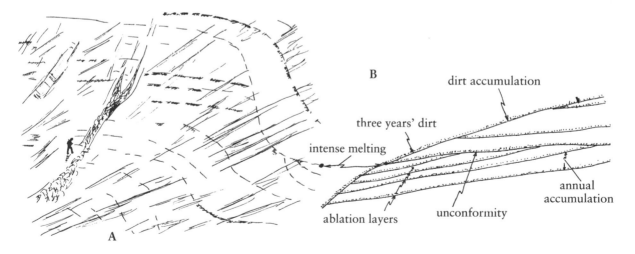

Figure 14-2. **Glacier Structure:** A—Sketch of the Middle Teton Glacier. Horizontal bands are ablation layers; diagonal lines are water grooves. B—Cross section of A showing annual accumulation layers, ablation layers, and an unconformity produced by a period of intense melting.

*Figure 14-3. **Sketch of the Enclosure Ice Couloir of the Grand Teton from the Serendipity Arete on Mt. Owen***

with hard *crystalline ice*. *Black ice* is old gully ice mixed with dirt and rock that has fallen down from above.

---

## Rime Ice

Rime ice forms when droplets of supercooled water impinge on rocks, snow, or other objects in their path above tree line, building exotic *ice feathers* that extend into the wind on rocks exposed to wet, cold winds on treeless summits. In Scotland and Patagonia, entire climbs can be on rime ice.

## Water Ice

The characteristics of a given section of water ice depend on whether it evolved from running water or from snow on ice (Figure 14-4). Climbers find water ice tenacious and difficult to penetrate, so it is sometimes called *hardwater ice*. An observant climber will note that different types of water ice may form adjacent to each other, within inches or feet, at the same time and on the same ice climb. On a particular climb, hand tools may easily penetrate the wet *plastic ice* formed where water is running over the surface, but ice screws placed in the same ice would probably not hold a fall. Only a few feet away, colder and more solid ice may take screws well, but shatter when struck by the Pockets of ice formed from snow on ice may allow hand tools to shear through the mass hold the tools well, depending on its state of transformation.

### Water-Ice Evolution and Running Water

Running water may form a glaze over rock, called *verglas*, which may eventually become thin—and then thick—sheets of water ice. Water dripping from overhangs can form stalactite-like candles, with rounded stalagmites below.

Ice can be transparent, white to milky white, blue-green to blue, or yellow. It can be brittle or plastic, and it can break into blocky pieces of *concrete ice*, or thin sheets called *dinner plates*. Alternating warm and cold weather can transform ice to a brittle concrete structure; longer spring days can make *snow cone ice*. Figure 14-4 provides a summary of water-ice evolution.

Water ice often begins to form as water flows from a groundwater seep over a cliff face. This situation occurs most readily if there is a snowpack above the cliff and if the air temperature is warm enough or the sun is strong enough for the snowpack to melt. Thin sheets of verglas form on the rock (you can see the rock through the ice) as the temperature drops. If accumulation continues, either during very cold weather or on a north-facing cliff, thick sheets of ice may form.

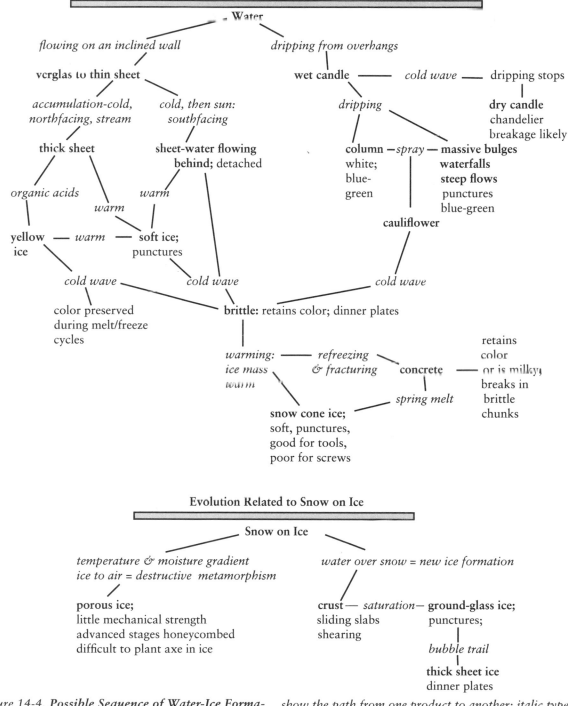

Figure 14-4. *Possible Sequence of Water-Ice Formation:* This diagram presents a model based on observation of ice formation; it is subject to redefinition with further investigation. **Bold type** indicates product; lines show the path from one product to another; *italic type* denotes process along the paths; and plain type describes the mechanical behavior and color of the ice.

If the cliff faces south and the sheets remain thin, the sun may warm the rock behind the ice and melt it. This melting becomes more pronounced as the days grow longer and the sun rises higher in the sky later in the ice-climbing season. As a result, thin ice that is climbable early in the day, before the sun strikes the cliff, may have water running behind it later in the day. This ice becomes detached or hollow, and cannot be climbed safely.

If the cliff has a small overhang, stalactites of ice begin to form, eventually meeting an ice bulge that started to form below. Many small stalactites or candles of downward-hanging ice may form. The individual candles are transparent to white, and the overall mass of the ice is also white. When forming, *candle ice* is wet, but in a cold period it dries out and becomes brittle. In either case, a significant part of the candle-ice mass consists of air pockets. It is relatively easy to bury an ice axe or ice hammer up to the head in wet candle ice, but climbing this mass is precarious because of the constant possibility that the tool may shear through the mass. When the mass is brittle, a hand tool or crampon shatters the candles with the tinkling sound of a breaking chandelier. You can sometimes climb candle ice by kicking tenuous footsteps or by breaking through the outer layer of candles if there is a more substantial mass of ice underneath.

Beneath the dripping candles, rounded masses of ice similar to stalagmites begin to grow upward, and eventually the two growing ice masses join to form *columns*. Associated with columns and dripping overhangs you find *cauliflower ice*, which results when water spray forms as dripping water strikes the lower surface. Cauliflower ice is rounded, resembling the vegetable for which it is named. Since it usually forms on a ledge, it often incorporates snow into its structure, while an ice crust forms on its outside.

During the spring an ice mass begins to warm and takes on a surface texture with the appearance and consistency of a snow cone, while the plastic ice of the interior gives good hand-tool purchase, which may tempt you to climb. Climbing would be dangerous, however, since ice screws do not hold well in the soft plastic ice, and running water between the ice and the cliff will have partially detached the ice.

Concrete ice is formed when ice warms and fractures as it freezes again. When warm, this ice is fun to climb because it is very plastic and ice tools stick with little effort. After a cold wave, concrete ice, which is milky white, is extremely brittle and breaks off in blocky chunks rather than in dinner plates when you hit it with hand tools. Crampons, unless recently sharpened, tend to skate even on low-angle concrete ice unless you work very hard. You can climb concrete ice, but it is difficult to do so because of the effort involved and the insecure tool placement.

*Ice Color and Consistency:* Ice color, which can vary on a climb, provides information about evolution, consistency, and potential response to tools. Yellow is the easiest color of water ice to understand, although its color is related to an external agent and not the nature of the ice itself. Yellow ice forms from seeps that have run over slabs beneath cedar bushes or other vegetation. Organic acids derived from the vegetation give the ice its pronounced dingy yellow color.

Transparent ice, white ice, milky white ice, and blue or blue-green ice take on their color because of interactions with and filtering of light as it passes through the ice. These colors do give some indication of how the ice will respond to tool placement.

Thin ice is transparent, but as it gets a little thicker it appears white. This white color is the mixture of all of the colors or wavelengths of visible light reaching our eyes, where they are mixed and then interpreted by the brain as white. As water continues to run over the ice surface and freeze, the ice thickens and begins to turn first blue-green and then blue. Blue ice appears blue whether you look at it in direct sunlight, shade, or even under a gray blanket of cloud and illuminated by the *incident* (scattered) light of the sky. John Tyndall, the nineteenth-century British scientist and climber, discussed the appearance and origin of the blue-green and blue color of ice in his delightful book *Glaciers of the Alps*.[1] Tyndall concluded, "When the rays of light pass through a sufficient thickness of ice the longer waves are, as in the case of water, more and more absorbed and the final colour of the substance is therefore blue." That is, the ice acts as a filter that only lets through light that we perceive as blue in color (Figure 14-5).

Blue ice is ice without internal fractures, but you may create some when you swing your tools. If it takes hand tools without much internal fracturing, it is plastic ice, but blue ice can become very hard and brittle on the outer surface as the air tem-

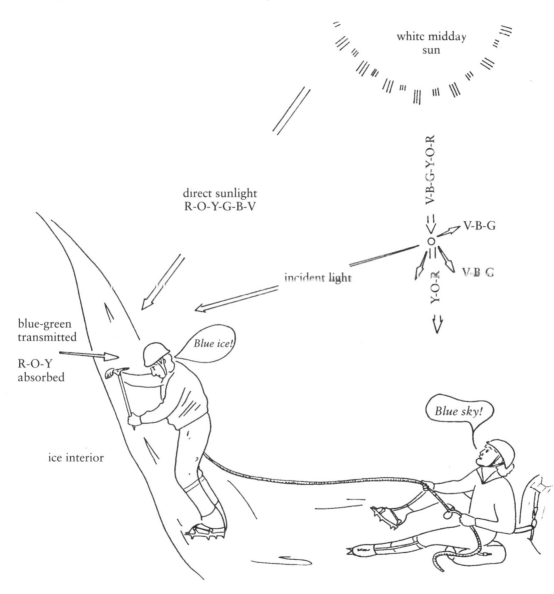

*Figure 14-5. **Blue Sky and Blue Ice:** When either direct sunlight or incident light hits ice, the ice absorbs (filters) longer wavelengths of red, orange, and yellow light and transmits wavelengths of blue. The light coming to our eyes from the ice is predominantly blue-green to blue, wavelengths to which the human eye and brain are especially sensitive. R = red, O = orange, Y = yellow, G = green, B = blue, and V = violet.*

perature drops. This surface shatters when struck, and dinner plates, with razor-sharp edges, break off. These are a threat to the belayer who, more often than not, is below in the line of fire. The lead climber can help, by trapping and breaking up the dinner plates into small pieces before allowing them to fall. Often, the more brittle ice is next to the surface, and you can find more plastic ice underneath into which you can securely sink your hand tools.

The milky white color of concrete ice apparently originates in the interaction of sunlight with many fractures formed in the ice as it freezes again after warming. All wavelengths of light, reflecting from these surfaces, come to our eyes, and our brain interprets them as white. Snow crystals that are individually transparent take on a white color in the snowpack because of similar reflections from crystal faces.

### Snow Alteration of Water Ice

Snow sitting over ice transforms the ice's appearance and properties. In a destructive *metamorphic* process, snow insulates the ice from the outside air, which is usually colder than the ice itself, causing a temperature and humidity gradient between the ice and the outside air, similar to that found in a winter snowpack. Moisture moves from the ice to the air, resulting in a porous ice mass that holds climbing tools and ice screws poorly. This situation is unfortunate because it means that you cannot use low-angle ice areas for practicing or teaching in heavy snow years, even if you go to the effort of clearing snow from the ice. It also means that as you exit from a vertical, difficult climb onto a snow-covered ledge, you may find porous ice with little integrity and will have difficulty getting good hand-tool placements over the top.

*Ice crust* (Figure 14-6) is formed when snow sits on ledges and adheres to steep surfaces. Water flows over the top, freezes, and forms a crust over the snow. When this crust occupies a large area at the bottom of ice bulges, it is a potential danger. It will perhaps support your weight, but more likely it will break, and you will fall into the snow on the ledge and may continue falling from the ledge.

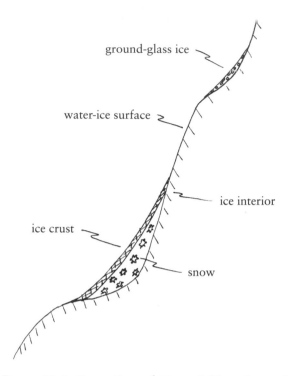

*Figure 14-6. Formation of Ground-Glass Ice and Breakable Crust*

It is best to break the crust purposely rather than to have it break unexpectedly. You also need to recognize ice crust because it sometimes has enough integrity for you to place ice screws but does not provide enough shear strength to prevent the screws from pulling out when loaded.

Where the crust forms over a few inches to a foot or so of snow, the snow may solidify as water percolates through. This situation produces *ground-glass ice*, which as its name implies, is an opaque white mass easily distinguished from the clearer brittle white ice surrounding it. As ground-glass ice turns into water ice, only a thin bubble trail may remain as evidence of its process of formation. Ground-glass ice holds ice tools far more easily than the brittle ice surrounding it, and recognizing it may save you untold amounts of energy while climbing relatively steep sections.

## References for Future Reading

Bentley, W. A., and W. J. Humphreys. 1962. *Snow crystals*. New York: Dover Publications, Inc.

Daffern, Tony. 1983. *Avalanche safety for skiers & climbers*. Seattle: Cloudcap Press.

Plummer, Charles C., and David McGeary. 1991. Glaciers and glaciation. Chapter 12 in *Physical geology*. Dubuque, Iowa: Wm. C. Brown Pub.

Post, Austin, and Edward R. Lachapelle. 1971. *Glacier ice*. Seattle: The Mountaineers and University of Washington Press.

Tyndall, John. 1860. *The glaciers of the Alps: Being a narrative of excursions and ascents, an account of the origin and phenomena of glaciers, and an exposition of the physical principles to which they are related*. London: John Murray,

_____. 1896. *The forms of water in clouds and rivers, ice and glaciers*. New York: D. Appleton and Company.

## Endnotes

1. Tyndall, 1860. The famous scientist John Tyndall did many interesting ascents of peaks, including the third ascent of the Matterhorn, during the golden age of alpine mountaineering. He solved various puzzles about glaciers and was the first to understand why the sky is blue.

# CHAPTER

# 15

# *Steep Ice*

## Rating Ice Climbs

Since modern ice ratings are more or less internationally accepted, an ice climb of a given grade is recognizable wherever you find it, within the context of local conditions. Ratings take into account average overall angle and length of the climb, the length of sustained vertical sections, and average ice conditions. Pluses and minuses are added to the rating to show variations in degree of difficulty. For example, in New England the relative shortness of climbs limits the upper end of the grading scale to 5+ in comparison to longer western Canadian climbs such as Polar Circus, a 6. A current trend to push the limits on "horror show" ice has raised the upper limit in western Canada to grade 6+ or 7. In addition to the ice rating, a commitment grade, similar to that used for rock, indicates how long the average competent party can expect to take to complete the climb.

Mixed routes involve both ice climbing and rock climbing (in rock portions, climbers hook reverse-curve tools and place crampons on nubbins). Mixed routes make the grading more complicated, but usually the ice ratings take account of these factors. Jeff Lowe has suggested incorporating the Yosemite Decimal System, commitment rating, and technical difficulty of rock climbing into a coherent system that would serve for pure rock climbs, pure ice climbs, or mixed climbs.[1] This method gives detailed information about climbs, which is particularly desirable when you are new to an area.

After gaining experience in a locale, you may find that the relative ratings—easy, moderate, and hard—tell you all you need to know about a climb. But with ice, the climb can vary enormously in difficulty—depending on the season, the day, the weather, the amount of ice and its quality—no matter what system is used.

## Climbing Steep Ice

Climbing steep ice is a relatively new sport. It began in the late 1960s when drooped picks, rigid boots, and ice hammers were developed. Previously, climbers boldly cut steps up steep ice and experimented with insecure ice daggers to maintain a precarious balance. The new tools allowed rapid front-point ascents of climbs that had previously taken several days.

Scout vertical ice before you attempt to climb it. It may contain concave sections with corners, grooves, or chimneys that allow stemming to take weight off your arms. The most strenuous section of vertical ice to climb will be a convex section that places you on the outside of a long bulge. Your arm muscles and arm bone structure have to do much of the work of keeping you on the climb. You may prefer long sections of uniform steepness that are not quite vertical to sections that start out at lower angles but require pulling over a bulge higher up.

When climbing vertical ice, you must place two hand tools very well indeed if they are going to provide security. Target a spot and keep hitting the target to get proper placement. The first blows may simply remove brittle or fractured surface ice, revealing better ice below.

Use the tool with the heaviest head in your off hand to provide momentum to penetrate the ice. Place the two hand tools above your shoulders and directly above your feet to maintain balance. Placing the hand tool well off to the side of the body provides little aid in balance unless you plan to move your feet underneath. Place the two tools at full arm extension well above your head. In this manner, you can move up to the tools and take them out while maintaining balance. If you move very high on the tools before taking them out, you will lose balance and fall backward. A good rule of thumb is to climb no higher than eye height on the tool heads. Placing the hand tools will take effort and concentration. It is essential to remember to use your crampons properly in the manner that you learned on less strenuous ice.

## Piolet Traction

*Piolet traction* is a technique used when ascending steep ice and bulges, and when traversing. The technique involves placing an ice tool's pick above your head, gripping the shaft near the spike, and pulling down on the shaft to provide a handhold. Climbers normally add wrist leashes to hang on to the axe.

### Wrist Leashes

A *wrist leash* is a sling loop, attached to the ice tool, that you wear over your wrist. A well-designed leash leading from the axe to your wrist helps to prevent fatigue on long vertical sections. Without a leash, you would have to hold on to the shaft of your ice axe very tightly to support your body weight, and your arm muscles would soon tire. With a leash, however, you can put body weight on the wrist loop, and the bone structure of your arms, rather than the muscles, will bear the weight.

A leash also allows you to retrieve and grip a dropped tool one-handed, slide your hand into position for use on snow and low-angle ice, and free both hands by hanging from an elbow to place an ice screw. The leash should also hold onto you, rather than requiring you to hold onto it, if you tire near the top of a long, strenuous climb.[2] Since you may use your ice axe on different-angle slopes, do not use the wrist leash on low-angle snow slopes, because doing so prevents you from transferring the axe to your uphill hand.

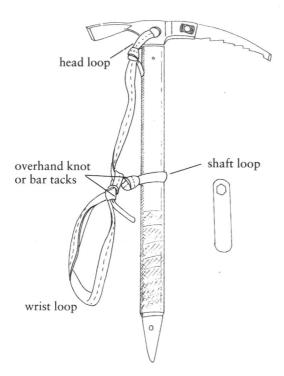

head loop

overhand knot
or bar tacks

shaft loop

wrist loop

*Figure 15-1.* ***A Custom Wrist Leash***

Wrist leashes that do all of these tasks are available commercially. A custom leash for a 60-centimeter tool (Figure 15-1) uses approximately 5 feet of half-inch supertape. A 50-centimeter tool requires about 4 inches (10 centimeters) less tape. You can replace the overhand knots with bar-tack stitching to produce a less bulky leash. The wrist loop should be sized so that when you twist it once or twice around your mittened or gloved hand, your hand will be at the proper position on the shaft. For more comfort, slide a piece of 1-inch tubular webbing over the wrist loop. The wrist loop should allow your arm to slide through it up to the elbow, so that you can use your elbow for balance while you are placing an ice screw with your hands (see Figure 15-8). The shaft loop may not slide on a rubber-coated tool, so you may wish to eliminate this loop or tie it larger. Minor adjustments in position of the grip are possible by altering the length of the head loop.

*Figure 15-2.* ***Traverses on Ice with a Bladed Tool (from Left to Right)***

### Normal Ice Traverses

Traverses on steep water ice are somewhat harder than on rock because of the difficulties of balance when a tool is off to the side, and because of the properties of picks that are blades (as opposed to picks that are tubes). An ascending diagonal line is always easier than a direct horizontal traverse, but many steep climbs require a few direct horizontal moves.

When you traverse, you need to place the axe above and off to the side, and the easiest way to do so is to use a diagonal cross-body swing. This diagonal placement, however, is undesirable. While a cylindrical pick would rotate, a bladed pick might bend as you step under the axe (you will feel as though you are holding onto a spring), and might shear from the ice or break altogether.

To avoid this problem, orient the axe so that the shaft is parallel with the fall line. You must not place the axe very far off to the side (Figure 15-2). Instead, you must make a series of short axe placements, and then move your crampons underneath

*Figure 15-3. **Traverse on Ice with a Hollow Tube Pick.** After Lowe, 1981.*

the newly placed tool. When you start to move, shift your weight in much the same manner as you would in traversing rock, but do not make long reaches. Put one foot out to the side and then shift your cen-

---

#### An Unusual Traverse on Ice

In its usual thin condition, the Black Dike of New Hampshire's Cannon Cliff requires a series of unique moves to pass the crux. After roping up beneath the narrow cleft, you ascend an easy 65-degree ice flow on ice thin enough to show the black rock of the dike below. This thin warm-up pitch brings you to an aerie high above the glacial trough of Franconia Notch and sets you up for the crux.

Leaving the belay, you venture left onto a rock buttress marked by two vertically stacked ledges, each large enough for one foot. From the upper ledge, you notice that the steep wall overhead has no holds for hooking the reverse-curve blade of the axe. Off to the left, a long arm's length away, a thin ice smear plunges vertically from a platform down a narrow chute. It does not seem that you can get to the ice from your

tiny ledge, since there are no holds overhead and no ice thick enough to take your axe. You are at the crux traverse!

This traverse does not yield to normal technique. It requires that you hook a waist-high rock flake on your right side and lean left on it. Leaning from the axe, you take little hop-steps to get as far left as you possibly can, to make room for your right foot on the hold. While still lying away off the axe, you throw your left foot across the void to a platform large enough for one set of front points. With a new stability, you lean left as far as possible and plant your blade in thin ice to give a minimal point of balance. Now stand on your left front point and do what you can with your right crampon and right ice axe to help you step up to the platform. Congratulations, you have passed the crux. Now protect and climb the steep, ugly black ribbon overhead to a wildly exposed belay.

ter of gravity over your foot before attempting to stand. (Refer to Figure 1-11 if you need a reminder.)

Because they rotate when securely placed in ice more than 1 inch thick, hollow tube picks allow you to lean farther and make cross-body placements with the shaft diagonally oriented to the fall line (Figure 15-3). The axe and hollow pick simply rotate as you traverse. Once you make a placement, shift your weight from left to right front points while doing a lieback on the axe with a straight arm. You can extend this technique to reverse steep ice pitches.[3]

### Ice Bulges

Ice bulges too high to step over are a challenge and may be more difficult than a steep wall. A bulge between waist and chest height presents much the same problem as the top of a nearly vertical ice climb. In order to pull over an ice bulge, reach over the top of the bulge as far as possible

A

B

C

D

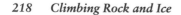

*Figure 15-4. Clearing a Waist-high Bulge: A, B, and C show a climber clearing a bulge. In D, the climber uses the axe as a cane to stand on top of the bulge.*

and place the ice axe securely. You must stand as close as possible to the ice, so that your feet almost touch the base of the bulge. A common mistake is to leave space between yourself and the ice. This space limits how far forward you can place the axe. If the bulge is not vertical, do not try to place the axe too far forward, or you will lean enough to rotate your front points and cause shearing.

Place your axe well enough to hold a short fall and lean back on it, as shown in Figure 15-4A. In this manner, you commit your safety to the axe. Leaning back ensures that you can see your front points and that you force them into the ice. If you lean forward, your front points will shear out and you will probably fall. In this committed but secure lieback position, walk your feet higher and higher.

The top of the bulge (Figure 16-4B, C) requires the most care and commitment to the axe. Continue to lean back with your posterior hanging out over space until you plant one foot on top of the bulge. Then, step up, smoothly shifting your weight onto the upper foot.

Note the role of your hands during this sequence. You begin gripping the axe with your hand in the leash's wrist loop. Place the other hand on the shaft of the axe, and slide it up the shaft as you climb higher. When possible, put the palm of the second hand on top of the axe to assist you as you mantle up onto the top of the bulge. Your wrist-loop hand will also slide up the shaft as you get higher. Stand on the top of the bulge (Figure 16-4D) and take the axe out, ready to move on. (Sometimes it helps you to stand if you remove the axe and use it as a cane.)

Bulges at the top of vertical ice climbs can be very troublesome if the top is horizontal, particularly if you are climbing with two reverse-curve tools. These tools are very difficult to place on a horizontal surface while you are front-pointing on a vertical surface. On the other hand, you can easily plant a tool with a normally drooped alpine pick, thus securing an easy exit. Some climbers use hand tools with reverse-curve picks in both hands for steep ice, and reserve a third tool with an alpine pick in a holster until the exit.

*Using a Short Ice Axe to Brace—Piolet Ramasse:* *Piolet ramasse* is the technique of moving over low-angle ice at the bottom or top of a steep climb by bracing with a short ice axe. The 45- to 50-centimeter axe that works best on steep ice is not the best length for cross-body bracing on low-angle ice. It would be nice if we could always depend on having the right ice axe for a particular slope, but in the absence of the perfect tool, we can adapt our technique to the tool at hand. This way, after ascending a long, steep ice column, you do not have to bend over awkwardly and continue using steep-ice technique on a 30-degree slope.

To adapt your bracing technique to a short axe, hold the shaft vertically instead of in the cross-body position while stepping over short bulges (Figure 15-5). Keep your hand on the ferrule and spike next to the ice surface, and press vertically down on the head of the axe. This position will give you additional security in those final few feet of the climb.

*Figure 15-5. **Bracing with a Short Ice Axe—Piolet Ramasse***

A — X-position from behind

B — rest position

C — stand

D — tensed right arm

E — X-position from side

*Figure 15-6. **The Monkey Hang:** A—Start in an X-position with your feet about shoulder-width apart. Reach up high and place the hand tools slightly off to the side to avoid getting hit with ice chips during placement (view from behind climber). B—Move both feet up to waist height. This unlikely position is a rest position: you are hanging mostly from bone structure rather than muscle. C—Stand slightly to loosen one axe (here, the left) while maintaining balance with the other arm tensed. D—Stand to full extension, place the loosened (left) axe higher, and then loosen the second axe and place it higher too. E—You have returned to the X-position and the beginning of the cycle (view from the side).*

### The Monkey Hang

On very steep ice where you cannot stem, move in a specific progression called the *monkey hang* (Figure 15-6). The object of the monkey hang is to transfer weight from your arm muscles to your bones.

If the base of the ice has an ice slope leading up to it, balance to the top of this starting slope using crampons and whatever natural handholds you find. In this way you can avoid three or four hand-tool placements and save your muscles for what lies ahead.

Place your right-hand tool as high as possible, then your left-hand tool. Seen from the rear, your body makes an X, with your arms and legs forming the crosspieces of the X (Figure 15-6A). Now bring both of your feet up to midthigh level so that you are in a squatting position on the vertical wall (Figure 15-6B). This position minimizes the effort of your arm muscles because most of your weight hangs from your arm bones and tendons. If you chip small platforms with your crampons, your front points will not skate down the ice. When you are secure in the squatting position, stand up (Figure 15-6C).

First, loosen your left-hand tool in its hole without removing it. Then stand partway up while hanging off your bent right arm (Figure 15-6D). This position is strenuous because your arm muscles are taking your weight. Remove the left-hand tool, reach as high as possible, and place the pick securely. Transfer your weight to your straight left arm and loosen the pick of the right-hand tool. Remove it, reach up as high as possible, and place the pick. You are back in the starting X-position (Figure 15-6E).

If preexisting pick placements are available, producing a kind of ice pegboard, you can save much energy by using them. Sometimes you may leapfrog the height of hand-tool placements rather than having both hand tools at the same level during the sequence. Experiment on a top rope and learn what works best.

## Fanging

Climbing steep ice with no hand tools, sometimes called *fanging*, can be an entertaining way to perfect technique or to keep in practice. You use handholds in the ice—flakes, pockets, etc.—as you would on rock. The technique requires excellent balance. Try it when the ice is dry but not too cold. (If the ice is wet, your gloves will get wet, resulting in rapid heat transfer. If it is too cold, you would have to use thick mitts that would hinder dexterity. Very thin gloves do not hinder dexterity.) Practice fanging on a tight top rope, but use the technique in leading when a move or two is actually easier without hand tools than with them—for example, on some thin-ice moves. Read the ice for the best line, looking for flakes, columns, and pockets to lieback; shallow concave surfaces and corners to stem; and one- and two-finger pockets to hook.

You will be amazed at what you can climb, less strenuously than when you use hand tools. For difficult moves, however, you spend a bit more time making secure front-point platforms than you do when using hand tools. Even overhangs yield to fanging, particularly if you can follow a corner that you can stem. Your balance will be more like that of rock climbing, and you will come to think of the ice-climbing movement in much the same way as you think of movement on rock.

## Leading on Steep Ice

Climbers have developed different strategies for leading ice than they have for leading rock. These strategies have changed with tool evolution, since ice climbing is tool-dependent. The fact that water-ice climbing takes place during short days and in cold temperatures also affects the choices, since climbers have a limited amount of time in which to finish a route, and they do not want to get too cold doing so. Unlike rock, ice is renewable and usually repairs itself in a day or two. An ice climb can change from being desperate to moderate or easy during the course of a season. Climbers routinely report the conditions under which they made an ascent, and wise climbers wait until the climb is "in shape" before setting out.

As long as it seems reasonable, you should attempt to move from one resting point to another and place protection at good stances. Many kinds of ice climbing require you to concentrate on good technique and to accept long run outs between stances. Pound-in ice pitons and the latest ice screws, coupled with good balance, allow you to place intermediate protection from front-point positions without resorting to direct rest or hanging from the hand tools. Climbers sometimes rest directly on ice tools, or purposefully aid from them, when climbing long stretches of steep ice. The first ascents of a number of now-classic long, steep ice climbs were done using *aiders* (slings in which to stand) attached to three Terrordactyls to make progress. As tools have evolved, more confident climbers have climbed longer and longer sections without hanging from the tools other than by wrist loops.

The ice leader can form holds to make the job of leading less strenuous and precarious. For example, it is often desirable to cut steps or enlarge natural footholds on steep climbs where you want to stop and place an ice screw. On climbs that are less than vertical, you can cut footholds or toe holds overhead with the adze of one axe while hanging on with the other. You can then move up to stand in the new hold. When starting a vertical section, it is sometimes helpful to chip front-point platforms overhead before leaving a stance. These chipped holds reduce the amount of muscle power needed and convert a strenuous climb into a balance problem.

### Protecting Yourself While Leading

When you use the rope to secure balance while placing protection, as in Figure 15-7, you can place it around the axe next to the ice to prevent leverage. The belayer then takes slack out of the rope to aid balance. Alternatively, attach a carabiner to the wrist loop of the ice axe and run the climbing rope through it.

You can also attach the secured hammer directly to the harness with a runner sling (or a keeper sling, described below). The wrist loop is not a good attachment point if you plan to hang directly from it, because you will stretch the loop flat, making it difficult to reinsert your wrist. These attachments provide security while you stand bal-

Figure 15-8. **Using the Wrist Leash to Place an Ice Screw While Balancing on Front Points**

A

B

to belayer

to climber

to belayer          to climber

Figure 15-7. **Temporary Belay with a Hand Tool: A—** *The rope drapes over the ice pick next to the tool to prevent levering. B—The rope attaches to the wrist loop with a carabiner.*

anced on one foot or on slightly larger stances, as you place an ice screw or pound-in for more reliable protection.

When the ice steepens to around 70 degrees, you can still balance on front points while placing an ice screw, but you will want to remain firmly attached to your axe. Use a wrist loop that opens up enough to allow your arm to slide up to the elbow (Figure 15-8) so you can use the axe for balance and your hand to help start the screw. Some steep-ice climbers use hero loops permanently attached to the screw to allow them to clip the rope when the screw is partway in. As the screw turns deeper into the ice, the security of the screw increases.

### Keeper Slings and Cows' Tails

You use *keeper slings* and *cows' tails* in order to rest on steep ice or as an emergency technique should something go wrong. A keeper sling (Figure 15-9A) is a permanently attached sling extending from an axe's spike hole to the rope-attachment point of your harness. If a rest becomes necessary, you can plant the tool firmly and hang from the keeper sling. In addition, hand tools with keeper slings are useful for safeguarding you when you set up a screw belay, and for backing up the belay. A cow's tail (Figure 15-9B) is a removable sling used whenever you want a rest. One end attaches to your harness and the free end has a *fifi hook* (a metal hook shaped something like a question mark) or a *sky hook* (a metal hook with a sharp bend) that you tuck away until you need it to connect to the axe. Carabiners do not work as well as hooks when you want to get out of an attachment to the hand tool because of difficulties caused by trying to open the gate while you are hanging from the tool.

Hanging from either a keeper sling or a cow's tail frees both your hands so you can place ice screws and gain a complete physical rest on very steep ice (although you may not mentally relax enough to enjoy it). To enhance your sense of security, make a two-headed cow's tail to distribute your weight to two hand tools firmly planted in the ice. Equalize a rappel ring in the middle of a loop

A

B

tool attachment

fifi hook

sky hook

harness attachment

*Figure 15-9. **Keeper Slings and Cows' Tails:** A—Keeper sling; B—Cows' tails.*

that has fifi hooks or sky hooks attached to both ends. Tie a short sling directly to the rappel ring and make a loop in its free end. This loop attaches to your harness with a locking carabiner, and the fifi hooks attach to firmly planted ice axes. Commercial versions of this rig are available.

The length of keeper slings and cows' tails may present a problem on low-angle ice and snow. For steep ice, slings should be long enough for you to place the hand tools overhead at full arm extension but no longer. If the sling is too long, you would lower too far below the tool when resting, so the tool might be out of reach. Then, in order to grip the tool, you would need to use a second tool to climb back up. On low-angle ice, however, a keeper sling dangles underfoot and threatens to trip you at every step.[4] Avoid this problem by clipping up the slack with a second carabiner, or by running a piece of elastic inside a tubular nylon sling that contracts and shortens the sling when it is not in use. You can also put the tool and keeper sling away and climb with a longer tool that is more appropriate for low-angle ice. Remove keeper slings on snow as they prevent you from transferring the axe to your uphill hand.

As with any technique you have not used before, experiment with keeper slings and cows' tails to determine what is suitable for your particular climbing style and needs. To experiment with these slings, find a column of steep ice placed so that you can stand at the bottom of it. Place your hand tools in the ice at full arm extension. Then slowly lower your body weight onto the keeper sling or cow's tail in such a way that you can quickly stand up again if the technique is not working.

### Reinforcing Ice Screws at Anchors

To supplement ice screws at a belay, attach a runner sling from the ice-tool wrist leash to the screw, as shown in Figure 15-10, or directly to your harness. When you are setting up a belay on thin ice, a driven hammer provides more security than the screws. When driven into the frozen mud found in cracks on thin-ice climbs, the tool gives you a sense of security, and perhaps some real value.

*Figure 15-10.* **Hand Tool Used as Anchor Backup**

Depending on the tool and its placement, you can optimize the strength of a tool belay by tying off the pick with a hero loop next to the ice like a tied-off piton. The security of a hero-loop belay is based on pick curvature, the presence of tie-off holes in the pick, the nature of the ice, and other factors. When you use a tool anchor of uncertain strength, make sure that your stance is secure enough to take the impact of a fall, to reduce force on the anchor.

You can use ice hammers and axes as temporary anchors while placing more permanent protection or to supplement screw anchors. When you arrive at a marginal stance, bury the pick of an axe or hammer in the ice. Northwall hammers work very well. If you carry an additional hammer as a third tool—and many climbers do—then use it to place the northwall hammer (Figure 15-11). Some hand

*Figure 15-11.* ***Securing a Hand Tool with a Hammer:*** *Some tools have a flange on the tool end of the pick to hit and drive the tool into the ice. Protect your eyes from flying ice chips.*

tools also have a raised flange at the head of the pick that you strike to drive the pick into the ice. The first few blows should be relatively gentle ones to set the hammer so it does not bounce out of the ice under a misguided blow. If you set the hammer too deeply, you will need to chop it out when you want to remove it. Note that hitting one tool with another will produce flying ice chips, so you will need to protect your eyes with sunglasses or gog-gles, or by looking away as you strike one tool with another.

## References for Future Reading

Barry, John. 1987. *Snow and ice climbing*. Seattle: Cloudcap Press.

Cinnamon, Charles. 1981. Hanging oneself. *Summit*. 27(4):4–7.

Cinnamon, Jerry. 1980. A versatile leash for hardwater ice tools. *Summit*.

Lowe, Jeff. 1979. *The ice experience*. Chicago: Contemporary Books, Inc.

_____. 1981. *Technical manual*. Lowe Alpine Systems: Broomfield, Colorado.

Wilcox, Rick. 1982. *An ice climber's guide to northern New England*. North Conway, New Hampshire: International Mountain Equipment, Inc.

_____. 1992. *An ice climber's guide to northern New England*. Second Edition. North Conway, New Hampshire: International Mountain Equipment, Inc.

## Endnotes

1. Lowe, 1979.

2. Cinnamon, 1980.

3. Lowe, 1981.

4. See Cinnamon, 1981, for things that can go wrong with axe keeper slings.

# 16

# *Avalanches*

## Avalanche Victims

There are about 15 avalanche fatalities per year in North America, and the survival statistics are sobering. One out of 10 people caught in an avalanche dies, and a person who is completely buried has one in three chances of surviving. The deeper a victim is buried, the smaller the chance of surviving: 46 percent survive when buried from 1 to 2 feet, 32 percent from 3 to 4 feet, 21 percent from 5 to 6 feet, and none when buried deeper than 7 feet.[1]

Two thirds of the victims die of suffocation, one-third die of internal injuries including head and neck injuries, and about 1 percent die of hypothermia. About one half of avalanche victims die if they are not recovered within 30 minutes, and realistic longer-term rescues of live victims appear to be in the range of 2 hours.[2]

Avalanche-related deaths can only be reduced if backcountry users avoid avalanches and if the avalanched party executes a rapid self-rescue. While it is important to educate backcountry users so they can avoid avalanches, attitude is crucial: many victims are knowledgeable but choose to ignore obvious warnings.[3] Self-rescue becomes more significant in backcountry situations, where 44 percent of the fatalities occur. These backcountry accidents involve climbers and others who, once caught, have trouble getting help fast enough to carry out an effective rescue.

Despite these deadly statistics, it is imperative to initiate a rescue. Even after 6 hours, approximately one victim in 40 is found alive. There is one documented case in which a victim lived after being buried under 5 feet of snow for 25½ hours. He had defied all odds; an airspace the size of a washtub around his head saved his life. Similar examples from the Alps indicate that survival times can vary, "so rescuers and victims should never give up hope."[4]

Dan, whose experience with an avalanche is featured in the box on page 228, made several mistakes. He was climbing early in the season, when the late autumn snowfall had not had time to bond well to the ice of the glacier. He was on the climb late in the day, when the snow-ice bond was weakened, and he set off the avalanche that then threatened to bury him. Like other lucky victims, he rescued himself, and he took out two health policies after his experience—traditional insurance to pay medical bills, and an educational policy to learn how to avoid avalanches.

## Mountain Geography and Avalanches

A mountain range triggers its own snowfall by the process of mountain, or *orographic*, lifting of moist air (Figure 16-2). The moist air cools as it rises over the mountain until water vapor forms snow that eventually falls. Warmer air can hold more moisture and give rise to heavier snowfall.

Once on the ground, snowfall is distributed by local winds (Figure 16-3), scouring in some places

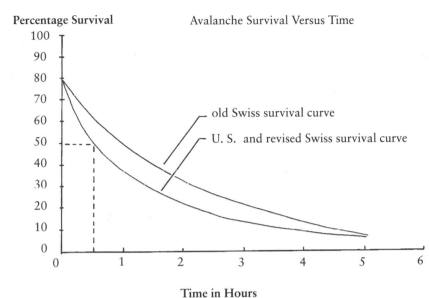

Percentage Survival

Avalanche Survival Versus Time

100
90
80
70
60
50
40
30
20
10
0

0   1   2   3   4   5   6

Time in Hours

old Swiss survival curve

U. S. and revised Swiss survival curve

*Figure 16-1. **Chances of Survival with Time.** Recent Swiss data include a greater number of short-duration rescues and now match those of North America. Note that both curves start at 80 percent, reflecting a 20-percent fatality rate due to multiple traumatic injuries. Swiss statistics from H. Jacomet,* The Avalanche Review.

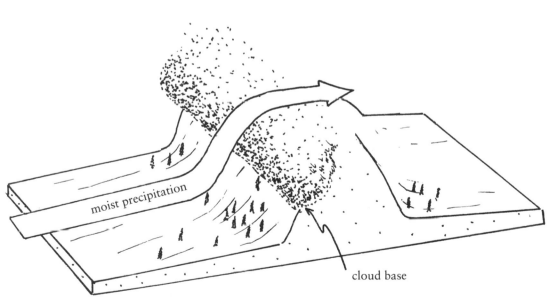

moist precipitation

cloud base

*Figure 16-2. **Orographic Lifting:** Moist air is lifted over the mountain and cools to the dewpoint. A cloud forms. Precipitation falls on the windward side of the mountain.*

and accumulating in others as wind speed and direction change in response to local ridges and valleys. Scouring occurs on the windward side of mountain ridges, leaving behind eroded slopes that are generally avalanche free. *Sastrugi*, a fluted snow surface formed by wind etching, often marks these eroded surfaces. The eroded snow is taken up to the ridge line, where it is deposited as cornices or

---

## Tobogganing the Tyndall Glacier

*Dear Jerry:*

*I was climbing the Tyndall Glacier in Rocky Mountain National Park and was about 40 feet from the top when the whole thing slid. There was around 4 or 5 feet of wind-packed snow covering the ice, around 50 degrees or so and maybe a little steeper as it topped out on a ridge between two peaks. The glacier is probably around 1,000 feet high and has a large basin at its base, which I had to climb down into to get to the glacier. It looked so beautiful, this huge expanse of smooth steep snow, I just had to climb it. I really didn't think I had to worry about it sliding, even though it was wind-pack, because it was so early in the season (Nov. 9).*

*It was right around 2:00 P.M., just enough time to top out, maybe bag one of the peaks, and then blaze on down and out to the car. I had to climb right up the center of the slope at the top because the sides were blocked by cornices. I was really close to the top and figuring that I'm home free even though it's getting steeper and all of a sudden something feels weird. I tried to self-arrest but I was going so fast and the ice was so hard, my axe just flew out of my hands. I knew I didn't want it dangling from my wrist so I tried to reach for it, or at least thought to do this, but it was futile. Then I remembered I had my crampons on and thought I should bend my legs; again this was futile. Then I remembered you're supposed to swim to try to stay on top but again, well, you guessed it. I was flying along the ice with a million tons of snow pummeling me. I was completely disoriented and everything was dark so I just went with it, pretty much my only option. It was weird. I really don't remember being scared or knowing if I was getting hurt or not.*

*After a while the snow started slowing down and I began to see light. Then all of a sudden I just sort of rolled to a stop and there I was, only halfway buried. I just lay there and freaked out for the longest time. Then I looked down at my body as I pulled myself free, and, amazingly, I was intact. My axe was dangling from its leash and my crampons (clip-on) . . . had been torn off and were all bent up! . . . I stood up and my whole left side was hurting. My ankle, hip, and elbow were really sore but I could just put some weight on the leg. I thought my arm was broken because it looked like hell and I couldn't move it. I turned around and was horrified to see that the whole glacier was no longer a beautiful white snow slope but an ugly green and dirty ice field. The snow had fractured right above where I had been and then the fracture line stepped down and around the whole glacier. The basin at the bottom, where I now stood, was filled to overflowing; the whole landscape had changed.*

*I knew I had to get out of there fast because I was alone, so I took a bunch of Advil and hobbled out. . . . No broken bones, just lots of bad bruises and two sprained ankles. A park ranger . . . and the doctor agreed that I was probably the luckiest person in the world that day. I have since ordered new crampons . . . and am more psyched than ever to head for the hills. I also got a health insurance policy . . . and signed up for an avalanche class.*

*Take care,*

*Dan*

decel.

acc.

decel.

acc.

transported to lee slopes, where it is deposited as an avalanche-prone windslab.

## Avalanche Classification

Avalanches are classified by type, trigger, size, and sliding surface (Figure 16-4).[5] You can recognize powder or *loose-snow* avalanches by the fact that they release from a point on a slope and spread out in a fan down-slope. There is little cohesion within the snow.

*Slab* avalanches usually occur in an accumulating snowpack that undergoes internal changes or metamorphism. These changes relate to settling as well as temperature and humidity gradients in the snowpack: some layers of individual snow grains are bonded together while others become cohesionless. A slab or layer of consolidated snow forms that is poorly connected to underlying layers. A *windslab* is a particular type of slab that forms from the accumulation of broken snow crystals that pack densely during and following a storm when wind speed exceeds 5 meters per second. The broken crystals do not interlock well with older snow and leave the slab less stable.

As the slab sits on a slope it *creeps* downhill under the influence of gravity. Since different parts of the slab creep at different rates, tension builds up and can be released by cracking within a slab and failure of cohesion between slabs, resulting in a slide. During the slide, the coherent slab breaks up. Climbers who start out on the surface may quickly become buried in the moving mass. Slab slides are recognizable after the fact by a vertical fracture line, the *crown surface*, that runs across the top of the slide. Broken-up pieces of slab often appear at the bottom of the slope.

Slabs are classified into *hard* or *soft* depending upon their resistance to probing with skis and how well they survive lengthy trips down-slope without disintegrating. Slab avalanches initiate at a crown surface and often have saw-toothed side boundaries, or *flanks*. They slide on a *bed surface*. The down-slope fracture, called the *stauchwall*, is

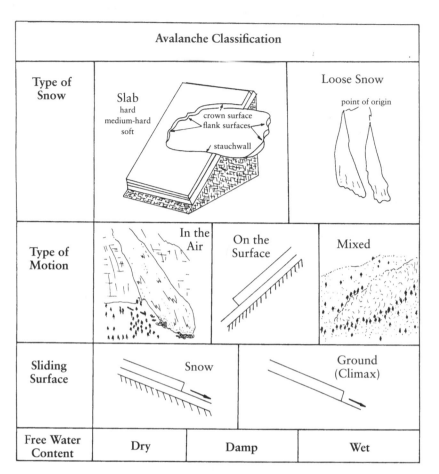

| Avalanche Classification | | | |
|---|---|---|---|
| **Type of Snow** | Slab<br>hard<br>medium-hard<br>soft<br>crown surface<br>flank surfaces<br>stauchwall | Loose Snow<br>point of origin | |
| **Type of Motion** | In the Air | On the Surface | Mixed |
| **Sliding Surface** | Snow | Ground (Climax) | |
| **Free Water Content** | Dry | Damp | Wet |

*Figure 16-4. **Avalanche Classification:** Based on* The Avalanche Handbook *(Perla and Martinelli, 1976) and the National Ski Patrol "Circle A" Avalanche Course Notes (Damon, 1986).*

often difficult to identify because it is usually over-ridden and obliterated by the sliding blocks.[6] A trigger, which is usually the victim in an accident involving people, disturbs the connection between these layers, and gravity pulls the slab downhill. Other triggers involve natural release, as well as various kinds of purposely controlled ski or explosive releases. The surface on which the slab slides can be either an old snow surface or the ground. Avalanches may vary in size from snow sluffs to whole mountainsides, but the average fracture (in a study of Colorado avalanches from 1951 to 1991) is 300 feet across and falls 700 vertical feet. Soft slabs accounted for 67.5 percent and hard slabs 26.2 percent of fatal episodes. Very large avalanches create an *airblast,* which is a strong and potentially destructive wind that can extend well out in front of the avalanche itself.

Small snow sluffs called *spindrift* are also of interest to climbers. Spindrift is small loose snow that slides down steep slopes during a snow storm. Spindrift can be a problem if enough loose snow builds up on a climb to force climbers backward off their stance. A quick rush of spindrift can also cause a lead climber to lose balance and fall. Of course, spindrift fills openings in clothing with cold snow and blinds climbers for short periods of time. When spindrift accumulates on gentler approach slopes below a climb it can build up slabs that avalanche. Since most avalanches occur within 24 hours of a storm, the presence of much spindrift indicates that climbers are endangering themselves by climbing at that time, especially if the rate of snowfall is heavy—exceeding 1 inch per hour—and if the temperature rose as the storm continued. A warming trend common to most storms, indicates

## Cornice Fall and Survival

*Dear Jerry:*

*The final 800 feet of the 3,000-foot-high hanging glacier looked like an easy romp up a narrow chute, but it was already 7 P.M. and darkness was pressing. To get to this point we had started at first light and soloed steep ice early in the morning. In the midday we had climbed four pitches of unprotectable disintegrating rock around an overhanging section of the glacier. With that crumbling vertical horror behind, we could see the top and hoped to beat darkness and undergo a cold bivouac near the summit. The chute started from the crevasse where Dan later landed at the end of his 300-foot fall.*

*At the end of the second lead Dan belayed in the middle of the ice groove that obviously channeled all falling things. There was good ice in the groove for an anchor and we would quickly be out of the line of fire when I led through. No rocks or ice had fallen off earlier in the day. We thought that if cornices were going to fall, they would have done so in the heat of midday. In retrospect, our reasoning was flawed; thick clouds and smoke blowing over the mountains from fires raging out of control in British Columbia combined to prevent normal cooling. It was too warm.*

*A section of the cornice the size of an 18-wheel tractor-trailer rig broke off. Giant blocks fell on top of Dan and pushed him down the slope like a hydraulic ram. An anchor carabiner broke, his axe keeper slings ripped out, and he unzipped the 32 bar tacks of a dynamic sling on a piece of protection before pulling the screw and finally collapsing a snow bridge over the crevasse that stopped his fall. This was a good landing place that provided dynamic deceleration. The tightly stretched rope cracked my ribs but did not completely cut me in two. After regaining consciousness, I rappelled down to Dan and we made our way to where we thought a helicopter could land or hover, because by now we knew that we needed help to get out alive. Dan's legs were not functioning and, in a freak side effect of the accident, I had lost most of the skin from my back and quickly became hypothermic. Dan's faith and activity kept us going throughout the cold night on the glacier. An alert warden realized that we had not signed back in from our climb and initiated a rescue the next day. Dan eventually quit climbing because of his damaged knees. Whenever I get near a cornice the scarred skin on my back starts to itch.*

*Take care,*

*Jim*

---

that wet, heavy snow may be sitting on a layer of loose, unconsolidated powder, producing the conditions in which a slab of new snow may slide.

---

## Cornices

Cornices (Figure 16-5) form at the crests of ridges. They blend with the mountain slope on the windward side but overhang steep, snow-laden slopes and are unsupported on the leeward side. Cornices form as the wind decelerates after passing over the crest. Angular ridge lines produce a more rapid wind deceleration than rounded ridge lines, and tend to promote the formation of cornices. Cornices are formed of broken crystals packed together so well that they create a density of about half that of glacier ice; new snow is usually much less dense.

Cornices are under tension and may fracture on the windward side well back from their crest. They

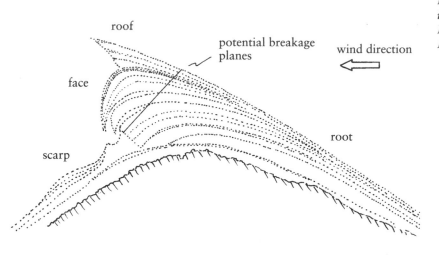

roof

potential breakage planes

wind direction

face

root

scarp

*Figure 16-5.* **Cornice Structure in Relation to Wind Direction.** *Modified from Perla and Martınelli, 1976.*

are a danger for at least three reasons. First, climbers approaching them from the windward side may wander onto them and cause them to break. The literature of mountaineering is filled with near-accidents, and the disappearance of a number of famous climbers is attributed to falling through cornices.[7] Unsuspecting climbers may not know that they are on a cornice until their ice axe or foot plunges through into open air below. Second, cornices may fall on climbers coming up leeward slopes. If the cornice does not fall during an ascent, it may break as climbers tunnel through the cornice to exit the climb. Third, a falling cornice can trigger a windslab avalanche on the slope below.

## Slope Steepness and Length

There is a relationship between slope steepness and the potential for avalanche. Slopes steeper than 60 degrees will sluff snow continuously. *Slopes 45 to 60 degrees will avalanche and should always be suspect.* Slopes of 25 to 45 degrees *may* avalanche and present the greatest danger because their stability is unknown.

Slopes less than 20 degrees are low enough in angle that they may not slide during the winter. If there is a steeper slope above, however, there can be a problem. One 1991 case involved three sledders on an 18-degree slope overlain by a 40-degree slope. The shallow-angled slope settled beneath the sledders and released the snow on the steeper slope above.[8]

People have a difficult time judging slope steepness and usually have to rely on clinometers (Figure 16-6A) or other measures. A simple observation of the angle between an upright ski pole and the slope will help give a realistic idea of the slope's steepness. If you mark one ski pole with tape and stand it vertically and use the second pole horizontally (Figure 16-6B), you can approximate the steepness of the slope.

Short slides kill as effectively and as frequently as long slides. Many victims (8 percent) are caught in slides of less than 100 feet, with the most frequent fatal slide falling 300 to 400 vertical feet (18 percent). Fully half (53 percent) of fatal avalanches fall less than 500 feet. Interestingly, in the Colorado statistics from which these figures are taken, there were no avalanches on slopes of 1,300 to 1,699 feet, but almost 14 percent of the fatal avalanches occured on slopes greater than 1,700 feet long.[9]

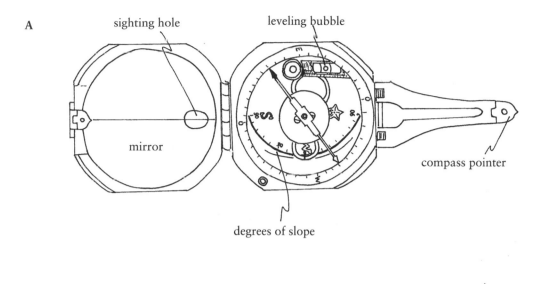

A
sighting hole    leveling bubble

mirror

compass pointer

degrees of slope

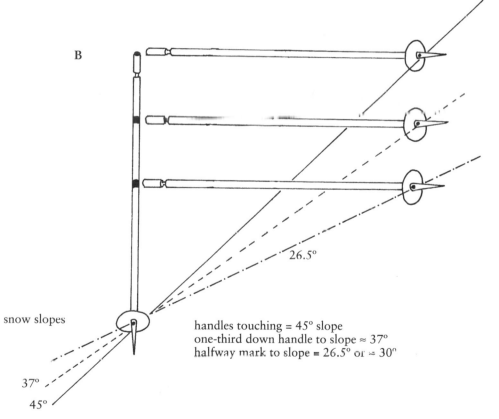

B

snow slopes

26.5°

handles touching = 45° slope
one-third down handle to slope ≈ 37°
halfway mark to slope = 26.5° or ≈ 30°

37°

45°

*Figure 16-6.* **Determining Slope:** *A—A clinometer built into a Brunton compass. It has a leveling bubble and a sighting hole in a mirror to measure the angle of long slopes. B—Ski poles used to determine snow slope. B is after Damon, 1986.*

## Concave and Convex Slopes

Snow slabs can be relatively rigid, and their tensile strength is affected by the slope profile (Figure 16-7). A concave slope tends to place snow in compression so that the maximum stress builds up at the base of the slope. This slope will release by sliding from the bottom. Convex snow slopes are in tension and tend to fracture in midslope where the release occurs. A uniform snow slope is more or less in tension throughout its length and can fracture at any point.

## Atmospheric Conditions

Atmospheric conditions are very important when you are considering traveling in avalanche country. Most avalanches take place within 24 hours after a storm. Heavy storms that have a snowfall of greater than 1 inch per hour are more likely to create unstable conditions rapidly. High winds—greater than 15 miles per hour—transport snow and form unstable windslabs on lee slopes. Rising tempcrature during the storm will place a layer of heavier snow on top of lighter, less dense snow, creating an unstable situation. Rain will increase the weight of the snowpack and increase the influence of gravity to promote sliding. Ample water from rain or sun melting can descend through the snowpack to a potential sliding surface, lubricate it, and promote detachment and sliding.

## Changes Within the Snowpack

The snowpack will undergo three types of change during a typical year: *equitemperature metamorphism, temperature-gradient metamorphism,* and *melt-freeze metamorphism.* Each change affects snowpack stability.

### Equitemperature Metamorphism (ET)

Equitemperature metamorphism is a slow change that takes place when the temperature from

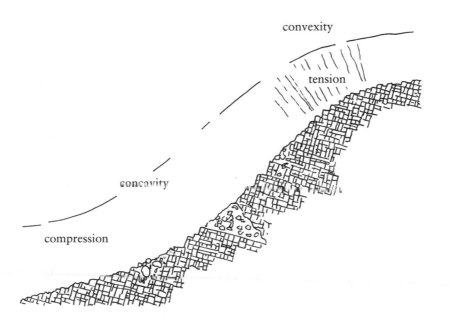

convexity

tension

concavity

compression

*Figure 16-7. **Slope Profile and Fracturing:** Compression occurs on a concave slope, and tension cracks appear in the middle of a bulging or convex slope. After Perla and Martinelli, 1976.*

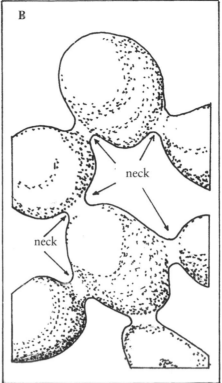

*Figure 16-8.* **Equitemperature Metamorphism:** *A—The weight of the snowpack presses ice grains together. If the temperature in the snowpack is equal, water molecules migrate into the concavities from convex regions.*

*B—This process, which rounds grains and joins individual grains together into a skeleton, is called* sintering. *After Perla and Martinelli, 1976.*

the bottom to the top of the snowpack is uniform. Mild days, with nights not much colder than freezing, promote this type of change.

If you examine individual grains of snow, you will see that angular, newly fallen crystals rapidly lose angularity and become more rounded. Water vapor migrates away from sharp points and convex bulges to the sharp valleys formed where individual grains touch, or to concavities. Due to lower vapor pressure in the valleys, water vapor deposits in the solid form, filling and strengthening the bond between particles. Equitemperature metamorphism creates strength and stability in the snowpack (Figure 16-8).

### Temperature-Gradient Metamorphism (TG)

The top of a snowpack is in contact with the air and exists at the prevailing atmospheric temperature. The bottom of the snowpack sits on ground. Small amounts of heat from within the earth, and heat retained in rocks and soils, are sufficient to keep the bottom of the snowpack around 32 degrees Fahrenheit (0 degrees Celsius).

In a thin snowpack during a cold snap, there is a very large difference between the temperature at the bottom and at the top of the snowpack (Figure 16-9). This temperature gradient will drive water vapor from the warm bottom to the cold top. As moisture leaves the bottom of the snowpack, the

cold

heat flux

warm

cup crystals

$H_2O$ vapor

$H_2O$ vapor

$H_2O$ vapor

*Figure 16-9. **Temperature Gradient in a Snowpack:** In temperature-gradient metamorphism, water vapor is deposited on the grains, leading to an increase in grain size and decrease in overall strength of the ice skeleton. Depth hoar develops, forming hollow cup-shaped crystals seen here in side view. After Perla and Martinelli, 1976.*

remaining snow becomes less dense. Snow crystals change, or metamorphose, to produce *depth hoar*—crystals that are not well bonded to their neighbors. These crystals might look like sugar to the unaided eye and appear as cup-shaped crystals under magnification. Depth hoar often forms directly on the ground or on an ice crust.

Since depth hoar has very little structural rigidity, its formation destroys the bonds to the snow slab above and creates a sliding surface. A significant thickness of depth hoar can form overnight under very cold conditions in a thin snowpack. One investigator observed a more than 12-inch thickness of snow converted to depth-hoar crystals overnight in a 24-inch-thick snowpack at temperatures of −40 degrees Fahrenheit.[10]

Equitemperature and temperature-gradient metamorphism produce radically different results in the snowpack. ET metamorphism tends to stabilize the snowpack and TG metamorphism tends to destabilize it. The temperature difference across the snowpack and snow density determine which type of metamorphism predominates. A loose, low-density snow allows vapor to flow easily, whereas higher-density snow reduces vapor flow. Higher elevations, shadowed north slopes, and very cold temperatures tend to promote temperature-gradient metamorphism. Climbers should keep track of storm and temperature patterns through-

out the winter, since early snowfall followed by cold periods will produce TG metamorphism. Thus, subsequent snow accumulation will be supported on an unstable foundation.

### Melt-Freeze Metamorphism (MF)

The melt-freeze process operates on the snowpack during spring and summer. Snow that survives into the summer, either on the ground or on glacier ice, continually melts in the daytime and refreezes at night. It is a simple process, with the grains becoming ever larger. It can, however, lead to deep instability because each grain in the melt cycle is surrounded and lubricated by water. A sudden shower or snow squall can add enough weight to initiate a slow-moving avalanche of very wet, heavy snow. Early in the morning, beware of a deep melt covered with a thin skin of frozen snow.

On the other hand, the melt-freeze cycle promotes stability in the snowpack in the frozen state because melting destroys weak depth-hoar layers produced during temperature-gradient metamorphism. Indeed the melt-freeze cycle is the only process by which temperature-gradient crystals are converted to a stable form.

### Surface Hoarfrost

If moist air moves over a snow slope and cools at night to below freezing, *surface hoarfrost* can form. This deposition is similar to that of dew during the summer except that thin ice crystals rather than dew drops are deposited. These hoarfrost crystals can persist during the daytime on shaded slopes or in gullies, where they form a beautiful sparkling surface. The hoarfrost layer is essentially frictionless and can act as a sliding surface if covered by new snowfall. If surface hoar is incorporated into the lower part of a snowpack, it becomes a weak layer that is difficult to detect because it is usually only a few millimeters thick.

## Indications of Slope Instability

There are certain signs to look for to determine quickly if a snow slope is unstable. Examine nearby snow slopes that have the same orientation as the slope in question for current or prior snow sluffs or avalanches. If avalanche debris is present on these slopes, then the slope in question may be unstable. Avalanche debris from a slab slide accumulates at the base of the slope as broken-up blocks of the former slab. The slab leaves behind both a sliding surface and crown surface at the top of the slope.

If cracks run across the slope, then the slope is under tension. If the cracks are deep, stay off the slope. Shallow cracks may involve only the thin upper layer, suggesting caution and further tests. Snow that emits a hollow sound or settles with a "whumphing" noise, which results from a rapid expulsion of air, is unstable.[11] You may also encounter hollow areas if you probe with an ice axe or ski pole. Cartwheel-shaped snow structures called *sunballs* rolling down the slope indicate that the layers involved are wet and unstable. Any open slope between the angles of 25 and 60 degrees should be suspect. If you know the slide history of the slope or observe trees with broken-off trunks, uprooted, or without branches on the uphill side, these are good indications the slope may be dangerous.

### Hasty Pits

The direct way to test a snow slope is to dig a *hasty pit*. This means that backcountry travelers must carry a shovel that is large enough for digging and keep it accessible, so that it will actually be used rather than simply carried. Dig hasty pits to ground level, if possible, or at least down to old snow surfaces. The pit will have vertical walls on three sides far enough apart for the tester to get into and perform a shovel shear or compression test, or a wedge-compression test, described below. Dig the first hasty pit on a smaller slope that has the same orientation and elevation as the questionable slope, or at the edge of the questionable slope. (The process of digging the hasty pit may trigger an avalanche.) You can dig subsequent hasty pits in the suspect starting zone of the slope in question, if conditions will allow. This can be a dangerous procedure and you should consider precautions, including safety lines to trees.

Once you dig the pit, you can carry out a number of tests. Bring out the *stratigraphy* of the snowpack by brushing the vertical rear wall of the pit with either a paintbrush or an evergreen bough. Brushing accentuates the differences in hardness of the individual layers and makes them more apparent. Ice crusts will stand out in relief and softer layers will recede. Remember that significant layers such as surface hoar or sun crust may be only a few millimeters in thickness.

You can determine the hardness of the individual layers by probing them in a direction perpendicular to the back wall. Hardness increases as you progessively use a fist, a finger, a pencil, or a knife to penetrate an individual layer. A particularly soft layer may indicate depth hoar, whereas particularly hard layers may be sun crust.

If you carry thermometers, you can test temperature gradients in the hasty pit between the ground and surface layers. This information will give a good indication of current temperature-gradient conditions, although it says little about past conditions.

You can examine the individual layers with an 8- to 10-power hand lens for faceted grains or "stepped" hoar temperature-gradient crystals, which might be the cause of any weak layer discovered in the hardness examination. You might first suspect these crystals to form at ground level in the snowpack, although a thorough examination can reveal them at any level in the pack.

### Shear and Compression Tests

You can test the overall structural integrity of the snowpack using a shovel test, or by means of the shear wedge (Rütschkeil) and shear block (Rütschblock) tests described below. All shear tests

*Figure 16-10.* ***The Shovel Shear Test:*** *Insert the shovel vertically until shear occurs on the weakest layer. As you insert the shovel pull it down-slope to reveal weak layers in the snow. Easy shear, particularly in the topmost layers, indicates that you should be cautious.*

take advantage of the downward-sloping layers of the snowpack to find weak layers. To carry out the shovel shear test, dig a pit as deep as possible and make a column of snow detached on three sides (Figure 16-10). As you continuously insert the shovel vertically at the rear of the column, weakly bonded layers will shear off.

You can test the bonding between each successive individual layer by inserting the shovel only to the depth of the topmost layer and pulling the shovel toward you until the layer slides. As you pull, be careful not to rotate the handle of the shovel and "pry" the block loose. After pulling off the current topmost layer, you then test the strength of the next layer, and so on until you reach the bottom of the pit.

If in your investigation you find that temperature-gradient metamorphism has formed a layer of depth-hoar crystals, you can use a shovel compression test to determine the compressive strength of the layer. Do not cut the back wall of the column, but bear down with the flat of the shovel or a ski on the upper surface of the column. The amount of force needed to collapse the TG layer gives an indication of the compressive strength of this layer.

For the shear wedge test dig a hasty pit and place a snow probe or upside-down ski pole equidistant from the side walls and about 6 feet behind the rear wall (Figure 16-11A). Now pass a length of avalanche cord, 5-millimeter kernmantle rope, around the ski pole to form a wedge-shaped pattern. To help this cord cut through the snow you can tie overhand knots in it about 1 foot apart to act as cutting teeth. Then jigsaw the cord down through the snow the length of the ski pole. This process cuts out a wedge-shaped block, which may spontaneously release, extending to the ski pole from the rear of the hasty pit.

The shear-block test is similar to the shear-wedge test except that you cut a rectangular snow block rather than a wedge (Figure 16-11B). Start by digging a hasty pit somewhat wider than a ski length. Next, dig trenches back into the snow perpendicular to the hasty pit wall for about the same distance. The remaining wall of the block is cut free by jigsawing the avalanche cord.

A                                                    B

Figure 16-11. **The Shear-Wedge and Shear-Block Tests:** *about a foot apart to act as cutting teeth.* **B**—*Cut three*
*A—An avalanche cord is used to jigsaw through the* *sides of the sliding block with a shovel and the remain-*
*back wall of a hasty pit to form a wedge that will be* *ing wall with the avalanche cord. From Damon, 1986,*
*increasingly weighed to check for potential slide sur-* *and Munter, 1985.*
*faces. The avalanche cord has overhand knots tied in it*

The shear wedge or shear block may release
spontaneously as it is cut. This indicates extreme
instability in the snowpack. If there is no spontaneous release, test the compressive stability of both
the shear wedge and shear block by stepping very
gently onto the upper surface. If the wedge or
block does not release, weigh it more heavily by
rapidly flexing both knees to transfer energy into
the snow. If the snow still does not slide, jump
onto the block. If this does not release the block,
take your skis off and gently weight the block with
one foot and then both feet. Finally, jump easily
and then vigorously. Any weak layer will fail at
some point during the testing and slide into the pit.
If the layer does not break until you are jumping

up and down on both feet, the slope is quite stable.
If failure occurs somewhere between easy and very
difficult, you must estimate the safety of the slope
based on experience and the need to cross it.
Needless to say, a spontaneous release signifies
maximum hazard.

## Route Selection in Avalanche Country

Potential avalanche slopes are stable much of
the time and many backcountry travelers ski and
cross them without incident. To cross safely over
a long period of time you need to be attuned to

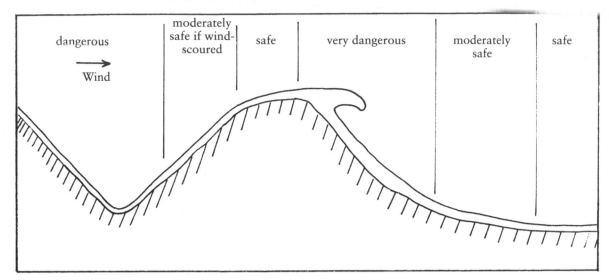

| dangerous | moderately safe if wind-scoured | safe | very dangerous | moderately safe | safe |

Wind →

*Figure 16-12.* **Travel Zones Related to Wind Direction for V-shaped Valleys and Ridges.** *After Daffern, 1983.*

microchanges in snow conditions and travel when the snowpack is stable. It is best to learn the skills of snow travel from an experienced backcountry traveler, but there are guidelines that you can follow.

Avoid going out for the first few days after a storm, since this is when most avalanches occur. Watch and probe the snow, looking for changes in slope and snow conditions that suggest instability. Travel between rocks or in dense timber stands, if possible. Be wary on sparsely timbered slopes that probably do not anchor the snow sufficiently. Dig hasty pits if you are suspicious, since pits do not take long to dig and provide critical information.

If you must cross suspect slopes, it is better to stay high on the slope above *starting zones* (zones of potential fracture), or keep to the side if you must climb the starting zone. Move quickly across the slope and travel one at a time, in the same track, in order to disturb less snow. Never violate the rule of traveling one at a time, and give the person ahead of you plenty of time to reach a safe island before you start out. Even if many members of the party have crossed safely, stay alert, because slopes may slide during the passage of the second, third, or tenth member. Many killer avalanches are relatively small—less than 100 meters in length

and somewhat narrower. You might belay a person crossing these slopes. If you do have to cross a suspect avalanche slope, go directly uphill and downhill. Do not crisscross or switchback the slope, and do not ski above another person lest you set off a slide.

### Travel Zones

In traveling through avalanche terrain, it is useful to think in terms of travel zones related to wind direction, valley slope, and ridge lines (Figure 16-12). Travel in V-shaped valleys is dangerous and probably a path of last resort because of the steep slopes on either side. Higher up on the slope, wind may have scoured the snow away, leaving behind a good crampon surface. However, in deeper snow this slope can develop depth hoar and become hazardous. Near the ridge line, but behind potential cornice fractures, is a relatively safe zone of travel. This area is above most of the snow, and the slope may flatten out at this point. The most dangerous zone lies on the lee side of the cornice, since this is where a decrease in wind velocity deposits much snow, and it is directly beneath cornices. The degree of safety increases down-slope on the lee side and becomes fully safe only when you are well away from the possible run out of spontaneous cornice falls and avalanches.

### Crossing Suspect Snow Slopes

When you cross suspect slopes, button up your clothing and put on a hat and gloves. Activate avalanche cords and beacons as discussed below. Have snow probes ready for use. Loosen ski bindings, pack belts, and safety straps, in case you need to jettison the equipment. Remove ski-pole wrist-straps so you can drop the poles. Skis are a mixed blessing when an avalanche occurs. On skis you might be able to move to the side, or your skis might stick up through the snow to indicate your position if you are buried. On the other hand, skis limit mobility and prohibit swimming motions,

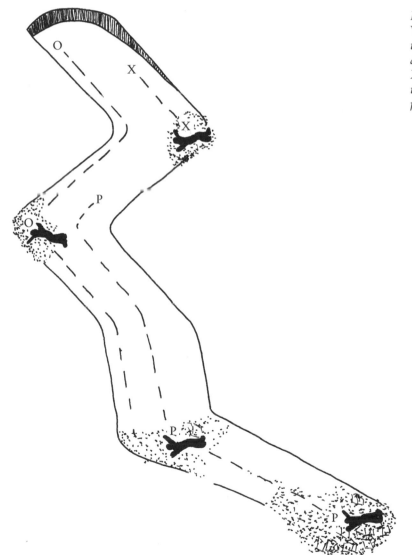

*Figure 16-13. **Fall Line of a Victim**: Avalanche victims tend to follow the local terrain and stop in corners like figures X and O, or on a bench or in the toe of the avalanche like figure P.*

which have proved effective for many victims of avalanches.

Interviews with avalanche survivors indicate that those people who tried to swim were somewhat successful. They tended to be able to control their movement upward in the snowpack. One survivor said, "I recall I was able to swim and did so as naturally as one would were he trying to surface in a pool of water."[12]

Martin Epp, a European mountain guide, feels that rolling is a better technique. "Although the passage of an avalanche can be compared to the flow of water, the analogy of swimming out is less effective, . . . than rolling like a cylinder or a bottle. Swimming tends to flatten you at the bottom of the avalanche. You will quickly be unable to move or breathe. But you can sometimes roll faster than the snow is moving."[13] Initially, he says, you should try to ski out to the side at a steep 45-degree angle, but if you are caught, begin to roll. Get rid of your skis and poles but retain your pack, since it gives you a greater volume per weight and helps bring you to the surface. (Retaining your pack is contrary to the advice usually given for attempting to swim since the pack restricts the swimming motion.) You should initiate the roll around your body's axis at a 45-degree angle to the path of the avalanche. As the momentum of the avalanche slows, try hard to remain on top. This technique should allow your nose and mouth to remain free of snow and allow you to breathe.

Whether you attempt to swim or roll, it is clear that you need to abandon skis and poles. Members of the party not caught in the avalanche and standing on the side of the avalanching slope can try helping victims initiate action by calling for them to swim or roll.

Most victims of avalanches suffocate because the moisture from their breath freezes in the snow around their mouth and cuts off further oxygen supply. To help increase air supply, you should get your hands out in front of your face and try to make an air space as you are coming to a stop. In addition, keep your mouth shut so it does not fill with snow and prevent breathing. Smutek noted a number of instances of survivors who had created an air pocket. He also noted that a snow ranger, who survived because he was found within two minutes of being buried, had tried to form an air pocket with his hand, but "the piling up snow forced it away."[14]

A few victims of avalanches owe their lives to having a hand above the snow. As the snow is coming to a stop, victims should attempt to thrust their hands toward the surface. "I noticed that it seemed lighter above me. I punched violently upward with my left hand and my fingers broke through the snow. It was this hand movement which was seen from the chairlift and led to my being quickly dug out by the rescue crew," said one survivor.[15]

Once the avalanche comes to a stop, the snow hardens, making it very difficult to make a breathing pocket or dig out victims.

If someone gets caught and buried in an avalanche, the remainder of the party activates a hasty search. Before initiating the search, however, safeguard the remaining members of the party so they do not get involved in further avalanches. Then, record the victim's fall line and starting location, the location of hats, packs, gloves, or skis that may have been dropped, and the last sighting of the victim. A person who has been caught by an avalanche will tend to follow the fall line in a direction determined by the terrain, as indicated in Figure 16-13. The victim may come to rest in corners or on benches as well as in the toe of the avalanche.

## Avalanche Cords and Beacons

Avalanche cords are 15 to 30 meters of brightly colored nylon cord marked along their length. In theory, at least part of the cord will remain on the surface after the avalanche and lead rescuers to the victim. In practice, in only 40 percent of burials will part of a cord remain on the surface.[16] Also, it may be very difficult to dig a buried cord back to the victim in snow that has set up after the avalanche. Avalanche cords may be useful, however, to maintain a straight-line probe during a rescue or to help cut a shear block from a hasty pit.

Avalanche rescue beacons have proven effective in rapidly uncovering victims. All members of a team of backcountry travelers must have beacons tuned to transmit to the same frequency in order for the system to work. Currently, beacons used in North America operate on a 2,275Hz audio-induction signal, whereas the European standard is 457kHz. The European standard, which transmits over a larger area than the 2,275Hz frequency, will become the sole acceptable standard as the American frequency is phased out, by December 1, 1995.[1] Dual-frequency beacons will be sold until that time.

If a victim is swept up in an avalanche, the remaining members of the party should stay out of the avalanche area while they switch their transceivers to receive, mark the last-seen area of the victim, post a guard to watch for additional avalanches, and prepare to switch back to transmit if there are new avalanches. If multiple searchers enter the search area, they move directly down- or uphill until detecting a faint beep.

A single searcher can more effectively cover ground by running directly uphill or zigzagging

*Figure 16-14. **Search by Right-Angle Pattern with an Electronic Transceiver.** Adapted from Perla and* Martinelli, 1976, *whose description is based on the* Skadi III Instruction Manual *by John Lawton.*

down. After detecting the initial beep (position 0 in Figure 16-14), the searcher stops and turns the handheld transceiver in three dimensions to its loudest position, with the volume control all the way up. This position is maintained with respect to the geographic area—not the searcher's body—as the searcher moves but is reoriented at stops as the search area narrows. At the first beep (0) the searcher begins tracking and backtracking (0 to 1, 1 to 2, 2 to 3) along a line, listening for volume changes; volume increases as the searcher nears the victim and fades as the searcher moves away. After discovering the loudest position (4) along the initial line, the searcher stops, reorients the transceiver for loudest volume, reduces volume setting, and turns at right angles to follow a new line, listening for volume fade (4–5) or increase (5–6) until fade begins (6–7). The searcher backtracks (7–8) beyond and returns to the loudest position (9) along this line. Here, the searcher reorients the transceiver, decreases volume to its lowest setting, and moves slowly at right angles (9–10) until passing the loudest position on the line, at which point a backtrack brings the searcher to the victim (11). In the last phase of tracking and backtracking, the searcher may remain in one spot with feet planted wide apart and move the transceiver back and forth in the search line just above the snow surface to pinpoint the victim's position.[18]

Avalanche beacon transmissions can be detected at distances between 75 and 125 feet when buried 3 feet. An experienced operator can find a victim within a 100-square-yard area in as little as 4 minutes. Searches with dogs can take 25 minutes, and it can take 20 probers up to 4 hours to coarse-probe the same area.[19] It is worth noting that finding the victim quickly may not be of much value unless you have shovels. Avalanched snow is extremely dense and difficult to penetrate even with shovels.

Wearing an avalanche transceiver does not automatically provide a greater degree of safety, because people wearing a transceiver may take more risks, and many survivors of avalanches are in a state of shock that considerably diminishes their ability to search and rescue. Only 35 per-cent of those completely buried while wearing an avalanche transceiver are rescued alive.[20] Obviously, the success of a transceiver is related to a high degree of training and the ability to function under stress. The transceiver clearly does not replace the judgment necessary to avoid avalanche terrain in the first place.

## Avalanche Probes

If there are surface clues, such as a hat, a limited number of probers can probe in likely spots immediately below the clue, hoping for a rapid recovery. However, probers will probably need to organize into lines and probe for long periods that will tax their strength and endurance. A line captain should see to the creature comfort of probers—water, food, and rotation with shovelers who dig all "strikes" by probers. Probing calls for discipline and concentration, and probers do nothing but probe, keep to the line, and listen to the line captain's commands without distraction. Strikes are investigated by shovelers who stand behind the line; stuck poles are left behind while the prober steps to the line with a new probe if possible. Ideally, probers use poles of rigid tubing 10 to 12 feet long, but you can use ski poles without baskets or other makeshift probes for shallow burials. It is critical to handle the probes with gloves to keep them from warming and icing. Icing will prevent the probes from penetrating the snow or cause them to become stuck in warmer snow.

Probes are either *coarse* or *fine*. A coarse probe, with which you begin, has about a 70-percent chance of striking a live victim. Completing a second coarse probe before initiating a fine probe significantly increases the chance of finding the victim and is faster than a single fine probe. Fine probes are more closely spaced but are too slow to expect live victim recovery, although they ensure almost 100 percent recovery.

Organize probe lines at the base of the avalanche slope and work uphill after first making sure that the working area will not undergo further avalanching. In organized probing, a line captain, aided by assistants at both ends, has the job of keeping line movement organized and straight. The line captain also observes the depth of the poles plunged by the line members. A pole that strikes a body will not go as deep into the snowpack as other poles, and will feel very different from a rock or ice layer.

You judge spacing for the coarse probe to a certain extent on the number of probers present and the area that you need to cover (Figure 16-15). Probers stand in a line, feet apart, elbow to elbow, hands on hips to determine sideways spacing. You insert the probe once at the center of your straddled span. Then, on a signal from the line captain,

line members together take one step up-slope. Another signal initiates probing. When the number of probers is limited, you use fingertip-to-fingertip spacing. You insert the probe first on one side of your body, say the left, and then on the other. You organize fine probing to insert the probe every 10 to 12 inches over the field that you wish to search.

Some experienced avalanche workers feel that individuals within a line can speed up their work by probing their section at their own pace. This method gives probers a chance to push in their probes as often as they can without waiting for commands.[21] Members of the probing line must be experienced enough to maintain the line as it advances. It is critical that there are shovelers to

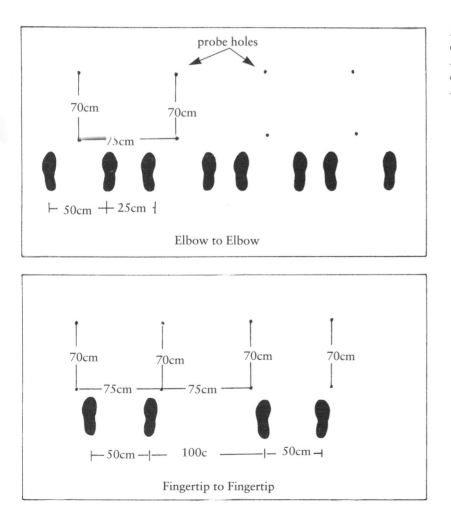

Figure 16-15. **Two Methods of Executing Coarse Probes:** *Methods used whenever live rescue is expected. After Perla and Martinelli, 1976.*

follow up sites that show resistance to probing. Areas already probed should be marked to prevent later confusion.

## Avalanche Scenario

The situation that follows illustrates the problems and decisions that you might make while traveling in avalanche country with a group of fellow climbers. You can work through the simulation by yourself, or gather two to four climbers[22] plus a moderator. The moderator should be someone who understands the information presented in this chapter or has had field work with avalanches.

The situation: You are completing a day climb or ski tour. Because of travel and routefinding problems, the trip has taken longer than expected. It is 45 minutes before sunset. In an attempt to be out before dark, you have deviated from the planned route and taken a shortcut that will allow you to reach your car in 30 minutes. In so doing, you have ventured into unfamiliar terrain. You have come to a slope that you fear may be unstable and avalanche-prone.

What information do you need to know? Review this chapter and discuss appropriate questions. Write the first question on a sheet of paper. The moderator will give you the answer; use the answer to ask a second question. After you get the second answer, ask a final question.

To conclude this simulation, use all three questions and answers to decide on a group plan. If you chose your three questions wisely, you should have gotten enough information to make a sound decision. If you need more information you can ask the moderator additional questions. Write out your plan on a piece of paper and discuss it with the moderator.

### Answers to Questions Your Group Might Ask

• "Do we have the equipment to survive a night out?"

Answer: You have what you would normally have for skiing or climbing in the backcountry. This means that you should be prepared to spend a night out.

• "How are we currently situated?"

Answer: You are situated in an extensive stretch of trees on the edge of a suspected avalanche slope. The slope, out in front of you, is about 2,000 feet high at an angle of 45 degrees. A cornice overhangs the suspect slope, but your current position is out of the fall line of the cornice.

• "Is there an alternative route?"

Answer: If you backtrack for about a mile, you will ascend a safe slope that will put you onto a ridge. You can follow the ridge out in about three hours. It will be difficult to follow the trail until you start up the correct slope leading to the ridge.

• "What is the current weather?"

Answer: Currently it is snowing very hard. Visibility is low, with snow blowing horizontally.

• "Are there any signs to suggest that the slope is currently unstable?"

Answer: There are no cracks, "woomfs," or current avalanches to suggest that the slope is currently unstable.

• "What do we find if we dig a hasty pit?"

Answer: The hasty pit reveals an extensive zone of depth hoar about 3 feet down. A shovel shear test produces sliding without much applied force.

• "Are we expected back before dark?"

Answer: Your friends expect to see you about one hour after dark.

### Possible Plans of Action and Probable Results

**1.** Travel directly across the slope.

You reason that the slope shows no obvious surface signs of sliding even though it is at a 45-degree angle and a cornice overhangs it. The snowfall, apparently at more than one inch per hour, seems to have produced no effect on the slope. Your friends will be worried if you are late, and you have only 45 minutes of light left, so you want to get out quickly. The slope is too wide to belay, but you figure that you can protect yourself by moving one at a time. Everyone checks that their avalanche beacons are turned to transmit, and the first person heads out across the slope.

This reasoning will lead you across a dangerous slope that is rapidly becoming more unstable as the storm progresses. Your party would probably trigger the slope. A hasty pit would have revealed an extensive sliding surface of depth hoar and the shovel shear test would have shown easy sliding conditions. At least one member of the party and perhaps the entire party would probably be caught in a big avalanche.

**2.** Climb up the side of the slope, traverse beneath the cornices, and head out.

You reason that the climb uphill will be tiring, but at least you will be above the avalanche slope. You decide to take a chance that the cornice will not fall off during the brief time that you are under it.

It is almost dark, however, and visibility is low, with snow blowing horizontally. You might easily wander onto the suspect slope. The climb uphill would have been exhausting. Even if everything else worked ideally, you would have to pass beneath the unstable overhanging cornice. Even if you were to reach the other side, you would face unknown difficulties in descending to a safe area.

**3.** Retreat immediately.

You decide that you will be safest if you return to your original route.

However, it is almost dark and visibility is low, so it would be difficult to follow the trail. You would likely get lost.

**4.** Stay where you are until morning.

This promises to be a cold experience, but it probably is the wisest choice. Being in the trees, you would be somewhat protected from both wind and avalanches. You would have the necessary equipment to spend the night out as you are routinely prepared to do this when climbing in the mountains. In the morning visibility would be better. You could then backtrack, ascend the safe slope to the ridge, which would be swept free of snow, and walk out. Your friends would have been worried, but they would have been greatly relieved that you chose the safe option.

---

## References for Future Reading

Armstrong, Betsy R., and Knox Williams. 1992. *The avalanche book*. Golden, Colorado: Fulcrum Publishing.

Atkins, Dale. 1991. White death: A review of fatal accidents in Colorado, 1950–91. *Avalanche Review*. 10(1).

Brown, Belmore. 1956. *The conquest of Mt. McKinley*. Boston: Houghton, Mifflin Company.

Couche, S. 1977. Avalanche awareness survey. *Mazama Journal*.

Daffern, Tony. 1983. *Avalanche safety for skiers & climbers*. Seattle: Cloudcap Press.

Damon, Roger. 1986. *The "Circle A" avalanche course notes*. The National Ski Patrol.

Diemberger, Kurt. 1991. *Summits and secrets*. Trans. by Hugh Merrick. Seattle: The Mountaineers.

Epp, Martin, and Stephen Lee. 1987. *Avalanche awareness for skiers and mountaineers*. London: The Wild Side.

Lawton, John G. 1969. *Instruction manual: Skadi III avalanche search and rescue system*. Buffalo, New York: Lawtronics.

Meiklejohn, Brad. 1988. Warm and dead. *Avalanche Review*. 7(2).

Perla, Ronald I., and M. Martinelli, Jr. 1976. *Avalanche handbook 489*. Washington, D.C.: U.S. Department of Agriculture Forest Service, U.S. Gov. Printing Office.

Setnicka, Tim. 1980. *Wilderness search and rescue*. Boston: Appalachian Mountain Club.

Simpson, Joe. 1988. *Touching the void*. New York: Harper & Row.

Smutek, Ray. 1977. Portrait of an avalanche survivor. *Off-Belay*. 36:8–12.

Steger, Will, and Jon Bowermaster. 1991. *Crossing Antarctica*. New York: Laurel-Dell Books.

Williams, Knox. 1975. *The snowy torrents: Avalanche*

*accidents in the United States 1967–71.*
Washington D.C.: USDA Forest Service General
Technical Report, RM-8, U.S. Gov. Printing Office.
_____. 1977. Portrait of an avalanche victim. *Off-
Belay.* 36:5–7.

# Endnotes

1. Williams, 1977.

2. Williams, 1975.

3. Atkins, 1991. The portrait of a modern avalanche victim
emerges from a study of 40 years of Colorado avalanche
data. "The typical avalanche victim is a 30-year-old male,
who is an advanced skier, either a tourer or out-of-bounds
lift skier, and who has had some avalanche training. The
accident is most likely to happen on a January day. . . . The
accident happens as the skier is traveling on a north- to
east-facing slope near or just above tree line. He triggers a
slab avalanche on a 38-degree slope. The avalanche fractures 300 feet across, failing on a weak old snow layer 3
feet below the surface. The slide races down the mountain,
falling 700 vertical feet. Some victims survive the ride, and
some do not. Most of those who do not are buried just over
4 feet deep in the debris."

4. Epp and Lee, 1987.

5. Williams, 1975.

6. Perla and Martinelli, 1976.

7. Perhaps the most famous fall through a cornice is that of
Hermann Buhl when he was on Chogolisa. This accident is
detailed in Diemberger, 1991. In 1988 Joe Simpson
described how his partner, Simon Yates, fell along with a
cornice that broke off 40 feet back from the crest, producing a break-line of vertical snow nearly 30 feet high.

8. Atkins, 1991.

9. *Ibid.*

10. This is an observation by Roger H. Damon, to whom
I am indebted for critiquing this chapter.

11. Steger, 1991, describes encountering "snowquakes" in
which areas the size of a large lawn or football field would
suddenly collapse and produce a loud noise that startled his
dogs. The physical cause of this collapse was not explained
in the text.

12. Williams, 1975.

13. Epp and Lee, 1987.

14. Smutek, 1977.

15. *Ibid.*

16. Perla and Martinelli, 1976, give a detailed description
of the search techniques as published by John Lawton,
1969.

17. The Ad Hoc Committee on Avalanche Rescue
Transceiver Frequencies of the American Association of
Avalanche Professionals has made this recommendation to
the Association.

18. Perla and Martinelli, 1976.

19. Damon, 1986.

20. Epp and Lee, 1977.

21. *Ibid.*

22. This simulation was created by Roger Damon of the
Eastern Division of the National Ski Patrol based on a sim-
ilar simulation presented by Doug Fesler at the National
Avalanche School. Damon's simulation was presented at the
1993 advanced avalanche course held at Pinkham Notch,
New Hampshire.

# PART FOUR

# *Climbing Program Concerns*

# 17

# *Top-Rope Site Management for Groups*

## Introduction

This chapter explores the problems and concerns of organized climbing programs for groups. Most of the climbing techniques used in programmatic climbing, such as anchor construction, are the same as those used by recreational climbers, although a few specific techniques have evolved for use with groups. What makes the management of a top-rope site different for groups than for individuals is that institutions must consider liability and risk management; they need to develop strategies for instructors who work with up to six beginners per intructor; and they should be concerned with methods of formally processing the experience.

Knowing how to make the climbing environment as safe as possible is also a part of site management. For this reason, it is also useful to know something about cliff formation.

## Liability in Climbing Programs

Climbing and mountaineering are not in themselves a cause of liability, and you do not need to avoid them simply because they might be dangerous. Liability arises when you teach climbing, thereby assuming the obligation to provide a safe environment by following accepted professional practices, and an injury occurs. Teaching beginners requires the most care, because they have the least understanding about what they are getting into and are least capable of being responsible for themselves.

The structure of the program affects the degree of liability. Liability may be less for a loose cooperative adventure (emphasizing individual choice and group cooperation in decision-making) and greater for a highly structured program such as a credit-bearing course with instructors.[1]

If you run a climbing program or if you teach in one, you must also be concerned with product liability. This liability involves the design of a product—a design that makes it hazardous—as well as defective workmanship or materials that cause an injury. Generally, unless you make, distribute, sell, lease, or rent the product, you need not be concerned with product liability so long as you use only equipment that is in good repair and designed for the activity, and use it in the manner specified by the manufacturer. In practice this means that climbing programs should only use ropes, helmets, harnesses, and other equipment that are approved by the *Union Internationale des Associations d'Alpinisme* (UIAA), an international organization of alpine clubs, and maintained in good condition. Equipment made for other purposes, such as construction helmets or yachting ropes, should not be used for climbing.

If you run an organization that sponsors climbing or other adventure activities, you should be familiar with the concepts presented here and consult an attorney concerning specific state laws and your individual situation. More detailed information is available from the references listed at the end of the chapter.

Owning a recreation site introduces separate liability concerns not discussed here. Many states have laws that protect the landowner who exercises ordinary responsibility toward the public. In general, you are not responsible for natural hazards, such as a cliff, but you may incur liability for hazards resulting from negligence, such as a poorly maintained or unsupervised climbing wall. Learn the laws of your state if you own a recreational site or wish to work with the owner of one.

One of the basic tenets of liability is *duty owed.* If you take individuals climbing, you are responsible for providing a safe environment. This responsibility exists whether your organization is for profit or nonprofit, and whether you are paid or unpaid. The duty owed is to provide a *standard of care* that has three major aspects: *supervision, conduct of activity,* and *environmental conditions.* The standard of care "is that of a 'reasonable and prudent professional' and asks what are the best practices (requires up-to-dateness) and what others who are knowledgeable and expert in the field do? By accepting a leadership role, a person holds himself to be competent."[2]

### Supervision

The site leader becomes the focal point of safety management after preliminary work is done and participants are at the cliff. Site leaders should be able to identify dangerous conditions and anticipate dangerous situations. They should provide for the proper rendering of first aid and know what to do in an emergency. They should have more experience than required for the activity at hand. They should be trained both in technical areas and in overseeing others. This additional experience gives them a cushion of knowledge and skill to prevent accidents and to handle the situation if anything should go wrong. They should observe the overall condition of participants and take specific steps to reestablish safe conditions if necessary. Just having experience in cooperative-adventure climbing does not qualify you to be a general supervisor of an organized climbing trip. However, there is every reason for individuals with good technical skills to contribute to the overall success of the trip under the leadership of individuals with broader experience.

### Conduct of Activity

Climbing or mountaineering in itself cannot be considered the cause of injury or liability. Whether you are deemed liable is determined by the manner in which you conduct the activity. Thus, it is reasonable to take a group climbing, provided that you meet certain standards: you must be capable of analyzing the skill level and performance of participants to enhance skills through a teaching progression and match these skills with challenges appropriate to their maturity, physical condition, and ability. Participants need to understand how rules relate to safety.

### Environmental Conditions

You should know the specific environment in which you are going to operate, either through personal visits or by talking to other leaders who have operated there recently. Visiting a cliff, cleaning loose rock annually, and inspecting for loose rock on each trip are aspects of meeting the environmental conditions portion of the standard of care. Program participants should have appropriate safety devices and protective clothing, including helmets and harnesses that are designed for rock climbing and that are in a good state of repair.

### Participants' Responsibility

Participants also bear responsibility for their own safety. In litigation, courts look to see if a "... plaintiff's conduct under the circumstances was that of a reasonable and prudent person exercising ordinary care for his own safety."[3] It is important, therefore, that participants be informed about the nature of the activity that they are going to undertake.

It is also important to discuss the inherent risk. Discussions should be specific and might take place each time you introduce new elements. Briefing sessions just before you enter the cliff area and when you change areas or activities provide good opportunities. You can present general information, such as slides of a previous group in action.

Even commercial climbing videos are useful to the extent that they help people understand what they will be doing. The object is to inform participants as fully as possible. As a participant becomes more experienced and skilled in an activity, he or she assumes a greater share of the risk.

### Assumption of Risk, Liability Release, and Medical Forms

*Assumption-of-risk forms* help to inform participants (and parents, if the participants are minors) of the nature of the activity and provide the climbing program with acknowledgment that participants have been informed about conditions, demands, and dangers of the program. Specifics are better than generalities. For example, rather than simply saying that climbing is dangerous, state that there is danger of falling rock and falls from rock, as well as other specifics. The assumption-of-risk form should also set out the program's rules and regulations and inform participants about the consequences—which may include expulsion from the program without refund or failure—of using drugs or alcohol, or not following reasonable instructions while on the trip. To ensure that participants understand the form, go over it verbally if possible, and have them (or their parents, if the participants are minors) read it and sign it. The assumption-of-risk form informs participants but does not relieve the program of its duty to meet the standard of care.

The *medical form* requests pertinent medical information such as prior injuries or frostbite, allergy, and other conditions related to the participant's ability to perform the activities in the program. It does no good to ask for this information, however, if you do not examine it and discuss potential problems with participants.

A *liability release* is different from an assumption-of-risk form. The release is a contract that excuses the provider of a recreational service from the duty owed—that is, the responsibility to protect the participant. These releases have been upheld when the signer is of majority age, when there are viable alternatives available to potential participants (including not participating), and when the release is signed voluntarily.[4] Viable alternatives might be similar but less strenuous activities, such as a less strenuous hike below tree line rather than a more strenuous and exposed hike above tree line; scraping and painting a building does not provide a viable alternative to the exposed hike.

## Risk-Management Programs

Organizations that sponsor climbing programs can reduce the potential for accidents by undertaking a risk-management program.[5] All program personnel—including the board of trustees, president, program directors, small-group leaders, logistics and equipment personnel, site leaders, instructors, and assistant instructors—have a role to play in promoting safety in all actions of the organization. Safety begins with establishing policies that are taught and implemented in hiring and training staff; purchasing, maintaining, and issuing equipment; scheduling; cleaning sites; and instructing.

All members of the organization should be involved in establishing written policies that undergo periodic review at all levels of the organization. "Any departure from specific safety policies must only be in emergency situations to significantly enhance safety, and involve a carefully developed, rational, and defensible plan."[6]

Safety should be subject to ongoing in-house reviews and periodic external reviews. Reviews should examine the integrity and effectiveness of the entire range of program components beginning with a statement of philosophy, goals, and learning objectives through staff training, staff/participant ratios, and health-care procedures, among others. Guides to conducting safety reviews are provided by *The Safety Review Manual* by Ian Wade and Michael Fischesser, and *Safety Practices in Adventure Programming* by Simon Priest and Tim Dixon.

## Qualifications for Climbing Instructors

If you are a climbing site leader or instructor working with a group, you must have the same general qualifications as any instructor of experience-based adventure programming; i.e., you must be competent in a broad range of skill areas.[7] You should be skilled in the techniques of climbing and know how to promote safety in a climbing program. You must be vigilant not just during the climb but at the time of assembly, travel to or from a climbing site, and when camping. To do this properly, you need to be physically and mentally fit enough to cope with the stresses of the program, and sometimes more fit than the participants. You need to be trained in first aid and cardiopulmonary resuscitation. You should teach low-impact methods of camping and traveling in the natural environment.

In addition to teaching climbing techniques, safety, and protection of the natural environment, you should also provide participants with an experience of general value that can be used in other settings. Instructors facilitate group debriefing at the end of an activity to help participants to clarify and learn from an experience.

Other responsibilities of the instructor include planning and budgeting, organizing food and equipment, and arranging transportation.

When you teach, you must be able to break skills down into basic components. When you initially teach climbing systems and procedures, you may want to use a *ground school*, run on flat ground, instead of placing participants on or near the cliff while they are learning. You must be capable of developing teamwork and cooperation among participants, and be skilled at crisis intervention and conflict resolution to deal with problems that arise in the stressful environment of climbing and group effort. This means that you can work with people and respect their rights, standards, styles, and values. The structure of the entire program and focus of individual instructors must allow participants to attempt a particular climb or defer it if they feel ill at ease. You may work with these individuals in a supportive manner but should not coerce them into attempting a particular climb. You must be mature, skilled, and confident as well as approachable, honest, and fun-loving.

You need to be able to communicate well with other instructors as well as with participants; give and receive feedback in a constructive, unthreatening manner; solve problems while under stress; and demonstrate a flexible leadership style that suits participants' needs under different conditions. In summary, climbing instructors need to be broadly experienced and demonstrate good judgment.

## Programmatic Practices

Site leaders have the job of organizing trips and supervising the climbing site and gear. For many programs, the site leader (1) inspects the site for loose rock at the beginning of the season and before each use; (2) selects and inspects gear, makes sure that gear is in good condition, initiates repairs, and orders new gear; (3) sets up and oversees all climbing-rappel systems and instructs course instructors in their use; (4) briefs instructors and students about the events of the day; (5) oversees the climbing progression; (6) debriefs the group at the end of the climbing day; and (7) oversees the dismantling of all climbing systems and return of gear to a storeroom at the end of the climbing day.

As with safety policies, every organization should establish its operating procedures in writing. Among the items covered might be:

There is a maximum of _____ (commonly six) participants to one instructor.

If there are two or more instructors, one should be designated the site leader.

Unroped climbing is prohibited.

First-aid material including litters and backboards must be available on-site.

Helmets are required for organized groups at climbing sites because of safety and liability concerns. Both instructors and students must wear helmets when climbing or when in designated areas at the base of a climb.

Safe-zone rest areas must be established well away from potential falling rocks, so that people can take their helmets off.

All safety rules apply to all climbers, including instructors. In addition to providing personal safety, course instructors are professionals who serve as role models for novices.

Helmets and harnesses used for climbing should be manufactured specifically for climbing and must be approved by the UIAA.

## Climbing Sites and Loose Rock

### Cleaning the Site

Inspect top-rope sites thoroughly at least once a year for dangerous loose rock. Freeze-thaw action during the winter may have loosened previously stable rocks. There are at least three categories of rocks of concern. First is the glacial material consisting of angular rocks called *erratics*, as well as finer till material dropped by a melting glacier. This material forms the soils and many of the large blocks on cliff tops in northern latitudes. Second are the exfoliation flakes that parallel surfaces of granite domes, and third are jointed blocks bounded by cracks.

Clean loose rock only when the cliff is secure, so that passers-by or workers will not be hit by falling rock. Communicate clearly with fellow workers to avoid misunderstanding. If you are doing the cleaning, do so on belay or while tied in, and remain uphill of the loose rock at all times. If you find high potential for an accident during cleaning, abandon the site and pick a different climbing area.

### Granite Exposure at the Surface by Uplift and Differential Erosion

It is helpful to know a little about how granite cliffs form. The process starts with the cooling of granite perhaps a mile underground. After cooling, very large regions of land, perhaps the size of New England, lift up above sea level as global-scale sections (plates) of the earth move. Stresses related to regional movements and their relaxations often give rise to parallel sets of fractures or cracks called *joints*.

In elevated land areas water weathers and erodes the land surface. As weathering proceeds, rock types surrounding the granite are often removed more readily than the granite itself, resulting in elevated granite hills or mountains, as shown in Figure 17-1. In northern latitudes glaciers have a dramatic effect upon these elevated lands with exposed granite outcroppings, transforming preexisting rounded peaks and valleys into a pronounced angular landscape.

*Exfoliation:* As a granite body in the earth uplifts the rock above, the rock surface erodes, releasing a tremendous pressure from the granite. This phenomenon, called *unloading*, allows the granite to expand upward, as shown in Figure 17-2. The outer part of the granite expands more than the inner part, and cracks called *sheet-joints* develop parallel to the outer surface. On cliff sides, gravity may cause the rock between the sheet-joints to break loose in concentric slabs or flakes from the underlying granite mass. Most climbers have routinely encountered these flakes and have been correctly concerned about the possibility of their breaking away, or *exfoliating*.

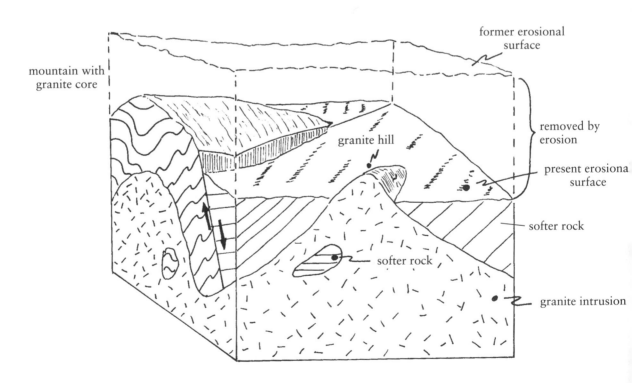

*Figure 17-1. Differential Equations and Isolated Granite Hills: A granite body undergoes regional uplift and differential erosion. Rain water, weathering, and* erosion remove the more easily eroded rock above the granite, exposing the granite as rounded hills.

A

several kilometers

B

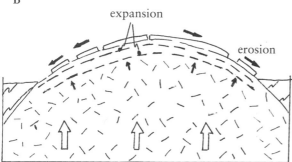

expansion

erosion

*Figure 17-2. **Exfoliation**: A—Granite intrudes into exist-ing rock as a liquid, cools, and hardens several kilome-ters underground. B—Regional uplift sets in motion ero-sion; erosion removes the rock over the granite, releasing pressure on the granite body and allowing upward expansion. Exfoliation occurs along sheet joints that are closely spaced at the surface (where expansion is greatest) and more widely spaced at depth. Modified from Plummer and McGeary, 1991.*

### A Perched Granite Block

Paul Piana and Todd Skinner completed the first free ascent of the Salathé route of El Capitan after thirty days of unmatched effort. *I was first over the rim and selected the best anchor I could find. We had already used this huge block, as had years of Salathé climbers. . . . When Todd jugged the pitch I used the block as a hauling anchor and as my tie-in as well. . . . We heard a horrible grating noise and, turning back, were horrified to see that somehow the block had come loose! . . . Todd remembers me putting my hands out at the block and yelling "No!" I do remember the two of us being battered together, and the hor-ror of seeing my best friend knocked wildly off the edge, and then a tremendous weight on my left leg as I was squeegied off the rim* (Paul Piana, in *Climbing*, 1988).

Because Paul Piana was "embarrassingly paranoid" while waiting for Todd to arrive, he tied off to a fixed pin in addition to the block. The bent ascenders and frayed ropes held, and the climbers managed to regain the rim, descend, heal, climb again, and tell the world about what it took to free the "great-est rock climb in the world."

Where exfoliation flakes have broken away, fresh gray rock that is surrounded by more highly oxi-dized rock of a red or pink color is often exposed. The expanding flakes found on many climbs are exfoliation flakes, and these flakes can be pried loose with camming devices. Rounded domes such as Half Dome of Yosemite Valley are rounded due to exfoliation.

***Perched Granite Blocks on Cliff Edges:*** Glaciers that covered large valleys, whole mountain ranges, and entire continents during the last ice age had a major hand in creating cliffs in northern latitudes. These glaciers quarried the cliffs along planes of

weakness and carried material down-ice, forming the cliff. Glaciers also picked up, carried, and then deposited blocks and finer material called till. After the glacier had vanished, other blocks came to rest on the till as they broke off nearby walls during frost expansion along joint-cracks. The blocks fell on till soils containing pebble and fist-size angular rocks set in a matrix of fine-grained ground-up rock. Granite blocks ranging up to many tons sometimes sit on top of till at the edge of an out-sloping cliff (Figure 17-3A).

Over a period of years, rain and frost expansion in the soil remove the finer-grained ground-up rock particles (soil) from the till beneath the blocks,

A

stable granite rock

till soil

B

precarious granite block

fines washed away from till soil

*Figure 17-3. **Perched Granite Blocks on Cliff Ledges:** A—A granite block has been broken off along joints by frost wedging and has fallen on top of glacial till soil on a cliff ledge. This block could also be a glacial erratic.*

*B—The fine particles of the soil washed away, leaving the block precariously perched on angular rollers at the edge of the cliff.*

leaving the blocks supported by fist-size rock "rollers" (Figure 17-3B). These massive blocks sit poised, ready to go over the cliff edge without very much force, as described in the accompanying box. While you may not encounter them everyday, these blocks are not rare. I have dislodged two, one that wiggled every time climbers stepped on it as they exited a popular top-rope climb, and the other at the top of a new route.

The easiest way to dislodge these blocks purposely, for site management, is carefully to pick out the rock rollers one by one from beneath the block as you attempt to push it over the edge. Both the person working with the block and anyone below must be extremely careful. *The best course of action may be to leave the block alone and just stay away since you can never be completely sure of safety while dislodging a block.* A site leader who has all pertinent site information will have to assess the situation and decide the best course of action.

An additional danger related to till soils (covered in detail in Chapter 6) is that trees growing in these soils on cliff ledges are not deeply rooted and should be suspect as belay anchors without rock protection backup.

## Top-Rope Site Practices

### Top-Rope Site Geography and Safety

The ideal top-rope site can be approached from the bottom, has a flat, boulder-free platform where climbers and belayers can belay and climb, is less than a rope-length high, and has good anchor locations near the cliff edge. It is also convenient to have a staging area, away from potential pebble-fall, which can be used for rest and lunch. The cliff itself should be free of loose rocks and pebbles. The top of the site should be flat, with a trail leading away from the cliff edge by which climbers can return to the bottom.

Since ideal sites are not always available, you may need to manage your location to make it safe. If, for example, climbers need to rappel to the base, as at a seaside cliff, then you must safeguard participants at the cliff top and give extensive help to climbers as they get to the bottom and back to the top. If the top of the cliff is rounded, and there are loose pebbles underfoot ready to act as ball bearings even after a reasonable amount of cleaning, you must make sure that participants do not slip over the edge.

*Figure 17-4. **Barrier on a Cliff Top***

Use control ropes for safety when groups are at the top of a cliff or on starting ledges above drop-offs. A couple of experienced climbers out on a cooperative adventure may be able to manage themselves safely in these situations, but the presence of inexperienced individuals in a group mandates ropes. Whether experienced or inexperienced, people clustered together on a cliff may bump into one another or react unexpectedly to a thrown or dropped object. Group behavior and reaction to events is very different from the behavior and reaction of an individual person.

There are two kinds of control rope. One type is simply a barrier to prevent access to the edge of the cliff (Figure 17-4). You can use this method when the top of the cliff is relatively flat and you establish a staging area at the top, or when a trail runs near the cliff edge. Climbers on the cliff side of the control rope are tied in at all times, while group members behind the control rope are free to walk around cautiously.

The second type of control rope safeguards traverses from the top of a climb, above exposed outsloping slabs, to a safe descent trail (Figure 17-5).

*Figure 17-5. **Traverse Line:** A novice climber who is traversing right to a safe zone and descent trail, has clipped into a traverse line with a sliding attachment. A climbing specialist, on the left, is coiling a top-rope and will throw it back to the ground for the next climber. The climbing specialist can oversee the top of a number of climbs as indicated by the two slingshot systems shown.*

The novice often climbs on a slingshot setup and unties from the rope at the top. The novice needs to be clipped into a safety traverse line by means of a sling and carabiner attached between the climbing harness and traverse line. A climbing specialist usually sets up the control lines and ensures that novices attach to the line. You may also use the traverse control rope when the starting area is exposed above a drop-off and participants are standing in an exposed position at the base of the climb.

### Leashes for Cliff-Top Management

When a number of slingshot systems are being operated with the belayers at the cliff base, a climbing specialist usually controls the cliff top. The specialist either helps climbers exit the climb to safe areas or works with rappellers. If belaying is done by instructors at the top of the cliff, away from the edge, the specialist serves as a communicator between the top belay and bottom tie-in points.

Instructors who are working in exposed positions must also be clipped to an anchor. A simple sling connection to the traverse line can suffice (Figure 17-5) when the top of the climb is within a few feet of the traverse line. If the top of the climb varies from zero to many feet away from the traverse line, however, you need a leash of variable length. Figure 17-6 shows how to make a variable-length leash from a length of climbing rope. You can tie to the leash directly with a knot. For greater mobility, attach by means of a mechanical ascender backed up with a knot tied at the end of the travel path of the ascender. Mechanical ascenders grip the rope with teeth that set into the outer rope sheath and release by means of a trigger, making it relatively easy to move the ascender. Only one ascender is required for the leash. How much mobility you need depends on cliff geography and the number of climbs you are overseeing.

Climbing programs often make use of low-angle cliffs, but participants still often get stuck, unable to climb up and unwilling to back down. If instructions and encouragement from below fail to help, you can rappel to the climber on a tied-off single-strand rope, safeguarded by also tying into the rappel rope. You can calm, instruct, and encourage the novice, then ascend using the rappel rope and one or more mechanical ascenders; clip your harness into the ascenders as well.

*Figure 17-6. **Variable-Length Leash with Mechanical Ascender:** The enlargement shows the ascender used to grip the rope. The climbing specialist ties the leash into his or her harness, and the tie-in serves as a backup to the ascender.*

### Ground School

Ground school provides basic instruction in climbing on flat ground where mistakes have little consequence. It can be part of a progression of instruction and is particularly useful in working with groups of beginners. If boulders are available, they can be incorporated into ground school to teach climbing movement. Ground school should address the various types of climbing movement and body position involved in liebacks, mantles, stems, and other basic moves.

Ground school should familiarize participants with the climbing system, preferably by duplicating on the ground the system to be used at the cliff site. Set up a belay anchor at a tree and then have the "climber" move away from the belay to simulate climbing. You can use top and bottom anchor points and either slingshot or top belays. With groups, locking carabiners provide the best security. Practice tying in to the climbing rope and into anchors; belaying, and giving climbing commands; clipping into a safety traverse line; lowering someone from a climb; and executing other safety procedures. Beginners who have practiced on the ground will be more comfortable dealing with exposure or movement problems on rock. Ground school can last two or more hours, and commonly occupies the morning hours before lunch, followed by actual climbing.

### Belay Systems for Groups

The belay system used for a group depends on the goals of the group. Groups that use belaying for a number of different elements, such as climbing and ropes courses, may wish to standardize belaying techniques. Often these groups will use either a waist belay or a mechanical belay plate that is consistent with the program goals. If the climber lowers back to the ground, as in a slingshot climbing system, a mechanical belay brake might be preferred over a waist belay to prevent friction burns. If you wish to focus on movement skills, you might consider having instructors do all belaying, while participants concentrate on climbing. However, as participants become familiar with basic movement skills, they often want to take part in belaying. This is a normal progression of learning, and you can teach belaying under close supervision as individuals are prepared to learn.

The novice backup belay shown in Figure 17-7

*Figure 17-7. **Novice Backup Belay***

gives responsibility to as many participants as possible and teaches belaying in a more structured progression. The primary belayer, a novice, gives a waist belay that is backed up by a safety belay provided by a second novice. An instructor oversees the two belayers and climbers. The primary belayer provides a normal waist belay and is fastened with a locking carabiner to an anchor. The rope is prevented from lifting from the primary belayer's waist by a carabiner. The backup belayer stands on the helping-hand side of the belayer with the rope in her hands, but not necessarily around her back. She allows enough slack, a few feet, so that she does not interfere with the primary belayer's manipulation of the rope. If the primary belayer forgets to brake the rope during a fall, the backup belayer can simply tighten the rope around the body of the primary belayer. The backup belayer may serve as apprentice to the primary belayer and become the new primary belayer when the former primary belayer climbs.

*A Belaying System for Beginning Rappellers:* When you work with inexperienced rappellers, you must take into consideration that they may not retain control of the braking hand. You can protect the rappeller by setting up a belay. The rappeller ties in with a bowline on a coil. If you attach the rope to an independent anchor, the belay system will be completely independent of the rappel anchor and the harness.

*Stuck Rappellers:* A belay can prevent out-of-control descents, but it does not help when a rappeller is stuck. Rappellers may become physically entangled in the rappel when a loose article of clothing such as a shirt or long hair is pulled into a mechanical rappel brake. Help rappellers to prevent these problems by reminding them to tuck in clothing and hair. Traditionally, these problems are solved by cutting away the offending shirt, hair, or knot with a knife, taking care, of course, not to cut the main rappel rope, which will part easily under the tension of the rappeller's body weight.

Stuck rappellers may also become more stuck if they use a prusik safety that is too long and becomes locked above an inaccessible overhang as they rappel.

There is a simple solution if a rappeller must be lowered. Place a figure-eight rappelling device on a sling around a tree (Figure 17-8). (For single-rope rappels you can also form a Munter hitch on a pear-shaped carabiner in place of the figure-eight brake.) Pass the rappel rope, either single or doubled, through this device and tie it to a second tree with a tensionless anchor. Wrap the doubled rope around the tree several times to gain friction, then pass the bight (formed in the wrapped end of the rope) around both segments of the rope to form an overhand knot; secure it with a locking carabiner. As long as there is sufficient rope between the figure-eight rappel device and the tensionless anchor, the entire rappel system including the stuck climber can be quickly lowered to the ground. Once on the ground, the rappeller can easily release himself or herself from the rappel device.

*Top or Bottom Belays for Safeguarding Rappelling:* Are top or bottom belays better for rappelling? The choice depends on program goals. It is clear that top belays using an anchor separate from that of the rappel provide the ultimate in safety for a novice rappeller. The bottom belay, applied by tensioning the bottom end of the rope and thereby adding friction in the belay brake itself, needs to be applied continuously and instantly if the rappeller loses control. Momentary inattention on the part of the belayer renders the belay ineffective, since the amount of braking force applied by this technique is small. This is not true of the top belay, where lapses in feeding out the rope simply prevent the rappeller from continuing. In addition, the top-rope belay system can be backed up by tying the novice to the belay rope with a bowline on a coil. This provides a separate tie-in from the rappel harness, the rappel brake, and the rappel rope itself. Programs that use rappelling to promote personal growth and character development

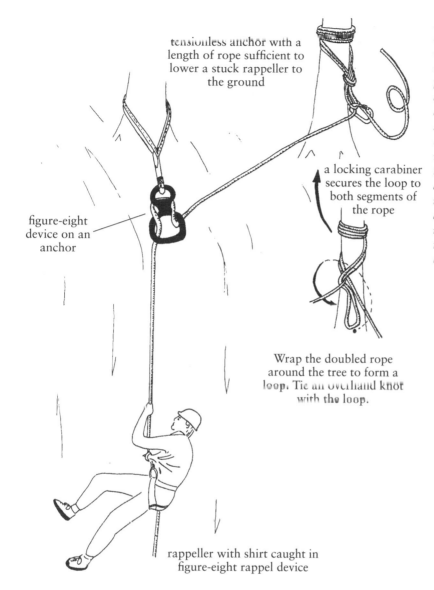

tensionless anchor with a length of rope sufficient to lower a stuck rappeller to the ground

figure-eight device on an anchor

a locking carabiner secures the loop to both segments of the rope

Wrap the doubled rope around the tree to form a loop. Tie an overhand knot with the loop.

rappeller with shirt caught in figure-eight rappel device

*Figure 17-8. **A Rappel Lowering System for Groups:** The rappel rope, either single or doubled, passes through a figure-eight rappel device and attaches to a tensionless anchor. The rope on the far side of the rappel device must be long enough to lower the rappeller and rappelling rope to the ground. Novices are usually given a top-rope belay using a bowline on a coil tie-in, and the belay is often done using an anchor separate from that of the rappel rope. This belay is not shown here.*

as a main goal would be safer to choose a top belay for rappelling.

Military programs often use a bottom belay for rappelling when a top belay, as from the platform of a helicopter, may not be possible. In addition, much military training is designed to simulate wartime situations where speed during a descent is essential for the safety of the mission. Here a bottom belay or no belay may be appropriate. Bottom belays are also used upon occasion by experienced recreational climbers to safeguard

each other when rappelling from overhanging lips or to assist an injured climber when they anticipate that control may be difficult.

## Equipment Logs

It is important to record the history of each piece of climbing equipment used in a climbing program, because hidden damage can occur from a number of causes. If various instructors use the same equipment, the history of the equipment cannot be stored in a single person's memory. Use a logbook to keep track of equipment and to document proper maintenance.

Ropes are the most likely piece of equipment to suffer invisible damage, and most benefit is gained from keeping a rope log. Give each rope a number and catalog historical data such as date of purchase, use, purpose, hours used, falls taken, and date of retirement. To keep track of individual ropes, before you store them attach a numbered tag that corresponds to the log number.

Since ropes retired from climbing are often useful for other purposes, such as for tie-downs, you should store them separately and mark them so that you do not mistakenly use them for climbing. Dipping the ends of the rope in black paint is an effective marker for ropes dead to climbing.

---

## Processing the Climbing Experience

Climbing enriches our lives in many ways. It gives a sense of physical well-being and of challenges met. It takes place in some of the most scenic spots on our planet. Experienced climbers consciously know that they renew themselves each time they touch rock. As instructors, we can help first-time climbers absorb their experience by reflecting on it. This allows individuals to be conscious of what they learned and to interpret and pattern events to give meaning.[8]

### Using Metaphors to Help Process the Climbing Experience

Throughout the actual climbing experience there are many opportunities for learning by drawing parallels from past and present experience. The learning can be unconscious or part of a structured experience. For example, a novice may be fearful before and during a climb, but elated at the top because he or she has achieved a difficult task. A climber who draws parallels with similar life experiences can generalize this learning and transfer it

to real-life situations, such as writing a paper required for school. Similar parallels may be drawn between the cooperation required between the belayer-climber team and that required between people in real life. Stephen Bacon calls this type of learning *metaphoric education.*[9] Metaphors work best when the metaphoric experience closely parallels, at least symbolically, the real-life experience.

A structured program can provide metaphoric experiences throughout the activities. In fact, in therapeutic programs, skilled therapists sometimes draw extensive metaphors for all aspects of the climbing experience.[10] These might take the form of narratives and anecdotes that accompany experiences. Stephen Bacon relates that he once asked his assistant instructor to tell two tales about his personal climbing experiences in great detail. One tale dealt with the fear, trembling, sweat, and turmoil that he experienced on a difficult climb. The second tale dealt with details of a successful climb in which everything went well. These stories were *isomorphic* (had the same form) with the experiences that the students were about to face and provided an opportunity for them to validate and examine their own feelings just before climbing.

Quotes selected from the instructor's favorite sources are useful in providing parallels between adventure and real life. For example:

*Let go and grow—*

*To climb, one hand must go*

*above the other.*

*So in life we succeed not by hanging fearfully to the old,*

*but by reaching out,*

*taking new handholds,*

*mentally accepting, welcoming,*

*adapting new and better ideas.*

*Hold fast—we fail.*

*Let go—we grow.*[11]

—Author Unknown

Other readings may not necessarily draw the parallels so tightly, but like the following will be obvious to adventure participants:

When you get into a tight place and everything goes against you, till it seems as though you could not hang on a minute longer, never give up then, for that is just the place and time that the tide will turn.[12]

—Harriet Beecher Stowe

Gather your own quotes or draw on published collections such as the Hurricane Island Outward Bound School's *Readings,* which explores self-reliance, challenge, wilderness, education, and leadership, or Project Adventure's *Golden Nuggets: Readings for Experiential Education,* which contains material on commitment, community, journey, leadership, and values, with humor, one-liners, and songs.

## Debriefing

Debriefing is a good way for small groups to learn from their experience. (Other teaching strategies and instructional processes are discussed by educator David Cockrell in *The Wilderness Educator.*) Debriefing is a verbal form of processing experience that works within a sequence of levels of thought—knowledge and comprehension, analysis, synthesis and evaluation, and transference:

• Knowledge and comprehension.[13] This level stresses concrete information and detailed recall of events. Questions such as *"What did we just do?"* and *"How do you understand . . .?"* explore knowledge and understanding using open-ended questions. The role of the group facilitator is to encourage participants to provide concrete, detailed answers, perhaps by having different participants describe different portions of the day.

• Analysis. This level of thought calls for participants to analyze their actions. Ask, *"Why do you think that you . . . ?"* *"Now that you have . . . how would you go about solving that particular problem in the future?"*

• Synthesis and evaluation. Synthesis leads to evaluation. Questions might be, *"What was the design of the course?"* *"In your opinion was the course well designed?"* *"What would you do differently if you were designing a climbing experience for beginners?"*

• Transference. This level follows synthesis and evaluation. One important goal of adventure education is to transfer adventure learning into constructive changes in everyday personal behavior. *"What have you learned about yourself?"*

An example of transference from an adventure to everyday behavior might involve communication. If you observed miscommunication during a climbing session, you can employ a sequence of questions to explore effective communication between participants.[14] For example, ask, *"Before you began to climb did you ask your belayer to keep a tight rope?"* *"How do you know that your belayer understood you?"* To explore whether the communication was effective when put into practice, you might follow with, *"While on the climb did your belayer's attention wander (away from the purpose of the communication)?"* *"If the belayer's attention wandered, what went wrong in the initial communication?"* *"What can you do differently next time to give a clearer message?"*

In his book, *Lasting Lessons,* Clifford E. Knapp makes many excellent suggestions for debriefing. Areas that are explored with sample questions include:

• communicating effectively,

• expressing appropriate feelings,

• deferring your judgment of others,

• listening,

• leading others,

• following others,

• making group decisions,

• cooperating,

• respecting human differences,

- respecting human commonalties,

- trusting the group,

- closure.

In conducting a verbal debriefing, ask clearly phrased and concise questions planned ahead of time. Give participants time to reflect and frame thoughtful answers, and listen carefully to them. Use follow-up questions to seek clarification and expand learning for other members of a group. Encourage students to ask questions so that group members, including yourself, may learn from them. Leading students into long-term learning through verbal debriefing is a skill acquired through practice. It many take only a few minutes or extended periods of time to reach course objectives.

### Writing about the Climbing Experience

Asking participants to react to specific readings by writing is also a useful way for them to learn about themselves. Provide a reading list that touches on the experiences of others related to climbing. If you provide more than one selection, have the participants treat the material as a coherent whole to promote analysis and integration. Through reading and writing, participants can reflect, metaphorically, upon their own recent experiences. Each individual will arrive at a unique analysis that reflects personal beliefs and prior experiences. Read what students write and share your own insights and experiences with them through notes in the margins or by brief discussions. These notes and discussions will validate the thoughts of participants and help them consider new ideas. Many students come to see climbing as a potential positive force in their lives. This type of analysis works well in concert with prior verbal debriefing.

Examples of readings that, at a surface level, touch on rules that climbers impose to keep climbs interesting, spiritual values, and technique include the selections by Lito Tejada-Flores, Benard Amy, and Michael Loughman, listed below under "References for Future Reading."

Reaction papers written by students show that they not only understand the surface significance of such material but also take away deeper personal meanings. Tejada-Flores's article shows how different types of climbing such as bouldering or cliff climbing may be viewed as different games with different rules designed to keep the outcome in doubt. This view of climbing provides an opportunity for many novices to see that their own desired outcome and self-imposed rules can lead to a personal definition of success. Amy's metaphoric story allows the reader to examine personal spiritual values within the context of a physical activity and draws gentle parallels with how one conducts one's own life. The Loughman book uses extensive photography and practical problems of body movement to teach technique. The strongest message in the book for many readers, however, is that women can climb well. Almost all of the photographs are of Amy Loughman, who serves as a strong, confident role model.

## References for Future Reading

Amy, Benard. 1972. The greatest climber in the world. In *The games climbers play*. Ken Wilson, ed. San Francisco: Sierra Club Books.

Bacon, Stephen. 1983. *The conscious use of metaphor in Outward Bound*. Denver, Colorado: Colorado Outward Bound School.

Cockrell, David. 1991. Environmental ethics and backcountry practices. Chapter 4 in *The wilderness educator: The Wilderness Education Association curriculum guide*. Merrillville, Indiana: ICS Books.

Direnfeld-Michael, Bonnie. 1989. A risk management primer for recreators. *Journal of Parks and Recreation*. March:40–45.

Gass, Michael. 1990. Transfer of learning in adventure education. In *Adventure education* by John C. Miles and Simon Priest, Venture Pub. Inc.

Hale, Alan. 1984. *Safety management for outdoor program leaders*. Bellefontaine, Ohio: National Safety Network.

Klokis, Holly. 1981. Outing centers—rowing, rollerskating & more. *College Union*. February: 13–16.

Knapp, Clifford E. 1990. Processing the adventure experience. In *Adventure education* by John C.

Miles and Simon Priest. State College, Pennsylvania: Venture Pub. Inc.

Knapp, Clifford E. 1984. Idea notebook: Designing processing questions to meet specific objectives. *Journal of Experiential Education.* 7(2):47–49.

_____. 1992. *Lasting lessons: A teacher's guide to reflecting on experience.* Charleston, WV: Clearinghouse on Rural Education and Small Schools, Appalachian Educational Laboratory.

Kuller, Alison Murray, ed. 1986. *Readings.* Rockland, Maine: Hurricane Island Outward Bound School.

Loughman, Michael. 1981. Movement. Chapter 3 in *Learning to rock climb.* San Francisco: Sierra Club Books.

Meier, J. 1980. Is the risk worth taking? In *High adventure outdoor pursuits.* Meier, J., et al., eds. Salt Lake: Brighton Pub. Co.

Miles, J. 1980. The value of high adventure activities. In *High adventure outdoor pursuits.* J. Meier, et al., eds. Salt Lake: Brighton Pub. Co.

Piana, Paul. 1988. Salathé wall. *Climbing.* 110:50–60.

Plummer, Charles C, and David McGeary. 1991. *Physical geology.* Fifth edition. Dubuque, Iowa: Wm. C. Brown Co.

Priest, Simon, and Tim Dixon. 1990. *Safety practices in adventure programming.* Boulder, Colorado: The Association for Experiential Education, Safety Committee.

Rivera, Margo, and Stacy Stefan. 1992. The metaphor of rock climbing in a psychiatric setting. In *proceedings manual of the 20th international conference of the Association for Experiential Education.*

Schoel, Jim, and Mike Stratton, eds. 1990. *Golden nuggets: Readings for experiential educators.* Hamilton, Massachusetts: Project Adventure, Inc.

Tejada-Flores, Lito. 1978. Games climbers play. In *The games climbers play.* Ken Wilson, ed. San Francisco: Sierra Club Books.

Van der Smissen, Betty. 1980. Legal liability-adventure activities. Las Cruces, New Mexico: New Mexico State University. Educational Resources Information Center (ERIC), Clearinghouse on Rural Education and Small Schools (CRESS).

_____. 1985. Releases, waivers, and agreements to participate. In *National Safety Network newsletter* 1 (4).

Wade, I. R., and M. Fischesser. 1988. *The safety review manual: A guide to conducting safety reviews for assessing and upgrading safety in outdoor adventure programs.* Greenwich, Connecticut: Outward Bound USA.

## Endnotes

1. Klokis, 1981.

2. Van der Smissen, 1980.

3. *Ibid.*

4. Van der Smissen, 1985.

5. Van der Smissen, 1980; Hale, 1984; Direnfield-Michael, 1989.

6. Priest and Dixon, 1990. This document is the standard reference of the outdoor recreation profession and has evolved in frequent revisions.

7. This section is adapted from the staff qualifications chapter of Priest and Dixon, 1990.

8. Knapp, 1992.

9. Bacon, 1983, explores the learning process of Outward Bound students.

10. Rivera and Stefan, 1992, discuss the extensive use of metaphors in the rock climbing sequence of a Challenge program in a dual-diagnosis psychiatric setting.

11. This is one of the favorite readings of Dr. Marty O'Keefe, from whom I took it. The original source is unknown.

12. From Kuller, 1986.

13. See Cockrell, 1991, pages 74–80, for a discussion of teaching strategies.

14. Clifford Knapp has a life-long interest in learning about and teaching others about the educational value of debriefing. Three references to his works are listed here.

# CHAPTER

# 18

# *Managing Risk*

## Introduction

From the very beginning, climbers have been concerned with accidents. A fatality occurred during the first ascent of the Matterhorn, on July 14, 1865. The party contained four gentlemen (Edward Whymper, Lord Francis Douglas, Mr. Hadrow, and Vicar Charles Hudson) and four guides (Michel Croz, Peter Taugwalder, and his two sons). On the descent the entire party tied together, but without attachment to the rock, to pass the difficult bit below the summit. Mr. Hadrow slipped off his feet onto his back; his feet struck Croz and knocked him over. The connecting rope jerked Hudson and then Lord Douglas from their steps, and they fell down the slope. Old Peter Taugwalder and Edward Whymper, upon hearing Croz's exclamation, held on as tightly as possible, but the oldest of their manila ropes broke. The men continued falling until they reached the glacier

4,000 feet below. From this time, mountain climbing, and by inference all kinds of climbing, were considered dangerous.[1]

Today we better understand why, when, how, and to whom accidents occur. The wilderness recreation community has kept statistics for many years as it strives to improve our understanding of how to manage associated risks.[2] Recently, a number of agencies and organizations have redoubled and systematized these efforts. We have learned that climbing and wilderness recreation as a whole hold dangers, but that these are significantly fewer than the dangers associated with many other normal activities. Driving to a climbing site and back home is more dangerous than rock climbing.[3]

Only a small percentage of climbers are involved in accidents. There are an average of 2.5 deaths and a few serious injuries in Yosemite each year, in comparison to about 25 deaths and 140 serious injuries among all climbers in the U.S. In addition, there are approximately 50 fractures, and 15 to 25 rescues annually in Yosemite Valley, out of perhaps 25,000 to 50,000 climber-days on the rock.

Indeed, rock climbing is less dangerous than operating a power lawn mower or playing high-school football. A recent survey of injuries occurring to participants in the National Outdoor Leadership School found that mountaineering and rock climbing were lower-risk activities than back-packing, which is generally considered a low-risk activity.[4,5] It is important to note that instructors sustained a higher rate of injury than students, which may be associated with greater dangers in leading multipitch climbs.

The generally low rates of climbing injury should not lull us into taking a casual attitude toward safety, since the fractures, head injuries, and internal traumas that occur in climbing accidents are potentially more serious than the sprains, strains, and soft-tissue injuries that result from backpacking.

The general public incorrectly perceives climbing as significantly more dangerous than high-school football and gymnastics, which have very high injury rates. Good statistical records will play a role in changing those perceptions as well as in educating climbers to the dangers that they do face.

In part, climbers have a good safety record because we know that climbing is dangerous if we do not manage the risk by taking precautions and safeguarding ourselves. We know that falls from rock, out-of-control slides on snow slopes, collisions, encounters with avalanches and lightning are the sources of injury. To deal with these dangers we have developed leadership techniques as well as engineering systems, and we are learning how the interactions of people and the environment contribute to accidents.

## Rock-climbing Accidents

An examination of accident records in Yosemite National Park from 1970 to 1986 by John Dill found that "[s]hort climbs and Big Walls, easy routes and desperate ones—all get their share of accidents," that "[m]ost victims are experienced climbers: 60 percent have been climbing for three years or more, lead 5.10, and are in good condition, and climb frequently," and that "at least 80 percent of the climbing fatalities, and many injuries were easily preventable. In case after case, ignorance, a casual attitude, and/or some form of distraction proved to be the most dangerous aspects of the sport."[6] The cause of many of the accidents in both Yosemite and the United States and Canada was human error. In Yosemite and the United States, these errors include those listed in the categories given below.[7]

### Learning to Lead

• Challenging oneself by learning to climb and protect at the same time. These are separate skills. Exceeding one's ability causes 12 accidents per year, and is a contributing cause for twice that number.

• Getting off route onto dangerous and/or difficult rock. Routefinding for longer climbs is a skill

in itself (discussed on page 269 under "Classical 'Rules' for Speed on Big Climbs"). Approximately 4 accidents per year are due to this cause.

• Becoming overconfident before (or after) one's skills are solidified.

### Leading

• Setting up a poor belay chain that turns an acceptable fall into an accident.

• Placing protection that failed when needed or was not placed frequently enough on easy run outs or to prevent groundfall. Approximately 38 accidents per year are due to no or inadequate protection or having a nut or chock pull.

• Trusting weathered fixed pins or bad bolts that pull.

• Falling after unroping to switch rappel anchors or to scramble on "easy terrain" to exit a climb.

• Being slow on long day climbs that turned into bivouacs followed by exposure and hypothermia.

### Descending

• Not learning ahead of time the easy way off a climb. Approximately 12 accidents per year are due to rappel failure or error.

• Using single-point anchors for belays or rappels that fail.

• Rappelling off the end of ropes and/or using prusik safety knots that melt.

### Equipment Choice

• Discovering that rain and bivouac gear is inadequate in a storm followed by a retreat in cold weather. Proper preparation requires getting a weather report before you climb, learning about local weather conditions in order to anticipate and recognize changing weather patterns, and taking appropriate gear.

• Not wearing a helmet (8 percent of injuries are to the head). A helmet increases survival chances, and lessens or eliminates injuries for some victims in some accidents.

### State of Mind

• Being unpracticed, unprepared, or uninformed about what to do when faced with a new task or situation.

• Being casual or inattentive; not taking climbing seriously.

• Being distracted, afraid, in a hurry, or argumentative with a partner.

### Loose Rock

• Climbing beneath another party.

• Allowing ropes to knock off loose rock.

• Anchoring in rotten rock.

A broader report of accidents has been published by the American Alpine Club since 1951 (jointly with the Alpine Club of Canada since 1977) as *Accidents in North American Mountaineering.* From 1951 through 1991, 4,040 accidents involving 7,149 persons with 985 killed are reported for the United States. Approximately 59 percent of these accidents occurred on rock, 37 percent on snow, 3 percent on ice, 0.3 percent in rivers, and 0.4 percent from unknown reasons in the United States. Accidents in Canada (1959 to 1991: 584 accidents, 1,289 persons, 203 killed) occurred about 50 percent on rock, 40 percent on snow, 9 percent on ice, 0.4 percent in rivers, and 0.9 percent for unknown reasons. Falls or slips on rock, snow, and ice account for about half of all accidents. Environmental hazards such as falling rock, avalanche, exposure, and lightning are listed as the direct cause of approximately 18 percent of accidents.[9]

Human error contributed significantly to these accidents. Among the factors were climbing unroped or alone (accounting for about a quarter of all accidents), exceeding abilities, and either using inadequate equipment, using equipment incorrectly, or trusting it mistakenly (pitons pulled). Climbers also set up rappels that failed,

and failed to follow established routes.

Many accidents happen to experienced climbers who make avoidable mistakes. In the United States as a whole, about 30 percent of accidents involve experienced people, and in Yosemite *most* victims are experienced (they have three years of climbing, lead 5.10 or more, and are in good condition) and climb frequently.

We must ask, then, why people make mistakes that result in accidents. Whatever we can learn will help us to protect ourselves. While this chapter explores risk management largely within the context of climbing, the question touches on human reactions to the many situations in which people find themselves while exploring the wild outdoors.

---

## Learning to Manage Risk

To learn to avoid making errors when we confront environmental hazards, we can draw on personal experience, education, and the experiences of others. Learning from one's own mistakes is a time-honored but self-limiting form of education. Participating in a structured program or working with a professional guide can teach us much, but here too the experience we can gain has practical limitations. An excellent way to learn without personal danger is by examining case studies that cover a multitude of situations. Sources that provide a starting point are listed below; detailed references appear at the end of the chapter.

Learning should result in a set of guidelines that you can store away until needed. These guidelines will never be the sole basis of decision-making, but they help you make decisions for the particular situation at hand. The process of internalizing a personal set of guidelines is a valuable one for future safety and may ultimately be as valuable as the written set presented here.

Chouinard, Yvon. 1978. "Speed and Safety," in *Climbing Ice.*

Dill, John. 1987. "Staying Alive," in *Yosemite Valley Climbs.*

Priest, Simon, and Tim Dixon. 1990. *Safety Practices in Adventure Programming.*

Synder, J. 1985. "A Collection of Accidents and Incidents to Learn from, Gleaned from the Records of the North Carolina Outward Bound School."

Walbridge, C. C., ed. *River Safety Reports.*

Williamson, John E., A. Harvard, P. Lev, C. Bangs, and B. Shaw. 1986. The Basecamp Program and the Mount Hood Accident. Reports of the Base Camp Inquiry Committee to the Board of Trustees of Oregon Episcopal School.

Williamson, John E., and O. Miskiw, eds. 1993. *Accidents in North American Mountaineering.*

Williams, Knox. 1975. *The Snowy Torrents: Avalanche Accidents in the United States 1967–71.*

### Classical "Rules" for Speed on Big Climbs

Climbers have developed safety "rules" for moving on glaciers, big cliffs, and in the mountains where hazards of terrain and weather, such as storms, rockfall, and avalanches, are vitally important.

Many climbers believe that the first "rule" of safety is *speed*, that the faster that you get up a climb and back down, the safer you will be. What does the maxim *speed is safety* mean in practice?

It applies to competent, experienced parties consisting of fit and acclimatized individuals. These individuals make correct routefinding decisions, use efficient rope-management procedures, carry light packs, and resolve technical difficulties efficiently.

Yvon Chouinard, in his book *Climbing Ice,*[9] gives 27 suggestions to increase speed that come down to being fit, experienced, and having a desire to push one's limits. To paraphrase and elaborate on a few of these suggestions:

• Train for aerobic endurance as well as strength; acclimatize on lower-elevation climbs, and push yourself when you are on high climbs.

• Learn routefinding on shorter routes before you do longer routes. Memorize descent routes as well as ascent routes.

• Learn weather principles and local conditions, and study the forecast before you start; know when to turn back.

• Start early to have a full day and to avoid having any party ahead of you or encountering an afternoon thunderstorm or avalanche.

• Carry gear appropriate to what you need to climb, survive, and get down safely, but not enough to force a bivouac. Keep gear and food for the climb in an outside pocket. Eat and drink frequently at belays rather than plan a big lunch stop.

• Use efficient gear—long ropes to cut down belays, buckle-type rather than tied harnesses.

• Move efficiently over snow. Use long axes instead of shorter ones; cut a few steps instead of putting on crampons; belay from bollards instead of deadmen; follow low-angle alpine ice on tension with no or one hand tool; keep your tools sharp.

These suggestions do not cover every possibility. Each new situation demands that the climber analyze the situation, adapt the "rules" according to personal experience, and take appropriate action. It is helpful to have a model for looking at how environmental conditions and people interact to produce accidents, and to form general guidelines to avoid undesirable interactions.

### Interactions of People and the Environment

The interplay of environmental and human factors creates accidents.[10] The guidelines discussed above help to prevent accidents by establishing a barrier between unwise human actions and environmental hazards. On the one side is the environment, with its steep slopes, avalanches, loose rock, gravity, storms, lightning, and other recurring natural hazards in an ongoing dynamic interaction. On the other side is what we take into the wilderness: knowledge and skill, personal goals, reaction to peer pressure and group dynamics, physical conditioning or fatigue, and a limited human perception of the time scale and processes involved in natural events.

A recurring accident at the Grand Teton National Park exemplifies how people make the same mistakes when they confront nature. The Symmetry Spire couloir is 2,500 feet long, with a rock cliff planted squarely in the middle a few hundred feet below the top (Figure 18-1). On the trip uphill, climbers usually scamper around this cliff using snow slopes on the cliff's left side. Above the cliff, climbers often cross a pronounced narrow groove in the broad upper fan and complete the ascent using the low-angle snow slope beneath Symmetry Spire.

From above, the view of the couloir appears somewhat different. A broad scoop leads down from the upper fan. Downhill, there is a long, gentle slope that seems to be made for sliding, but the center of the scoop is very icy and the slope becomes steeper as the scoop narrows to a trough just above the cliff. It is difficult to self-arrest in the

icy center of the scoop, so the scoop funnels climbers over the cliff.

Below the cliff the snow melts away from the rock during the spring to leave a moat, which may be dry or filled with water. If there is water, the out-of-control glissader will instantly submerge and suffer immersion hypothermia or drown. If the moat is dry, the glissader's fall may result in head injuries. Several fatalities have occurred in this particular place.[11] At least one glissader has escaped serious injury by jumping from the top of the cliff across the moat onto the snow slope below.

Being caught up in a terrain trap is one of many undesirable interactions with the environment that can lead to an accident. Individuals can develop guidelines to avoid these interactions and to manage risk.

Risk-management guidelines are presented below along with a few simplified case studies meant to illustrate these guidelines. A proper analysis of these case studies requires reading the original sources, which are often complex and bring to the analysis knowledge tempered by expe-

Figure. 18-1: *The Terrain Trap of Symmetry Spire Couloir*

### Anticipating Potential Danger

A group of outdoor leaders examined a rappel accident in which a member of an organized class fell to his death during his second rappel when the rope "popped" off the anchor rock.[12] They noted that anchor systems composed of two or more anchors that back up each other prevent failure of the entire system in case one anchor fails, and that it is common practice to belay beginning rappellers with a top-rope throughout the beginning session and on the second rappel. They agreed that leaders need experience and knowledge of systems and people operating in groups to deal with situations that arise in the course of the outing. Leaders may be knowledgeable in one area but not in another; one of the hallmarks of good leaders is to know their own limitations and operate within them.

rience. The original sources are listed as references. Many of the case studies involve near-misses that did not result in injury, since we know that accidents are often preceded by a number of near-misses, these reports should lead to better judgment.

These guidelines are those of this author, tempered by the wisdom of others. Readers should ask their own questions, based on their own education and experience, in response to these and other examples. The guidelines that you form will serve you in any difficult situation. Remember, the purpose is to prevent accidents—not to criticize the mistakes of others.

## Some Guidelines for Risk Management

*Leaders' Reserve of Experience:* Leaders should have more experience, knowledge, and skill than required for the activity at hand. This additional experience gives the leader a cushion of knowledge and skill to anticipate what might go wrong, take steps to prevent an accident, and handle the accident if it occurs.

This reserve of experience and skill is one component of what we call good judgment. We base good judgment on experience and the analysis of each specific situation, rather than written rules to be followed to the letter. Another component of

---

### Pushing the Limit

*On New Hampshire's Mt. Washington, my partner and I had spent the evening in the Harvard cabin at tree line and awoke to a chilly 10 degrees inside the cabin. We fixed breakfast and noted that with an outside temperature of −20 degrees Fahrenheit our climbing would be limited. Still, since we had the day, we walked the mile or so to the base of Huntington Ravine, where we emerged from the trees. There was no wind and the sky was clear. We hiked up the lower fan to the base of Damnation Gully, which is 1,500 feet long, mostly low-angle snow and a few ice bulges.*

*Before entering the gully we checked for wind and reasoned that we could easily reverse the next few hundred feet of climbing. After reaching a short vertical ice bulge midway, we again checked for wind. We did the crux and decided that we could retreat easily if necessary. We found no frostbite, which would occur if any wind were present. Although we were in a sheltered gully, we could see no snow trails blowing off the Alpine Garden or summit that would indicate wind overhead. The air was wonderfully still.*

*The climb of the upper gully was long and uneventful. The gully ended in a short, steep wall that changed abruptly to the flat surface of the Alpine Garden. As we exited, we discovered that we had been climbing totally sheltered from the unheard and unseen jetstream winds blowing from the west across the summit and Alpine Garden. A blast of this wind flattened Scott, who emerged before me, and then I was knocked down in turn. I stood up and was knocked over again. Scott's cheek was frostbitten as he helped me pull up my jacket over my climbing helmet. The new position of the jacket exposed my Adam's apple and it was instantly frostbitten by the −75-degree windchill. Covering ourselves, we raced the quarter mile to a simple downclimb and dropped out of the wind into the now calm −20-degree air. Because we were skilled at ice climbing, experienced on this mountain in winter, and constantly alert, we were willing to operate where all factors combined pushed us against a critical safety barrier. We crossed that barrier in an instant, and were lucky to get down with as little injury as we had.*

*—letter from a friend*

good judgment is self-knowledge. Leaders may be skilled in one area and not in another; they should know their own limitations and act as leaders only within their area of competency.

*Approaching the Limits of Our Abilities:* While the dangers of exceeding our abilities are clear, we need also to understand the dangers of approaching our limits, especially when we are entrusted with the lives of others. Maintaining a large margin of safety and being extraordinarily well prepared can prevent a small setback from becoming life-threatening.

The line between life and death is narrow. We can perhaps learn more from near-misses than from fatal accidents (since in the latter case we can never know what people were thinking at the time). The accompanying case study (see box, page 271) represents a near-miss that may have a similar origin to that of a fatal accident on New Hampshire's Mt. Washington.[13] In the fatal accident, two experienced climbers completed a difficult climb in subzero conditions but were forced to bivouac at the top as jetstream winds prevented their escape to the normal descent route. After a night of extreme cold, they fell to their deaths as they attempted to descend another climb.

---

### A Novice and His Partner

*I was in the Tetons seeking a partner. This was to be my first mountain route, although I had moderate experience rock climbing. I found a partner who had just climbed the North Ridge of the Grand and a number of other notable climbs, and I considered him experienced. We bivouacked at the base of the East Ridge, started out at first light, and did some interesting climbing throughout the long day. The highlight was the final 800-foot-high snow field adjacent to the 3,000-foot North Face. But in mountaineering, getting to the top is only half of the story. We had to return to the base of the ridge, which we did by crossing over the mountain and going down the regular Owen-Spalding route, then traversing the base of the mountain along the Black Dike Traverse.*

*At the end of the traverse, we reached the Tepe glacier after the light had left it. The soft surface of the sunlit glacier had quickly frozen into hard ice demanding crampons, an excellent glissading technique, or at least a few ice screws for belays. My partner started down, skiing on his feet. I followed but had not mastered the technique and repeatedly fell. I was wearing a smooth nylon "foam-back" cagoule that, combined with my lack of skill, acted as a runaway*

*sledge. I self-arrested properly, but the steep glacier was fluted with alternating ridges and grooves extending up and down the glacier. With my axe in a ridge, I slowed but then my travel path would take me across a groove and my axe would be in the air. I needed to self-arrest again. Sometimes I was airborne, sometimes I did somersaults to self-arrest, but always after a few seconds of slowing, my axe was in the air above the groove. This situation continued for a thousand very rapidly descended feet until the glacier became gentle enough for the self-arrest to work. I stood up and was miraculously unhurt, although my forearm was "pumped up" from hanging onto the axe. My partner, far above at the end of the slide, caught up and then passed me on the way, asking, "Who told you that you should wear nylon when glissading?" I later found out that this glacier was named for the climber who first died in a similar slide. I have also heard of a number of wiser parties who spent sleepless but safe nights at the top of the col looking down at their sleeping bags below. In the morning, after the sun softened the snow, they safely descended what had been a dangerous slope only hours before.*

*—letter from a friend*

---

*Novices and Mentors:* A mentor can make a significant difference to a novice's well-being. A mentor, whether leader, instructor, or experienced partner, needs to have technical skills, people skills, knowledge of the environment, and knowledge of the rules of safety. In a group, the mentor's leadership style may have a direct impact upon safety.

In one situation (see box on page 272), two climbers shared a common adventure without a designated leader, as is common with many climbing teams. In this case each climber is responsible for his or her own safety as well as the safety of the team, but in practice the more experienced climber probably has a better understanding of the needs of the team and an ethical if not a legal responsibility for its safety. Most climbers accept this responsibility and pass their knowledge and skills on to their partners. Here, communication is the key to a safe outing.

In this near-miss, the experienced climber made an unrealistic assumption about the ability of his partner to undertake a technical glissade, and both climbers communicated poorly. They should have explored their differences in ability and experience more thoroughly by talking at greater length. If they had climbed a less committing route as a warmup, they might have gotten a better sense of each other's abilities and experience and had a chance to discuss techniques and options.

### Guidelines for Groups

*Objectives:* Frame objectives to fit the physical fitness and abilities of the group, whether it is an organized group or an informal group joined for a common adventure. One group may be goal-oriented, wanting for example to hike a particular trail; another may place primary emphasis on education.

Groups are normally goal oriented, which may be positive or negative. Since goal orientation seems such a prominent part of group behavior in the outdoors it might successfully be dealt with openly. Goal orientation is negative if a group is locked into a goal and continues to attempt to accomplish it without realistically considering alternatives in the face of environmental hazards.[14]

The goal need not be a summit; it might be pushing on through fatigue to camp at a particular site. Many of us have done this even though we could easily have camped earlier and proceeded the next morning when the group was fresh. Consider establishing acceptable alternatives or contingency plans before starting out to avoid locking into an inappropriate goal.

In small groups, members will benefit by discussing decision-making procedures before heading out. This discussion will help establish consultation as an important procedure in decision-making.

*Group Size:* The number of people in a group influences its dynamics. Gregarious by nature, we often think there is safety in numbers, but more important is how well we, as individuals and team members, respond to situations that we encounter. Traveling in a group in a wilderness environment can test us all.

The advantages and disadvantages of large and small groups remain debatable. Undoubtedly, decision-making and organizational details are harder and more time consuming in large groups of inexperienced climbers who do not operate by a linear command structure, so size can give a false sense of security. On the other hand, having at least four in the party may be critical in an emergency: if a person is injured, two individuals can summon help while one remains with the victim. To evacuate a person, even with a minor injury such as a sprained ankle, requires several people to assist the injured person.

On the other hand, a small group may be able to evacuate itself more easily than a large group in a storm. When there are severe injuries requiring extensive medical care and mechanical evacuation, initial group size seems to be of more limited importance than obtaining outside help. While there are no sure answers, wilderness travelers need to consider how group size in combination with experience might strengthen or hinder them for any given trip.

*Peer Pressure:* Peer pressure is ever present in our outings with others. It can be negative when one climber talks another into undertaking a climb that is too hazardous, and an accident occurs. Negative peer pressure usually involves the lack of resolved communication between climbers—a partner squelches or ignores a climber's concerns without the give and take of thoughtful debate. The incident described in the accompanying box is an example of how peer pressure can bring pleasure.

Peer pressure is a normal function of individuals in a group. Look for and openly discuss the concerns of party members before undertaking the activity whenever a single person opens the discussion. Members of a party may quickly reject voiced concerns as invalid, and the rejected person continues against his or her own best interest in order to remain a member of the group. In a structured group, leaders need to act in the group's best interest in order to avoid this tendency. Individuals with doubts concerning a peer group's course of action need to analyze the consequences to themselves and the group as a whole if they were to choose another course of action.

---

### A Great Climb

*Two friends and I bivouacked at 11,500 feet in the Teton range. After a sleepless night, we awoke before first light and ate a cold breakfast of greasy sausage. About 5:30 A.M. we began working our way uphill into increasingly technical terrain. I was stiff with cold and sick to my stomach. The term nausea doesn't do it justice. I felt like quitting, but continued. After a half hour, I felt better and we had a good climb. Two years later, in a relaxed social atmosphere, I told this story to my friends, who revealed that they had felt the same way at that time. If anyone had brought up the idea of stopping at just the right (or wrong) moment, we all might have turned around and missed a great climb.*

—letter from a friend

---

*Time:* Groups on a time schedule might consider picking at least two worthwhile potential goals, one of which all members of the group can achieve in almost any weather conditions. If the group does split up, each group should be under competent leadership and contain enough internal strength to reach its goal safely.

The desire to achieve a goal within the limited time span of a vacation contributes to many accidents. Individuals and groups often are not willing to wait the two days needed for new snow to consolidate before skiing, or until unsettled weather clears before going high. Often, they expose themselves to avalanches, storms, and lightning in order to achieve goals conceived months earlier in their living rooms. To avoid this mind-set, it is useful to pick more than one original goal: for example, a summit on a fair day or a difficult but dry rock climb underneath an overhang in a drizzle. Or, take a cross-country ski trip through wooded terrain instead of venturing above tree line if avalanche conditions prevail. What is important here is that the participants believe both alternatives are worthy. They need to be ready to back away from one goal if it is no longer appropriate. We always need to remind ourselves that we are visitors in an environment that we cannot control.

In a program, participants should climb because they want to, not because they will fulfill some requirement. Programs also need to tailor the activities to the participants' abilities and give participants desirable options. Participants should always choose whether to take part in high-adventure activities that are potentially dangerous.

*Staying Together :* A basic rule of safety in backcountry travel is that members of the party not lose sight of one another, but it takes effort and organization to do so. To organize this effort, some groups assign functions to members as "guides," who find the way, and "sweeps," who bring up the rear without letting anyone out of sight at any time. To learn more about this technique, consult Paul Petzoldt's *New Wilderness Handbook* and "Adventure Skills and Travel Modes," Chapter 8 in *Wilderness Educator.*

Many accidents stem from uncoordinated movement when one member of a group suffers injury. Individuals can become separated from the group and subsequently injure themselves in a fall or suffer hypothermia. In an unusual case described in *Snowy Torrents*,[15] a member of a group was buried by a very small avalanche while he was close to other group members. The avalanche ran about 50 feet and the uninvolved members of the group skied past the buried victim shortly after the slide. The victim might well have survived if group members had seen that he was caught in the slide.

*Established Practices:* Established practices can be a cause of accidents (see box below). If you have initial doubts about an activity but the first trip succeeds without incident, you may dismiss your doubts. This produces a cyclic reasoning process that allows the activity to continue on the basis of its prior usage even though you suspect it may be unsafe. Breaking the cycle is difficult once it becomes established.

Other incidents have led to fatalities. One accident involved a routine long-established practice of guided parties eating lunch under a cornice because that was the only flat spot in the area. After many years the cornice fell off, resulting in a number of deaths.

Periodic safety review seems to be the only way to change established practices. In-house review panels can and probably should be established for ongoing review. Outside reviewers can have a more objective view of practices as they see these without prejudice due to historical development.

---

## Summary

All climbers must be concerned about accidents because sooner or later most of us will be involved in one, either directly or indirectly. Accidents happen to experienced and highly skilled individuals as well as to the unwary novice. You should understand your own vulnerability and be committed to learning to climb safely.

Classic "rules" and guidelines tell us the best way to move safely and swiftly through the mountains, but these rules are ultimately not enough. As individuals and members of a group, we need to recognize what human behaviors we bring into the wilderness. We need to understand how these behaviors interact with environmental hazards and plan our climbs accordingly.

Climbing safely means gaining personal skills and experiences in technical matters, learning about the natural environment, accepting our limits as human beings, and interacting in positive ways with climbing partners and others that we encounter while climbing. We need to be constantly on guard because everything can change quickly. This very alertness and the concentration that it demands makes climbing interesting and challenging enough to last a lifetime. By concentrating on safety we do not necessarily become

---

### Crossing the Train Trestle

A serious near-miss occurred to an Outward Bound group[16] following an established procedure, when two instructors were accompanying students on a final expedition.

*As Alan and Anne were partway across the Catawba River Railroad trestle (150 feet long and 30 feet above the river) a train suddenly appeared. At the far end of the trestle, Alan ran to get off the bridge and either leaped for the bank or was hit by the train. He sustained mild abrasions and a concussion and was consequently hospitalized overnight. He was X-rayed for possible head, neck, and spinal injuries. Anne was trapped in the middle of the trestle as the train appeared, jumped the railing and hung on to a parallel beam with her pack on until the train passed. She was shaken but did not require hospitalization. . . .*

—"A Collection of Accidents and Incidents to Learn From" by Jane Synder obsessed with it, but simply see potential danger where others may not see it.

# References for Future Reading

Chouinard, Yvon. 1978. *Climbing ice*. San Francisco: Sierra Club Books in Association with the American Alpine Club.

Cinnamon, C. G. 1989. Risk management in high adventure outdoor pursuits. In *Proceedings of the 1988 National Conference on Outdoor Recreation*, J. Gilbert and E. Brunner, eds. University, Mississippi: The University of Mississippi, Department of Health, Physical Education and Recreation.

Cinnamon J., and Ed Raiola. 1991. Adventure skills and travel modes. Chapter 8 in *The wilderness educator: The Wilderness Education Association's curriculum guide*. David Cockrell, ed. Maryville, Indiana: I.C.S. Books.

Cockrell, David. 1991. *The wilderness educator: The Wilderness Education Association's curriculum guide*. Maryville, Indiana: I.C.S. Books.

Couche, S. 1977. Avalanche awareness survey. *Mazama Journal*.

Dill, John. 1987. Staying alive. In *Yosemite climbs* by George Meyers and Don Reid. Denver, Colorado: Chockstone Press.

Gentile, Douglas A., John A. Morris, Tod Schimelpfenig, Sue M. Bass, and Paul S. Auerbach. 1992. Wilderness injuries and illnesses. *Annals of Emergency Medicine*. 21(7):854–861.

Hale, Alan. 1984. *Safety management for outdoor program leaders*. Bellefontaine, Ohio: National Safety Network.

Hunt, Tom. 1988. Yosemite Valley: Study challenges common assumptions. *Climbing*. 108:116–117

Meyer, D. 1979. The management of risk. *The Journal of Experiential Education* 2(2):9–14.

Petzoldt, Paul. 1984. *The wilderness handbook*, rev. ed. New York: W. W. Norton & Company.

Priest, Simon, and Tim Dixon, 1990. *Safety practices in adventure programming*. Boulder, Colorado: University of Colorado, The Association for Experiential Education, Safety Committee.

Roberts, David. 1986. Reflections on Mount Hood. *Outside*. September: 39–41.

Roskelly, John. 1986. Tragedy on Mt. Hood. *Backpacker*. September:51–53.

Smutek, Ray, ed. 1972. Symmetry Spire—a very bad year. *Off-Belay*. January–February:44.

Snyder, Howard. 1973. *The hall of the mountain king*. New York: Scribners.

Synder, Jane. 1985. A collection of accidents and incidents to learn from, gleaned from the records of the North Carolina Outward Bound School. Mankato, Minnesota: in partial fulfillment of an M.S. in Experiential Education, Mankato State University.

Wade, Ian R. 1991. *Safety management in adventure education*, John C. Miles and Simon Priest, eds. State College, Pennsylvania: Venture Publishing Co.

Walbridge, Charles C., ed. 1986. "Fatal accident on the North Fork, American River." In *River Safety Report*, 1982–1985. Newington, Virginia: American Canoe Association, Inc.

Whymper, Edward. 1880. *The ascent of the Matterhorn*. London: John Murray.

Wilcox, Joe. 1981. *White winds: America's most tragic climb*. Los Alamitos, California: Hwong Publishing Co.

Williams, Knox. 1975. Mt. Cleveland. In *The snowy torrents: Avalanche accidents in the United States 1967–71*. USDA Forest Service, General Technical Report RM-8.

_____. 1975. Slide Mtn. Nevada. In *The snowy torrents: Avalanche accidents in the United States 1967–71*. USDA Forest Service, General Technical Report RM-8.

Williamson, John E., ed. 1983. Rappel failure, inadequate protection, Utah, Diamond Fork. In *Accidents in North American mountaineering*. New York: The American Alpine Club and Banff: The Alpine Club of Canada. 4(6):36, 58.

_____. 1983. Fall on snow, fall into moat, inadequate equipment, inexperience, Wyoming, Tetons. In *Accidents in North American mountaineering*. New York: The American Alpine Club and Banff: The Alpine Club of Canada. 4(6):36, 67.

Williamson, John E., A. Harvard, P. Lev, C. Bangs, and B. Shaw. 1986. The base camp program and the Mount Hood accident, reports of the base camp inquiry committee to the board of trustees of Oregon Episcopal School. The Oregonian Publishing Co. 136: 44, 821, Friday, July 25, 1986, sunrise edition.

Williamson, John E., and E. Whalley, eds. 1980. Fall on snow, and ice, exposure, darkness, New Hampshire, Mt. Washington. In *Accidents in*

*North American mountaineering.* New York: The American Alpine Club and Banff: The Alpine Club of Canada. 4-3-33, 36.

Williamson, John E., and J. Whitteker, eds. 1987. Preface. *Accidents in North American mountaineering.* New York: The American Alpine Club and Banff: The Alpine Club of Canada.

_____. 1988. Statistical tables: *Accidents in North American mountaineering.* New York: The American Alpine Club and Banff: The Alpine Club of Canada.

Williamson, John F., and O. Miskiw, eds. 1992. Statistical tables: *Accidents in North American mountaineering.* New York: The American Alpine Club and Banff: The Alpine Club of Canada.

# Endnotes

1. *The Ascent of the Matterhorn* (Whymper, 1880) describes the race between two parties attempting to reach the summit of the Matterhorn on the same day. When Whymper and his party reached the summit, they saw the competing party far below on a different route and rolled rocks from the summit to catch their attention. The accident during the descent is described in the book.

2. See especially Meyer, 1979; Hale, 1984; Dill, 1987; Wade, 1991; and Williamson and Whitteker, 1988.

3. Meyer, 1979.

4. Williamson and Whitteker, 1987.

5. Results and conclusions are taken from a study of injuries and illnesses occurring in the National Outdoor Leadership school over a five-year period, September 1984 through September 1989. See Gentile et al., 1992.

6. Dill, 1987, and Hunt, 1988.

7. U.S. data are from statistical tables in Williamson and Miskiw, 1992.

8. *Ibid.*

9. Chouinard, 1978, page 153.

10. Hale, 1984.

11. Smutek, 1972; Williamson, ed., 1983, pg. 67.

12. Williamson, ed., 1983, pg. 58. Outward Bound, with over 19,000 participants and 1,000 instructors, has been able to reduce its accidental death rate seven fold in the last decade to achieve safety results comparable to the risk of everyday life. See Wade, 1991.

13. Williamson, John E., and E. Whalley, 1980, pg. 36.

14. Williams, 1975, pg. 102. As an example of an accident that might be related to goal orientation, see the case study on Mt. Cleveland.

15. Williams, 1975, pg. 56.

16. Snyder, 1985.

# First-Aid Programs

## Wilderness First Aid

Wilderness travelers can gain skills and the critical personal confidence required to administer first aid by completing a Wilderness First Responder (WFR) or Wilderness Emergency Medical Technician (WEMT) course. There is a growing list of nationally recognized schools now offering basic and advanced wilderness first aid for backcountry travelers. These courses teach basic life-support techniques, how to stabilize a spine, and how to recognize and treat head injuries, shock, and hypothermia. Most important, they teach you to think about potential changes in a victim's condition over the few hours after an accident and what you can do to stabilize the victim's condition.

## First-Aid Schools

Stonehearth Open Learning (SOLO), RFD 1, Box 163, Conway, New Hampshire 03818.

Wilderness Medical Associates (WMA), RFD 2, Box 890, Bryant Pond, Maine 04219.

The Wilderness Medicine Institute, Inc. (WMI), P.O. Box 9, Pitkin, Colorado 81241.

# Fitness

## Physical Fitness and Climbing

Being physically fit enables you to climb at your best and to avoid soreness, fatigue, and injury. These pages do not outline a complete fitness program, which could fill a whole book, or offer personalized advice such as you can get from a sports trainer, but rather aim to get you started in the proper direction.

To achieve fitness you can train for cardiovascular (aerobic) endurance; muscular endurance, flexibility, strength, and power; balance, agility, and coordination; and body composition. You can also pay attention to proper nutrition in order to reach peak performance. Before undertaking more than a generalized training program, have fun climbing and develop good technique and concentration while gaining experience. When you do start a generalized training program, do so to improve your entire body rather than concentrating on only a few specific muscle groups.

If you have any doubts about whether to start a fitness program, given your age and health, consult your physician. To help you get started and to understand the principles underlying many forms of fitness, refer to Hoeger's *Lifetime Physical Fitness and Wellness*, and Hoeger and Hoeger's *Fitness and Wellness*. (All publications mentioned in this appendix are listed under "References for Future Reading.")

Once you are motivated and are well into a fitness program, do not overdo your training, because this can result in injury. Once injured, you must avoid training until you heal, and you will be susceptible to further injury.

### Aerobic Endurance

Endurance is important on each pitch and allows you to function well pitch after pitch. Aerobic, meaning *with oxygen*, fitness is necessary for the muscular endurance required during longer climbs. Aerobic endurance will help avoid soreness that comes from prematurely calling upon your less efficient *anaerobic* energy system. The objective of aerobic training is to strengthen your heart, lungs, blood vessels, etc., so that your body can collect, transport, and use oxygen efficiently at the cell level, where it helps produce energy. Aerobic training involves groups of large muscles, mainly your legs or upper body and legs combined, in a sustained effort. The aerobic system is the body's most efficient system for delivering energy to muscle cells and provides the main source of energy involved in any sustained effort.

Mountain biking on rough trails, for example, gives good general aerobic training and uses the upper body as well as the lower body. This form of exercise is easy on the knee joints, while it strengthens the muscles of the legs, back, and arms. Other aerobic activities include taking long walks, hiking, running, road bicycling, and cross-country skiing. Enjoying the training activity is important, since good results require that you train systematically for eight to twelve weeks at about 75 to 80 percent of maximum effort before the climbing season starts.

### Stretching

The object of stretching is to extend the operating range of a muscle group so that you can use and strengthen the muscles throughout their entire range of motion. Before stretching, warm up by engaging in an aerobic activity for five minutes to increase the temperature of your muscles. This activity will also increase the blood supply to these muscles and remove waste products produced in exercise more efficiently. If you are stretching as part of an aerobic workout, stretch lightly before exercising and spend more time stretching during a cool-down phase of your exercise. Stretching should occur statically—hold a muscle in a slightly extended position, where there is some muscular discomfort but no pain. Stretching by bouncing can tear muscles, ligaments, and tendons.

The standard work on stretching is *Stretching*, by Bob Anderson, which includes a pretraining routine for weight training and running.

### Muscular Endurance Training

Generalized training should work on the muscles of your upper, middle, and lower body. The easiest and most enjoyable generalized training to prepare for climbing is to boulder on large holds two or more times a week in hour-long sessions. Vary the aerobic-workout intensity by the size of footholds that you use, and the workout duration by the length of time spent without touching down. You are unlikely to injure your tendons if you stay away from repeated laps on small holds. Injury often results because muscles of your shoulders, arms, and forearms strengthen more quickly than tendons connecting these joints. You will quickly be strong enough to pull harder with these muscles than the connecting ligaments and tendons can sustain[1], so they will tear instead. A slow buildup in an eight- to twelve-week training program will allow your tendons and ligaments to get stronger slowly, keep up with increases in muscular strength, and thus help prevent injury.

When you get into the gym, incorporate into your program exercises where you push or pull against a solid object. Push-ups, sit-ups, curls, squats, dips, pull-ups, and chin-ups fall into this group. Lifting light weights 15 to 20 or more times is another type of muscular endurance training. Muscular endurance depends upon both muscular strength and aerobic conditioning. Muscular strength programs, discussed later, depend on prior muscular endurance programs to succeed. *Weight Training for Life* by James Hesson, *Climbing Fit* by Martyn Hurn and Pat Ingle, and *The Outdoor Athlete* by Steve Ilg are good guides for muscular endurance and strength training; *Climbing Fit* was written specifically for climbers. A video on training for rock climbing is also available from the Vertical Club.[2]

### Muscular Strength

At some point when you climb a steep wall, your aerobic energy production system may begin to overload and your anaerobic energy system kicks in. Operating without oxygen, you can put out sustained energy for only a few minutes. The anaerobic system also produces lactic acid as a by-product, which remains after exercise and promotes soreness. When you train to improve muscular endurance, you are trying to elevate the critical effort level at which your anaerobic system comes into play, and improve the ability of your body to remove lactic acid once it has been created.

Muscular strength is gained by anaerobic training, which relies on the overload. If you overload specific muscle cells beyond their normal use, they will increase in size, strength, and/or endurance. Women who weight-train show increases in muscular strength, but do not experience large increases in muscular size.[3] To increase strength systematically, progressively, and without injury, increase the demands placed upon your muscles over a planned period of time involving a training program. Your body needs rest periods of 48 hours or longer between workouts, so that its aerobic systems can repair damaged tissue and build new cells. Insufficient rest between workouts prevents improvement and may lead to injury. Normally you should work out a set of muscles only every second or third day, depending on your personal rate of recovery.

To stimulate strength development in weight training, you should use a weight that you can lift 6 to 12 times before momentary failure. This might be between 70 and 80 percent of your body weight, with the higher resistance levels more likely to lead to injury. Refer to listed references for specific training exercises, techniques, and lifting patterns.

### Training Programs

Programs of training involve both aerobic and anaerobic training and accompanying stretching exercises. A training program might be the equivalent of running three miles, three times a week,[4] and spending two days a week strength training. Advanced climbers may benefit from strength training on three days each week. Each session might begin with stretching to warm up, then training, followed by cool-down stretching. Be sure that you allow 48 hours of rest or longer between strength-training sessions. When you plan to climb, be sure to rest or only train lightly the day before.

Year-long muscular training programs begin during the winter when you spend most of the time building endurance and strength in the gym.[5] As rock season comes around, you gradually spend more time climbing, with weekly trips to the gym to maintain your strength. When you begin to spend all your time on the rock and reduce strength training, you will find that your performance level picks up and peaks. After you peak, you probably will be mentally and physically stale for a while, so train and climb less intensely until you are ready to begin the cycle again.

### Injuries

The most common climbing injuries are to tendons and ligaments of the elbow, shoulder, or fingers. Treatment begins with rest; do not climb. You can help reduce swelling and promote healing in a sore joint by applying ice frequently throughout the day. Move the ice around and take care not to cause cold-induced nerve damage. When the pain from the injury goes away, your joint may not be inflamed or swollen, but it has not healed. You need to wait a few more weeks before beginning to train at a level appropriate to the injury and stage of healing.

A complete program of recovery that avoids reinjury may require eight weeks or longer to work back to a high level of fitness. Adopt a slow, systematic increase in activity while avoiding the movement or error that caused the original injury. Start with a full range of motion stretching followed by high-repetition, low-weight isolation exercises, such as using dumbbells, after you experience no pain during stretching. Continue to ice after each session.

Dr. Mark Robinson, a physician and a climber, recommends that you add "eccentric" exercises once you regain 80 percent of your lost strength. For example, he recommends that you lower from a bar, stretching your muscles slowly and controlling your descent. Take care, as these exercises are stressful, and limit them to once every three to five days. Your first climbs should be on low-angle, big-hold slabs. As you continue to recover, emphasize improving balance, flexibility, and smooth static moves on steeper climbs with large holds. Rehabilitation is not training, and you can easily reinjure yourself by following routines suitable to an uninjured climber or by attempting dynamic moves to small holds. Seek help in dealing with the complex steps of recovery by consulting a physician or trainer who specializes in sports injuries.

---

## References for Future Reading

Anderson, Bob. 1980. *Stretching*. Bolinas, California: Shelter Publications.

Cooper, Kenneth H. 1968. *Aerobics*. New York: Bantam Books.

_____. 1982. *The aerobics program for total well-being: Exercise, diet, emotional balance*. New York: Bantam Books.

Hesson, James L. 1991. *Weight training for life*. Englewood, Colorado: Morton Publishing Co.

Hoeger, Werner W. K. 1989. *Lifetime physical fitness & wellness: A personalized program*. Second edition. Englewood, Colorado: Morton Publishing Co.

Hoeger, Werner W. K., and Sharon A. Hoeger. 1990. *Fitness and wellness*. Englewood, Colorado: Morton Publishing Co.

Horst, J. Eric. 1989. Happiness is a pair of big guns. *Climbing*. 116:118.

Hurn, Martyn, and Pat Ingle. 1988. *Climbing fit*. Seattle: Cloudcap.

Ilg, Steve. 1985. Weight training for rock climbers. *Climbing*. 91:58–62.

Robinson, Mark. 1988a. Fingers: Get a grip on injury prevention and treatment. *Climbing*. 109:108–113.

_____. 1988b. The shoulder: A powerful joint with a delicate construction. *Climbing*. 111:111–116.

_____. 1989. The elbow: Understanding a common "sore" subject. *Climbing*. 113:130–137.

_____. 1992. Climbing injuries to fingers and forearm. *Climbing*. 138:141–150.

Smith, Nathan J., and Bonnie Worthington-Roberts. 1989. *Food for sport*. Palo Alto, California: Bull Publishing Co.

## Endnotes

1. See Robinson, 1988a and b and 1989.

2. This video is hosted by Christen Griffen and includes stretching, bouldering, proper use of hang boards, and weight exercises to prevent shoulder injuries. Available from the Vertical Club, Inc., Seattle, Washington; (206) 283-8056.

3. Hesson, 1991, indicates that this may be related to low levels of the hormone testosterone and high levels of the hormone estrogen.

4. See Horst, 1989, for a general rundown on training.

5. See Robinson, 1988a and b and 1989.

APPENDIX

# C

# *Lightning*

## Introduction

Lightning is the leading direct meteorological cause of casualties in the United States. Snowstorms cause more indirect deaths and tornadoes cause more property damage, but lightning kills about 100 and injures about 300 Americans each year. For this reason, lightning is of concern to all who use the outdoors for recreation.

Rock climbers and mountaineers, of course, play a part in the statistics. Thirty-seven mountaineering accidents involving lightning were reported in the United States from 1951 to 1991.[1] Lightning encounters by mountaineers in Canada appear to occur at a lower rate, with only six incidents reported between 1959 and 1991.

Lightning occurs when warm moisture-laden air is lifted into the atmosphere and water vapor condenses to form thunderstorms. Towering *cumulonimbus thunderclouds* contain the up and down air currents associated with heavy rain, hail, wind gusts, and lightning. Orographic or mountain lifting (Figure C-1) is of particular interest to climbers and hill hikers alike. In summer, by afternoon, the solar heating of moist air during the morning coupled with air rising over a mountain range produces thunderstorms and lightning. After an hour or two, its energy dissipated, the storm blows over and the sky clears.

The weather in many major alpine areas follows this pattern in summer, affecting rock-climbing areas located in the mountains or at their base. Climbers who do not wish to get caught climbing in the midst of a storm ascend their route and descend by early afternoon, before the storm begins.

Other kinds of thunderstorms are those associated with cold fronts, air-mass heating, and severe thunderstorms (that can spawn tornadoes). Frontal thunderstorms originate as a cold air mass burrows under a warm air mass along a boundary that may extend over many states. These storms can occur at any time of the day or night throughout the year and often last for half a day or longer. Air-mass thunderstorms occur in the afternoon of a hot summer day, when warm moist air is heated and lifted within an air mass that may cover an area that is the size of many states. This air-mass lifting may assist mountain lifting, but it may also produce thunderstorms over flat areas. Severe thunderstorms are associated with fairly unique conditions of colliding air masses, shear between air layers and spin, and strong air flow aloft. These storms are of interest to climbers because they may lead to serious weather changes in specific locations at specific times, but climbers must cope with the thunderstorms produced by mountain lifting on a daily basis. Lightning usually occurs during the mature stage of the thunderstorm. As a cumulonimbus cloud develops, charge separations occur in it very quickly (Figure C-2), making the middle of the cloud negative and the top positive.

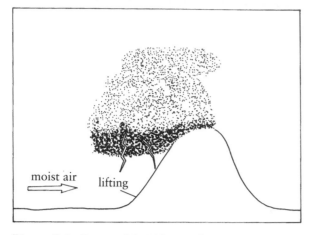

*Figure C-1. **Orographic Lifting of Warm Moist Air:** Mountain lifting often produces summer afternoon thunderstorms with hail, a torrential downpour, and lightning.*

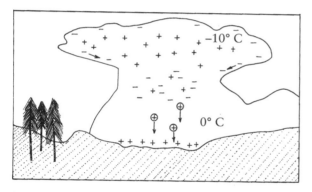

*Figure C-2. **Thunderstorm Charge Distribution:** Charge separation occurs in the middle of the cloud, the upper part becoming positively charged (+) and the lower part negatively charged (--) The ground takes on a positive charge and the air acts as an insulator to the flow of electricity. After Uman and Krider, 1989.*

Lightning, a transient high-current discharge with a path length kilometers long, can occur within clouds, from cloud to cloud, from cloud to air, and from cloud to ground. Discharges connecting clouds and the earth are of primary interest because of the possibility of injury and death associated with them. There are four identified types of lightning connecting cloud to earth, categorized by whether the initial discharge (leader) moves downward or upward and whether the initial leader is positive or negative. The most common discharge initiates in a cloud and connects the negative charges in the middle of the cloud to positive charges induced at ground level, like a shadow, by the negative charges in the lower part of the cloud. A small percentage of the cloud-to-ground leaders are positive. Upward-initiated leaders usually occur from mountain peaks and tall structures, with the most common having a positive leader.[2]

### Charge Separation and Updrafts

The origin of the charge separation that leads to lightning is not fully understood. It must relate to the rapid vertical movements, updrafts, and formation of frozen precipitation within the building cumulonimbus cloud. The processes of freezing and melting produce charged particles. Collisions between falling pea-size white ice pellets (called *graupel*), ice crystals, and supercooled water drops appear to be important in producing the distribution of charges.[3] In laboratory experiments, when the temperature is below a critical value called the charge-reversal temperature, $T_R$, the falling graupel particles acquire a negative charge in collisions with the ice crystals. At temperatures above $T_R$, they acquire a positive charge. $T_R$ is thought to be about 5 degrees Fahrenheit (–15 degrees Celsius). This reading coincides with the temperature of the region in thunderclouds where the main negative charge is found. When graupel falls below this altitude, to a region of higher temperature, it picks up a positive charge. There is evidence that these positively charged graupel particles form a small lower positive region of the thundercloud that lies beneath the main negative region.

### The Lightning Stroke

The lightning flash, which is the total discharge from the cloud, is actually a sequence of strokes. Each stroke lasts about a millisecond, and the separation between strokes is typically several tens of milliseconds. The sequence of cloud-to-ground flash is illustrated in Figure C-3. The primary breakdown in the cloud may occur when a flow of electrons (negatively charged particles) from the middle of the cloud rushes toward the base. The

## Lightning on the Chouinard-Becky

On August 3 . . . two climbers left the Bugaboo Hut and climbed in good weather to the base of Great White Headwall on the Chouinard-Becky route on the west face of the South Howser Tower (3,300 meters). The following day the pair reached the start of the lower-angle summit ridge immediately following the tension traverse pitch. The weather had deteriorated over the preceding half hour with scattered squalls moving through the area, but none affecting the Howsers. Continuing over the summit and down the standard route seemed preferable to rappelling the ascent route. They were not far below the summit when a nearby small pinnacle on the ridge began to hum. The climbers got rid of their hardware and sat on their packs and ropes in a notch beneath the pinnacle. Then the humming stopped, and they did not feel the prickling skin or hair sensation that would indicate a gathering charge. But within one or two minutes, there was a sharp crack, and both climbers were hit by ground current.

Afterward, one climber had lost feeling in both legs, and his right leg was paralyzed. Later, entrance and exit wounds were found on his right hip and on both sides of his ankle. The other climber had generalized numbness and muscle weakness. His right forearm was painful, and he could see holes burned through several layers of clothing. Entrance and exit wounds were later found on both sides of his forearm and on his right ankle. In addition to the small full-thickness burns at the entrance and exit wounds, there were patches of superficial burns where his polypropylene underwear had ignited.

The climbers gradually regained motor control over the next half hour, and they rappelled their ascent route. They then hiked back to the Kain Hut where their burns were cleaned and dressed. (From Williamson and Whitteker, 1988; original source: J. Bird and C. Atkinson, Bugaboo Glacier National Park.)

Analysis: The climbers did all the classic, right things. They were not on the summit or under overhangs. They insulated themselves by sitting on their packs.

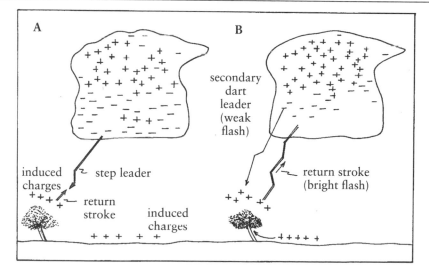

*Figure C-3.* **Steps in the Lightning Stroke:** *A—A step leader (discharge) initiates the stroke from the base of the cloud, ionizing the air. When the step leader has almost reached the ground, a return leader leaps up to meet it. B—The return stroke lights up the sky and neutralizes the lower part of the cloud. Higher in the cloud a secondary dart leader begins its path toward earth, taking electrons with it, repeating the earlier sequence.*

initial stroke is the first of a series of stepped leaders. *Stepped leaders* are tens of meters long and last about a millionth of a second; there is a pause of 20 to 50 millionths of a second between steps. The average downward speed of propagation is about 200,000 meters/second; our eyes cannot distinguish the individual steps at this speed.

As the tip of the leader nears the ground, the electrical field increases until it exceeds the resistance of air at sharp objects or at irregularities on the ground. The earth and cloud join by an ionized path. Up this path rushes a return stroke that imparts energy to the atoms and molecules of the air, which in turn give off light to the branches of the descending step leader. The *return stroke* somewhat neutralizes the cloud, since the initial stroke only discharges the lowest portions of the cloud. The drama of discharge continues as a secondary return occurs through the ionized channel, prepared by the initial strike, to discharge higher and higher regions of the negatively charged portion of the cloud. This secondary return is the dart leader, of which there are usually three or four. The elapsed time from step leader to final dart leader occurs in about a second—too fast for our eyes to see individual steps, although high-speed photography has captured them on film.

### Upward Lightning

Lightning is sometimes initiated by upward-moving leaders that arise from TV towers and from tall mountain peaks. Upward-moving leaders can be distinguished from downward-moving strokes because the flash branches upward (Figure C-4). These leaders are usually positive and produce a more or less continuous flow of current at the ground. In about half of the upward-initiated events, however, the continuous current is followed by a sequence of dart leaders and return strokes that are similar to those following the first strokes in natural cloud-to-ground discharges.[4]

### Thunder

Thunder is a direct effect of lightning. Lightning heats the air in a narrow channel to around 54,000 degrees Fahrenheit (30,000 degrees Celsius) as it

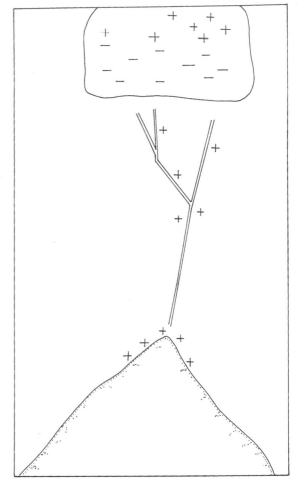

*Figure C-4. **Upward Lightning:** Lightning may sometimes be initiated by upward-moving discharge leaders. These discharge leaders are usually positive and can produce a continuous flow of current, or a sequence of dart leaders and return strokes. This phenomenon is well documented in association with TV towers and appears to occur on tall mountains. Modified from a figure by Uman and Krider, 1989.*

propagates earthward. This heating causes explosive expansion of the air, producing the sound that we call thunder. Thunder rumbles because different parts of the lightning stroke are different distances away from the observer.

We can use the different rates of travel for light and sound for the practical purpose of calculating how far away we are from a lightning storm. Light travels so fast that a flash from a lightning stroke

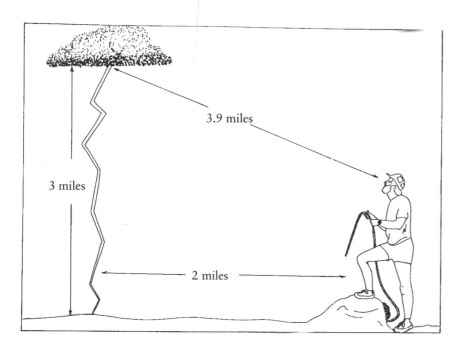

Figure C-5. *Thunder, or Maybe We Shouldn't Do This Climb:* Because sound waves from the lower part of the lightning stroke reach the observer before those from the upper part of the stroke, the thunder appears to rumble.

3.9 miles

3 miles

2 miles

appears to an observer almost as it happens. However, sound travels at a much slower rate—about 4.8 seconds per mile, or approximately one-fifth mile per second. In Figure C-5, the sound of the bottom portion of the stroke reaches the observer in about 10 seconds, whereas sound from the top part of the stroke takes about 19 seconds to arrive. The rumbling "sound on sound" effect results from the sound traveling different distances. The lag time between lightning and thunder is approximately 5 seconds for each mile that the storm is distant from the observer's position. A lag of 10 seconds between lightning and thunder thus indicates that a storm is 2 miles away. This 10-second lag is a strong warning to seek safety.

## Lightning Dangers

During a lightning storm, climbers are in direct danger from the storm's electricity in three ways: (1) a direct lightning strike, (2) induced currents in the vicinity of a strike, and (3) ground currents.

### The Direct Strike

If you cannot descend from a mountain or leave the area before a storm, you should avoid locations that might be hit by a direct strike. Seek a place where nearby projections, such as a pinnacle, are above your own head. Such projections provide a 45-degree cone of protection (Figure C-6). On an exposed ridge with trees, the safest shelter is amid the shorter trees in the middle of the ridge. Avoid trees at the edges or shoulders of the ridge. On a bare mountain top it might be possible to use the peak itself as a lightning rod to take the direct strike, but it is always preferable to get lower, out of the strike zone, before the storm begins.

### Induced Currents

In a cloud-to-ground lightning strike, a climber may be the projection that takes on the induced positive charge (Figure C-7). (A climber can also be the chief discharge point for a lightning flash in ground-to-cloud lightning.) In either case, the air

*Figure C-6. **The 45-Degree Cone of Protection from Lightning Strike:** The climber sits halfway between the top of the rock pinnacle and the edge of the cone. The projection should be 5 to 10 times the climber's height.*

around the climber will become ionized and lose its insulating ability. It can give off a crackling noise, known in the Alps as the "buzzing of bees," and the distinctive odor of ozone may be present. If the climber's hair stands on end and crackles, and ice axes, carabiners, and other metal tools discharge, giving off a bluish glow or corona called St. Elmo's Fire, lightning is about to strike.

The literature on mountaineering suggests that climbers usually toss aside ice axes, carabiners, and other gear when they hear and see these phenomena in an attempt to avoid the lightning stroke,[5] returning to pick up their gear when the storm is over. While it is realistic to be afraid of a lightning storm, climbers should also fear doing dangerous things to get out of the path of a storm. You can get hurt as seriously by falling when your rappel anchor fails or while running down a mountain as when you get hit by lightning.

### Ground Currents and Body Position

Your major concerns in a lightning storm are to avoid a direct strike and prevent the passage of ground current through your body. Two factors determine the extent of human injury caused by

*Figure C-7. **Induced Charges on a Climber:** The climber is in immediate danger of experiencing a lightning strike. The climber may hear the "buzzing of bees" and smell ozone. The climber should immediately get below the summit and seek a cone of protection, leaving the axe where it can be found after the storm has passed.*

ground currents: the quantity of current and the part of the body affected. A current passing from one hand to the other, through the heart or lungs, or from head to foot through the brain and other organs, is most dangerous, since vital functions can be impaired. As the boxed excerpt on page 285 indicates, you can also suffer burns at entry and exit points, as well as medical shock.

To avoid the worst effects of ground currents, assume one of the body positions illustrated in Figure C-8. You may crouch low in a balanced position on a doubled insulated pad. Both feet should be together and touch the pad so that lightning cannot enter one foot, travel through the

Figure C-8. **Body Positions to Minimize Damage from Lightning Storm:** *All positions keep the climber low to avoid direct strikes. The feet are held together to make one entry point for ground currents, and to prevent the body from providing a conducting path.*

**A**
incorrect

**B**
incorrect

**C**
incorrect

**D**
correct

Figure C-9. **Placement on a Rock Ridge in a Lightning Storm (A, B, and C are dangerous):** *A—Leaning against wet rock (currents go in one arm and through the body); B—Sitting under a shallow overhang or cave (currents jump the gap and go through the body); C—Sitting in a* depression *(currents pass through wet soil or water and through the body).* **Better Placement:** *D—Sitting on a rock—with added insulation—above the surface of a shelf and well below the direct strike zone (ground currents may pass beneath the climber).*

body and exit via the second foot. Because the crouching position is difficult to hold for very long, you may need to sit if the storm continues. In the sitting position, the feet are together, and feet and buttocks touch the pad. Hold arms out to the side or wrap them around the knees for stability. (It is difficult to hold the arms out to the side for any period of time, but theoretically ground currents are less likely to pass through the heart and lungs in this position.) Both sitting positions are intended to keep you low to avoid a direct strike, and require less balance and muscular control than to maintain a crouching position.

### Ground Currents and Positions on a Peak

When an electrical discharge strikes a point, electricity flows outward. On rock, the major path of flow is along the wet surface, because water is a better conductor than rock. Electricity travels down wet cracks, through depressions with saturated soils, or along water-rich vegetation. Electrical currents can jump short gaps, such as from the roof to the floor of a shallow cave, so you should not seek shelter from storms in the shallow caves and overhangs normally found on peaks. Figure C-9A, B, and C illustrate three dangerous choices: leaning against a wall (ground currents may pass through heart and lungs), sitting underneath a shallow overhang (the climber provides a path for ground currents from roof to the floor), and sitting in a depression (the climbers provide a shortened path for ground currents and a pool of conducting water may accumulate). Figure C-9D shows the only position that is potentially safe: the climber sits on an insulating pad (a pack would also serve) on a shelf, above the path of ground currents, which should pass safely underneath.

## First Aid

Any climbers who are struck directly by lightning or have ground current pass through their body will need first aid and subsequent examination by a physician. Common effects of severe electrical disturbances to the body are burns, stoppage of respiratory and cardiac functions, severe muscular contractions, and even functional failure of the brain. In addition, the victim may experience serious secondary injuries from a fall.

The fact that lightning is a high-voltage event of very short duration leads to characteristic patterns of injury. Second-degree burns from lightning usually cover skin surfaces and do not normally lead to entrance or exit wounds, which do occur from contact with alternating-current power lines. The short encounter also protects victims from the excessive internal burning associated with alternating currents.

It is important for rescuers to realize that victims of lightning do not retain any electrical charge. You can safely touch victims to give first aid immediately after they are struck.

Look first for signs that lightning has interfered with heart and lung function. If respiratory and cardiac arrest occur together, you can revive the victim by prompt action. In some victims who experience both heart and lung arrest, the heart may spontaneously start up, leaving them only in respiratory arrest. In other victims, only respiratory arrest occurs initially, but cardiac arrest follows if they are not promptly revived. Individuals who are only in respiratory arrest can be saved with prompt ventilation at a rate that makes their chest rise and fall normally after establishing an open airway.

Climbers and others who spend time adventuring outdoors need to know rescue breathing and heart massage as taught in American Red Cross or American Heart Association cardiopulmonary resuscitation (CPR) courses. Since lightning can strike a CPR-trained member of a climbing team, all climbers should learn CPR to safeguard each other.

Other injuries and symptoms that can occur in lightning encounters include strong muscular contractions, related to the electrical impulse of lightning, that can lead to fractured bones and muscular injuries. Approximately half the victims of direct lightning strikes also have at least one eardrum ruptured. Amnesia, postconcussion swelling of the brain, and even paralysis may occur. Victims of direct strikes can literally have their clothes blown off as the lighting current explosively vaporizes skin moisture. Because of possible hidden complications that may not present for hours after injury, all victims of lightning encounters should undergo observation by a physician in a hospital after first aid has been administered.

## References for Future Reading

Peters, Ed, ed. 1982. *Mountaineering: The freedom of the hills*. Fourth edition. Seattle: The Mountaineers.

Uman, Martin A., and E. Philip Krider. 1989. Natural and artificially initiated lightning. *Science*. 246: 457–464.

Williams, Earle R. 1988. The electrification of thunderstorms. *Scientific American*. November: 88–99.

Williamson, J. and J. Whitteker, eds. 1988. *Accidents in North American mountaineering*. New York: The American Alpine Club and Banff: The Alpine Club of Canada.

Williamson, John E., and O. Miskiw, eds. 1992. *Accidents in North American mountaineering*. New York: The American Alpine Club and Banff: The Alpine Club of Canada.

## Endnotes

1. Williamson and Miskiw, 1992.

2. Uman and Krider, 1989.

3. Williams, 1988.

4. Uman and Krider, 1989.

5. This is my observation as well.

# APPENDIX

# D

## *Pulley System Basics*

## Introduction

Pulleys connected by rope form a system, often called a *tackle*, that provides leverage for lifting or lowering heavy objects. There are a number of reasons why climbers might want to know about pulley systems. A pulley system is commonly used to rescue climbers from a crevasse and for the construction of hauling systems for big-wall rescues.[1] Knowing how to set up pulley systems will allow you to lift heavy panels single-handedly if you build a climbing wall—or to pull your car out of the mud at the base of the climbing site.

Pulley systems create *mechanical advantage* by using a tensioned rope that changes direction at the pulleys, making it possible to lift people or gear. The stresses pulleys produce can break ropes and anchors because tensioned ropes are suscepti-

ble to cutting or breaking. Hence, belays and backup systems are important when using pulleys for rescues. And be sure that you do not climb again on a rope after you destroy its shock-absorbing character by using it in a pulley system.

Mechanical advantage is defined as the ratio of the weight to be lifted divided by the applied force, or:

$$\text{Mechanical advantage} = \frac{\text{Weight to be lifted}}{\text{Applied force}}$$

The mechanical advantage is normally written as a ratio—3:1, 2:1, 1:1. No units are involved. In the ideal mechanical-advantage systems examined in this appendix, friction does not exist, though of course it does in real systems, where the friction of pulleys reduces work efficiency to 70 to 93 percent of the theoretical value. If you use carabiners in place of pulleys, efficiency drops to less than two-thirds of the theoretical value.[2] For example, a 3:1 mechanical advantage is reduced to less than a 2:1 advantage when carabiners take the place of pulleys in the system.

## Single-Pulley Systems

### *1:1 Systems*

In a one-to-one system a single rope supports the load. When you directly lift a weight, as the climber does in Figure D-1A by using her arm and shoulder muscles, the lifting force equals the load, and the lifting force is in the direction of the applied force. The same 1:1 advantage occurs when you lift a weight by means of a pulley and a rope (Figure D-1B). The rope on the right side of the pulley does not give any additional lifting force, but it does offer the advantage of a change of direction of the applied force.

The climber using the pulley system finds lifting the weight easier than the first climber because pulling down on the rope after it changes direction at the pulley allows her to

applied and lifting force

lifting force

applied force

Figure D-2. **2:1 Systems**

A             B

employ her muscles more efficiently; she uses her legs, both arms, and her shoulder, chest, back, and stomach muscles to lift the weight. When the climber using the pulley system suspends the load in the air without moving, the load is in a state of *equilibrium*: a balanced state between the force of gravity trying to pull the load downward and the force of the climber trying to lift the weight. To upset equilibrium and lift the weight, the climber has only to supply a small additional force.

### 2:1 Systems

If two people lift the same weight, a new situation occurs (Figure D-2A). To share equally in lifting the weight, they each must lift one-half the total. They do this by compensating for differences in height and strength by conscious *coordination*. If we substitute a rope for the climbers' arms (Figure D-2B), there are still two "arms" supporting the weight. The climber in Figure D-2B can now lift the weight from its position of equilibrium by lifting one of the rope "arms." The rope automatically coordinates sharing the weight between the two supporting rope arms. In general, if two "arms" support a weight (in this case, the two arms of rope in the pulley system), they create a 2:1 advantage. If the climber runs the rope she holds through a second pulley at the ceiling, she can change the direction of the applied force again, so that she can use her leg, shoulder, arm, and back muscles to help lift the weight, as in Figure D-1B.

### 4:1 Systems

Now imagine that four people get together to lift the weight, as shown in Figure D-3A. We could call this a 4:1 people-advantage system. Of course, four people have to coordinate their efforts to raise the weight. The coordination problem is simplified by using a rope and pulleys as illustrated in Figure D-3B. In this 4:1 mechanical-advantage system, the rope provides continuity. When the weight and system are at rest, one person supports just one-fourth of the total weight, while three-quarters of the weight is supported by the other "arms" of the system. When she pulls with slightly

more force, she unbalances the system and starts the weight moving upward.

## Pulley System Notation

Pulley systems employ two different types of pulleys, those that are fixed in position and those that are free to move. A *fixed pulley,* such as that of Figure D-1B, attached to a structural support simply provides a change of direction. A *floating pulley* (Figure D-2B) moves as the load moves while providing a change of direction. Pulley systems that give higher ratios of mechanical advantage use both types of pulleys, as illustrated by the 4:1 systems of Figure D-3B. Here, one fixed pulley and two floating pulleys alter rope direction to provide four rope "arms" to support the weight; these floating pulleys replace the two sticks in Figure D-3A.

As more pulleys, changes of direction, and "arms" are added to pulley systems, it is useful to employ a system of notation to describe the system and to calculate mechanical advantage provided by

Figure D-3. **4:1 Systems**

the system. We use a system that denotes properties of pull, or *tensional force* (T). A subscript to the right the T (for example, $T_a$) indicates the *location* of a specific tensional force; a number to the left of the T (for example, 2T) gives the *size* or *magnitude* of the tensional force. Hence, $2T_b$ is a tensional force of size 2 at the location b.

In Figure D-3B, the rope producing forces of $1T_a$, $1T_b$, $1T_c$, and $1T_d$ replaces the pulls or tension provided by the four arms of the young people.

## Pulley Systems with Prusiks

A prusik knot can be used to enhance the mechanical advantage of a pulley system. Systems with prusiks have mechanical advantages with ratios of 3:1, 6:1, or 9:1, and so on. The prusik knot is purposely made of a smaller and weaker rope so that if you overload the system, the prusik—not the main rope—will break. Because

Figure D-4A. **3:1 System Using a Prusik Knot to Increase Efficiency**

Figure D-4B. **Function of the Floating Pulley in the System**

there is a backup, the lifted load will not drop if the prusik breaks.

This section explains the theory of how pulley systems with prusiks work. In the field, of course, there are many practical considerations when you use these systems for safeguarding yourself or for rescues. Because rescue can be (and is) the topic of entire books, coverage here has been limited to the theoretical aspects.

### 3:1 Systems

The climber in Figure D-4A provides the initial pulling or tensional force that passes to the rope at $T_a$. The tensional forces on the rope labeled $T_a$, $T_b$, etc., act much like the human arms in the previous examples in supporting and lifting the weight. The initial pull force at location a is assigned a value of 1, giving $1T_a$. $1T_a$ passes around the floating pulley unaltered in magnitude so that $T_b$ has the same value as $T_a$, namely 1. These two pulling forces act through the floating pulley and its associated prusik sling to exert a force of $1T_a + 1T_b = 2T_c$ on the weight in the direction indicated by the arrows. If we isolate subparts of the system (by not showing part of the rope), the result would be as shown in Figure D-4B: $1T_a$ and $1T_b$ each share equally in holding the total load.

The rope passes from location b around a fixed pulley on the tree (Figure D-4A) to change the rope's direction. Now consider positions b and d in Figure D-4C. Here there is another pull on the load, $1T_d$, that owes its existence to force $1T_b$, in that $1T_b$ transfers around the fixed pulley on the tree to create $T_d$. This means that the total lifting force on the weight is the combination of $[(1T_a + 1T_b) = 2T_c] + 1T_d = 3T_e$. Thus, the system is a 3:1 mechanical-advantage system, and the climber needs to apply a force slightly greater than one-third of the load's weight to start it moving upward.

In examining the system note that the direction of pull arrows may actually be in a different direction than the rope moves as it maintains coordination between various parts of the system. These opposed directions are illustrated at position b (Figure D-4A), where the tensional forces act to pull the floating pulley to the left, while the rope runs to the right as the climber pulls on it.

In any pulley system you need to pull an

Figure D-4C. **The Fixed Pulley's Contribution**

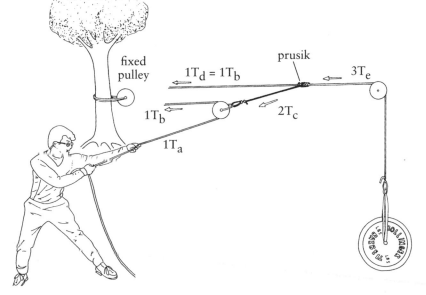

fixed pulley

prusik

$1T_d = 1T_b$

$3T_e$

$1T_b$

$2T_c$

$1T_a$

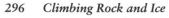

amount of rope through to raise a weight a given distance: the weight rises a distance that is inversely proportional to the mechanical advantage of the system. In a 3:1 system, the weight rises only 33 feet for every 100 feet of rope pulled through. The climber in Figure D-4 does not have to exert a lot of effort to lift the weight, but he has to pull in lots of rope.

When you pull a rope to raise a weight using a pulley system, prusik knots and floating pulleys move toward fixed pulleys until they touch, or until mechanical advantage is lost by removing changes of direction at the pulleys. As a result, you must periodically restore the system or reset it to its original state.

*Z-Drag Systems:* A Z-drag system is a 3:1 pulley system combined with prusik knots that maintain the load in a lifted position while you release tension on the system to reset it. A Z-drag system should also provide anchors for rescuers who work around a crevasse lip or are endangered while operating the system. When you use the Z-drag for crevasse rescue, friction is caused by the rope cutting into the lip of the crevasse. To prevent this you pad the edge, cut away any protruding lip, and possibly use ice axes laid horizontally to keep the rope from cutting into the edge. In addition, you need to safeguard pads, ice axes, and people working at the edge. Another way to avoid the problem of edge friction is to suspend a pulley in the air directly above the middle of the crevasse. Attach this pulley to anchors on the opposite side of the crevasse to the 3:1 pulley, as shown in Figure D-5. In order to gain the full mechanical advantage of this system, you must pull the rope parallel to the system's arms, and not at an angle, which would destroy mechanical advantage.

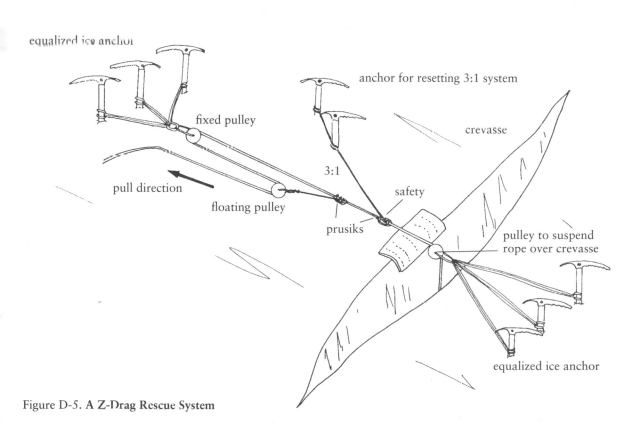

Figure D-5. **A Z-Drag Rescue System**

# Higher Ratios of Mechanical Advantage

Higher ratios of mechanical advantage make it easier to lift heavy loads with fewer people. These systems are rescue systems that tax the strength of prusiks and ropes and require safety backups for the system as well as for people working with it. They commonly use specially made rollers to reduce friction where the rope passes over an edge.

Higher systems are formed by combining either a simple system with one that uses prusiks, or two-prusik systems. For example, a 2:1 system pulling a 3:1 system gives rise to a 6:1 system of mechanical advantage, a 3:1 system pulling a 3:1 system gives rise to a 9:1 system of mechanical advantage, and so on. To help you learn to analyze these systems, their description is set up in the form of problems to solve. After working on both problems, turn the page to compare your analyses to those presented here.

## Problem One

Our climber has set up a higher ratio of mechanical advantage in Figure D-6A. He wants to determine what mechanical advantage exists for

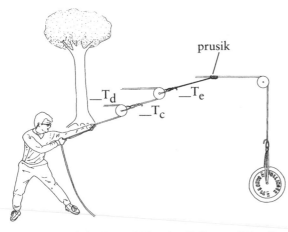

Figure D-6A. **A System of Higher Mechanical Advantage**

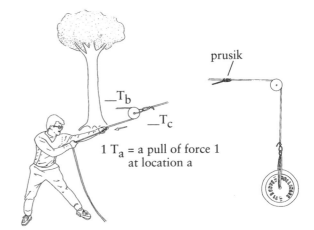

$1\,T_a$ = a pull of force 1 at location a

Figure D-6B. **The System Related to the First Floating Pulley**

Figure D-6C. **The Second Floating Pulley and Prusik**

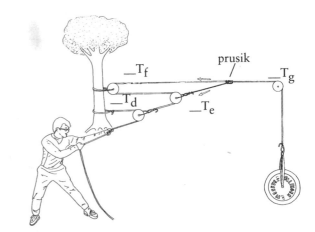

Figure D-6D. **The Fixed Pulley and Total Mechanical Advantage**

the total system: Is this a 6:1 system, a 12:1 system, or a system with some other ratio of mechanical advantage? We will analyze each subpart in turn to understand the total system.

First look at Figure D-6A; then, on Figure D-6B, fill in the pull forces encountered for each side of the pulley on the blank lines labeled __$T_x$. The initial pull force has a value of 1T at location a in the direction indicated by the arrow. Next, use the pull forces or T values, derived in Figure D-6B, to determine those in Figures D-6C and D-6D in turn. Use arrows to show pull directions for each rope segment. Finally, fill in the final value of mechanical advantage at $T_g$, located to the right of the prusik knot in Figure D-6D.

Therefore, to lift a weight of 60 pounds you need to exert a starting force of ____ pounds to offset equilibrium and to cause lifting to start. This system is an example of a ____ : ____ mechanical-advantage system.

### Problem Two

Draw the hook-up, showing rope travel, pulleys, prusiks, trees, and weights required to set up a 9:1 mechanical advantage system. Label the forces exerted on the subparts of the system.

This problem tests your understanding of the main points discussed thus far. If necessary, review the material presented above. When you do begin, try a number of combinations of fixed and floating pulleys and figure out the mechanical advantage on scrap paper. Put the result of this trial-and-error figuring below before turning the page.

### Answer to Problem One

(A) Figure D-7 shows the completely sketched setup of problem one of Figure D-6. This is basically a 2:1 system pulling a 3:1 system to give rise to a 6:1 system of mechanical advantage.

(B) Starting with a pull of force 1T at a, the pull is transferred by a change in direction at the first free-floating pulley to an equal pull of 1T at b. This means that there is a pull on the rope attached to the first free-floating pulley at c of 1T + 1T = 2T. Note that the arrows at the lettered positions show the direction in which the pull is exerted, not the direction in which the rope is moving. Indeed, the rope is moving in the direction of the pull at a, but in the opposite direction at d.

(C) The pull of strength 2T calculated above for c transfers around the second free-floating pulley by the continuous rope to the opposite side at d. This means that there is a pull of 2T + 2T = 4T at e on the second prusik sling.

(D) At the prusik sling at e is a pull of 4T. In addition, the pull of 2T at d changes direction at the fixed pulley on the tree and exerts a force of 2T

directly on the weight at f. When you add up these tensional forces, the weight is being pulled with 4T (e) + 2T (f) = 6T at g.

(E) This is a system of 6:1 mechanical advantage. If you use it, you can lift a weight of 60 pounds with a starting force of slightly more than 10 pounds, neglecting friction. With a fair amount of friction the mechanical advantage is lower, possibly about 4:1.

### Answer to Problem Two

This is a 9:1 mechanical-advantage system (Figure D-8) that is basically one 3:1 system pulling another 3:1 system. Begin the analysis at a, where 1T is the amount of pull. This also occurs on the left side of the lowest free-floating pulley at b. The combined effect of these two pulls, of 1T each, on the prusik sling at c produces a pull of 2T on that sling.

Each of the pulleys fixed to the tree is a 1:1 system that alters the direction but not the amount of pull. Therefore, the force on the far side of these pulleys is the same as on the near side. The 1T pull of b transfers around the lower fixed pulley to become 1T at d. This combines with the 2T pull on

Figure D-7. A **6:1 System**

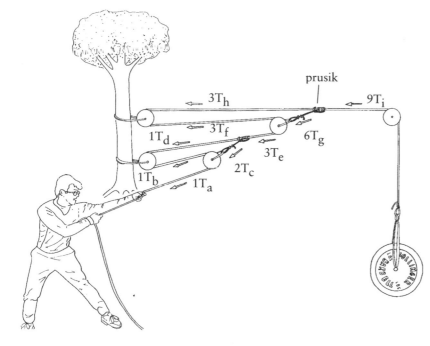

Figure D-8. A 9:1 System of Mechanical Advantage

the prusik in c to exert a combined pull of 3T on the second free-floating pulley at e.

This 3T pull occurs on both sides of the higher of the free floating pulleys, at both e and f, producing a combined pull of 6T on the higher prusik at g. The 3T pull at f transfers around the upper fixed pulley as a 3T pull at h. This 3T pull of h combines with the 6T pull of the prusik at g to give a total of 9T at i. The components of this system up to e comprise a 3:1 system that pulls on a second 3:1 system from e to i.

In a frictionless system, you might be able to initiate a pull of 50 pounds or more, allowing you to lift 450 pounds, using this imaginary system. In a real system, friction would reduce this advantage considerably—perhaps by one-third—limiting the weight being lifted to a maximum of about 300 pounds.

## References for Future Reading

May, W. G. 1973. *Mountain search and rescue techniques*. Chapter 26, Hauling systems. Boulder, Colorado: Rocky Mountain Rescue Group, Inc.

Setnicka, Tim. 1980. *Wilderness search and rescue*. Chapter 19, Raising systems, Boston: Appalachian Mountain Club.

Selters, Andy. 1990. *Glacier travel and crevasse rescue*. Seattle: The Mountaineers.

Smutek, Ray, ed. 1977. Notes on equipment & technique: Efficiencies, advantages, and factors. *Off-Belay*. 36:8–19.

## Endnotes

1. May, 1973; Setnicka, 1980.

2. Smutek, 1977 lists the two-thirds value. This article includes a letter by John Lawton commenting on test data by Don Wenzel. A value of approximately 60 percent is listed in Appendix D of the Ontario Rock Climbing Association Safety Manual.

# *Index*

Note: Numbers in **boldface type** refer to illustrations.

El Capitan, 31–32, 255
Eldorado Canyon, 117
Epp, Martin, 242
equilibrium: in pulley system, 293–294
erratics, 253
etrier protection (ladder slings), 119, 136
exposure/hypothermia, 267–268, 270, 275
eye protection/lenses, 165, 225

face climbing, 1–18; balance and progression, 5; combined techniques, 14; protection for, 123; ratings, 121; shoes for, 28
face mask: for winter climbing, 164–165
face stance, 111–112
Fall Arrest, 103
fall factor, 53, 153–157; fall rating of rope, 58–59
fall forces, 69, 153–162; and camming devices, 93–94; and dynamic slings, 103–104; braking friction and (belaying), 70–72, 74–75, 77, 161–162; distribution/absorption during fall, 49–51, 153, 161–162; fall factor, 153–157; impact forces, 156–161; on protection pieces (belaying), 125–126
falls: causes of in liebacking, 8–9; fall distances, 128, 132–134; fall factor and, 153–155; harnesses and, 47–49, 51; impact on rope strength/serviceability, 52–53; of leader, 65, 77, 137–138, 158; severity, 158; turning upside down, 47, 51; tying off fallen climber, 137–138
fatigue: cautions, 105, 115, 138, 269
fear: controlling, 138
fifi hook, 223–224
figure-eight descender (used in braking/rappelling), 74–76, 78, 106–107, **108**, 159, 260–261
figure-eight loop, 40
figure-eight retraced (follow-through), 40, **41**, 49–51, 149
finger grip, 4–5
finger holds, 3–5, 18
finger lock, 19–20
firn, 207
first aid, 290; for lightning victims, 290–291; in climbing programs, 253; instructor training, 250, 252; wilderness medicine programs, 278

fist cracks: jamming techniques, 21–22; taping for, 25–26
fitness, 269, 279–282; aerobic endurance, 279; anaerobic training, 281; injuries, 281; muscular endurance, 280; muscular strength, 280–281; stretching, 280, 281; training programs, 281
flakes, exfoliation, 8, 23, 100, 253–255
flaking (rope), 56–57
flanks (of avalanche), 229
flat-footing (Eckenstein or French technique), 167, 169–171
flow, sense of, 139–140
food and water, 164, 269
Foot-Fang, 167–170
footholds, 2, 11 *See also* stepcutting
foot sequences/exchange: in face climbing, 11–13
foot stacking, 23
footwear *See* boots, shoes
forces *See* braking force, counterforce, fall force, friction/braking force, impact forces, loading forces, outward force, shear forces, shock loads/forces, static loads/forces, tensional force, torquing forces
Forest, Bill, 103
free climbing, 84, 139; fixed protection for, 94–95, 267; leading, 126, 139; ratings, 121
free-fall, 105
freezing rain, 206
friction holds/moves, 2–3
frictioning, 3
friction knots, 42
friction melting, 99, 267
friction/braking force: distribution of energy, 161–162; in belay brakes, 73–75, 77, 260; in camming action, 93; in pulley systems, 292; in rappelling, 106, 109, 111, 113–114; in waist belays, 69–72
Friend, 29, 84; Friend of a Friend, 92–93
front-pointing (Austrian technique), 167, 171–174
frostbite, 169, 271

Gilman, Bradley, 84
girth hitch, 68
glacial till, 78–79, 253, 255–256
glaciated cliffs: belaying on, 78–80
glacier ice, 204, 206–207
glaciers: and cliff formation, 254–256

glissading, 186, 187, 270, 272–273
goals, and managing risk, 273–275
Grand Teton, 83, 117, 186, 207–208, 270, 272
granite: exposure, erosion, and exfoliation, 254–255
granite blocks, perched, 255–256; anchoring cautions, 255
grapevine (double fisherman's) knot, 116; tying, 42; untying, 42, **43**
graupel, 284
gravitational slack/loops, 133–134
gravity, center of: in face climbing, 5, 11, 13–15, 17–18
Grigri (Petzl) belay plate, 77–78
grips, 3–5
Grivel, Laurent, 167
grooves, shallow: stemming, 10
ground belay, 113–115
ground currents, 285, 288–290
ground-glass ice, 212
ground school, 252, 259
groups, safety guidelines for, 273–275; evacuating injured climber, 273, 275; group size, 273; peer pressure, 273–274; staying together, 274–275; time and goals, 273–274 *See also* climbing programs, top–rope site management
guidebooks/route descriptions, 29, 120, 138–139
guide hand: in rappelling, 110–111
guide services, 119
gullies *See* couloirs

hand cracks: jamming techniques, 20–21; taping for, 25–26
handholds, 1–5, 11; absence of in face climbing, 8 *See also* stepcutting
hands: preventing injury in crack and face climbing, 5, 20, 25–26
hand traverse (on slab), 5–6
harnesses, 47–51, 253; chest, 136–137; safety tips, 156; sewn with buckles, 47–49, 269; sit, 47; tied, 47–48, 269; tie–in for, 49–50; waist, 47
Harrer, Heinrich, 172
hasty pits, 237–238, 240, 247
hedging, 170
helmets, 164–166, 192, 253, 267–268
helping (feeling) hand: in belaying, 61
Henderson, Kenneth, 84
hero loops, 96–97, 204, 224

Spectra cord, 92
speed and safety, 269
Spider Mitts, 20, 25–26
spindrift, 230–231
sport climbing, 77, 97, 119
sport mode: belay technique, 77, 159
spreading the crack, 23–24
spring-loaded camming devices
(SLCDs), 84, 88, 90–94; for
offwidths, 94; overcamming, 91;
placing and setting, 90–94;
removing, 92–93; safeguarding in
horizontal cracks, 92; stems of,
91–92
St. Elmo's Fire, 288
stacking fingers: in jamming, 5, 19
stacking rope, 56–57
stake, ice axe used as (*piolet
manche*), 179, 193
stalactites, ice *See* candle ice
standing part, 39
starting zones, 240
static belays, 74, 78, 157–159
static foot exchange, 11–13
static loads/forces: on anchor
systems, 144, 152; on rope,
157–158
static ropes, 58
stauchwall, 229–230
steep faces: rappelling on, 111–112,
114; rest/balance on, 14–15;
stemming on, 9–10
steep ice, 206, 214–225; belay
protection, 203; climbing
techniques, 214–221; leading on,
221–225; rating, 214–215;
vertical, 214–215
stemming: on a steep rock face, 8–10
stepcutting: in ice, 180–182, 269; in
snow, 179–180; pigeonhole steps,
180–181; side step, 180; slab
step, 181; slash step, 179
stepkicking, 178–179
Sticht plate, 74–78, 157, 159–160
sticky rubber, 27–28
stoppers, 84
stratigraphy (of snowpack), 237
strength, 38
style, 139
sunballs, 237
swami belt with leg loops, 269; tie–in
for, 50–51; tying, 47–48

tackle, 292
tail (free end of rope), 39
tapers, 84–85; setting and removing,
88–89; slings/slinging, 86–87;

spring–loaded, 89–90
taping ("palmless glove" pattern),
25–26; removal, 26
temperature–gradient (TG)
metamorphism, 235–238
tensional force: in anchor systems,
143–144, 152; in belay chain,
159–161; in pulley systems,
295–297
tensionless anchor, 260–261
Terrordactyl, 177
thin cracks: jamming techniques,
19–20
three-cam units (TCUs), 90, 97
thumb-down position: in jamming
techniques, 19–20
thumb-up position: in jamming, 20
thunder, 286–287
thunderstorms, 269, 274, 283–287
toeholds, **9**
toe jams, 20–21
Toft, Murray, 205
top rope, 57
top-rope anchors, 146, 148–150
top-rope climbing, 116, 148–149
top-rope site management for
groups, 249–264; belay/rappel
systems, 259–261; cleaning loose
rock, 251, 253–256; cleaning the
site, 253; control ropes and
leashes, 257–258; equipment,
250–253, 261–262; granite
exposure, erosion, and
exfoliation, 254–256; ground
school, 252, 259; processing
climbing experience, 262–264;
site geography and safety,
256–258
top-roping waist belays, 66–72
torquing forces: in jamming, 19, 23
traversing, 130–134; hand traverses,
5; on snow and ice, 179, 182,
216–218; traverse line (control
rope) for groups, 257–258;
weight shifts, 11
tree anchors, 68–71, 260–261;
cautions, 78–80, 116, 256
triaxial loading, 68
Tricams, 29, 90, 97
twin-rope technique, 52, 128
Tyndall, John, 210–211
Tyndall Glacier, 228

unconformity structure, 207
underclings, 8, 14
Underhill, Robert, 83–84
unroped climbing, 134, 253, 268

unzipping (of protection), 131–133

verglas, 208–210
vertical cracks: jamming, 20;
liebacking, 8–9; placing
protection, 91
vertical grip, 3–4
vertical ice, 214–215
V-hitch, 68
Vibram lug pattern, 26

waist (body) belays, 61–72,
159–160; limitations of, 72, 159;
sitting, 69–70; standing, 69–70
waist harness, 47
water ice, 193, 198, 204, 208–212;
bulges in, 202–203, 209–210,
212, 214–215; color and
consistency, 210–212; snow
alteration of, 212; various types,
208–210
water knot, 40, 47, **48**
weather conditions: avalanche risk,
234, 240, 269, 274;
lightning/thunderstorm risk, 267,
269, 274, 283–284
webbing, flat, 84; tying knots in, 40,
47, **48**
webbing, tubular nylon, 42; tying
knots in, 39; used for swami belt,
47, **48**
weight shifts, 11
Weis, Mike, 199
Wellman, Mark, 31–32, 37
wheelchairs, people in: high ropes
courses for, 35–36
whipping rope ends, 54–55
White Mountains, 32, 83
Whitney, Hassler, 84
Whitney-Gilman Ridge, 81, 84
Whymper, Edward, 266, 277
Wilts, Chuck, 84
windchill factor, 271–272
windslab snow, 181, 206, 228–229
winter rock climbing, 94
working elongation (rope stretch), 58
wraps, 3–5
wrist leashes: for ice axes, 215–216
wrists: preventing injury, 25–26

Yaniro, Tony, 23
Yates Screamers, 103–104, 160
Yosemite Decimal System, 121–122,
214
Yosemite Valley, 52, 83–84, 266–268

Z–drag rescue system, 297